4.17.69

J. Hillis Miller

CHARLES
DICKENS:
The World of
His Novels

A MIDLAND BOOK

MB 124

$2.95 / 25s. net

RUNK
Pre-

l. Beer by Retail

# CHARLES DICKENS

## THE WORLD OF HIS NOVELS

# CHARLES DICKENS

## THE WORLD OF HIS NOVELS

*J. Hillis Miller*

INDIANA UNIVERSITY PRESS
*Bloomington and London*

1506153

TO

GEORGES POULET

# INTRODUCTION

He made out of Victorian England a complete world, with a life and vigour and idiom of its own, quite unlike any other world there has ever been. (Humphry House, *The Dickens World*)

N recent years a good many important studies of Dickens ave appeared.[1] These have approached Dickens from the most iverse points of view, though there has been generally an implicit agreement with Edmund Wilson's belief that "we may nd in Dickens' work today a complexity and a depth to which ven Gissing and Shaw have hardly . . . done justice — an ntellectual and artistic interest which makes Dickens loom ery large in the whole perspective of the literature of the West." [2] While recognizing the measure of justice in the raditional charges against Dickens' novels (that they are melodramatic, falsely pathetic, didactic, repetitive, and so on), various critics and scholars have attempted to assess what is authentic in his fiction. One can distinguish several different modes f approach in these recent studies, though there is of course a ood deal of overlapping. There are biographical studies, culminating in Edgar Johnson's probably definitive book. These iographies have put our knowledge of the facts of Dickens' fe and their relation to his work on solid ground. Other scholrs have explored the relation of Dickens' work to the political, oral, and social realities of the Victorian age, while still others have examined Dickens' overt opinions about art, politics, morality, and have shown us how Dickens was a much more eliberate and calculating writer than we had thought. The later scholars have most often found their evidence in Dickens' tters and prefaces, and in the nonfictional pieces he wrote or

[1] A selected bibliography will be found at the end of this book.
[2] Edmund Wilson, "Dickens: The Two Scrooges," *Eight Essays* (New rk, 1954, pp. 11–91), p. 13.

accepted for the periodicals he edited. Similar studies hav
shown the relation of Dickens' opinions and practice as a nov
elist to Victorian theories and practice generally, or have stud
ied the history of the criticism of Dickens' novels. More in th
direction of literary criticism have been investigations of th
relation between Dickens' life and his fiction. The best suc
study is the brilliant essay by Edmund Wilson, though on
might also include an introduction to *Little Dorrit* by Lione
Trilling, and the biographies by Jack Lindsay and Edgar Johr
son. But Trilling's essay is really one of the best examples of
kind of study closer to my own approach: the discussion c
Dickens' novels as autonomous works of art. Such criticism ha
frequently used one form or another of the method of analys
associated with the "new criticism." Trilling's essay, howeve
like most such studies, is limited to the discussion of a sing
novel.

All these recent investigations are taken for granted her
and without them my own study could never have been unde
taken. However, I have attempted to do something slightly di
ferent from any of them: to assess the specific quality of Dic
ens' imagination in the totality of his work, to identify wh
persists throughout all the swarming multiplicity of his nove
as a view of the world which is unique and the same, and
trace the development of this vision of things from one novel
another throughout the chronological span of his career.

Though it is true to say that a work of literature is rooted i
its age, in the life of its author, and in his conscious theori
about art and morality, and though, in the other direction, a
single novel by Dickens can legitimately be viewed as ind
pendent of all these factors and as standing on its own as
self-contained entity, there is still another way of looking
Dickens' work, a way which to some degree reconciles the d
chotomy between these extreme approaches. This way revers
the usual causal sequence between the psychology of an auth
and his work. It sees a work of literature not as the mere sym
tom or product of a preëxistent psychological condition, but
the very means by which a writer apprehends and, in son
measure, creates himself. The given conditions of a writer's lif

including his psychological nature as well as the culture he lives in, are merely the obstacles or materials which he transforms and vanquishes by turning them into novels or poems, that is, by giving them a different meaning from the one they had in themselves. The attitude I have here taken, then, also reverses the usual relation between the spirit of the age and a work of literature. Rather than seeing the former as wholly the cause of the latter, so that the work becomes a symptom of the age and altogether determined by it, this approach remembers the other side of the truth and sees Dickens' own creative vision as in part determining the "Victorian spirit" itself.

This study presupposes that each sentence or paragraph of a novel, whether it is presented from the point of view of the narrator or of some imagined character, defines a certain relationship between an imagining mind and its objects. A passage of interior monologue or of reminiscence, passages describing characters in action, or portraying an imaginary scene, will reveal unsuspected similarities if each is taken as the definition of a certain relation between mind and world. Juxtaposed, these apparently distinct elements can clarify one another and be brought to reveal their profound harmony. Taken all together, all the unit passages form the imaginative universe of the writer. Through the analysis of all the passages, as they reveal the persistence of certain obsessions, problems, and attitudes, the critic can hope to glimpse the original unity of a creative mind. For all the works of a single writer form a unity, a unity in which a thousand paths radiate from the same center. At the heart of a writer's successive works, revealed in glimpses through each event and image, is an impalpable organizing form, constantly presiding over the choice of words. This form, if we can discover it, will be a better clue than any biographical data to the writer's intimate relation to the material world, to other human beings, and to himself. For a novel is not simply an external structure of meaning, an objective narrative which we can understand from the outside. It is also the expression of the unique personality and vital spirit of its author. It is the embodiment in words of a certain very special way of experiencing the world. The pervasive stylistic traits of a writer, his recurrent words and images, his special cadence and tone, are as personal to him as his face or his way of walking. His style is his own way of living in the world given a verbal form. So in literature every landscape is an interior landscape, just as each imaginary man or woman is also a figure in the writer's own private world of perception or memory, longing or fear. A poem or novel is indeed the world refashioned into conformity with the inner structure of the writer's spirit, but at the same time it is that spirit given, through words, a form and substance taken from the shared solidity of the exterior world. It is in this sense that the words of the work are themselves the primary datum, a self-sufficient reality beyond which the critic need not go. For in literature what is hidden and without visible form is made visible and communicable to others.

The chapters presented here have as their goal the exploration of the imaginative universe of Dickens, and the revelation of that presiding unity hidden at the center, but present everywhere within his novels and partially revealed there in the embodied disguises of particular characters, actions, interiors, landscapes, and cityscapes. The imaginative universe of a great writer is an infinite domain, and an infinite number of critical paths might traverse it profitably. The view from certain roads, however, is more complete and less distorted, and I have chosen what seems to me a salient approach to Dickens, the theme of the search for a true and viable identity. Wishing to respect the unity and fullness of particular novels and yet to remain within some bounds of length, I have chosen to explore in detail six novels spanning Dickens' career: *Pickwick Papers, Oliver Twist, Martin Chuzzlewit, Bleak House, Great Expectations,* and *Our Mutual Friend.* Each of these novels represents an important segment of the curve of Dickens' temporal development, and all of them together include much of Dickens' most important work. However, I do not mean to imply that these six novels are far more important or excellent than the others. To bridge the gaps between the detailed studies I have interspersed much briefer discussions of all the other novels. These concentrate on the special contribution of the omitted novels to the development of Dickens' creative vision.

Where I have multiplied quotations expressing the same attitude or idea it has been to show, through the juxtaposition of passages from widely separated points in a novel, the pervasive presence of a certain organizing form. Only through such evidence of recurrence can a mode of sensation or thought be shown to be a permanent law of the world of a novel, and not an isolated and fortuitous exception. And if I have made little reference to the work of other scholars and critics, it has been to achieve a maximum of concentration upon Dickens himself. But I am anxious to acknowledge here my great debt to all the many students of Dickens' life and work, and especially to those more recent critics who have approached him in ways near to my own. I also want to thank Professors Douglas Bush and Albert Guerard, Jr., of Harvard University. They directed my doctoral dissertation on Dickens, and have continued to give me help and encouragement. Professor Bush read the manuscript of this book, and made extremely helpful suggestions for revision. My deepest debt, however, is to Professor Georges Poulet of the University of Zurich, formerly at The Johns Hopkins University. The example of Professor Poulet's own criticism, the inspiration of his friendship, and his patience and generosity in discussing this book with me and reading drafts of it are more responsible than anything else for such virtues as it may have.

J. Hillis Miller

The Johns Hopkins University

## A NOTE ON REFERENCES

For Dickens' novels and letters I have used *The Nonesuch Dickens,* edited by Arthur Waugh, Hugh Walpole, Walter Dexter, and Thomas Hatton (Bloomsbury: The Nonesuch Press, 1937, 1938). Since this edition, though it is the best and the most complete, is not readily available, I have put in parentheses after each quotation the chapter number, in Arabic numerals, rather than the page number, or, in the case of novels which are divided into books, I have put the book number, in Roman numerals, followed by the chapter number in Arabic. With this mode of reference, the reader may use whatever edition of Dickens he wishes. I have used the following abbreviations, where necessary:

*Sketches by Boz:* SB
*Pickwick Papers:* PP
*The Old Curiosity Shop:* OCS
*Barnaby Rudge:* BR
*American Notes:* AN
*Martin Chuzzlewit:* MC
*Dombey and Son:* DS
*David Copperfield:* DC
*Bleak House:* BH

*Oliver Twist:* OT
*Nicholas Nickleby:* NN
*Hard Times:* HT
*Little Dorrit:* LD
*A Tale of Two Cities:* TTC
*Great Expectations:* GE
*Our Mutual Friend:* OMF
*The Mystery of Edwin Drood:* ED
*Letters: Let.*

# CONTENTS

# THE WORLD OF DICKENS' NOVELS

Representing London — or Paris, or any other great place
— in the new light of being actually unknown to all the people in the story, and only taking the colour of their fears and
fancies and opinions. So getting a new aspect, and being unlike itself. An *odd* unlikeness of itself.
(Dickens' "Memorandum Book" (1855–65), *Let.*, III, 788)

What does it mean to speak of "the world of Dickens' novels"?
The "world" is the totality of all things as they are lived in by
all human beings collectively. For Dickens the concrete embodiment of this totality is the great modern commercial city, made up
of millions of people all connected to one another without knowing
it, and yet separated from one another and living in isolation and
secrecy. Dickens was fascinated by the city, any city, by London
most of all, but also by Paris or Boston or Genoa. In each city he
visited he went to prisons, morgues, workhouses, markets, and the-
aters, and walked for hours through the streets. He wanted to
know each city by seeing it from every possible point of view. For
example, while he was visiting Paris in 1847, he wrote in a letter:
"I have been seeing Paris — wandering into hospitals, prisons,
dead-houses, operas, theatres, concert-rooms, burial-grounds, palaces, and wine-shops. . . . [E]very description of gaudy and
ghastly sight has been passing before me in a rapid panorama"
(*Let.*, II, 9). Dickens' novels are a transposition into fiction of his
assimilative way of living in the real world, his attempt to see
everything, know everything, experience everything in the city for
himself. The most striking characteristic of his novels is their
multitudinousness, the proliferation within each one of a great
number of characters, each different from all the others, and each
living imprisoned in his own milieu and in his own idiosyncratic
way of looking at the world. For the city is "actually unknown to
all the people in the story," and becomes in the eyes of each "an
*odd* unlikeness of itself." Though each individual reaches out to-

ward a comprehension of the city, the essential quality of the city is its transcendence of any one person's knowledge of it. Each individual's knowledge is partial, baffled, askew. And yet it was the city as it really is, in all its unknown and perhaps unknowable complexity, which Dickens wanted to know and to encompass in his work. Or, rather, Dickens wanted to absorb the city into his imagination and present it again in the persons and events of his novels. But how could he reach the real city, the city hidden from all the people who are distorting the world by interpreting it in terms of their fears and fancies and opinions? Perhaps he could transcend the limitations of any single point of view by presenting as many as possible of the limited persons, and of the new aspects which the city gets when seen through their eyes. The truth thus reached would be Dickens' own truth too, the truth of his deepest sense of the nature of the world. From novel to novel throughout his career Dickens sought an ever closer approach to the truth hidden behind the surface appearance of things. But he sought this truth not so much by going behind the surface as by giving an exhaustive inventory of the surface itself. For the truth behind appearance is unavailable by any direct aproach. And to reveal the secrets in the hearts of his characters is not to approach any closer to the truth of the unknown city, for the truth is hidden from each of them too. The special quality of Dickens' imagination is his assumption that he can get behind the surface by describing all of it bit by bit. For each limited event, each person trapped in his distorted view of the city, contains as well as hides the truth. And when enough of the isolated parts are described, and their relations discovered, the truth behind each, it may be, will be liberated — a truth at once particular and universal. Then Dickens' novels will no longer be merely a collection of "odd unlikenesses," but a true likeness, an authentic image of the world.

# CHARLES DICKENS

## THE WORLD OF HIS NOVELS

# Chapter I

## PICKWICK PAPERS

### I

WHAT a study for an artist did that exciting scene present! The eloquent Pickwick, with one hand gracefully concealed behind his coat tails, and the other waving in air, to assist his glowing declamation; his elevated position revealing those tights and gaiters, which, had they clothed an ordinary man, might have passed without observation, but which, when Pickwick clothed them — if we may use the expression — inspired voluntary awe and respect; surrounded by the men who had volunteered to share the perils of his travels, and who were destined to participate in the glories of his discoveries. ( 1 )

THE consciousness of Pickwick and the consciousness of Dickens do not coincide. It is not a question here, it goes without saying, of the biographical "consciousness" or subjective identity of Dickens as he lived it in his own life. That consciousness is, for the most part, beyond recovery, since, even in Dickens' letters, it exists only as expressed in words, that is, in a changed form. No, when we say "consciousness of Dickens" we mean the elusive and pervasive consciousness which is expressed and embodied in the words of the novel, present everywhere, and recoverable as the persistent tone or note we apprehend as we read the novel through. It is easiest to think of this consciousness as the stance or position of the narrator in relation to the events and personages of the story.

Dickens, present here only as the voice of the narrator who tells the story, has been very careful to remove himself from direct involvement, and to recount events from the point of view of detached objectivity. The full title of the novel is, after all, *The Posthumous Papers of the Pickwick Club*. The nar-

rator tells us in the first paragraph that he is only the *editor* of
certain papers, secretary's reports and so on, which have come
into his hands. And even when this pretense is dropped or forgotten, the narrator keeps his stance of objectivity. This objectivity is evident in a mild and not very subtle irony which per-
meates the style of the early part of the novel. Pickwick's tights
and gaiters really did "inspire voluntary awe and respect" in the
secretary whose report the narrator uses, but behind the fatuity
of the secretary we can easily perceive the consciousness of the
narrator, of Dickens himself, making fun of the journalistic
style which describes with ridiculous solemnity the appearances
of so-called great men. At the beginning, then, the narrator is
separated from Pickwick, and sees him from the outside, from
the point of view of an uninvolved spectator. He is not caught
up in the events, but sees each one as an "exciting scene," as a
"study for an artist." He does not apprehend the thoughts and
feelings of the characters from the inside.

The perspective of the narrator is, one recognizes, precisely
that necessary to a comic view of things. To see some action or
person as comic, one must be in some sense detached and removed from what one sees. So, Pickwick's adventures and his
feelings are attributed to him. They are perceptible in his expression, gesture, and words, but they are not experienced from
the inside, with sympathetic identification. As a result, the
reader feels superior to Pickwick, and sees him as the object of
his delighted laughter. At once we must say, then, that the
novel is a unity because it is the verbal expression of Dickens'
mood, or sensibility, or spiritual state, at the time he wrote the
novel, and we must say that this sensibility, the unique expression of a certain stage in the development of Dickens' creative
genius, is not to be identified with the subjective experience of
any character or characters. The consciousness of Dickens,
ironically amused and detached, intervenes everywhere between the reader and the consciousness of the characters, and
is the true spiritual and tonal unity of *Pickwick Papers*.

If this consciousness is present at all within the events and
people of the novel, it is present covertly. When Pickwick encounters Sam Weller cleaning boots in the yard of the White

Hart Inn, innocence encounters wisdom, but we can also say that Pickwick encounters the embodiment of the author in the novel, the character who protectively supervises Pickwick's adventures, and sees to it that he is not really hurt. Sam knows all that Pickwick does not know. A child of the streets, like Dickens himself, he knows that appearances are not realities, expects people to try to fool him, lives by his wits, and even accepts with a kind of wary generosity the absurd and inexplicable things about the world. But the presence of Dickens in Sam Weller is a masked presence. It is hidden behind Sam's self-effacing deference and behind the brilliance of his talk. (It is perhaps as much in his gift for anecdote as in his knowledge of the world that we can detect Dickens in Sam.) Hidden behind Sam Weller's *savoir faire,* and surreptitiously present in the ironic style of the narrator, Dickens' own consciousness and judgment, then, are not directly present in the novel, and Dickens seems, as hidden both in Sam and in the narrator, to be a mere servant of the central characters, to watch and describe their actions with detached objectivity.

But the events and characters do not, after all, have an objective existence. They were invented by Dickens himself. Dickens, we come to see, is present in the novel in two ways, both covert. He is present in the detachment of the narrator who sees the characters as a comic spectacle. But he is also present in the comic characters themselves, as he invents them and plays one role after another. Dickens is not the spectator of a real world, but the spectator of an interior drama which he is inventing as he goes along. And this invention takes the form of imaginative role-playing, as, for example, Dickens plays the part of Pickwick, the comic old man with the innocence and ebullience of youth, or as he invents one of Jingle's magnificent monologues. The attitude of the narrator toward the characters is not that of complete detachment and cold objectivity. Rather the narrator (and hence the reader) is both inside and outside the characters, inside enough to imagine their feelings and thoughts with a certain degree of sympathetic identification, outside enough to find these thoughts and feelings amusing.

Moreover, the various comic characters and situations remain within a certain limited range of possibilities. There are only so many possible kinds of people which Dickens is able to imagine the narrator as seeing, and only so many kinds of adventure he can imagine the characters as having. These as much reveal the nature of Dickens' inner world when he wrote the novel as does the mode of consciousness of the ironic spectator.

The experiences of the characters tend to occur in a certain constant succession, to form themselves in an order which suggests a whole, a single adventure which happens over and over in different ways throughout the novel. Though Pickwick himself is the central embodiment of these experiences, each stage of his adventures is matched by parallels in the lives of other characters, who, it may be, experience only a part, a truncated version, of the whole. In what follows I shall try to describe in detail this basic sequence of possibilities, made by putting together moments from many different parts of the novel. These moments are drawn from the experience of many personages, though chiefly from the adventures of the immortal Pickwick himself. When I speak in the following pages of "Pickwick," I must be understood to be using the term in a Pickwickian sense, and to be including within that term all Pickwick's avatars in the novel, all those characters who have analogous experiences.

II

. . . the sun . . . had just risen, . . . when Mr. Samuel Pickwick burst like another sun from his slumbers, threw open his chamber window, and looked out upon the world beneath. (2)

. . . he was . . . awakened by the morning sun darting his bright beams reproachfully into the apartment. Mr. Pickwick was no sluggard; and he sprang like an ardent warrior from his tent — bedstead. . . . Mr. Pickwick thrust his head out of the lattice, and looked around him. (7)

The beginning of Pickwick's life is the simplest act imaginable. This beginning is repeated again and again throughout his adventures. Awakened from his slumbers by the sun, the hero, with a burst of youthful energy, like another sun, throws open his bedroom window and looks out at the world. Before this, enclosed in his darkened chamber, sunk in his slumbers, he has had no life; he has not really been Pickwick: "the earlier history of the public career of the immortal Pickwick" is "involved" in "obscurity" (1). Only when he breaks through the secure walls of his room, and begins "to penetrate to the hidden countries which on every side surround it" (2) does his real life begin. The structural axis of *Pickwick Papers* is the age-old motif of the quest. This motif precedes the modern novel, but is fundamental to it, from *Don Quixote* and the early picaresque novels onward. Quest for reality, quest for truth, it is also implicitly a quest for oneself, since one can only know oneself by knowing how one is related to the world.

But it is not enough simply to open the window. Pickwick must leave the safe world of his privacy and go forth into the sunlight to encounter the reality of experience. To remain inside looking out is to see only what Pickwick sees through his chamber window on the day his adventures begin, a bland homogeneous world, entirely without surprises, stretching as far as the eye can see, everywhere exactly like itself, a world of pure surface: "Goswell Street was at his feet, Goswell Street was on his right hand — as far as the eye could reach, Goswell Street extended on his left; and the opposite side of Goswell Street was over the way" (2). If one wishes to penetrate beneath this false surface and discover "the truths which are hidden beyond" (2), experience must be actively encountered. Rather than "be[ing] content to gaze on Goswell Street for ever" (2), one must move through the world in "pursuit of novelty," "mixing with different varieties and shades of human character" (57): "High-roads and by-roads, towns and villages, public conveyances and their passengers, first-rate inns and road-side public houses, races, fairs, regattas, elections, meetings, market days . . . were alike visited and beheld, by the ardent Pickwick and his enthusiastic followers" (Advertisement from the "Athenæum," March 26, 1836, reprinted in *PP*, p. ix). The proper image for the start of Pickwick's life, then, is not the opening of a chamber window, but the opening of the window of a *coach,* symbol of the constant peregrination of the hero as he makes his inventory of the various forms human reality can take. Only when Pickwick is in motion, and only so long as he keeps in motion, will he have a chance really to see: "Mr. Pickwick saw, on popping his head out of the coach window . . ." (50).

Pickwick's quest is not without specific motivation, and not without certain a priori assumptions. He does not begin like a Lockean *tabula rasa*. He is not like Adam newly turned out into the brave new world, forced to translate sensations into perceptions, and to give names to all the creatures. Nor does he begin, in accordance with the germ idea of *Pickwick Papers*, with the assumptions of an English sporting gentleman, in the tradition of Surtees' *Jorrocks*.[1] When Dickens "thought of Mr. Pickwick," [2] he thought of someone who was to have the motivations of a *scientist*. The scientist is a special case of the fixed character who fits his experience into a preconceived mold. Pickwick's companions are rigidly formed personages who find everywhere in the world opportunities to reconfirm their *idées fixes*. Whatever happens to them will be interpreted in terms of these ideas, love for Tupman, poetry for Snodgrass, and sport for Winkle. But Pickwick, "his telescope in his great-coat pocket, and his notebook in his waistcoat, ready for the reception of any discoveries worthy of being noted down" (2), has a different hobbyhorse. He makes it his business to remain always disengaged, to regard the world from the outside, as a note-taker. Pickwick's "restless and inquiring spirit," and his "insatiable thirst for Travel" (*PP*, p. ix) were to be stimulated by his desire to investigate and report objectively on all the variety of the world. Pickwick was to be a parody of the good scientist who, rejecting received opinions, goes beyond the immediate appearances of things and extends the frontiers of

[1] "The idea propounded to me was that the monthly something should be a vehicle for certain plates to be executed by Mr. Seymour, and there was a notion, either on the part of that admirable humorous artist, or of my visitor (I forget which), that a 'Nimrod Club,' the members of which were to go out shooting, fishing, and so forth, and getting themselves into difficulties through their want of dexterity, would be the best means of introducing these" (Preface to the first cheap edition, 1847, PP, p. xviii).

[2] *Ibid.*, p. xviii.

knowledge: ". . . inestimable benefits . . . must inevitably result from carrying the speculations of that learned man into a wider field, from extending his travels, and consequently enlarging his sphere of observation, to the advancement of knowledge, and the diffusion of learning" (1).

Like a good scientist, Pickwick confronts experience with detachment. He studies the world coolly, and describes what he sees. His initial attitude is one of idle curiosity, mixed with a kind of genteel interest:

They were very motley groups too, and well worth the looking at, if it were only in idle curiosity. (45)

Mr. Pickwick stood in the principal street of this illustrious town, and gazed with an air of curiosity, not unmixed with interest, on the objects around him. (7)

On the one hand there is Pickwick, observant and calm, making himself a kind of camera eye, and on the other hand, at a distance, there is all the multiplicity of the world, which he regards as a spectacle. Only so long as he remains absolutely unmoved by, and removed from, what he sees will he be able to examine it minutely, and take mental notes. His prototype is the good reporter, such as the author of *Sketches by Boz,* as well as the scientist. Pickwick's relation to the world is wholly dispassionate, the frailest of relations, intellectual rather than emotional. Even in the midst of turmoil and confusion, he does not lose his head: "It was a beautiful sight, in that moment of turmoil and confusion, to behold the placid and philosophical expression of Mr. Pickwick's face" (9).

Pickwick goes forth to encounter experience with an apparently unshakable calm because, again like the scientist, he does not expect that what he sees will involve or change himself. His researches will not, he thinks, tell him anything about his own intimate life and destiny. Nothing of his own security or complacency is at stake. His discoveries will involve no risk. They will be safely useless, like Pickwick's previous work, "Speculations on the Source of the Hampstead Ponds, with some Observations on the Theory of Tittlebats" (1).

But Pickwick can assume that his journeys will involve no

risk only because he believes that nothing he meets will really surprise him. The enclosed chamber from which he sallies forth is not empty. It is furnished with a priori assumptions about the constant and universal nature of man. Pickwick goes out to visit "all the scenes . . . at which different traits of character may be observed, and recognised" (advertisement from the "Athenæum," *PP,* p. ix). To observe is the same as to recognize. Whatever is seen will be simply the fulfillment in real experience of what has already existed as theoretical knowledge. Whatever Pickwick encounters will be assimilated into the system he already knows, the systematic structure of his mind. The world fits his mind. Pickwick already knows what he is going to find. So, Pickwick describes a scene outside his window "after the most approved precedents," and before he has even looked at it (7)! And in the same way, before he has even met Ben Allen and Bob Sawyer, he asserts that medical students are "fine fellows . . . ; with judgments matured by observation and reflection, and tastes refined by reading and study" (30).

Parallel to the naïveté and detachment of the scientist who expects all the evidence to confirm his hypotheses is the naïveté of the innocent man who expects everyone to be good and to tell the truth. The latter expects appearances to conform to realities. The a priori of science is equated with the a priori of an ethical optimism which believes that people are essentially good and that things in the social world are what they seem. So, when a cabman tells Pickwick a collection of outrageous lies about his horse, Pickwick "enter[s] every word of this statement in his note-book, . . . as a singular instance of the tenacity of life in horses, under trying circumstances" (2). And, in the same way, the drunken soldiers in the streets of Stroud, Rochester, Chatham, and Brompton are seen by an eye wholly unacquainted with evil: "It is truly delightful to a philanthropic mind, to see these gallant men staggering along under the influence of an overflow, both of animal and ardent spirits; more especially when we remember that the following them about, and jesting with them, affords a cheap and innocent amusement for the boy population" (2).

Pickwick, then, begins with a double assumption of the natural goodness of the human heart, and of the immanence of a benign Providence in everything which happens in the world. He believes that he can safely travel everywhere and to every level of society, certain to find everywhere confirmation of his prejudgments, and certain that all of his experiences will be without danger for him. Like the holy fool, he thinks he lives in an unfallen world. Pickwick's assumptions are ironically epitomized in Sam Weller's Leibnizian maxim: "Wotever is, is right" (51). They are, in a sense, the presuppositions of the eighteenth-century novels which nurtured Dickens' imagination in childhood. It is these assumptions which are put to the test by Pickwick's adventures.

### III

The smile that played on Mr. Pickwick's features was instantaneously lost in a look of the most unbounded and wonder-stricken surprise. (22)

. . . he stood perfectly fixed, and immovable with astonishment. (42)

. . . he . . . gazed with indescribable astonishment on the faces before him. (19)

Instead of the calm recognition which he had expected, Pickwick and analogous characters, when they encounter the world, are plunged into "mute perplexity and bewilderment" (45). "Bewildered and amazed" (16), Pickwick is wholly unable to understand what is happening within him and without. His astonishment is an instantaneous and absolute transformation of his subjective state. If he is not "wholly bereft of speech" (45) by the change, he is reduced to the most primitive language, exclamation: "expressions of astonishment . . . burst spontaneously from his lips (48); " 'Can such things be!' exclaimed the astonished Mr. Pickwick" (13). Pickwick's "terrified surprise" (9) is caused not so much by the physical danger to him of what he sees as by its complete unpredictability. Nothing is recognizable, nothing can be understood in terms of the preconceived ideas with which the hero armed himself. He is "quite stupefied by the novelty of his situation" (41). Consequently, nothing is intelligible. Each thing is simply there before him. Its causes, its nature, its meaning, are wholly hidden from the spectator. His astonishment is not yet an involvement in the world. It is rather an experience of separation. He is simply surprised, and in being surprised he affirms his essential distance from the incomprehensible spectacle which he sees.

In the moment in which Pickwick becomes astonished he leaves completely behind him the cool detachment of the scientist. Instead of an intellectual lucidity, he has only "a confused consciousness" (41). In fact, he leaves everything of his previous life behind him. His surprise is "overwhelming and absorbing" (45). Everything is forgotten but the immediate scene. In this state, the hero no longer knows where he is because he can no longer remember how he came to be where he is: ". . . he sat down and gazed about him with a petrified stare, as if he had not the remotest idea where he was, which indeed he had not" (50).

Bit by bit, the disengagement of this initial astonishment gives way to a different kind of surprise. Finally the hero is engulfed by the sensations caused by the scene. His surprise is no longer to be distinguished from these sensations, because he can remember nothing different from them:

> The noise and bustle which ushered in the morning, were sufficient to dispel from the mind of the most romantic visionary in existence, any associations but those which were immediately connected with the rapidly-approaching election. (13)

> . . . looking upwards, he beheld a sight which filled him with surprise and pleasure. (4)

## IV

What the hero sees is, first of all, a world in which each thing and each person is, like those in *Sketches by Boz,* idiosyncratic. *Pickwick Papers* is a long succession of scenes in which Pickwick and his friends meet, one after another, characters who surge up suddenly and vividly within the field of our immediate vision, command all of our attention for a brief span of time, and then disappear altogether, never, for the most part, to reappear. Instead, each figure or scene is merely replaced by others. Each character is detached from all the others and incommensurate with all the others. Each appears momentarily at the focus of vision, enacts his brief pantomime, and then leaves the stage for good. The general effect is of a swarming multiplicity, of an inexhaustible fecundity of invention. The characters appear suddenly from nowhere, and there seems to be an endless supply of them. The entire novel, then, is not unlike the dream of the bagman's uncle: "The queerest thing of all, was, that although there was such a crowd of persons, and although fresh faces were pouring in, every moment, there was no telling where they came from. They seemed to start up, in some strange manner, from the ground, or the air, and disappear in the same way" (49).

Throughout the novel, character after character is described, each with his own unique peculiarity of appearance and manner:

He was a shortish gentleman, with very stiff black hair cut in the porcupine or blacking-brush style, and standing stiff and straight all over his head; his aspect was pompous and threatening; his manner was peremptory; his eyes were sharp and restless. . . . (51)

They were curious-looking fellows. One was a slim and rather lame man in rusty black, and a white neckerchief; another was a stout burly person, dressed in the same apparel, with a great reddish-black cloth round his neck; a third, was a little weazen drunken-looking body, with a pimply face. (40)

Each such person is "a character" (44), as Sam Weller calls the prisoner who sleeps under a table because it reminds him of a four-poster bed. The spectator is at the mercy of each of these "characters." Their gestures, action, and appearance hold him in fascinated concentration. Other people are traps who absorb the spectator in absorbing his attention. Again and again, a specimen is picked out of the mass, and put before us "as if he were catalogued in some collection of rarities" (2). Each specimen can only be defined by its queerness, by its devi-

ation from any type: "a queer sort of fresh painted vehicle
drove up, out of which there jumped with great agility . . .
a queer sort of gentleman, who seemed made for the vehicle,
and the vehicle for him" (40). Since it is the "singularity of
the thing" which makes it a "matter of surprise" (43), and
since Pickwick has no access to the inner lives of the queer
characters he meets, they must be caught at the moment when
they are displaying themselves in farcical action, the women
flying into hysterics, the boys and men spinning round and
round, like Tupman when he hears that Jingle has eloped
with Miss Rachel (9). The art which invents and describes
these objects and people is an art of hyperbole, in which, for
example, "a particularly large fire" is "vehemently stirred"
"with a particularly small poker" (31). In such a novel, Sam
Weller must announce his presence, not by a mere cough, but
by making "sundry diabolical noises similar to those which
would probably be natural to a person of middle age who had
been afflicted with a combination of inflammatory sore throat,
croup, and hooping-cough, from his earliest infancy" (39),
and two city men are described in a cascade of superlatives:
"Both gentlemen had very open waistcoats and very rolling
collars, and very small boots, and very big rings, and very little
watches, and very large guard chains" (55).

Dickens' art in this novel is also an art of pantomime. People in *Pickwick Papers* communicate not by speech, but by a
"complete code of telegraphic nods and gestures" (43). World
of hyperbole and pantomime, it is also a world of pure surface.
The characters in this perpetually changing vaudeville exist
entirely as their appearances. Everything that it is possible to
say about them can be quickly said. Their outer idiosyncrasies
remain the same, and they apparently have no private inner
lives at all. They are what they appear, their gestures and expressions. After they have once come out strongly as themselves, they can only be allowed to disappear, or be shown as
repeating themselves over and over.

It is impossible to relate oneself to such characters, or to discover something like oneself in them. They do not respond to
the spectator or engage in real dialogue. Everyone simply enacts

himself, side by side with all the others. The world of *Pickwick Papers* is a swarming plurality of isolated centers of vitality, each endlessly asserting himself as himself. There is no real communication, and nothing outside any one of these characters, except his immediate material possessions, which supports him as what he is.

Moreover, each of these characters keeps his secret. Each remains incomprehensible, inscrutable. His motivations, the reasons he does what he does, remain absolutely hidden. Since the world is seen entirely from the outside, it remains essentially mysterious. What a character does can be seen, but why he does it, or who he is beneath his costume, cannot be known:

". . . Wot are they, then?"

"Clerks," replied Sam.

"Wot are they all a-eatin' ham sangwidges for?" inquired his father.

" 'Cos it's in their dooty, I suppose," replied Sam, "it's a part o' the system; they're alvays a doin' it here, all day long!" (55)

"And who was he?" inquired Mr. Pickwick.

"Wy, that's just the wery point as nobody never know'd," replied Sam. (41)

In the end, even though each character is altogether different from all the others, we come to feel that they are all alike. The immense proliferation of personages only makes them all eventually seem to be representations of one another. Since they are completely idiosyncratic, they are unthinkable. There is no basis of comparison or contrast, and Dickens can only tell us, not show us, that they are queer. Where there is no possibility of classification, there is no possibility of differentiation. All of these characters are equal, since they are all equally beyond comprehension. What Pickwick or his fellow innocents see with such "unbounded astonishment" (55) is, literally, "impossible to describe" (28).

v

But the plurality of the world of *Pickwick Papers* is not always simply successive. It is also a simultaneous plurality.

Each item in the scene before one is multiplied inexhaustibly within the moment to produce, it may be, a world of delightful plenitude. Sometimes this is a plenitude of nature, a visual, auditory and olfactory space filled with an infinite variety of perceptible forms:

Hedges, fields, and trees, hill and moorland, presented to the eye their ever-varying shades of deep rich green; . . . the songs of birds, and hum of myriads of summer insects, filled the air; and the cottage gardens, crowded with flowers of every rich and beautiful tint, sparkled, in the heavy dew, like beds of glittering jewels. (19)

The hundred perfumes of the little flower-garden beneath scented the air around; the deep-green meadows shone in the morning dew that glistened on every leaf as it trembled in the gentle air; and the birds sang as if every sparkling drop were a fountain of inspiration to them. (7)

It may also be a multitude of human forms which delights the eye and produces a social "scene of varied and delicious enchantment" (15) parallel to the natural one: ". . . look where you would, some exquisite form glided gracefully through the throng, and was no sooner lost, than it was replaced by another as dainty and bewitching" (35).

But, as the last passage suggests, this spectacular world is unstable. It is full of movement and action, a movement and action which can pass through stages of being a kind of swirling multiplicity mingling discordant sounds and sights, and reach a point at which it explodes disastrously in all directions. What had been pleasant multitudinousness approaches sheer chaos:

Dirty slip-shod women passed and re-passed, on their way to the cooking house in one corner of the yard; children screamed, and fought, and played together, in another; the tumbling of the skittles, and the shouts of the players, mingled perpetually with these and a hundred other sounds; and all was noise and tumult. (45)

Stage coaches were upsetting in all directions, horses were bolting, boats were overturning, and boilers were bursting. (1)

This exploding world is at first a mere succession of unrelated objects rushing by with accelerating velocity — "Fields,
trees, and hedges, seemed to rush past them with the velocity
of a whirlwind" (9); "Houses, gates, churches, haystacks, objects of every kind they shot by, with a velocity and noise like
roaring waters suddenly let loose" (49) — but in the end the
scene which had at first been so full of distinctly perceptible
objects becomes a mere undifferentiated blur, perhaps "a
bewildering coruscation of beauty and talent" (15), perhaps the "one deep murmur" into which "all the busy sounds
of a mighty multitude instinct with life and occupation"
"blend[s]" (44).

Such visions are nightmarish, a restless flitting to and fro
of objects and people who can no longer be distinguished from
one another. The scene becomes a formless agitation, perpetually fluctuating, in which nothing remains stable for a moment, but either changes into something else, or disappears
altogether. No beginning, orientation, or ending is apparent.
The aimless eddying of the phenomenal scene corresponds to
an increasing anxiety and even delirium on the part of the spectator. No order or meaning can be found in this world of
vertiginous change:

The whole place seemed restless and troubled; and the people
were crowding and flitting to and fro, like the shadows in an uneasy dream. (45)

Scenes changed before his eyes, place succeeded place, and
event followed event, in all the hurry of delirium. (21)

One's inner condition becomes, then, more and more a
match for the aimless motion of the world. This interior turmoil, a swirling mélange of contradictory thoughts and feelings, is perfectly congruent with the exterior world as one
discovers it to be constituted. One becomes like the exterior
world: a "restless whirling mass of cares and anxieties, affections, hopes, and griefs" (45).

This nightmare is, at its climax, a nightmare of eyes. The
entire visible world becomes, in every direction, a solid mass of
gleaming eyes: "Brilliant eyes, lighted up with pleasurable ex-

pectation, gleamed from every side" (35). The turning point
of the experience which Pickwick so naïvely sought is the mo
ment when the spectator becomes himself a spectacle, and finds
himself utterly at the mercy of the looks of others. The world
no longer remains a passive scene. It is human, alive, and i'
threatens to force the spectator to yield his secret. The world
is not so much a physical as a spiritual danger. It turns on the
spectator and begins to invade and destroy his self-possession
and, finally, even the integrity of his being:

> . . . an immense crowd of mail coach guards swarmed round
> the window, every one of whom had his eyes earnestly fixed upon
> him too. He had never seen such a sea of white faces, red bodies
> and earnest eyes, in all his born days. (49)

> There were insects too, hideous crawling things with eyes that
> stared upon him, and filled the very air around: glistening horribl'
> amidst the thick darkness of the place. The walls and ceiling were
> alive with reptiles — the vault expanded to an enormous size —
> frightful figures flitted to and fro — and the faces of men he knew
> rendered hideous by gibing and mouthing, peered out from among
> them. (3)

But one's terror is caused not so much by the multiplicity o
eyes, as by the mere experience of being looked at. A single
pair of eyes caught "glancing eagerly" (47) at one is definitive
proof that it is impossible to remain uninvolved. To leave one'
secure chamber is to yield oneself to the inexplicable threat in
the glances of strangers. The hero, transformed in a wholly un
expected way by this experience, leaves for good his passivity
and actively engages himself in the world.

VI

This engagement at first takes the form of a complete trans
formation of the hero's inner state. Beneath "that perfect cool
ness and self-possession, which are the indispensable accom
paniments of a great mind" (4), there is continually present
potential excitement. The scenes he beholds, or his rapid mo
tion through them, generate at first simply stunned surprise
but this is transformed bit by bit into an actualized emotion, "
state of excitement and agitation" (28), "feelings of the mos

ntense delight and indignation" (13). There is no real dis-
inction here between delight and indignation. What is created
by the "exhilarating sight" (52), or by "the exciting influence
of the morning" (7), or even by "the influence of [an] exciting
iquid" (19), is simply the most generalized form of intense
emotion. A violent inner turmoil replaces "torpor" with "a fever
of excitement" (7). This excitement may be linked, according
to circumstances, with "admiration" (13), with "anxiety"
(38), with "rage" (9), or with "indignant amazement" (50),
but the general condition of inner disturbance is more important than its *differentia*. Compared to the unmoved intel-
ectual lucidity with which Pickwick began, his state of inner
onfusion is not far from the state of the madman who says:
I felt tumultuous passions eddying through my veins" (11);
strange feelings came over me, and thoughts, forced upon me
y some secret power, whirled round and round my brain"
11). Pickwick, like everyone else in *Pickwick Papers*, is, in
pite of his philosophical calm, "a gentleman of an excitable
emperament" (53). "Roused" (15) by the "exciting spec-
acle" (52), which "light[s] up a glow of enthusiasm within
im" (11), he "start[s] into full life and animation" (1).

At first spectators and event still remain separate. On the
ne hand, the spectators are already "in a state of the highest
xcitement" (19), but their excitement is an empty frenzy, a
enzy of anticipation, an excitement which reaches out toward
scene which remains at a distance, or toward an event which
as not yet happened, and prepares to match it by a kind of
remonitory disturbance. So, on the day of the grand review,
t]he whole population of Rochester and the adjoining towns
ise] from their beds at an early hour . . . , in a state of the
tmost bustle and excitement" (4). But, on the other hand,
ere is in the scene itself "as much bustle as the most excitable
erson could desire to behold" (40). What causes one's "fever
excitement" (13) is a scene of multiplicity poised for the
cceeding burst of activity. Or, rather, it is a scene in which,
in the spectators, there are anticipatory movements which
athwart the poised stasis: "The appearance of everything
the Lines denoted that the approaching ceremony was one

of the utmost grandeur and importance. There were sentries posted to keep the ground for the troops, and servants on the batteries keeping places for the ladies, and sergeants running to and fro. . . . Officers were running backwards and forwards . . . ; and even the very privates themselves looked from behind their glazed stocks with an air of mysterious solemnity, which sufficiently bespoke the special nature of the occasion" (4).

There is "a moment of awful suspense" (13), or "a breathless silence" (7), as the turmoils, within and without, remain for an instant longer separated, the spectator poised "on the verge of a strong burst of indignation" (47), or of some other passion. And then, carried away by surprise and by the uncontrollable emotion it generates, the hero, in spite of his detachment, loses his head, and throws himself into the scene with the utmost frenzy. It is now both a violence of emotion and violence of action. The "ebullitions of feeling" (41) into which the hero's detachment has suddenly been transformed expand in a moment into a violent action of engagement in the world. Pickwick, in the "impetuosity of his passion" (9), precipitates himself blindly into the scene of swirling activity which confronts him:

Mr. Pickwick, without the slightest intimation of his purpose, sprang vigorously out of bed; . . . gasping . . . from excitement . . . . (41)

Mr. Pickwick was a philosopher, but philosophers are only men in armour, after all. The shaft had reached him, penetrated through his philosophical harness, to his very heart. In the frenzy of his rage, he hurled the inkstand madly forward, and followed up himself. (10)

. . . he darted swiftly from the room with every particle of his hitherto-bottled-up indignation effervescing, from all parts of his countenance, in a perspiration of passion. (2)

As spectator and scene make direct contact at last there is a "moment of turmoil and confusion" (9). "To describe the confusion that ensue[s] would be impossible" (7), for it is too close to be understood. Nothing can be distinguished but a confused and multiple actuality. Moreover, such direct contact with the world coincides with self-forgetfulness. Pickwick no longer exists as passive watching, or even as surprise. He exists as his action, and as the frenzied emotion which goes with it. The hero identifies himself with the scene, is inextricably merged with the confusion and excitement which he had at first merely watched from a distance. Forgetful of himself, Pickwick is not really aware of the scene either. He is nothing but a double violence of emotion and action, a violence which does not allow him enough distance from himself or from the world to be aware of them. Nothing exists but the indescribable bewilderment and confusion in which his separate existence is lost. When Pickwick finally encounters reality he is literally bowled over and momentarily annihilated by his shattering contact with the world. His subjective response to the intense and physical pressure of the world is itself so physical that it cannot be described in psychological terms. It is a purely material contact between self and world, and transforms the hero, for the time, into an inanimate object. His involuntary motions are comic. They exemplify the Bergsonian comedy of the change of a person into a passive body subject to the impersonal laws of physics. In the same way, the huge meals which occur so often in *Pickwick Papers* and come to a climax at the famous Christmas dinner at Dingley Dell are occasions for forgetting the gap that separates one from the world. Rather than being, as in Rabelais, Flaubert, or Balzac, a way of assimilating the world into oneself, eating and drinking in *Pickwick Papers* are ways of assimilating oneself to the world, ways of overcoming the detachment of mere spectatorship. Overrun by a review, turned over in a coach, absorbed by Christmas festivities, or caught up in an electioneering mob, Pickwick, at the very moment when he should have the most to report of his experiences, is wholly unable to make any report whatsoever. He cannot tell where he is, what is happening, to whom, or why:

[There were] a very few seconds of bewilderment and confusion, in which nothing but the plunging of horses, and breaking of glass, could be made out . . . . (9)

He describes himself as being surrounded on every side, when he could catch a glimpse of the scene, by angry and ferocious countenances, by a vast cloud of dust, and by a dense crowd of combatants. He represents himself as being forced from the carriage by some unseen power, and being personally engaged in a pugilistic encounter; but with whom, or how, or why, he is wholly unable to state. (13)

## VII

After the turmoil, withdrawal, detachment. Very quickly, the hero's "excitement subside[s]" (42). The frenzy of passion and action rapidly exhausts itself, burnt up by the very excess with which Pickwick or his fellows engage themselves in experience. This is true even of the passion of love, as Wardle tells us in the execrable verses of his Christmas Carol: ". . . when love is too strong, it don't last long,/As many have found to their pain" (28). The inner turmoil, of whatever sort, returns quickly to the state of inertia from which it has been roused. Sometimes, indeed, the emotion disappears before it has even had time to be carried into action: "Mr. Pickwick's temporary excitement began to sober down a little, as he reflected upon the inconveniences and dangers of the expedition . . ." (9). The excitement is never more than "temporary," and it is continually in danger of being destroyed by the voluntary or involuntary return of reflection and self-control. Sometimes the passion is deliberately bottled up, as when "Mr. Pickwick paused, bottled up his vengeance, and corked it down" (9). But more often the intense moment of action and feeling passes, and there is an involuntary return of self-awareness which detaches the hero from the world and returns him to his self-enclosed calm. A moment's reflection will destroy his frenzy and recall him to himself:

. . . the first effervescence . . . subsided. (27)

Mr. Pickwick . . . was a quick, and powerful reasoner; and a moment's reflection sufficed to remind him of the impotency of his rage. It subsided as quickly as it had been roused. (10)

As the "momentary passion" "gradually melts" (15), night falls, and Pickwick and his friends, utterly used up by the ex-

eriences of the day, or, perhaps, "dismally depressed with
pirits and agitation" (32), yield themselves to repose: "Slowly
nd sadly did the two friends and the deserted lady, return
ext day in the Muggleton heavy coach. Dimly and darkly had
he shadows of a summer's night fallen upon all around, when
hey again reached Dingley Dell, and stood within the en-
rance to Manor Farm" (10).

But when morning comes again, the hero is completely re-
reshed, completely ready to face again, with no memory what-
oever of the past, the surprises the new day will bring. Since
e was not really conscious in the midst of his experiences, he
annot remember them. And he is protected by this absence of
nemory from being affected at all by his experiences. A night
f sleep returns him altogether to his original state, and he is
eady to go forth on his adventures again with exactly the same
nnocence he had when he first opened his chamber window
nd looked forth on the world:

. . . although the bodily powers of the great man were thus
npaired, his mental energies retained their pristine vigour. His
pirits were elastic; his good humour was restored. Even the vexa-
ion consequent upon his recent adventure had vanished from his
nind . . . . (17)

A night of quiet and repose in the profound silence of Dingley
Dell, and an hour's breathing of its fresh and fragrant air on the
nsuing morning, completely recovered Mr. Pickwick from the
ffects of his late fatigue of body and anxiety of mind. (11)

Thus Pickwick at first yields himself to a life made up of un-
elated adventures separated from one another by a vacancy of
leep and forgetting. These experiences have very little con-
ection with one another. Each adventure has a real duration,
ith a beginning, middle, and end linked together in a rhyth-
ic continuity. The stages of this rhythm are the sudden dis-
overy, when the window is thrown open, of a new experience
nto which Pickwick throws himself with youthful efferves-
ence, the evaporation of this bubbling excitement, a return to
xhausted calm, and, finally, the blotting out, through sleep, of
ll that has happened. Each such adventure is complete in it-

self, but all of them together do not form an interconnected
whole, a total duration whose length is the length of the
novel. Rather, each episode starts again from a new beginning
and each episode culminates in its own obliteration. The novel
like a traveling side show, as Dickens himself said, "keep[s
perpetually going on beginning again, regularly, until the end
of the fair" ("Address from Part X," *PP,* p. xiii). It must per
petually begin again because each adventure consumes itself in
its own violence of action and feeling and leaves nothing but
"a clear stage" (28) ready for the next adventure. The total
rhythm of the novel is apparently not really a rhythm at all, but
rather a discontinuous succession of experiences whose only
unity is that they happen to the same person. The emptiness
of Pickwick's innocence is filled by one adventure after an
other, but each is only substituted for the last. They do not
build on one another. Sam Weller's anecdotes, like the inter
polated stories, introduce characters who do not even exist on
the first level of reality in the novel. These interpolations only
increase the discontinuity, as does the emphasis in the novel on
the accidental nature of encounters or changes of feeling—
as when Sam Weller is "suddenly stricken filial and affection
ate" (27).

*Pickwick Papers,* then, is Victorian picaresque. Like the
novels of Charles Lever, it is more akin to *Peregrine Pickl*
than to *Middlemarch.* But Lever's novels are in at least one
way post-romantic. The piquancy of *Charles O'Malley,* the spe
cial turn it gives to the picaresque mode, is its alternation of
farcical adventures in the eighteenth-century style with pas
sages which express delicate feelings of reminiscence or roman
tic longing. *Pickwick Papers,* on the other hand, seems to be
purely in the manner of the eighteenth-century novel. Its "ob
ject," as Dickens said, was simply "to place before the reader
a constant succession of characters and incidents" (Preface to
the first edition, 1837, *PP,* p. xv). Such a fragmented novel
can be defended in two ways. It has, after all, illustrious models
in the history of the English novel: ". . . if it be objected to
the *Pickwick Papers,* that they are a mere series of adven
tures, in which the scenes are ever changing, . . . he can only

content himself with the reflection, that . . . the same objection has been made to the works of some of the greatest novelists in the English language" (*ibid.*). But *Pickwick Papers* is also, Dickens says, a true representation of real life. In real life too "the scenes are ever changing," and the novel, in presenting characters who appear briefly before us and then disappear for good, is only imitating the perpetual transformations of the real world. It is not really a confession of failure to say that in *Pickwick Papers* "the characters come and go like the men and women we encounter in the real world" (*ibid.*). A good novel, like the real world, must be less an organic whole than a collection of disparate parts which resists all our attempts to reconstitute it into a unity.

## VIII

But can we even say that such a novel is held together by having a single central character to whom most of the adventures happen? Are we justified in saying that Pickwick remains the same person? If, in each episode, he loses himself in the scene before him, and forgets everything but what is immediately present, it would seem that to the discontinuity of adventures corresponds a discontinuity of feelings, and, ultimately, a radical fragmentation of the person who is created by these feelings.

Apparently Pickwick will be a person who lives entirely in the moment, and is constantly reborn as a radically new self. Such a character is never the same self from situation to situation. He passively becomes what his situation makes him, and since his situation is constantly changing, his identity changes too. It changes without pain and without any awareness of transition, since what he was during the previous episode of his life is utterly forgotten. His identity is "inspired by the occasion" (39). Thus Sam Weller, after his first day in the Fleet, is "as much at home as if he had been bred in the prison, and his whole family had vegetated therein for three generations" (44).

The archetype of this mode of existence is "Alfred Jingle, Esq., of No Hall, Nowhere" (7). The breathless and broken quality of Jingle's staccato speech repeats in miniature the disjointed quality and rapid pace of the novel as a whole. Jingle can speak only in brief spurts of verbalization, each followed by a pause, followed by another brief exclamation. His language is made up mostly of nouns and adjectives. It does not move enough to permit the use of verbs, but consists of motionless disconnected names with their qualities attached. These phrases are thrown at the reader pell-mell: ". . . glorious pile — frowning walls — tottering arches — dark nooks — crumbling staircases — Old cathedral too — earthy smell — pilgrim's feet worn away the old steps . . ." (2). Jingle's speeches are a sequence of empty clichés. Moreover, he is a liar and a shape-changer. He is constantly reinventing himself to fit his situation. What is involuntary for the other characters is deliberate for Jingle. He fits himself instantaneously into each new situation, and initiates a new role for himself with the facility of a skilled actor: " 'Friend of yours! — My dear sir, how are you? — Friend of *my* friend's — give me your hand, sir,' — and the stranger grasped Mr. Wardle's hand with all the fervour of a close intimacy of many years" (7). And just as Jingle invents his identity as he goes along, so he invents a past to fit it. The past does not really exist for him as something stable and finished. It can be remolded and manipulated at will, or a wholly fictional past can be substituted in its place, as when Jingle invents a fabulous story about a cricket game in the West Indies (7).

But the very fact that Jingle manipulates deliberately the possibilities of the world in which he finds himself should warn us against assuming that there is no continuous substratum in his personality. Jingle is one of the minor characters in *Pickwick Papers* who is encountered again after we first meet him. And each time he reappears we recognize him immediately as the same person, with the same idiosyncrasies of appearance and speech, and the same ability to adapt himself to a new situation. The very flexibility of Jingle's character is a permanent and indestructible trait. And even Pickwick himself does not really change from episode to episode. His detachment after involvement in the world does not mean simply a forgetting of the event. It also means a return to himself. All the characters whom we can observe through time in *Pickwick Papers* remain recognizably the same through all their adventures. They confront each new experience as persons with intrinsic identities which can never be changed by any adventure.

Moreover, the characters have never really ceased to be themselves even in the midst of the violence of their emotion and action. The external event is the occasion of emotion, but it does not determine that emotion. The emotional effect is not commensurate with its cause. An external event merely makes it possible for Pickwick to manifest the "innate good feeling" (16) which characterizes him at the beginning and throughout. Each person's excitement is his own idiosyncratic emotion, his own inalterable personal tone. Although an external event may be required to bring it into being, it has already existed potentially, and it remains essentially the same whatever the situation which calls it out. Contact with other people, for example, cannot cause substantial change in the characters of *Pickwick Papers* because there is no real possibility here of intimate subjective relations. There is no loss or change of identity through love. Love relationships are entirely external. They no more cause one to change one's identity than do the other causes of excitement, such as the huge festival meals. The great celebrations in *Pickwick Papers* are not really occasions of communion. They are a being together around a third impersonal thing, the food, the drink, the mistletoe, or the songs. These produce in everyone a feeling of well-being, an escape from self-consciousness and the cares of everyday life. But no real contact with other people is made at these festivities. Each character is simply forced by excitement to manifest himself in his true nature. There is truth in wine, just as in any other stimulus of excitement. Drink merely brings out Pickwick in all his innate benevolence. "Yielding by degrees to the influence of the exciting liquid" (19), he simply reveals the uncaused and unchangeable quality of his character: "Mr. Pickwick . . . produc[ed] a constant succession of the blandest and most benevolent smiles without being moved thereunto by any discernible cause or pretence whatsoever" (8).

If there is any essential change in the characters it is primarily in our apprehension of them, though it is also true to say that Dickens' conception of his protagonists changed and deepened as he wrote the novel. By the end Winkle, Snodgrass, and Tupman have almost completely shed their comic masks and costumes — though Tupman in the last chapter still projects his "humor" on the world around him, and thinks Pickwick "contemplate[s] a matrimonial alliance" (57). Bit by bit, though more rapidly at first, the central characters become more or less three-dimensional persons, able to share at the end of the story in the ideal society Pickwick creates. And Pickwick himself changes from an oversimplified comic façade to a living person who is the object of sympathy rather than of laughter. But the explanation of this change offered by Dickens himself is at least plausible: "It has been observed of Mr. Pickwick," says Dickens, "that there is a decided change in his character, as these pages proceed, and that he becomes more good and more sensible. I do not think this change will appear forced or unnatural to my readers, if they will reflect that in real life the peculiarities and oddities of a man who has anything whimsical about him, generally impress us first, and that it is not until we are better acquainted with him that we usually begin to look below these superficial traits, and to know the better part of him" (Preface to the first cheap edition, 1847, *PP*, p. xix). The appeal again is to "real life." It is the sole criterion Dickens will overtly recognize at this stage of his career. Furthermore, Dickens reminds us that we, as readers, are in a particular position in relation to the characters. We are outside as spectators, able to see a character's appearance and actions, and to hear him speak. We reach his inner life primarily through these avenues, though Dickens will permit himself direct expression of Pickwick's thoughts or feelings. We are both inside and outside, but we are outside first, as we are with real people in the real world, and only slowly reach an understanding of what a character is like subjectively. The change in Pickwick or in the other characters, Dickens claims, recapitulates this drama of progressive understanding. It is our comprehension of the characters which changes rather than the characters themselves.

The characters in *Pickwick Papers* cannot, then, change — except perhaps to discover what the world outside themselves is really like. It is not any "artfully interwoven or ingeniously complicated plot" which unifies the various episodes of the novel in "one tolerably harmonious whole, each leading to the other by a gentle and not unnatural progress of adventure" (Preface to the first edition, 1837, *PP*, p. xv). The true dramatic center of *Pickwick Papers* is not the unraveling of any plot, nor is it the change of Pickwick or of any other character. It is Pickwick's gradual discovery of the real nature of the world.

## IX

The discontinuity of the world of the eighteenth-century novel was made tolerable not only by the inalterable permanence of the characters during all the vicissitudes of their emotions and adventures, but also by the assumption that the external world, though fallen, is guided by a benign Providence, or at least by a capricious Fortune which tends to reward the naturally good who have learned prudence. The world may appear to be meaningless and malign, but behind appearances it favors a certain kind of goodness, and, moreover, everyone has a given place in it. Tom Jones, after his adventures have matured him, finds a ready-made place for himself in society, and society itself is justified, for Fielding, by supernatural sanctions.

Pickwick too begins by assuming that God conducts all things for good. The novel remains comic, in both senses of the word, and Pickwick's expectations are, in a way, fulfilled. But the prevailing comic tone and the happy ending should not blind us to the darker side of Dickens' portrait of society. *Pickwick Papers* is a comedy played against a somber backdrop. The adventures in which Pickwick becomes involved, and especially the stories he hears, introduce him to a world without Providence, a world of dog-eat-dog aggression, a world in which people are driven by fortuitous circumstances, not guided by a providential power. Pickwick discovers that the reigning principles of large portions of the world are disorder and injustice. God is apparently not present in these areas at all, and to leave one's protected enclosure may be to put oneself at the mercy of merciless forces. The city is the special place of danger. In the urban world, the world of law or commerce, people are, like Mr. Winkle's bullets, "unfortunate foundlings, deprived of their natural rights, cast loose upon the world, and billeted nowhere" (19). There, direct contact with society brings one into the arena of a battle. Either I shall deceive and exploit the other, or he will deceive and exploit me. The latter will certainly happen to the naïve characters like Pickwick who expect people to be good. And, even though the inner natures of people cannot change, they can be slowly and irrevocably worn down by the world. The interpolated stories in *Pickwick Papers* present characters who are driven by destructive forces in their environments. This submission to evil forces is expressed in several of the stories by hallucinatory, nightmarish visions in which the phenomenal world is a dark enclosure, swarming with ghosts or monsters. These creatures rush in toward the delirious protagonist to possess him and destroy his sanity. Or, one may be slowly destroyed, worn out, used up by a world in which one has no place. The innate characters of Jingle and Job Trotter are not changed by imprisonment, but they are physically transformed, and other victims of the cruelty of society are in various stages of deterioration, like the prisoner of whom Dickens says: "the iron teeth of confinement and privation had been slowly filing him down for twenty years" (42) In the city, everyone is alone, as much alone as the prisoner who says: "My loneliness . . . , in all this noise and riot, has been very dreadful. May God forgive me! He has seen my solitary, lingering death" (44). Even Pickwick is "alone in the coarse vulgar crowd" (41). This isolation in the midst of a hostile crowd is the essential human condition in *Pickwick Papers* for those who are not lucky enough to have money or a snug place in the country or in the suburbs.

But how can Pickwick be brought to recognize and accept

this fact? As we have seen, to engage oneself in adventures is not to discover the real nature of the world. It is only to discover one's own identity, the color of one's own inner fire. Pickwick is not really taught by his encounters with people who are being destroyed by injustice, and he is not really taught by the education which Sam Weller tries to give him.

The turning point of *Pickwick Papers* is the moment when Pickwick becomes involved in the case of Bardell versus Pickwick, and must say: "We are all the victims of circumstances, and I the greatest" (18). When Pickwick himself becomes "a dreadful instance of the force of circumstances" (18), he is no longer merely shaken out of his detachment into a state of surprised excitement which is really only an affirmation of himself. He begins to be driven by the same forces that have destroyed the prisoners, the strolling player, and the madman. He becomes implicated in a process which might end, as it has in so many of the interpolated stories, if not by changing the innate character of Pickwick, then by impersonally destroying him, seizing his possessions, throwing him into prison, and leaving him there to rot. Pickwick only truly understands the world when he becomes involved in it. Only then does he finally recognize that he is really in danger, that innate goodness is not armor enough in this world: ". . . old men," he says at last, "may come [into the Fleet Prison], through their own heedlessness and unsuspicion" (42).

At this point Pickwick's life begins to have a cohesive duration, and the novel a real plot. Pickwick can no longer reënact in a kind of eternal childhood the rhythm of his innocent adventures. He must now either extricate himself from his situation or be destroyed by it.

The dramatic center of *Pickwick Papers* is Pickwick's discovery that much of the world is indifferent or even a positive threat to his life and to his goodness. Even if there are centers of good, like Mr. Wardle's Dingley Dell, where he is safe, these are no certain protection. Their power of good does not extend beyond their own frontiers. Far from containing anything which sustains him in his innate identity, the world tends to deny that identity. He is dependent on himself alone. The

prisoners in the Fleet are restless and do not know what to do
with themselves: ". . . they all lounged, and loitered, and
slunk about, with as little spirit or purpose as the beasts in a
menagerie" (45). But Pickwick too has no real direction in his
life, though at first he does not recognize the significance of
this fact, and at one point can say: " . . . we may as well see
Ipswich as any other place" (20). Neither the prisoners nor
Pickwick have any real place in the world. There is nothing
in the world outside which tells them what they ought to do.
To involve one's life in the world may be not to have that life
enhanced, but to lose it, to have it slowly crushed out of existence.

x

If a man wished to abstract himself from the world — to remove himself from within the reach of temptation — to place
himself beyond the possibility of any inducement to look out of
the window — he should by all means go to Lant Street. (32)

There is only one way to protect oneself: permanent withdrawal. One must enter a sequestered place where there will
be no temptation to look out of the window. One must refuse
to have any complicity in the world. It is extremely dangerous
to leave home at all. The hero therefore withdraws from the
world, shuts himself up in himself. But now he is no longer
able to forget what he has discovered the world to be like. He
is completely cured of his "pursuit of novelty."

Pickwick withdraws first by refusing to pay the damages
after the suit is decided against him. His refusal to take part
in the unjust proceedings of the law makes him a kind of
Thoreau. Pickwick too believes that there are times when the
only place for a good man is behind bars. The institutions of
organized society are corrupt, and when there is a choice between one's own inner knowledge of what is right, and obedience to an unjust decision, there is only one choice to make.
One chooses to be true to oneself, though this means passive
resistance to the law of the land.

But Pickwick's refusal to pay only involves him more. He has already gone too far, and must suffer for it. Society seizes him, incarcerates him. In jail he experiences for the first time the full impact of the world he so innocently entered at the beginning of his adventures. And here the definitive act of withdrawal takes place:

Mr. Pickwick wandered along all the galleries, up and down all the staircases, and once again round the whole area of the yard. . . . There were the same squalor, the same turmoil and noise, the same general characteristics, in every corner; in the best and the worst alike. . . .

"I have seen enough," said Mr. Pickwick, as he threw himself into a chair in his little apartment. "My head aches with these scenes, and my heart too. Henceforth I will be a prisoner in my own room." (45)

And after he has paid the costs of the suit, the necessary price of his education, and has escaped from the prison, Pickwick reaffirms this withdrawal by giving up his "rambles." He buys a house which is an enclosed retreat, and ends his life as the center of a world from which all danger has been carefully excluded. It is only by creating a private domicile protecting one's identity that one can safely exist. A person is safe only because of the fixity of his nature, and because this nature, if it happens to be good, has an inexhaustible power to create an enclosed milieu of goodness radiating from the good person at the center. Such a milieu is a little circle of good in the midst of a dangerous world: "He saw those who had been delicately nurtured, and tenderly brought up, cheerful under privations, and superior to suffering, that would have crushed many of rougher grain, because they bore within their own bosoms the materials of happiness, contentment, and peace" (29).

But Pickwick is not really withdrawn and alone, or, rather, he is both withdrawn and not withdrawn. It is true that he plans to spend his declining years in "peaceful retirement," cut off altogether from the outer world. But he will live these years "cheered through life by the society of [his] friends" (57). He does not isolate himself from all mankind, and live like Fielding's old man of the hill. At the end of the novel

Pickwick is the center of a little society, a perfect social organism which he has created.

A long tradition in the eighteenth-century English novel, extending even down to Scott's *The Heart of Midlothian,* was based on a pattern of exit from some earthly paradise into a fallen world, followed, after many adventures, by a return to that paradise. But, for the eighteenth-century novel, the earthly paradise was ready-made and preëxistent. It was the rural remnant of a good traditional society, and it was sustained by divine principles inhering in it and justifying it. So Tom Jones returns after his education to Paradise Hall, and to the benevolent protection of Squire Allworthy, and so the good but innocent Dr. Primrose, in *The Vicar of Wakefield,* wins happiness for himself and for his family not through his own actions, but through the benevolence of Sir William Thornhill. Sir William acts as a kind of earthly providence, an avenue through which the Divine Providence can act in the world. But Pickwick must be both Primrose and Thornhill at once. He is himself the founder of his own earthly paradise. It does not preëxist, nor will anyone else make it for him. Moreover, he cannot depend on any direct help or justification from God. The ideal society he makes is wholly self-contained and self-sufficient. It derives altogether from Pickwick, or, if from God, only from Pickwick's nature as God has initially made him. The world outside Pickwick offers him no support for his establishment of a good social order. Pickwick must, in a way, be his own God. At the end of the novel Pickwick is like God in the center of his universe, diffusing benevolence all around, and receiving it back in reciprocal influences and reflections:

And in the midst of all this, stood Mr. Pickwick, his countenance lighted up with smiles, which the heart of no man, woman, or child, could resist: himself the happiest of the group: . . turning round in a different direction at every fresh expression of gratification or curiosity, and inspiring everybody with his looks of gladness and delight. (57)

The goodness of Pickwick's little heavenly city is defined by the intuitive knowledge which its citizens have of one another through the radiations of love emanating from Pickwick, or, rather, its perfection is determined by the sympathetic confidence which they have in one another. This confidence, based upon emotion, makes them feel that they understand one another. The perspicuity of Sam Weller, which might see through all this and return the characters to their isolation, must be relegated to a subordinate position. Pickwick's ideal community is thus doubly in jeopardy. It depends altogether upon Pickwick's own human benevolence (and upon his money). The barriers resisting the threats from outside are fragile, and will collapse when Pickwick dies. Moreover, the problem of communication and love has only been evaded. It has not really been faced. The eighteenth-century concept of the man of feeling goes back to the Shaftesburian idea that one can pattern oneself sympathetically to match the universal order of nature. This kind of sympathy made possible a sympathetic understanding of other people, and also made possible the projective power of the sympathetic imagination. The possibility of love and understanding between people depended upon the idea of a pervasive transhuman harmony and goodness, available everywhere to all men. But it is just this concept of a divine order and goodness, transcendent and yet available to man, which is lacking in *Pickwick Papers*. Pickwick's benevolence is wholly human, and wholly enclosed within himself. There is nothing but its own power which guarantees its ability to flow outward to pierce the barriers separating people, and to create a milieu of communication and love for them to inhabit.

Nevertheless, *Pickwick Papers* accepts the miracle as accomplished, and the wisdom of Sam Weller is effaced by the effervescent optimism and good spirits of Mr. Pickwick. The inextinguishable *élan* of Pickwick's benevolence survives even this transition from innocence to wisdom. It is only later on, for example in *Martin Chuzzlewit,* that Dickens faces the problem posed by his sense of the isolation and irreducible idiosyncrasy of each human being. Moreover, the effacement of Sam Weller corresponds to an extraordinary change in the tone of the novel as it progresses toward its conclusion. For initially, as I have said, the consciousness of the narrator and therefore of the reader are not identified with that of Pickwick. At the beginning we see Pickwick from the outside as comic, even as farcical, more the object of laughter than of sympathy. But as the novel proceeds, the relationship between narrator and protagonist changes radically. It is not simply that Pickwick develops into a fuller, more human character. More important is the way Dickens is progressively attracted by his own creation. Just as Pickwick arouses in Sam, Dickens' covert representative in the novel, an unwonted devotion and fidelity (for whom but for Pickwick would Sam go to prison?), so Dickens, as the novel progresses, is taken by his own invention, and more and more believes in him and loves him. Pickwick has a power to transform those around him, and to change the situations in which he finds himself into a representation of himself, irradiated by his goodness. But the most startling example of his magical power is the change in the attitude of the narrator himself. With this change the tone of the novel changes too. Bit by bit the distance and objectivity, with which the narrator at first watched Pickwick with ironic amusement, is replaced by sympathy and belief. This progressive destruction of a dry comic tone and its replacement by warmth and sympathy is, one might say, the hidden drama of the novel. What had been an interior play in which Dickens watched without sympathy another part of himself invent and enact the role of Pickwick becomes the mysterious attraction and domination of the author or narrator by his own creation. The narrator becomes fascinated by Pickwick, and, in the end, the narrator (and the reader) are wholly within the charmed circle of warmth and benevolence which derives from Pickwick and transforms everything around him. The reader and the narrator, then, become believers in Pickwick, and, tempted to remain forever within his safe enclosure, we leave him reluctantly. We leave him living at the center of his own world, radiating a goodness which derives from himself alone, giving his friends in marriage from his own house, acting as godfather to their numerous children, and idolized by the whole neighborhood (57).

Pickwick is thus safe and happy in the end, but *Pickwick Papers* itself, seemingly so closely linked to eighteenth-century optimism, is really a farewell to the eighteenth century. The crucial event of the novel is Pickwick's discovery that transcendent power and goodness are no longer immanent in the world. The failure of the attempt to revive Pickwick and Sam Weller in *Master Humphrey's Clock* is a good indication that the cycle of Pickwick's adventures corresponded to a decisive transformation of Dickens' own inner world. Once Dickens had written *Pickwick Papers* there was no real possibility of ever going back again to its beginning. In dramatizing this definitive exit from innocence the novel raises by implication the fundamental questions of all Dickens' novels: How is a person who cannot withdraw going to avoid being destroyed by the evil forces in the world? How is someone who begins as an outcast going to discover anything which will be a support for his identity and the source of a coherent life? It is this problem to which Dickens addresses himself in *Oliver Twist,* begun while *Pickwick Papers* was yet appearing in monthly installments.

## Chapter II

## OLIVER TWIST

I wished to show, in little Oliver, the principle of Good surviving through every adverse circumstance, and triumphing
at last. (Preface to the third edition, *OT*, p. vii)

I

A T first Oliver Twist is not at all aware of himself or of his
situation. He is simply a kind of animate object, inhabited by a
will to live. He is a "millstone . . . round the parochial
throat" (4), passed indifferently from institution to institution,
"brought up by hand" (2), put out "To Let" (3) as though he
were a piece of real estate.

But self-awareness does come to Oliver eventually, and it returns intermittently even in the midst of his life of animal-like
suffering and abjection. When it does come it appears spontaneously in a form which is simple and all-embracing. It is a
consciousness of his total solitude:

. . . a sense of his loneliness in the great wide world, sank
into the child's heart for the first time. (2)

"I am a very little boy, sir; and it is so — so — . . . lonely,
sir! So very lonely!" (4)

He was alone in a strange place; and we all know how chilled
and desolate the best of us will sometimes feel in such a situation. (5)

Oliver's desolation is the absence of a primary human requirement, some relation to something human or material out-

side oneself. His interior life is, as a result, formless. It is nothing but the prolonged monotonous repetition of a moment which is simply emptiness. "Gloom and loneliness . . . [surround] him" (3), and nothing can be seen or experienced but this gloom and this loneliness.

Oliver's story begins and the moment of his becoming potentially human occurs when he becomes aware of his solitude and in the same moment becomes instinctively aware that it is intolerable to him. Oliver's experience of solitude is not posited upon a prior experience of its opposite. He has never known any other condition: "The boy had no friends to care for, or to care for him. The regret of no recent separation was fresh in his mind; the absence of no loved and well-remembered face sank heavily into his heart. But his heart *was* heavy, notwithstanding" (5). It is only because Oliver's heart *is* heavy notwithstanding, only because he has an awareness of his state which does not depend on anything outside himself, that he can turn now to the outside world and demand from it some form of that love which he feels to be his natural right as a human being.

But when he turns to the world he finds something very different from the first undifferentiated gloom. He finds that the world does not simply leave the outcast in the open to die. It aggressively addresses itself to the destruction of the helpless being to which it gives no place. Once the decision is made that the outcast has no reason for existing, the world sets about deliberately to fill up the vacuum it has created by a legislative fiat. For even the space he takes up is needed. The world rushes violently in to bury him away out of sight, to take back the volume he occupied, and even to consume the very substance of his body. The characters of *Oliver Twist* find themselves in a world in which they are from the first moment and at every moment in extreme danger. Not how to "succeed," how to "rise in the world," but how to live in this world at all, is their problem. Neither the social world nor the world of nature is willing to give them the means of life. The thieves would have starved to death either in or out of a workhouse if they had not turned to crime, and Oliver's most pressing need is not the status and comfort of a recognized place in society, but simply breathing room and food.

The outcast is likely to be starved or smothered or crushed to death by mere accident, for the world goes on as though he were not in it. So parish children are often "overlooked in turning up a bedstead, or inadvertently scalded to death when there [happens] to be a washing" (2). And so Oliver is in danger of being beaten or crushed to death. "Grind him to ashes!" says Monks (33). The board of the workhouse thinks of sending Oliver to sea, "the probability being, that the skipper would flog him to death, in a playful mood, some day after dinner, or would knock his brains out with an iron bar" (4).

Or, the outcast may be starved to death. The fame of the scene in which Oliver asks for "more" derives, one feels, from the way it expresses dynamically Oliver's revolt against the hostile social and material world. Oliver's request is total. He demands not simply more food, but recognition of his right to live. The workhouse authorities respond to his demand by imprisoning him in a "dark and solitary room." Later on, when Oliver revolts again, he is again assigned to a windowless underground room, the universal scene of his incarceration throughout the novel.

In the windowless room, one may suffocate. The fear of enclosure and the fear of choking to death are closely related motifs in the central imaginative complex of *Oliver Twist*. When Oliver is born there is "considerable difficulty in inducing [him] to take upon himself the office of respiration" (1). Parish children are, we have seen, often turned up in beds and smothered by accident, and Oliver is nearly apprenticed to Mr. Gamfield, a chimney sweep, who reluctantly admits that "young boys have been smothered in chimneys before now" (3).

But when the "gentleman in the white waistcoat" predicts of Oliver, "I know that boy will be hung" (2), we meet for the first time a version of the motif of suffocation which dominates the novel. Hanging is the inescapable destiny in *Oliver Twist* of all those who attempt to live outside the world of honest men. It is Oliver's destiny too if Fagin succeeds in making him

a thief. The characters in *Oliver Twist* are obsessed with a fear of being hanged, a fear which is expressed with hallucinatory intensity in the description of Fagin's "last night alive" and is fulfilled in the death of Sikes (52, 50). In the narration of both of these deaths the motif of hanging is merged with the image of a dark suffocating interior. Hanging is a frightening mixture of two fears which operate throughout *Oliver Twist* — the fear of falling and the fear of being crushed or suffocated. A man is hanged out in the open, in full view of the crowd, and the executioner drops him into the air. But beneath his black hood the victim is as completely alone, enclosed in the dark, as if he were in the depths of a dungeon. And what more proper symbol of the crushing, suffocating violence of the hostile world than the instantaneous tightening of the noose? Fagin and Sikes merely act out the death which has threatened Oliver from the beginning, and has, in his case too, been connected with the image of close imprisonment in a dark room. When Oliver is locked in the "dark and solitary room" after he has asked for "more," Dickens comments: "It appears, at first sight, not unreasonable to suppose, that, if he had entertained a becoming feeling of respect for the prediction of the gentleman in the white waistcoat, he would have established that sage individual's prophetic character, once and for ever, by tying one end of his pocket-handkerchief to a hook in the wall, and attaching himself to the other" (3).

But there are other striking passages in *Oliver Twist* which combine the contrary actions of falling and being crushed: "A great many of the tenements had shop-fronts; but these were fast closed, and mouldering away; only the upper rooms being inhabited. Some houses which had become insecure from age and decay, were prevented from falling into the street, by huge beams of wood reared against the walls, and firmly planted in the road" (5). Or, in another place, we see: "tottering house-fronts projecting over the pavement, dismantled walls that seem to totter . . . , chimneys half crushed half hesitating to fall" (50). These buildings seem inhabited with a will to fall, to plunge down and smash themselves to bits. It is not a question here, as one might expect, of a fear that the roof will cave in and crush one. The windowless prison, dark and seemingly underground like a cave or grave, is really suspended over a void, and is kept only by a few insubstantial props from plunging down with all its inhabitants. It is the upper rooms of these houses which are inhabited. However solid the prison appears from the inside, the bottom may at any moment drop out. It encloses, entombs, but offers no substantial support, and its most dangerous potentiality may be to fall *with* its prisoner, crushing him. Enclosure in an absolutely dark underground room is, paradoxically, not total imprisonment, immobilization. For if one is wholly alone in the dark and cannot even see the surrounding stone walls, it is as if there were no walls there and one were suspended in nothingness or even falling endlessly through an indistinguishable gloom. One reaches out to touch even the imprisoning walls. They are at least something solid, something which will support, however coldly, the isolated being: "when the long, dismal night came on, [he] spread his little hands before his eyes to shut out the darkness, and crouching in the corner, tried to sleep: ever and anon waking with a start and tremble, and drawing himself closer and closer to the wall, as if to feel even its cold hard surface were a protection in the gloom and loneliness which surrounded him" (3).

The image of the dark, dilapidated house which strives constantly to fall of its own weight is one of the recurrent configurations of the imagination of Dickens. It reappears in the slum houses of Tom-all-Alone's in *Bleak House* which come crashing down with no warning, killing the paupers within, and it reappears most strikingly as one of the central motifs of *Little Dorrit:* the gloomy, heavy, apparently solid house of the Clennams which is secretly mined from within and falls at the climax of the novel.

There is another variation of this destructive plunge, a variation which haunted Dickens throughout his life and of which *Oliver Twist* contains striking examples. The fall may be into the dirty, suffocating, rending water of the rapidly flowing river. Dickens was, as has often been observed, obsessed by the river Thames and by the daydream of death by drowning, a daydream which was both repulsive and attractive at the same

time. But it has not been so often noticed that an important part of Dickens' imaginative landscape of the river was the image of a nook at the edge of the water or of a house towering over the river bank or built in the mud of its shores and in the process of sinking gradually into the shore:

> The old smoke-stained storehouses on either side, rose heavy and dull from the dense mass of roofs and gables, and frowned sternly upon water too black to reflect even their lumbering shapes. (46)

> . . . a scattered little colony of ruinous houses . . . [was] erected on a low unwholesome swamp, bordering upon the river. (38)

Nancy tells the secrets of Fagin's gang at a midnight meeting with Rose Maylie and Mr. Brownlow in a "dark and dismal hole" (46) formed by the landing-stairs going down to the river from London Bridge on the Surrey bank. Behind them are the dark stones of the bridge, before them is the dark water, and concealed in an angle of the stairs is the watcher sent by Fagin whose report of her infidelity will cause Bill Sikes to murder her. The scene is like all the black, suffocating interiors in the novel except that the floor is formed by the dark water which, Nancy says, is her destined deathbed. Nancy is actually crushed to death, but Dickens has her die in imagination the death by water which so fascinated and repelled him: "Look at that dark water," says Nancy to Rose Maylie. "How many times do you read of such as I who spring into the tide, and leave no living thing, to care for, or bewail them! It may be years hence, or it may be only months, but I shall come to that at last" (46).

Death by drowning is not, for Dickens, a soft and easy death. The drowning man does not melt away fluidly into the water. The plunge into the dark river ends in the same violence as hanging or as the fall of the windowless room. The meeting between Monks and the Bumbles is held in a room high up in a large abandoned factory. The image of the tall unstable tenements is repeated, but this time it is the river into which the building might fall: ". . . a considerable portion of the building had already sunk down into the water; while the remainder, tottering and bending over the dark stream, seemed to wait a favourable opportunity of following its old companion" (38).

The imminent fall of the building is, however, only an analogue of the corresponding human fall. Through the secret trap door Monks shows the horrified Bumbles a glimpse of "the turbid water, swollen by the heavy rain, . . . rushing rapidly on below" (38). It is into this turbulent water, which will both swallow up its victim and "cut [him] to pieces" (38), that Monks throws the locket and ring which are the only evidence of Oliver's identity, the symbolic vessels of that selfhood Oliver seeks.[1] And just as Oliver is in danger of being hanged, crushed, or suffocated, so he is in danger of being drowned. When Sikes is taking him through a dark misty night the boy hears "a dull sound of falling water not far off": "The water!" he thinks, "He has brought me to this lonely place to murder me!" (21).

Apparently there is no escape. One demands life from this world only to be met by even more determined hostility. Against this calculated effort to destroy him, Oliver has for defense only what Bumble calls his "artificial soul and spirit" (7). Only the "good sturdy spirit" "implanted" "in Oliver's breast" by "nature or inheritance" (2) will keep him alive. It is both nature *and* inheritance, both the self that Oliver has inherited from his unknown parents, and his "natural goodness." Both are necessary to keep Oliver alive at all.

But at the heart of the novel is the fear that this "good sturdy spirit" will seize by violence what belongs to it by right — status and the goods of this world — and thus transform its innocence into a guilt which no longer deserves approval and status. He is saved by the fact that he is naturally "grateful and attached" (32), as Rose Maylie calls him, and, far from planning to seize by force the goods and status he lacks, is simply looking for someone to whom he can be related as a child to the parents who seem to him the source of all value and the absolute judges of right and wrong.

There is little active volition in Oliver, no will to do something definite, to carve out for himself a place in the solid and hostile world, to choose a course oriented toward the future and follow it out without regard to the sacrifices necessary. No, all

[1] See Monks' boast: ". . . the only proofs of the boy's identity lie at the bottom of the river" (49).

Oliver's volition is the volition of passive resistance. Oliver wills to live, and therefore resists violently all the attempts of the world to crush him or bury him or make him into a thief. But at the center of this fierce will there is passivity, the passivity of waiting, of expectation, of "great expectations." Oliver will not seize for himself a place in the world, nor will he join in the attempts of the thieves to create a society in the depths of the slums. But neither will he allow the world of honest men to destroy him. He resists the crushing walls of his prison because he expects that somehow they will turn into a soft protecting enclosure, into a cradle, a comfortable nook where he will be securely cared for.

But before this can happen Oliver must endure a long trial, a sequence of experiences which is essentially the detailed exploration of the world as it is for the outcast. And without any external evidence at all that he is other than he seems to be, gallows' bait, Oliver must act as if he were what he wants to be, a good boy, the son of a gentleman.

## II

Apparently there is no escape. No novel could be more completely dominated by an imaginative complex of claustrophobia. No other novel by Dickens returns so frequently to images of dark dirty rooms with no apparent exit. At various times Oliver is imprisoned in "the coal-cellar" (2), in a "dark and solitary room" (3), in a "little room by himself" (3), in a "cell" "in shape and size something like an area cellar, only not so light. It was most intolerably dirty" (11). He is almost apprenticed as a chimney sweep, and is finally taken on by an undertaker who begins by pushing him "down a steep flight of stairs into a stone cell, damp and dark: forming the ante-room to the coal-cellar" (4). He sleeps in the workshop among the coffins: "The shop was close and hot. The atmosphere seemed tainted with the smell of coffins. The recess beneath the counter in which his flock mattress was thrust, looked like a grave" (5).

When Oliver reaches London it is to live in a world of dark rooms, rooms which seem to be underground even though they may be high above the earth. These rooms are reached by unlighted staircases and narrow corridors, crooked passageways which make it impossible to orient the rooms to which they lead with the street one has just left. The rooms which Oliver enters are usually lit, if at all, by a single candle which burns dimly in the gloom, or lit and warmed at once by a fire over which crouches Fagin, the evil power of the London underworld, guarding his treasure like some fabled dragon. In London Oliver is introduced to an entire society which lives in the total exclusion he has experienced alone in Mr. Sowerberry's coal cellar.

The time of Oliver's passage from the street to these entombed interiors is of especial importance. Not only is it the time when he loses his sense of direction and his knowledge of the whereabouts of the open street; it is also the period when he has a special awareness of his plight and of his surroundings. Here, for a moment, several distinct entities can be distinguished: the street from which Oliver is being excluded, the room toward which he is going, and the dark passage which forms an absolutely impassable barrier between the room and the street. It is impassable at least by the mind, for it is a space of absolute unintelligibility between the street and the buried room. The two latter have no connection with one another because they are separated by a blank, but for a moment, in the midst of that blank, it is possible at least to juxtapose what one has just left and what one is entering. In one direction there is the street from which one is being shut out, but the place where one is now is totally obscure: "The passage was perfectly dark. . . . it was impossible to distinguish even the form of the speaker in the darkness" (16); "Look sharp with the light, or I shall knock my brains out against something in this confounded hole" (26); "Oliver, groping his way with one hand, and having the other firmly grasped by his companion, ascended with much difficulty the dark and broken stairs" (8). But in the other direction, at the end of the dark passage, the room toward which one is going can be dimly seen: ". . . the light of a feeble candle gleamed on the wall at the remote end of the passage; and a man's face peeped out, from where a balustrade of the old kitchen staircase had been broken away" (8).

If the darkness of the passage gives way to light it is only to reveal a series of rooms which cut one off more and more completely from the open street, and lead one to feel more inextricably buried within, deep underground: "They looked into all the rooms; they were cold, bare, and empty. They descended into the passage, and thence into the cellars below. The green damp hung upon the low walls; the tracks of the snail and slug glistened in the light of the candle; but all was still as death" (26).

At last one enters the inner room itself, the interior of the interior, beyond which it is impossible to go further. At first this inner room appears merely as a place which is lighted rather than dark. It is hardly possible to distinguish anything more: "The room was illuminated by two gas-lights; the glare of which was prevented by the barred shutters, and closely-drawn curtains of faded red, from being visible outside. The ceiling was blackened, to prevent its colour from being injured by the flaring of the lamps; and the place was so full of dense tobacco smoke, that at first it was scarcely possible to discern anything more" (26, and see 15). But finally one makes out in the dim light various objects, the debris of civilization and communal living, perhaps "a smoky fire, two or three broken chairs, a table, and a very old couch" (22), perhaps merely "a broken arm-chair, and an old couch or sofa without covering" (26). Dickens' precise enumeration of the contents of these low dark rooms only makes their essential desolation more apparent. These objects, old and broken as they are, must be named because they are the only things in sight except the blackened walls. They form the total world of the inhabitant; he is by now psychologically so far removed from the open street that it is as if nothing but this room and its battered furniture existed.

Along with the light and furniture which make this room a parody of a human habitation, Oliver sees, in some cases, the people who live there. But the discovery of the underworld society is described as the transition from an almost total obscurity to the perception of a crowd of people which is merely confusing and unintelligible to the observer. It no more relates it-

self to him or tells him anything about his place in the world
than do the broken chairs and tables of the empty rooms: "By
degrees, however, as some of [the smoke] cleared away through
the open door, an assemblage of heads, as confused as the
noises that greeted the ear, might be made out; and as the eye
grew more accustomed to the scene, the spectator gradually became aware of the presence of a numerous company, male and
female, crowded round a long table: at the upper end of which,
sat a chairman with a hammer of office in his hand; while a
professional gentleman, with a bluish nose, and his face tied up
for the benefit of a toothache, presided at a jingling piano in a
remote corner" (26). The gloom clears only to reveal the interior landscape of a dream — a group of people carrying on
some mysterious ritual or revelry as though the spectator were
not there at all. The spectator can see only that the inhabitants
are like the scene in which they live, and that the same taint, a
taint which is both physical and spiritual, covers in one way or
another both animate and inanimate objects: "for depravity, or
poverty, or an habitual acquaintance with both, had left a taint
on all the animate matter, hardly less unpleasant than the thick
greasy scum on every inanimate object that frowned upon
it" (43).

This world is wholly incomprehensible to Oliver. The exterior confusion of sights and sounds is matched by an interior
bewilderment. Oliver's state of mind as prisoner of the thieves
in these underground interiors is usually that of semi-conscious
anxiety. He has little awareness or understanding of his plight.
He has merely a vague knowledge that he is living in a kind of
earthly hell, not the least unpleasant part of which is the fact
that he does not comprehend most of what is going on around
him. This failure to understand actually protects Oliver from
the complicity of too much knowledge of the thieves' world.
But this is another of the things he does not know, and he remains aware only of the confusion itself and of his failure to
understand it:

Oliver tried to reply, but his tongue failed him. He was deadly
pale; and the whole place seemed turning round and round. (11

Oliver looked at Sikes, in mute and timid wonder; and drawing a stool to the fire, sat with his aching head upon his hands, scarcely knowing where he was, or what was passing around him. (22)

Over and over again we see Oliver simply falling asleep in these "foul and frowsy dens, where vice is closely packed and lacks the room to turn" (Preface to the third edition, *OT*, p. ix). Cut off altogether from the past and the future, enclosed in a narrow shadowy present which does not make sense, he loses consciousness altogether, so exhausted is he by anxiety and by his failure to comprehend what is happening to him. More precisely, he is reduced to the simplest and most undifferentiated form of consciousness, sleep.

. . . he was sick and weary; and he soon fell sound asleep. (16)

The boy was lying, fast asleep, on a rude bed upon the floor; so pale with anxiety, and sadness, and the closeness of his prison, that he looked like death. (19)

Weary with watching and anxiety, he at length fell asleep. (20)

. . . quite overpowered by fatigue and the fumes of the tobacco, [he] fell asleep. (21)

But Oliver is unable always to escape by sleep or bewilderment. As he slowly becomes acclimated to his new environment he comes to recognize that, for its inhabitants, this underground world has a certain logic and a certain coherence. Even in his very first glimpse of this world there was visible, along with the dirt and closeness, another quality, a quality which makes life to some degree tolerable and even pleasant for these outcasts: "The walls and ceiling of the room were perfectly black with age and dirt. There was a deal table before the fire: upon which were a candle, stuck in a ginger-beer bottle, two or three pewter pots, a loaf and butter, and a plate. In a frying-pan, which was on the fire, and which was secured to the mantleshelf by a string, some sausages were cooking; and standing over them, with a toasting-fork in his hand, was a very old shrivelled Jew, whose villainous-looking and repulsive face was obscured by a quantity of matted red hair" (8). There are two contradictory values in this passage: Fagin's den is both a dungeon and a place of refuge. It is dark, dirty, and absolutely shut off from the outside world, but it is also a parody, at least, of a home, that place where one lives safely by one's own fireside, protected from the outer world, and where one has food, light, warmth, and a circle of other human beings with whom one feels at ease. Fagin's den is a "snug retreat" (43), and inside its walls we find a society leagued for common protection against the hostility of the outside world. It is a situation well imaged by the single candle which so often appears shining dimly in the gloom.

Fagin expounds the apparent philosophy of this hidden society within society to Noah Claypole: ". . . you depend upon me. To keep my little business all snug, I depend upon you. The first is your number one, the second my number one. The more you value your number one, the more careful you must be of mine; so we come at last to what I told you at first — that a regard for number one holds us all together, and must do so, unless we would all go to pieces in company" (43).

But the life of Fagin's gang does not always recall its origin in a Hobbesian contract. Dickens shows Oliver discovering and being attracted in spite of himself by the cheerfulness and camaraderie of their existence. He and the other boys laugh until the tears run down their faces at Fagin's imitation of a prosperous old gentleman taking a walk, and when Fagin tells them comic stories of his robberies, "Oliver [cannot] help laughing heartily, and showing that he [is] amused in spite of all his better feelings" (18).

Fagin's gang is an authentic society and provides the security and sense of belonging to a community which Oliver has never before known, but these goods are not won without a price. The price is the permanent loss of the kind of life among honest men of which Oliver instinctively dreams: ". . . the wily old Jew had the boy in his toils. Having prepared his mind by solitude and gloom, to prefer any society to the companionship of his own sad thoughts in such a dreary place, he was now slowly instilling into his soul the poison which he hoped would blacken it, and change its hue for ever" (18). Oliver among the thieves is, in fact, totally excluded from the life of pro

ected security he desires. He is as truly outcast as if he were starving in the open, however warm and comfortable and even cheerful the interior of Fagin's den may be. Oliver's situation in the world is to be at once "hedged round and round" (20) and abandoned in the open. His relation to the thieves leads him inevitably to the moment when, left behind by Sikes after the failure of a robbery, he lies unconscious in a ditch in the rain (28).

But it is in Dickens' treatment of the lives of the thieves themselves rather than in his treatment of Oliver that we can see most clearly why he rejects the attempt by the outcasts to create an autonomous society of their own.

In the first place, the thieves' society is unstable. It is built on the principle of internal treason, and it is constantly threatened by destruction from the outside. If the least chink in the walls lets the beams of the hidden candle out into the night, the society of the "upper world" will rush in and destroy the hidden society of outcasts. The two qualities of disloyalty and danger from without are causally related. It is because the thieves live through raids on the world of honest men that they are, ultimately, disloyal to one another. They are inevitably disloyal because only by caring more for their own individual safety than for their common safety can they survive. It is Fagin who lives most deliberately by a philosophy of "every man for himself," and it is Fagin, consequently, who lives longest.

Fagin's apparent philosophy of one for all hides an actual philosophy which sacrifices all for one. He lives only by condemning others to death. If he does not do this, they will turn him in. Just as he moves from den to den, so he must constantly replace the members of his gang. A society defining itself as evil, that is, as the denial of all social laws, can only live by perpetual metamorphosis. Fagin is accordingly a shape-changer, a master of disguise, but his best disguise is the constantly changing membership of his gang. He can only survive by being nothing and by doing nothing himself, that is, by committing his crimes only by proxy and remaining himself the empty center of all this crime, the void of evil itself. For positive evil in this world is inevitably punished; the man who sets himself up against society always comes to be hanged. The periphery around Fagin, all the boys and adult thieves who work for him, are one by one plucked away and hanged or transported. It is only by maintaining this solid wall of active evil committed by others between himself and the world of good that Fagin can continue to live at the center of his dark hollow den.

The true relation of the thieves to one another is given not by the image of a mutually loyal group crouching around their single candle in an underground room, but by the recurrent motif of spying. Fagin himself spies on Oliver and on other members of his gang; Nancy finds out the secrets of Oliver's birth by spying on Fagin and Monks; Nancy herself is spied on by Fagin's representative. Her betrayal of the thieves is thus discovered and her death brought about. And Oliver is spied on by Fagin and Monks as he dwells in what he assumes to be the total security of Mrs. Maylie's country home. All the thieves are in constant fear not only that someone in the outside world will observe and identify them but that they will be observed and betrayed by one of their own number. Oliver's share in the general fear of the unseen look that steals one's secret is a measure of the degree of his participation, in spite of himself, in the thieves' psychology. For the world of honest men the thieves' world is invisible. When Oliver takes Dr. Losberne to the house where he has been with the thieves, everything is changed. They are met by "a little ugly hump-backed man" whom Oliver has never seen before, and when they enter the house "not an article of furniture; not a vestige of anything animate or inanimate; not even the position of the cupboard [answers] Oliver's description" (32). Only Oliver, with his unwilling complicity in the underworld, sees the dwarf's "glance so sharp and fierce and at the same time so furious and vindictive, that, waking or sleeping, he could not forget it for months afterwards" (32).

The thieves, then, are constantly threatened, within and without, by the possibility that their secret will be revealed. But the attempt to assume one's isolation publicly and thereby make it the source of one's identity is equally unsuccessful. T

Artful Dodger attempts to achieve selfhood by assuming the alienation forced upon him by society: "I wouldn't go free, now, if you was to fall down on your knees and ask me," says the Dodger to his captors. "Here, carry me off to prison! Take me away!" (43). But the Dodger realizes that this defiance is hollow. It is a kind of comic role he plays: "I'm an Englishman, ain't I?" he asks. "Where are my priwileges?" But he knows, and everyone else knows, that he has no privileges, that he has no attorney "a-breakfasting this morning with the Wice President of the House of Commons." All his defiance and all his pretense that he wills his punishment do not hide the fact that he has been caught by the law and will be treated as his captors wish. His attempt to will defiantly to be a thief does not permit him to escape from the process whereby society imposes upon him whatever identity it chooses, once it has dragged him out into the daylight.

But if the attempt to escape from isolation through a relationship to the world of good men is a failure, so equally is the attempt to establish relationships inside the underworld. The tragic end of the Sikes-Nancy liaison is final judgment on the futility of the attempt to keep love alive within a society which is excluded from the daylight of law and convention. Within such a society all voluntary relationships are evil. They are evil because there is nothing outside of themselves which justifies them. They cannot be other than illicit. Sikes and Nancy are inevitably destroyed by their guilty love, a love that is guilty because it is outside social sanctions. The only alternatives for them are death or separation and reintegration into the honest world: "Bill," pleads Nancy a moment before Sikes murders her, "the gentleman and that dear lady, told me to-night of a home in some foreign country where I could end my days in solitude and peace. Let me see them again, and beg them, on my knees, to show the same mercy and goodness to you; and let us both leave this dreadful place, and far apart lead better lives, and forget how we have lived, except in prayers, and never see each other more" (47).

Dickens, at this stage of his career, is willing to sacrifice all, even faithfulness in love, to the need to escape from social ostracism. For the outcast, it seems, is in an impossible dilemma. He is now nothing, because society has chosen to reject him utterly. But if he tries to take a place he will be even more certainly defined as an outlaw and all the more surely destroyed. Oliver's only hope is somehow to escape from the underground society altogether. But this seems impossible.

### III

It was a very dirty place. The rooms up-stairs had great high wooden chimney-pieces and large doors, with panelled walls and cornices to the ceilings; which, although they were black with neglect and dust, were ornamented in various ways. From all of these tokens Oliver concluded that a long time ago, before the old Jew was born, it had belonged to better people, and had perhaps been quite gay and handsome: dismal and dreary as it looked now.

. . . and often, when it grew dark, and he was tired of wandering from room to room, he would crouch in the corner of the passage by the street-door, to be as near living people as he could. . . . (18)

This passage marks Oliver's transition to an active search in the *external* world for the meaning of his plight and for the identity and security he obscurely seeks. He has been recaptured by Fagin and locked all alone in an empty house. He has had a brief glimpse of the world of honest people, and has been strangely moved by the sight of a picture which is, although he does not know it, a portrait of his mother, who died when he was born. Apparently his new prison is merely a repetition of all the interiors he has already known, interiors which offer no avenue of escape and which contain no clue whatsoever as to the meaning of his suffering. Oliver studies his new surroundings with a child's wonder. Everything seems larger than life-size. The chimney-pieces are high, the doors large, and the perspective is that of someone looking upward. But this interior is different. Oliver is no longer at the very center of the darkness. He can watch from the outside as the mice "scamper across the floor, and run back terrified to their holes" (18). It is as though he were a good man watching the thieves run for cover in their secret dens. Moreover, his new prison is not only dirty

nd enclosed. It also contains the decayed signs, almost the
rcheological remains, of another way of life. Oliver sees un-
nistakable evidence of a happy existence once lived within the
ery walls of his prison. And this prison is more than a single
oom reached by a dark corridor or by a series of rooms of in-
reasing interiority. He can wander from room to room and ex-
lore each one for signs of the past happiness it seems indis-
inctly to reveal. The present is no longer wholly enclosed in
tself. In the very midst of the present in all its dirt and dark-
ess there are indications of a past that was wholly different.
'erhaps if the present world is wholly intolerable there was
evertheless once in the past a "gay" life. All Oliver's life is ori-
nted, without his knowing it, toward the discovery of a world
nterior to his life, a life where he can, it may be, recover his
st identity and the happiness he has never known.

Moreover, the life which existed in the past may exist also in
he present outside the walls. Oliver crouches in the corner, as
ear to the outside world as he can get, but he has a new aware-
ess of what this outside world might contain. And the present
self, perhaps because of this very discovery of the past and of
n outside life very different from his own, ceases to be the
ind endurance of a moment which simply repeats those which
recede or follow. Now it has become a real duration. At least
ere is an awareness of the passage of time and of its empti-
ss: Oliver "would remain [crouching by the street door], lis-
ning and counting the hours" (18). Furthermore, this prison,
like the others, lets in a little light from the outside. It has
tiny aperture through which Oliver may dimly descry the
orld of freedom and study it:

In all the rooms, the mouldering shutters were fast closed: the
rs which held them were screwed tight into the wood; the only
ht which was admitted, stealing its way through round holes
the top: which made the rooms more gloomy, and filled them
th strange shadows. There was a back-garret window with rusty
rs outside, which had no shutter; and out of this, Oliver often
zed with a melancholy face for hours together; but nothing was
be descried from it but a confused and crowded mass of house-
s, blackened chimneys, and gable-ends. Sometimes, indeed, a

grizzly head might be seen, peering over the parapet-wall of a dis
tant house: but it was quickly withdrawn again; and as the win
dow of Oliver's observatory was nailed down, and dimmed with th
rain and smoke of years, it was as much as he could do to make ou
the forms of the different objects beyond, without making any a
tempt to be seen or heard, — which he had as much chance of be
ing, as if he had lived inside the ball of St. Paul's Cathedral. (18

If there is any single image which we remember longes
from *Oliver Twist* it is the picture of the lost boy, deprived c
all knowledge of his forebears, imprisoned all alone in a laby
rinthine ruin of a house, peering "with a melancholy face fc
hours together" through a high clouded window at a world h
cannot understand, and with which he has seemingly n
chance of making direct contact. Oliver's exploration of th
outside world is here only that of passive and detached observa
tion. There is an obscuring veil, the deposited layers of "th
rain and smoke of years," between him and the world outsid
so that he can hardly distinguish one object from anothe
What has cut him off from the past, the years of which he ha
no knowledge and cannot break through, cuts him off also fro
the outside world by depositing a veil of dust and cobwebs c
the window. And, if the inside world is dark and unintelligibl
if it offers to his gaze merely the same blank walls, black wi
age and dirt, or glistening with subterranean moisture, the ou
side world is unintelligible because of its jumbled multiplicit
Oliver sees only a "confused and crowded mass of house-top
blackened chimneys, and gable-ends." There seems to be r
order in this confusion, and it seems to be related in no signi
cant way to himself. It is simply there before him, a bewilde
ing collection of objects in the midst of which the figure of a
other human being makes a brief and mysterious appearan
only to be "quickly withdrawn again." But, even though Oliv
has no chance at all of being seen or heard, of making conta
with this world, he is at least aware now that he is not buri
deep underground out of all proximity to the outside world. F
is as near to it, as close and yet as far, as if he were enclosed n
underground but high in the air — as if he were enclosed
the ball of St. Paul's Cathedral. He spends long hours studyi

this disordered world, as if he had some faint chance of forcing it to yield up its secret, a secret which might be *his* secret too, the secret of his identity and the meaning of his life.

More than once Oliver does escape and is able to explore the external world, to make an active search for its meaning. Does this world have the same hostility that the walls of the dark interior world possessed? The windowless room corresponded to Oliver's interior darkness, to the semiconscious stupor which was his initial condition. Perhaps the exterior world may be controlled by understanding it. Perhaps it may be held at arm's length, may be comprehended, may even be forced to correspond exactly to his inner state and thus to offer an escape from the total separation between inner and outer worlds imaged in Oliver's melancholy gaze out the back garret-window at the "confused and crowded mass of house-tops, blackened chimneys, and gable-ends."

At first the exterior world seems as dark and indistinct as the interior one. The image of a cold dark foggy night, a night in which no object can be clearly seen, is repeated again and again in *Oliver Twist*. In this obscurity, one is aware that what one sees is as much a projection of one's fear as an accurate perception of objects in the external world: "Every object before him, substance or shadow, still or moving, took the semblance of some fearful thing" (48, and see 21). But the mist may be simply opaque and impenetrable, and perhaps this is even more frightening. The fog simply mirrors back to the lost boy his own lostness, his total inability to understand where he is or who he is or what is the meaning of the objects which surround him: "The night was dark and foggy. The lights in the shops could scarcely struggle through the heavy mist, which thickened every moment and shrouded the streets and houses in gloom; rendering the strange place still stranger in Oliver's eyes; and making his uncertainty the more dismal and depressing" (16, and see 19, 28, 46).

But when the obscurity gives way somewhat to light, when "the objects which had looked dim and terrible in the darkness, [grow] more and more defined, and gradually [resolve] into their familiar shapes" (28), the hero can look around him for the first time. The first thing he observes is that he is apparently totally alone in a world of objects which are closed to him or which exist statically at an unattainable distance:

It was a cold, dark night. The stars seemed, to the boy's eyes, farther from the earth than he had ever seen them before; there was no wind; and the sombre shadows thrown by the trees upon the ground, looked sepulchral and death-like, from being so still. (7)

. . . the windows of the houses were all closely shut; and the streets through which they passed, were noiseless and empty. (21)

The window-shutters were closed; the street was empty; not a soul had awakened to the business of the day. The sun was rising in all its splendid beauty; but the light only served to show the boy his own lonesomeness and desolation . . . . (8)

This new state of isolation is in a way more desperate than the first. The walls of Oliver's prison were at least close to him and were a kind of comfort in themselves. And the outcast can no longer be consoled by the idea that everything will be all right if only he can escape from his prison. The outside world is revealed as simply the opposite extreme from the inside world. Instead of being close and suffocating it is absolutely open. And what can be seen at a distance in the clear light forms a kind of solid barrier just as hostile as the damp walls within which Oliver has been immured. It is now a hostility of withdrawal and silence rather than of active violence against Oliver. The world constitutes itself still as a solid wall, but it is now a wall of indifference rather than of hate. In the distance between himself and the closed shutters or the cold stars Oliver can see for the first time his total isolation. It is an isolation which is both material and social. He is cut off from the community behind the closed shutters as much as from the stars or the trees.

There is only one avenue of action left, only one thing the hero can do now that he could not do when he was locked in: he can run "hurrying through a labyrinth of streets" (45) seeking some escape from his exclusion: "They crossed from the Angel into St. John's Road; struck down the small street which terminates at Sadler's Wells Theatre; through Exmouth

Street and Coppice Row; down the little court by the side of the workhouse; across the classic ground which once bore the name of Hockley-in-the-Hole; thence into Little Saffron Hill; and so into Saffron Hill the Great . . ." (8). The labyrinth at first reveals itself as simply the repetition of the scene of empty desolation which had appeared when the fog cleared away. Now, however, this desolation has a geography. There are paths marked out in it, and walls at the sides which limit the indefiniteness of space, and indicate specific directions to be taken. But the careful precision with which Dickens names the streets of these itineraries only serves to emphasize the fact that each of these streets is merely a different version of the first. It is Dickens himself, or the detached narrator of the story, who knows the names of the streets, not Oliver. He has no idea where the Dodger is taking him. And the place names are simply superficial facts; they do not serve to relate Oliver to his environment.

The urban labyrinth turns out to be nothing more than an endless daedal prison. As in a dream, Oliver wanders through intricate streets which are different but which do not seem to lead anywhere. And the darkness, narrowness, muddiness, crookedness of this maze make it difficult to distinguish it from the underground prison in which the hero first found himself. The hero and his avatars are as much lost and as much enclosed outside as they were inside, and there is repeated over and over the sequence of a rapid walk, sometimes a flight, through streets which get narrower and narrower and dirtier and dirtier and more and more intricate and finally lead to the doors of one of the subterranean interiors I have described:

They walked on, for some time, through the most crowded and densely inhabited part of the town; and then, striking down a narrow street more dirty and miserable than any they had yet passed through, paused to look for the house which was the object of their search. (5)

To reach this place, the visitor has to penetrate through a maze of close, narrow, and muddy streets. . . . (50)

He kept on his course, through many winding and narrow ways, until he reached Bethnal Green; then, turning suddenly off to the left, he soon became involved in a maze of the mean and dirty streets which abound in that close and densely-populated quarter. . . . He hurried through several alleys and streets, and at length turned into one, lighted only by a single lamp at the farther end. At the door of a house in this street, he knocked. . . . (19)

At the deepest imaginative level the London of *Oliver Twist* is no longer a realistic description of the unsanitary London of the thirties but is the dream or poetic symbol of an infernal labyrinth, inhabited by the devil himself: "The mud lay thick upon the stones, and a black mist hung over the streets; the rain fell sluggishly down, and everything felt cold and clammy to the touch. It seemed just the night when it befitted such a being as the Jew to be abroad. As he glided stealthily along, creeping beneath the shelter of the walls and doorways, the hideous old man seemed like some loathsome reptile, engendered in the slime and darkness through which he moved: crawling forth, by night, in search of some rich offal for a meal" (19). Fagin is as much dream as reality. He is often called the devil (19, 44), or shown in a pose that recalls the devil: crouching over a fire with a toasting fork (8), or other implement (20, 25), or gloating over his hidden treasure (9). Dickens had been reading Defoe's *History of the Devil* with great interest while he was writing *Oliver Twist,* but his reading, it seems evident, only reinforced the image of the archetype of evil which was already present in his imagination. Fagin is imagined too vividly in his combination of supernatural and animal qualities to be the mere copy of traditional and literary representations of the devil: ". . . Fagin sat watching in his old lair, with face so distorted and pale, and eyes so red and bloodshot, that he looked less like a man, than like some hideous phantom, moist from the grave, and worried by an evil spirit. . . . and as, absorbed in thought, he bit his long black nails, he disclosed among his toothless gums a few such fangs as should have been a dog's or rat's" (47).

At the center of the labyrinth, then, is Fagin, the personified principle of the world cut off altogether from the light and the good. There he crouches, greedy to possess Oliver altogether by making him a thief, but hiding, perhaps, the secret that will make possible Oliver's permanent escape from the labyrinth. The only escape from the prison, it may be, is to descend into its very heart and to wrest from the darkness its secret. Oliver does not know this, of course. He only knows that there is a centripetal force which seems to pull him toward the center of the labyrinth, however hard he tries to escape. When Oliver flees from his living grave at Sowerberry's it is not outward through the maze to freedom, but into the intricacy of London, toward the dark center of the labyrinth — Fagin's den. And when Oliver's rescuer sends Oliver out on an errand he has only to turn down a bystreet by accident (15) to be plunged back into the labyrinth and recaptured by Fagin.

The true meaning of the labyrinth image is perhaps revealed in a phrase Dickens uses about Nancy: "Fagin . . . had led her, step by step, deeper and deeper down into an abyss of crime and misery, whence was no escape" (44). Movement in the Dickensian labyrinth is always inward and downward toward the center, and never outward toward freedom. The labyrinth is really an abyss, a bottomless pit of mud and darkness in which one can be lost forever, forever separated from the world of light and freedom. And the labyrinth is also a moral abyss. It is the world into which Oliver will be permanently plunged if the thieves succeed in hardening him and making him into one of themselves.

But thus far the labyrinth has seemed to be entirely uninhabited, or at least there has been no direct contact with its inhabitants. Its walls have been, so to speak, blank — simply endless repetitions of the same muddy, damp, featureless stones or planks. There have appeared neither people to whom the frantically searching wanderer might relate himself nor objects which he might separate out from the whole and scrutinize for their possible meaning. But there are several labyrinthine progressions in *Oliver Twist* which replace the journey through intricate streets to a gravelike interior with a journey through the obscurity of fog into streets that are at first empty but are then gradually filled up with a great crowd, a crowd either of distinct objects or of human beings. The blank walls

take on distinct features and the visual field becomes a heterogeneous mass of details rather than a single homogeneous blur:

> In . . . filthy shops are exposed for sale huge bunches of
> second-hand silk handkerchiefs, of all sizes and patterns. . . .
> Hundreds of these handkerchiefs hang dangling from pegs outside
> the windows or flaunting from the door-posts; and the shelves,
> within, are piled with them. . . . Here . . . stores of old iron
> and bones, and heaps of mildewy fragments of woollen-stuff and
> linen, rust and rot in the grimy cellars. (26)

> To reach this place [Jacob's Island], the visitor has to penetrate
> through a maze of close, narrow, and muddy streets, thronged by
> the roughest and poorest of waterside people, and devoted to the
> traffic they may be supposed to occasion. The cheapest and least del-
> icate provisions are heaped in the shops; the coarsest and common-
> est articles of wearing apparel dangle at the salesman's door, and
> stream from the house-parapet and windows. (50)

These scenes present a world in chaotic action, a world in
which the undifferentiated fog has resolved itself into a mass of
perceptible objects, into multitudinous motion and cacopho-
nous noise. But it is still a world which does not relate itself to
the spectator. He remains a passive observer who takes no part
in all this action and is ignored by all the people he sees. The
"drunken men and women" "wallowing in filth" (8) pay no
more attention to him than do the crowd of handkerchiefs
which wave in the wind. The inanimate and animate objects
seen are strictly equivalent and remain at a distance as pure
spectacle. This spectacle is simply a great swirl of mingled
sense perceptions, of things seen, heard, and smelled. Everything is in the plural, and multiplies itself inexhaustibly. Not
only are there innumerable distinct objects, there also seems
to be an endless supply of each species. The cellars are stuffed
with "stores" and "heaps" more of what is displayed outside;
each house seems to contain enough unseen drunkards to fill
the streets even if all the visible ones were cleared away; and
the "commonest articles of wearing apparel" "stream from the
house-parapet and windows" as though flowing from a bottomless reservoir. These are scenes of profusion and excess, of the
endless accumulation of heteroclite details. But in the end

this multiplicity gives way to a fluidity in which everything seems to be surging liquidly up from the interior. Since each detail is multiplied indefinitely it appears to be constantly replaced by its fellows, and the entire series forms a continuous "stream" in which what had been hidden a moment ago makes its momentary appearance only to be replaced without transition by the next in line. It is consequently a world which is inside out. All that should be secret is out in the open; wearing apparel, the evidence of lawbreaking, unseemly behavior, all is revealed. And yet the spectator finds that he is no nearer the real secret than he was before.

Even if the chaotic crowd remains harmlessly at a distance, its effect is malign. When Sikes takes Oliver off in the early morning to try to make a thief of him, at first the streets are empty. Gradually, though, the streets begin to fill with a motley crowd of men and women. Oliver and Sikes move toward the center of the city, toward the dense source of all this multiplicity and movement. At the center of it all, Smithfield, the distinct sounds are so numerous that they begin to blur and "swell" "into a roar of sound and bustle" (21). Each sound and each sight is still distinct, but each has become exactly the equivalent of all the others and thus, in the end, fuses into a single indistinguishable blur or roar. The multitudes of distinct sense perceptions destroy one another by their very abundance, and the spectator is left face to face with a single vertiginous cacophony in which nothing can be distinguished clearly because all the thresholds of clear sense perception have been exceeded: "the whistling of drovers, the barking of dogs, the bellowing and plunging of oxen, the bleating of sheep, the grunting and squeaking of pigs, the cries of hawkers, the shouts, oaths, and quarrelling on all sides; the ringing of bells and roar of voices, that issued from every public-house; the crowding, pushing, driving, beating, whooping, and yelling; the hideous and discordant din that resounded from every corner of the market; and the unwashed, unshaven, squalid, and dirty figures constantly running to and fro, and bursting in and out of the throng; rendered it a stunning and bewildering scene, which quite confounded the senses" (21).

At first the "tumult of discordant sounds" had filled Oliver "with amazement" (21), but in the end he is "stunned," "bewildered," his senses are "confounded." He is, in fact, reduced by his exploration of the exterior world to exactly the same state he was in when he lay in a half-conscious stupor in the darkness and solitude of his prison. And the world of distinct objects mingled together in an unintelligible mass is shown to be in the end the exact equivalent of the world of total darkness. A light too bright is invisible, and a world of sheer multiplicity is shown to be the same as a world in which nothing at all exists or in which nothing at all is perceptible. Both worlds mirror back to the alienated hero his own subjective confusion, his own bewildered inability to tell where he is or who he is.

Until the very end of the novel all the characters are living in the midst of experiences which have the total opacity of the present and cannot yet be seen in retrospect as having the logical structure of a destiny. The mystery, the unintelligibility, of the present is perfectly expressed by these scenes of multiplicity in a state of rapid, aimless agitation. The exterior scene is exactly matched by the state of mind of the inhabitants of this world of bewildering uncertainty and unpredictable change. Rose Maylie's interview with Nancy "had more the semblance of a rapid dream than an actual occurrence." She sinks into a chair and endeavors "to collect her wandering thoughts" (40). Fagin's violent thoughts when he learns he has been betrayed follow "close upon each other with rapid and ceaseless whirl" (47). At a crisis in the story Mr. Losberne and Mr. Brownlow hastily separate "each in a fever of excitement wholly uncontrollable" (49), and we see Oliver "in a flutter of agitation and uncertainty, which [deprives] him of the power of collecting his thoughts" (51).

But there is one case in *Oliver Twist* in which a character seeks out such a scene, and succeeds in losing his self-consciousness by identifying himself with the violent agitation of the world. When Sikes, after the murder of Nancy, has wandered through the countryside attempting to lose himself and his past, but lingering obsessively "about the same spot," he succeeds for a few hours in forgetting himself and his crime at the scene of a great fire (48). Sikes can forget himself momentarily because he has found an external scene which corresponds exactly to his inner state and can be intermingled with it. The objective fire is matched by Sikes' internal fever, and at the height of his "ecstacy" he is as much inside the fire as the fire is inside him: "in every part of that great fire was he" (48). Only if a person is in a state of self-destructive disintegration, consuming himself with some inner conflict, will the multitudinousness of the world be an appropriate projection of the self. Only then will self-forgetfulness be possible. And even this transcendence of the subject-object cleavage is only momentary: "This mad excitement over, there returned, with tenfold force, the dreadful consciousness of his crime" (48). The external fire is burned to "smoke and blackened ruins," but Sikes' inner fire burns on, and would be satisfied not by any mere chaotic swirling of the world such as bewildered Oliver at Smithfield, but by a gigantic holocaust which would consume the whole world in consuming him.

But perhaps the seemingly chaotic world can be kept at a distance and its details studied carefully for the meaning they may reveal. The spectator can, it may be, achieve a kind of detachment, put the world in brackets, and study it as pure phenomenon. So Fagin in the courtroom where he is on trial for his life: "He looked up into the gallery again. Some of the people were eating, and some fanning themselves with handkerchiefs; for the crowded place was very hot. There was one young man sketching his face in a little note-book. He wondered whether it was like, and looked on when the artist broke his pencil-point, and made another with his knife, as any idle spectator might have done. In the same way, when he turned his eyes towards the judge, his mind began to busy itself with the fashion of his dress, and what it cost, and how he put it on. . . . [He] pursued this train of careless thought until some new object caught his eye and roused another" (52). However, this detached study of events in the external world only shows that as pure phenomena they are utterly meaningless. To study the world in detachment is to study it *idly,* and to be led at best to a "train of careless thought" which is inconsequential speculation about the sheer facts of its mechanical operation. If this speculation goes behind the superficial appearances of things it is only to imagine more of the same absurd details: "He wondered within himself whether this man had been to get his dinner, what he had had, and where he had had it" (52). The real relationship of the world to Fagin, the relationship he is vaguely aware of even as he studies the scene from the point of view of a detached spectator, is the relationship of executioner to victim: "Not that, all this time, his mind was, for an instant, free from one oppressive overwhelming sense of the grave that opened at his feet; it was ever present to him, but in a vague and general way, and he could not fix his thoughts upon it. Thus, even while he trembled, and turned burning hot at the idea of speedy death, he fell to counting the iron spikes before him, and wondering how the head of one had been broken off, and whether they would mend it, or leave it as it was. Then, he thought of all the horrors of the gallows and the scaffold — and stopped to watch a man sprinkling the floor to cool it — and then went on to think again" (52). There is an extraordinary alternation here between Fagin's vague awareness that he is involved and threatened, and the clear vision of detached observation. At one moment Fagin sees things as if he were not part of them, as if he had all the time in the world and could watch forever the slow or rapid changing of the perceptible scene. At the next moment he remembers that he is involved in time and in the world, involved in them in the specifically human way, by reason of his awareness of his own inevitable death. His vision of the world as something separate and harmless, something which may be safely studied in its trivial detail for the satisfaction of mere idle curiosity, is false. The world is in reality hostile. Fagin can read in no face that stares at him "the faintest sympathy with himself, or any feeling but one of all-absorbing interest that he should be condemned" (52). The faces are, in fact, the exact equivalent of the stone walls of a prison: "He could glean nothing from their faces; they might as well have been of stone" (52). The human world is as inhuman as stone or as distant stars. For the solid opaque enmity of blank walls is substituted

a world which is an infinitely repeated *look,* a look which piti-
lessly devours Fagin with its glance, now that he has been
dragged at last from his den into the light of day: "The court
was paved, from floor to roof, with human faces. Inquisitive
and eager eyes peered from every inch of space. From the rail
before the dock, away into the sharpest angle of the smallest
corner in the galleries, all looks were fixed upon one man —
Fagin. Before him and behind: above, below, on the right and
on the left: he seemed to stand surrounded by a firmament, all
bright with gleaming eyes" (52).

The search through the labyrinth, then, has come face to
face with the absolute impasse of a world which, hovering at a
distance, regards one with an implacable stare. It is a universe
which has become all eyes, eyes which see into every corner of
one's soul, and do not leave any recess which is free or secret.
But worse is to follow. Three times in the novel for three different characters the direction of the labyrinth changes, the
seeker becomes the sought, he who had rushed frantically
through endless crooked streets seeking some escape now flees
even more frantically from the active enmity of the mob. The
labyrinth is turned into a hostile crowd which, no longer remaining at a distance, turns on the protagonist and hunts him
down:

"Stop thief! Stop thief!" The cry is taken up by a hundred voices,
and the crowd accumulate at every turning. Away they fly, splashing through the mud, and rattling along the pavements: up go the
windows, out run the people, onward bear the mob, a whole audience desert Punch in the very thickest of the plot, and, joining the
rushing throng, swell the shout, and lend fresh vigour to the cry,
"Stop thief! Stop thief!"

"Stop thief! Stop thief!" There is a passion *for hunting something* deeply implanted in the human breast. One wretched breathless child, panting with exhaustion; terror in his looks; agony in his
eyes; large drops of perspiration streaming down his face; strains
every nerve to make head upon his pursuers; and as they follow on
his track, and gain upon him every instant, they hail his decreas-
ing strength with still louder shouts, and whoop and scream with
joy. (10)

Here the entire world seems to have turned animate and to be chasing Oliver down the endless dreamlike corridors of the London labyrinth. And the aim of the mob is not simply to catch him, but to "crowd" him to death. The crowd "jostles" and "struggles" centripetally toward Oliver, and will suffocate him or crush him if it can: " 'Give him a little air!' 'Nonsense he don't deserve it' " (10). In the same way the crowd tries to tear Fagin to pieces like a pack of wild animals when once he is dragged out of his den into the light of day (50), and another crowd, beside itself with rage and hatred, presses like a "strong struggling current of angry faces" around the house where Sikes is at bay, "to curse him" and kill him if they can (50).

The similarity of these three passages impresses upon us forcibly the kinship between Oliver and the thieves. Fagin dies "for" Oliver the death he would have died. The embodiment of all the evil in the novel, he is the scapegoat whose death, even more than Sikes', destroys all that evil, and makes it possible for Oliver to "live happily ever after." The description of his "last night alive" and of Oliver's visit to the condemned man forms the penultimate chapter of the novel, coming just before the account of Oliver's subsequent happiness and preparing for it. In this scene, Fagin says, quite correctly, that Oliver has betrayed him and caused his death: "He has been the — the — somehow the cause of all this" (52). In the delirium of his fear Fagin claims a secret friendship and even kinship with Oliver, tells him where the papers containing the clue to the mystery of his life are hidden, and tries to get Oliver to smuggle him out of the prison. The few steps toward the gallows Oliver and Fagin take together testify to their profound consubstantiality. Oliver, by accepting the identity among honest men imposed upon him by the discovery of the secrets of his origin, has betrayed the identity as a pariah which was apparently his from birth. It is Oliver himself who is the real spy in the novel. Fagin dies the death Oliver would have died, but in choosing Mr. Brownlow's "little society" Oliver must betray and destroy the underground society which Fagin has created for protection against a world in which he and the other thieves are use less and despised, "the very scum and refuse of the land" (Preface to the third edition, *OT*, p. x).

Another kinship between Oliver and the thieves, the identity of their initial natures, is strongly implied in the preface to the third edition of *Oliver Twist*. Whereas Oliver is to represent "the principle of Good surviving through every adverse circumstance," the thieves are described not as initially evil, but as an original good which is, in the case of Sikes, finally destroyed, or is, in the case of Nancy, so corrupted that it remains only as "the last fair drop of water at the bottom of the dried-up weed-choked well" (*OT*, p. xi). Sikes is one of those "insensible and callous natures that do become, at last, utterly and irredeemably bad" (*OT*, p. x). In the version of the preface for the Charles Dickens edition of 1856 this became "utterly and incurably bad," evidently to remove the theological implication of "irredeemably." Dickens did not want to deny God's power to redeem even those who are apparently hopelessly evil. But even in the earlier version he did not leave unqualified his assertion that all good is wholly dead in such people: "Whether every gentler human feeling is dead within such bosoms, or the proper chord to strike has rusted and is hard to find, I do not know" (*OT*, p. xi). Moreover, the good feelings of Nancy are "emphatically God's truth, for it is the truth He leaves in such depraved and miserable breasts; the hope yet lingering behind" (*ibid.*). Whatever Dickens at this time felt to be the original source of human evil (and it is a crucial problem for him later on), it is clear that he did not believe the thieves were "naturally evil," just as Oliver was "naturally good." Though the world is fallen, evil is, initially, extrinsic to any individual. There is no acceptance of the doctrine of original sin in Dickens' anthropology. Each human creature comes pure and good from the hand of God and only *becomes* evil through the effects of an evil environment. Some are, however, like Oliver, paradoxically more naturally good than others, or more invulnerably so, "by nature or inheritance," and are thus able to withstand the pressure of evil surroundings, surroundings which slowly and inevitably taint, corrupt, and ultimately destroy all the others who are exposed to them. One might say that the fable of *Oliver Twist,* the father's will, the lost inheritance, and the lost identity, were devised to make this paradox plausible. But Oliver's special position does not prevent Dickens from sympathizing more or less openly with the thieves.

Indeed there is a good deal of covert sympathy even for Fagin, especially in the description of his capture and death. Fagin in jail is as much a figure to be pitied as hated (52), and it is clear that Dickens strongly identified himself with Fagin, and in writing of his death lived with intensity the death of the outcast, utterly cut off from society, hated by all the world, and implacably destroyed by it. It was, one feels, because he could imagine so vividly the life of the outcast that he strove so desperately in novel after novel to prove that the outcast was not really outcast, that there was a hidden identity waiting for him among the honest men who enjoy with complacency a secure status and the comforting sense that, like Dr. Losberne, they can act upon impulse and yet do no wrong because they are naturally and incorruptibly good (32).

Oliver, then, is in the same situation as Sikes or Fagin. For all three the human or material world is not simply unintelligible multiplicity in agitated motion. It is a great solid force which rushes in toward the isolated one at the center. There is escape neither underground nor out in the open for the outcasts. Both inside and out they are threatened by the remorselessly hostile wall of a world which converges on the central figure. ". . . the great, black, ghastly gallows clos[es] up their prospects, turn them where they may" (Preface to the third edition, *OT,* p. viii). They seek in vain for a tiny aperture through which they may escape.

The main axis of the nuclear structure of *Oliver Twist* is a fear of exclusion which alternates with a fear of enclosure. Between these two poles the novel oscillates. On the one hand there is the fear that one will be completely cut off from the world and from other men. Thrust into an empty world from which everything has receded to an unattainable distance, one is left only with a need, a lack, the need to be related to the world, to find a ground to stand on and a roof over one's head. On the other hand, there is the fear that the world will ap proach too near, that one will be buried alive, squeezed to death, or suffocated, that freedom and even life itself will be crushed out. At a level beneath the superficial coherence of narrated events, at a level where all the characters reduce themselves into isomorphic representations of a few basic possibilities, *Oliver Twist* is the search for a way of life which will escape from these two extremes. For the extremes of enclosure and exclusion come in the end to the same thing, from the point of view of individual existence. They are the failure to *be* someone, and to have that identity recognized by the outside world, to be someone in security and without guilt. The extreme of exclusion images that failure in a total evaporation of the self into a murky world where nothing can be distinguished clearly or where everything has retreated to an unattainable distance. The extreme of enclosure images the loss of identity in a narrowing down of the limits of selfhood until finally one ceases altogether to exist — like a snuffed candle flame. Oliver requires some firm ground to stand on and a warm protective covering, material or human, around him and above him. In a world in which there is nothing but himself and a dark unsubstantial mist he is nothing, and he would rather be related to the world as a slave among slaves than not be related at all. But on the other hand the world must not approach too close. It must be a protective and approving gaze, not a suffocating coercion, a secure foundation, not the solid enclosure of the prison, or the grave: "Mother! dear, dear mother, bury me in the open fields — anywhere but in these dreadful streets. I should like to be where you can see my grave, but not in these close crowded streets; they have killed me." The passage is from the *Sketches by Boz,* but there, as in *Oliver Twist,* the city is the place where one is crushed to death by the walls and the crowds or suffocated by the "closeness."

Oliver's search, then, is for a physical and social world which will offer support but not coercion, protection but not imprisonment, which will be tangibly *there,* but there at a certain safe distance. It is a world of which he has had no knowledge except in his dreams.

## IV

Suddenly Oliver is extricated. He wakes to find himself in a kind of world he has never known. Both times when Oliver is transported into the good world there is an interval of unconsciousness between, followed by a period of serious illness. When he sinks into unconsciousness from the strain of his intolerable life there seems no possible escape. When he comes to his senses again he is in a transformed world. There is an absolute discontinuity between the two worlds. The movement from the bad world to the good one is as mysterious and as unpredictable as his initial incarceration in the dark world or as his redescent into the inferno when Fagin recaptures him. He simply finds everything suddenly changed. At first he does not know where he is, and the absolute transmutation of scene makes possible an absolute transmutation of self: "What room is this? Where have I been brought to? . . . This is not the place I went to sleep in." He has collapsed in the police office of the horrible Mr. Fang. He awakens to see "a motherly old lady, very neatly and precisely dressed" (12), sitting at needlework in an armchair by his curtained bed. All his past life seems a nightmare from which he has finally awakened to a life anterior to anything he has known in his actual life: "Weak, and thin, and pallid, he awoke at last from what seemed to have been a long and troubled dream" (12).

What are the characteristics of the new world in which Oliver so suddenly finds himself? Is it simply the opposite of the dark world of his initial interment? Is it freedom, openness, light, intelligible order rather than darkness, enclosedness, and incoherence?

At first it seems that the country world which is paradise on earth to Oliver is merely the diametrical opposite of the city world: "In the morning, Oliver would be a-foot by six o'clock, roaming the fields, and plundering the hedges, far and wide, for nosegays of wild flowers . . ." (32). For the first time, Oliver is in a world where he can wander freely and without danger. There is even a passage which is a benign version of the frenzied race through the labyrinthine city streets: "Swiftly

he ran across the fields, and down the little lanes which sometimes divided them: now almost hidden by the high corn on
either side, and now emerging on an open field, where the
mowers and haymakers were busy at their work . . ." (33).
Here all the narrowness and the threatening complexity of the
city labyrinth have disappeared. The calm repose which is one
leitmotiv of the country scenes seems caused simply by the
openness they substitute for the suffocating narrowness of
city streets or city interiors: "Who can describe the pleasure and delight, the peace of mind and soft tranquillity, the
sickly boy felt in the balmy air, and among the green hills and
rich woods, of an inland village! . . . It was a lovely spot to
which they repaired. Oliver, whose days had been spent among
squalid crowds, and in the midst of noise and brawling,
seemed to enter on a new existence there. The rose and honeysuckle clung to the cottage walls; the ivy crept round the
trunks of the trees; and the garden-flowers perfumed the air
with delicious odours" (32). This seems simply to oppose the
openness of the "balmy air, and . . . green hills and rich
woods, of an inland village" to "crowded, pent-up streets." But
what of the rose and honeysuckle which *cling* to the cottage
walls, and the ivy which *creeps round* the trunks of the trees.
Are not these images of protective enclosure rather than of
complete openness? Are they not images which suggest domestic refuge rather than the empty sky and expansive landscapes of complete freedom?

Indeed, it soon becomes apparent that the country world is
rather the reverse of the subterranean city world than its opposite. The country world combines the freedom Oliver had
when he lay dying in the open with the enclosedness of the
claustral interiors to produce a protected enclosure which is yet
open to the outside and in direct contact with it. It is a paradise
not of complete freedom but of a cosy security which looks out
upon openness and enjoys it from the inside: "The little room
in which he was accustomed to sit, when busy at his books, was
on the ground-floor, at the back of the house. It was quite a
cottage-room, with a lattice-window: around which were clus-
ters of jessamine and honeysuckle, that crept over the case-

ment, and filled the place with their delicious perfume. It
looked into a garden, whence a wicket-gate opened into a small
paddock; all beyond, was fine meadow-land and wood. There
was no other dwelling near, in that direction; and the prospect
it commanded was very extensive" (34, and see 14). The ideal
situation in *Oliver Twist,* then, is to be securely enclosed in a
refuge which is yet open to the outside, in direct contact with
the outside air and commanding an *extensive* view into the distance. Here Oliver possesses the entire surrounding world,
*commands* it, by being able to see it, and yet he is secluded from
view himself. He possesses intimacy, security, and expansion,
openness, breadth of view: "The great trees . . . converted
open and naked spots into choice nooks, where was a deep and
pleasant shade from which to look upon the wide prospect,
steeped in sunshine, which lay stretched beyond" (33).

The world of desirable enclosure differs from the subterranean interiors in being the place of tranquil repose and order
rather than of anxious imprisonment. But this world is *like* the
underground realm in being unintelligible. Oliver understands
the world of the Brownlows and Maylies no more than he understood the world of Sikes and Fagin. He only knows that the
walls have receded to a safe distance and that they now have
apertures through which he can safely watch the outside world.
But he is no more aware of having any right to enjoy this protected and modified enclosure than he felt that he was justly
punished by incarceration in the scenes of entombment. The
world remains unfathomable, opaque, in either case: "And
thus the night crept slowly on. Oliver lay awake for some time,
counting the little circles of light which the reflection of the
rushlight-shade threw upon the ceiling; or tracing with his
languid eyes the intricate pattern of the paper on the wall. The
darknesss and the deep stillness of the room were very solemn . . ." (12).

Oliver imprisoned by Sowerberry, Bumble, or Fagin, or
threatened by the crowd in the street, had no time to study so
carefully the aspect presented to his eyes by the surrounding
world. The world has ceased to push vertiginously upon the
hero, and he can lie at his ease calmly studying the pattern it

makes. But this pattern has no meaning for him. It is merely "intricate," and the number of little circles of light is merely a number. It has no significance for Oliver. Oliver is capable of being in the same state of bewilderment after he is saved as he was before: "[He] looked at the strangers without at all understanding what was going forward — in fact, without seeming to recollect where he was, or what had been passing" (31).

The image of Oliver languidly tracing the meaningless outlines of the world which presents itself to his vision is strangely like the passage quoted above in which Fagin, on trial for his life, is, so to speak, hypnotized by the very intensity of his fear into looking at what surrounds him with detachment and calm, as though it had nothing whatever to do with him. But just as Fagin is in fact about to be condemned to death, so Oliver is in great danger even in the midst of these scenes of protected repose. He is recaptured almost immediately by Fagin when Mr. Brownlow saves him, and his life with the Maylies is punctuated with appearances in the midst of his new environment of the dark world he was born in, appearances which only he can see. The vindictive glance of the hideous dwarf is glimpsed only by Oliver. He no sooner leaves the Maylies' cottage alone, than Monks starts up before him.

But the most important case of the appearance of the dark world in the midst of the good has a deeper significance.

Oliver falls asleep one evening in his little cottage room, sitting close by the lattice window from which he can see so much without being seen. There follows an experience which seems to prove the total insecurity of Oliver's present happy state. It is a passage which is, for Dickens, strangely deliberate and analytical. Apparently it is the statement of a doctrine about dreams, or, more precisely, about a certain state between sleep and waking in which the imaginary world of dreams is not cut off from the real situation of the sleeper but is mingled with it: "There is a kind of sleep that steals upon us sometimes, which, while it holds the body prisoner, does not free the mind from a sense of things about it, and enable it to ramble at its pleasure. So far as an overpowering heaviness, a prostration of strength, and an utter inability to control our thoughts or power of mo-

tion, can be called sleep, this is it; and yet, we have a consciousness of all that is going on about us, and, if we dream at such a
time, words which are really spoken, or sounds which really
exist at the moment, accommodate themselves with surprising
readiness to our visions, until reality and imagination become
so strangely blended that it is afterwards almost matter of impossibility to separate the two" (34). Earlier in the novel an
almost exactly similar experience, defined in the same way —
"There is a drowsy state, between sleeping and waking, when
you dream more in five minutes . . . than you would in five
nights with your eyes fast closed" (9) — had been explicitly
defined as proof of the mighty power of the human mind to
transcend its ordinary limitation to a single time and a single
space. "At such times, a mortal knows just enough of what his
mind is doing, to form some glimmering conception of its
mighty powers, its bounding from earth and spurning time and
space, when freed from the restraint of its corporeal associ-
ate" (9). For a moment, while such an experience lasts, a mortal is freed from his mortality and from his imprisonment in his
body and in the present moment.

But the special interest of this state for Dickens is that it
links an "imaginary" world to the actual present world, whereas
an ordinary dream is entirely free, and has no direct relation
whatever to the present. Even if we are not at all aware
through sensation of what is there in reality as a "mere silent
presence," it will magically determine the nature of our dream:
"It is an undoubted fact, that although our senses of touch and
sight be for the time dead, yet our sleeping thoughts, and the
visionary scenes that pass before us, will be influenced and ma-
terially influenced, by the *mere silent presence* of some external object; which may not have been near us when we closed
our eyes: and of whose vicinity we have had no waking consciousness" (34).

Nevertheless, the most important peculiarity of this half
waking state is not, it turns out, that it links a real state to an
imaginary state, but that it links a *present* state to a *past* state.
In the earlier experience Oliver was perfectly aware of what
was going on in the room around him and "yet the self-same

senses were mentally engaged, at the same time, in busy action with almost everybody he had ever known" (9). In fact, what was perceived by Oliver's "half-closed eyes" was not only an immediate reality but a reality which seemed to contain, although Oliver was only vaguely aware of it, a hidden reminiscence, extending even prior to "everybody he had ever known." For what Oliver sees is Fagin gloating over his stolen jewels, and "poring long and earnestly" over a tiny trinke which may be a clue to his origin, and to his lost identity. Th: trinket functions as a magic talisman in whose presence th half-dreaming Oliver is put in touch with his past. But hi mysterious sense that what he is doing or perceiving now is somehow a repetition of something from long ago is at this point wholly incomprehensible to Oliver.

In the second of such experiences the earlier time which the present repeats is definitely recognized: "Oliver knew, perfectly well, that he was in his own little room; that his books were lying on the table before him; that the sweet air was stirring among the creeping plants outside. And yet he was asleep. Suddenly, the scene changed; the air became close and confined; and he thought, with a glow of terror, that he was in the Jew's house again.. There sat the hideous old man, in his accustomed corner, pointing at him, and whispering to another man, with his face averted, who sat beside him" (34).

Oliver wakes to find his dream reality: "There — there — at the window — close before him — so close, that he could have almost touched him before he started back: with his eyes peering into the room, and meeting his: there stood the Jew!" (34). The dream that is suggested by the "mere silent presence" of Fagin and Monks is not a free fantasy but is the total and exact reliving of Oliver's past as the prisoner of Fagin. The real theme of this striking passage is the possibility of that affective memory which forms, with many variations, a central theme of romanticism. Here a peculiar psychological state caused by something directly present brings about the total recovery of a certain epoch of the past not as a faint memory but as an intimately relived experience. The past invades and altogether replaces a present which it is like. Or rather, the two times, past and present, are superimposed and inextricably mingled, and Oliver for a moment lives in a time which is neither past nor present but is somehow a universal and atemporal experience of being imprisoned by Fagin and subjected to his look. It is an experience which sums up his entire life since his birth.

But what Oliver endures is a very special variant of affective memory. He is perfectly aware that he is in his own little room, and suddenly he is in the Jew's house again. And yet when he wakes in terror he finds that Fagin and Monks are really there. What had seemed a fearful dream is literal actuality, and the present is in reality a reënactment of the past. The past has been recaptured. Here, though, there is no Proustian escape from the burden of an intolerable present through the ecstatic identification of a present moment and a past moment. Oliver has known no blissful infancy, and the past which comes back to dominate and to destroy his present happiness is the past of his subterranean life. Even though Oliver had thought himself secure in his new life with the Maylies, Fagin now reappears in the very midst of his most secure moment and invades his most secure place. Fagin comes as if to reclaim Oliver, as if to remind him that he really has belonged permanently to the dark underground world from his birth, and has never really escaped. A glance of "recognition" passes between Oliver and Fagin, like the look between Oliver and the dwarf, a look which seems to seal forever Oliver's secret identification with the world into which he was born, however completely he may seem to have left it behind: "It was but an instant, a glance, a flash, before his eyes; and they were gone. But they had recognised him, and he them; and their look was as firmly impressed upon his memory, as if it had been deeply carved in stone, and set before him from his birth" (34).[2] When Oliver's friends look for footprints in the garden where he has seen Fagin and Monks, they can find none. This may suggest

---

[2] Compare: ". . . the boy's eyes were fixed on his in mute curiosity; and although the recognition was only for an instant — for the briefest space of time that can possibly be conceived — it was enough to show the old man that he had been observed" (9).

that Fagin is the devil who leaves no footprints, but more importantly it shows that only Oliver is threatened by these sudden incursions into his happy present of a past from which he can never be free. Only Oliver is perpetually insecure because that past is "as firmly impressed upon his memory, as if it had been deeply carved in stone, and set before him from his birth." Oliver's past is permanently part of him and cannot be escaped by any movement into the future in the retrospectively oriented world of the novel.

Oliver knows now what he wants — a present which will be a protected repose combining freedom and enclosure. But he does not know how to possess this paradise on earth in permanent security. It seems to be in perpetual danger of being at any moment overrun and replaced by the dark past. The present, then, is altogether intolerable for Oliver, whether he is in the midst of a dark enclosed world which is accelerating toward his destruction, or whether he is in a calm protected world which may at any time be invaded and destroyed by the other world. The present in *Oliver Twist* is characterized by a failure to know who one is or to attain any acceptable identity. It is also characterized by a failure to understand the outside world. Oliver can only submit passively to a succession of present moments which do not relate coherently to one another. The world imposes a random rhythm of escape and capture. Oliver has only his "sturdy spirit" to defend himself, and because of the taboo against taking matters into his own hands he can use that spirit only to keep himself alive by passive resistance. Time in this unrelieved present either "steals tardily," slows down, coagulates, and freezes into an endless present of suffering, bewilderment, and interior emptiness, or, like a broken clock, it accelerates madly under the impulsion of fear toward the death that seems rushing out of the imminent future: "The day passed off. Day? There was no day: it was gone as soon as come — and night came on again; night so long, and yet so short; long in its dreadful silence, and short in its fleeting hours. . . . Eight — nine — ten. If it was not a trick to frighten him, and those were the real hours treading on each other's heels, where would he be, when they came round again!

Eleven! Another struck, before the voice of the previous hour had ceased to vibrate. At eight, he would be the only mourner in his own funeral train; at eleven — " (52). The future then is a blank wall — an inevitable death by hanging. Only one dim hope appears. The present is able to be, through the phenomenon of affective memory, the reliving, the recapturing, of a past time.

V

Three distinct forms of repetition through memory of a past time may be distinguished in *Oliver Twist*.

First, there is the experience already described which links a present with a past moment in Oliver's own life. There is no escape here. Oliver is merely plunged back into the procession of enclosed and threatened moments which began with his birth and is carrying him implacably onward, even when he seems to have escaped, toward an outcast's death.

But there is another form of memory, a form which seems to connect the present with a supernatural paradise, a paradise which is anterior to all Oliver's present life, but which the present seems somehow to reveal. And it is revealed as a promise, the promise of an eventual escape out of this world of pain and suffering.

*Oliver Twist* abounds in intimations of immortality. In Mr. Brownlow's revery there were "faces that the grave had changed and closed upon, but which the mind, superior to its power, still dressed in their old freshness and beauty, . . . whispering of beauty beyond the tomb, changed but to be heightened, and taken from earth only to be set up as a light, to shed a soft and gentle glow upon the path to Heaven" (11). Rose Maylie's tears upon Oliver's forehead cause him to stir and smile in his sleep, "as though these marks of pity and compassion had awakened some pleasant dream of a love and affection he had never known" (30). But this dream is no mere fantasy; it is the recollection of a prenatal paradise, as "a strain of gentle music, or the rippling of water in a silent place, or the odour of a flower, or the mention of a familiar word, will sometimes call up sudden dim remembrances of scenes that never were, in this life; which vanish like a breath; which some brief memory of a happier existence, long gone by, would seem to have awakened; which no voluntary exertion of the mind can ever recall" (30). Memory, then, can be an intense sensation of *déjà vu,* a sensation which is no longer the reliving of a past moment in one's own earthly life, but is the faint apprehension of "some remote and distant time" which is not of this world at all and which seems to be one's real home: "The memories which peaceful country scenes call up, are not of this world, nor of its thoughts and hopes. . . . there lingers . . . a vague and half-formed consciousness of having held such feelings long before, in some remote and distant time, which calls up solemn thoughts of distant times to come . . ." (32).

But this is not what Oliver wants. All the intimations of a supernatural state of bliss which Oliver receives from the earthly world only serve to accentuate the shortcomings of the latter. What Oliver wants is to possess his heaven on earth. The "memories" of a prior state of bliss called forth by "peaceful country scenes" only separate more radically the present real earthly world and the distant unattainable paradise. ". . . heaven is," as Oliver says, "a long way off; and they are too happy there, to come down to the bedside of a poor boy" (12). Graham Greene has spoken of the "Manicheanism" of the world of *Oliver Twist,* and indeed there does seem to be initially an absolute breach between heaven and the intolerable earthly world — which is a kind of hell. But the problem of the novel is precisely how to join these two apparently irreconcilable worlds, how to bring heaven to earth. It seems, though, that the only way to reach heaven is through death. Again and again any state of calm happiness, any beautiful landscape, and even any state of complete moral goodness is equated with death:

. . . he wished, as he crept into his narrow bed, that that were his coffin, and that he could be lain in a calm and lasting sleep in the church-yard ground, with the tall grass waving gently above his head, and the sound of the old deep bell to soothe him in his sleep. (5)

Gradually, he fell into that deep tranquil sleep which ease from recent suffering alone imparts; that calm and peaceful rest which it is pain to wake from. Who, if this were death, would be roused again to all the struggles and turmoils of life; to all its cares for the present; its anxieties for the future; more than all, its weary recollections of the past! (12)

He felt calm and happy, and could have died without a murmur. (30)

The city men go to the country to die; little Dick dies the death Oliver would have died and the news is brought to Oliver in the very moment when his happiness is at last secure (51); Dickens has no sooner got Oliver to the pleasant country cottage with the Maylies than he has Rose Maylie nearly die because she is too good for this world. The narrative of this event is characterized by that maudlin sentimentality of language which Dickens often slips into when he writes about either beautiful and pure young women or about heaven: " 'A creature,' continued the young man, passionately, 'a creature as fair and innocent of guile as one of God's own angels, fluttered between life and death. Oh! who could hope, when the distant world to which she was akin, half opened to her view, that she would return to the sorrow and calamity of this!' " (35). The falsity of the language here is a sign that Dickens rather wishes for the heavenly world than wholly believes in it. His real allegiance, it may be, is to the dark world, the world which he so fears is the real and only world that he writes novel after novel whose dramatic action is the attempt to escape from it.

But still Dickens can be caught up in the vision of a natural innocence which is brought into this world at birth from a prenatal heaven and which is regained at death after passing through a world which is predominantly evil: "Alas! How few of Nature's faces are left alone to gladden us with their beauty! The cares, and sorrows, and hungerings, of the world, change them as they change hearts; and it is only when those passions sleep, and have lost their hold for ever, that the troubled clouds pass off, and leave Heaven's surface clear. It is a common thing for the countenances of the dead, even in that fixed and rigid

tate, to subside into the long-forgotten expression of sleeping
nfancy, and settle into the very look of early life . . ." (24).
Heaven, then, is the place where all that has been lost in this
fallen world is regained, and it is a place of which one may
have glimpses momentarily athwart the almost totally unrelieved gloom of this world.

There seems no escape from this world but by death.

However, one final form remains of the repetition through
memory of a past state: one may find signs in the present of a
secret past life which existed *on this earth* before one was born.
When those signs are understood, their revelations may be accepted as a definition of what one really is. Then it will be
possible to live ever afterward in a kind of paradise on earth, a
paradise regained which is the present lightened and spiritual-
ized because it is a repetition of one's prenatal earthly past. If
*Oliver Twist* is in one sense Oliver's procession through a sequence of opaque and meaningless present moments, it is in
another sense the slow discovery, in the midst of that confusion, of a secret which will make all seem orderly and significant. As in all of Dickens' novels, there is a mystery at the center of apparently unrelated events which will make them turn
out in retrospect to be orderly and intelligible. Here the mystery
is the secret of Oliver's birth. When it is solved he can live
happily ever after because now he knows who he *is*. He discovers his essence, his intrinsic nature, and with it acquires a
place in society.

But the total dramatic pattern of *Oliver Twist* suggests that
Oliver can have happiness so completely in the end only because he has lost it so completely at the beginning. If there had
not been an absolute break in the chain of time which determines each person's present identity by an ineluctable series of
causes and effects, and if there had not been an absolute break
in the chain of community relationships by which parents and
adults own, control, and judge, as well as protect, their children, would the secure life Oliver covets have been so desirable after all? Does not Dickens secretly enjoy the situation
of the outcast, with an enjoyment nonetheless intense for being
hidden far beneath the surface? If the outcast is, in one sense,

entirely coerced, in another sense he is entirely free, entirely
untrammeled by any direct ties to any other human being. Even
if Oliver secretly and almost unconsciously believes that he is
something other than the "bad 'un," destined for the gallows
which everyone names him, that belief has no evident source in
the external world. It depends only on Oliver himself for its
existence. And Oliver can claim his inheritance only after he
has proved that he really is who he is in a world which does not
give him any reflection or recognition of that identity. Oliver
can only become himself by forming a relation between what
he is initially, a wholly independent self, depending on and sus
tained by nothing external, and the self he discovers himself al
ready to be. The distance between these two selves is absolutely
necessary. Hence the extreme importance of the clause of
Oliver's father's will providing that he shall inherit the money
"only on the stipulation that in his minority he should never
have stained his name with any public act of dishonour, mean
ness, cowardice, or wrong" (51).

Dickens, then, in a manner contrives to have both his con
tradictory needs simultaneously. Oliver is self-determining in
that, without any knowledge of who he really is, he has had to
defend his essence from the world that tries to make him a
thief. But in the end he is entirely the protégé of the outside
world, and submits without quarrel to a life under the approv
ing eyes of Mr. Brownlow and the Maylies. Finally, when all
the secrets are out, having been wrested by force from the
heart of the dark world, Mr. Brownlow adopts Oliver "as his
son," and Oliver has what he wants at last as a member of
"a little society, whose condition approached as nearly to one
of perfect happiness as can ever be known in this changing
world" (53). He has the landscape of reconciled enclosure
and freedom, now personified in Rose Maylie, literally his aunt
but in a way mother and sister to him too, and described in
language which identifies her with the ideal scene of the novel:
"I would show Rose Maylie in all the bloom and grace of early
womanhood, shedding on her secluded path in life soft and
gentle light, that fell on all who trod it with her, and shone

into their hearts" (53). And he has the selfhood he has sought, a selfhood which he has not chosen or created, but which has been given to him from the outside: "Mr. Brownlow went on, from day to day, filling the mind of his adopted child with stores of knowledge, and becoming attached to him, more and more, as his nature developed itself, and showed the thriving seeds of all he wished him to become — . . . he traced in him new traits of his early friend, that awakened in his own bosom old remembrances, melancholy and yet sweet and soothing . . ." (53).

Oliver has at last what he wants. He has reconciled freedom and the desire for self-determination with the desire not to choose what he is to be, to have the choice made for him, and then to be protected and accepted by society. Mr. Brownlow *fills* the empty spirit of Oliver with those "stores of knowledge" which will make him an authentic member of the middle class, but this education only reveals that Oliver has been all along potentially what Mr. Brownlow wants to make him in actuality. His selfhood is both made for him by Mr. Brownlow and yet prior to Mr. Brownlow's education of him. And this reconciliation of contradictory needs is possible because Oliver is willing to exist as the image of his father, willing to take as the definition of his essential selfhood those traits which are the repetition of his father's nature. He is willing to accept an idenfication of himself which does not derive, ultimately, from anything he has done, but only from what his parents were. In order to escape from the harsh world into which he has been born, a world in which the extreme of enclosedness combines with the extreme of isolation, Oliver is willing to live out his life facing backward into the past, spending with Rose Maylie whole hours . . . in picturing the friends whom they had so sadly lost" (53). He escapes from an intolerable present and a frightening future by making the present a reduplication of a past safely over and done with, and by turning his back altogether on the future and on autonomous action. He lives happily ever after, but only by living in a perpetual childhood of submission to protection and direction from without.

The ending of *Oliver Twist* is a resolution of Dickens' single great theme, the search of the outcast for status and authentic identity, but it is a resolution which is essentially based on self-deception and on an unwillingness to face fully his apprehension of the world. It is a resolution which will not satisfy him for long.

## Chapter III

# NICHOLAS NICKLEBY
# THE OLD CURIOSITY SHOP
# BARNABY RUDGE

BETWEEN *Oliver Twist* and *Martin Chuzzlewit* Dickens wrote three major novels: *Nicholas Nickleby, The Old Curiosity Shop,* and *Barnaby Rudge.* Taken together these might be seen as preliminary statements of the themes and problems which occupy him in *Martin Chuzzlewit.* They move Dickens' attention from the perspectives of those altogether outside society at either end of the scale (Pickwick and Oliver) to characters who are within the open arena of the world, but who still lack security or status. A brief discussion of these novels will show where Dickens was at the beginning of the composition of *Martin Chuzzlewit,* and will prepare for a more elaborate investigation of that novel. This chapter, like Chapters V and VII, is not meant to be a full analysis of the novels discussed. It is rather an interchapter outlining Dickens' development between *Oliver Twist* and *Martin Chuzzlewit,* and suggesting what I find to be central in the three novels which intervene.

Without question, the most striking thing about these novels is the inexhaustible proliferation, within them, of grotesque characters who are altogether unique, each vivid and distinct, each living as the perpetual reënactment of his own peculiar idiosyncrasies. Dickens in these novels shows us again and again that "all men have some little pleasant way of their own"

(*NN,* 33). As Henry James perceptively observed, speaking of the Cruikshank illustrations for *Oliver Twist,* which seem so intrinsic to Dickens: "the scenes and figures intended to comfort and cheer, present themselves . . . as but more subtly sinister, or more suggestively queer, than the frank badnesses and horrors." [1] Squeers, Newman Noggs, the Mantalinis, Lillyvick, Mr. Vincent Crummles, Quilp, Dick Swiveller, the Marchioness, Miss Miggs, John Willet — Dickens' power to improvise multitudes of inimitable, slightly insane personages was never greater. These novels are animated by an immense energy, the spiritual energy of Dickens himself, as he personifies each character, and plays each part with the skill of a great comic actor. This energy, while any one character holds the stage, is completely confined within the limits of that character. Each one, while we see him, remains altogether himself. The characters do not overlap or repeat one another. They have in common only the unashamed force with which each one enacts himself, and the fact that each is incommensurate with all the others. The genius which invokes these characters and gives them continuing life is an extravagant linguistic power, ceaselessly inventing for each character gestures, action, and speech which are always different, yet always the same, as, for example, in the magnificent nonsense of the speeches of Squeers: " 'It only shows what Natur is, sir,' said Mr. Squeers. 'She's a rum 'un, is Natur. . . . I should like to know how we should ever get on without her. Natur,' said Mr. Squeers, solemnly 'is more easier conceived than described. Oh what a blessed thing, sir, to be in a state of Natur!' " (*NN,* 45). Indeed, we feel occasionally, as Dickens invents a scene, plays it with incomparable energy, taking all the parts, and then tells us in a moralizing passage what to think about it, that he does not really need us, that we have come accidentally upon a private theatrical, being acted by Dickens for his own personal amusement.

But, whereas such extravagant grotesques were, in *Pickwick Papers,* most often seen from the outside, as they presented

[1] "A Small Boy and Others," *Autobiography,* ed. F. W. Dupee (New York, 1956), p. 69.

themselves to the bewildered regard of the secure rich man, and were seen, in *Oliver Twist,* from the perspective of the equally bewildered outcast, in *Nicholas Nickleby, The Old Curiosity Shop,* and *Barnaby Rudge,* they are seen from the point of view of someone without security who is nevertheless within society. We are now altogether out of Oliver's cellar, and out of Pickwick's enclosed chamber. We are in an open world, in which people are available to one another as gesture, speech, and action in a purely comic space. Within this space, everyone accepts the absence or unattainability of a private subjective life in other people. The characters *are* what they appear, and are accepted by one another, for the most part, without surprise or curiosity.

To the uniqueness of the grotesque characters corresponds the uniqueness of the narrative moment. Such is Dickens' fertile invention of detail, such is the vividness with which the immediate scene is represented, that the structure of the novel as plot is often forgotten, as, for example, in the narrative of the Kenwigs' anniversary party (*NN*, 14). The individual scene swells out of all proportion to its significance in the whole, and we abandon ourselves to what is immediately present, without memory or concern for the intrigue of the novel. One pole of these novels is fascinated and exclusive attention, under the pressure of some extreme situation, whether comic or melodramatic, to what is perceptible in the present moment. What is seen impresses itself indelibly on the memory in all its detail, but is without past or future of its own, without depth, like a landscape glimpsed momentarily from the window of a speeding vehicle, or like objects which senselessly absorb our attention when we are lost in a daydream:

The cracks in the pavement of his cell, the chinks in the wall where stone was joined to stone, the bars in the window, the iron ring upon the floor, — such things as these, subsiding strangely into one another, and awakening an indescribable kind of interest and amusement, engrossed his whole mind . . . . (*BR*, 62)

Still, he lacked energy to follow up this train of thought; and unconsciously fell, in a luxury of repose, to staring at some green stripes on the bed-furniture . . . . (*OCS*, 64)

There are times when the mind, being painfully alive to receive impressions, a great deal may be noted at a glance. (*NN*, 53)

Perhaps a man never sees so much at a glance as when he is in a situation of extremity. (*BR*, 58)


In this universe of the moment and of the idiosyncratic nothing can have a significant existence because nothing can be related to anything else, or supported in its existence by anything else. There is no scale of categories, essences, or species organizing the whole. Everything is what it is, and no more can be said about it. It is not really even possible to say that the characters are a little mad, for there is no concept of sanity by which they may be judged, and the objects too refuse to reveal themselves as ordered in any pattern or hierarchy, though large numbers of the same object may exist together. These things and people are simply there before the spectator's eyes.

The procedure of nominalism (which reaches the general by abstraction from many particulars) is present, in a way, in Dickens' treatment of comic characters. Each appearance of a comic personage is unique and concrete. But we slowly come to realize, through our recognition of the repetition of obsessional phrases, modes of speech, or gesture, that the character really exists as a kind of generalized form or abstract idea of himself. This universal is in each concrete action or speech embodied in an individual and unique form. Beginning with the individual moments we work toward an atemporal form which endures unchanged throughout the character's life, rather than, as in "realist" novels (e.g., those of Trollope or George Eliot), beginning with a general sketch of the character and then seeing this abstract idea embodied in various concrete instances. But this universal "idea" of each character is wholly special to him, and cannot be compared or related to any other. Dickens' comic characters, with their obsessional tics of speech or manner, are related rather to Sterne's hobbyhorse riders or to the characters in Jonson's plays, each with his peculiar humor, than to the typified personages of the seventeenth-century "character" sketches.

In the end the world of these novels reveals itself as, like that of *Oliver Twist,* a sheer chaos, an inextricable jumble of objects and people in ceaseless motion, multiplied inexhaustibly, without order or direction. The city is, for Dickens, a Dance of Death:

> Streams of people apparently without end poured on and on, jostling each other in the crowd and hurrying forward, scarcely seeming to notice the riches that surrounded them on every side; while vehicles of all shapes and makes, mingled up together in one moving mass like running water, lent their ceaseless roar to swell the noise and tumult.
>
> As they dashed by the quickly-changing and ever-varying objects, it was curious to observe in what a strange procession they passed before the eye. Emporiums of splendid dresses, the materials brought from every quarter of the world; tempting stores of everything to stimulate and pamper the sated appetite and give new relish to the oft-repeated feast; vessels of burnished gold and silver, wrought into every exquisite form of vase, and dish, and goblet; guns, swords, pistols, and patent engines of destruction; screws and irons for the crooked, clothes for the newly born, drugs for the sick, coffins for the dead, churchyards for the buried — all these jumbled each with the other and flocking side by side, seemed to flit by in motley dance like the fantastic groups of the old Dutch painter, and with the same stern moral for the unheeding restless crowd. (*NN, 32*)

Coherent existence is impossible for human beings in such surroundings. To the ever-changing multiplicity of the phenomenal scene corresponds a continual metamorphosis of the self. This is shown in two ways in these novels: from the point of view of the spectator seeing the characters from the outside, and from the point of view of the characters themselves.

Nicholas Nickleby's experience among the provincial actors of Crummles' company is of great importance as a critique of the way of life of all the characters here. Crummles, Lenville, Miss Snevellicci, and the other actors have no solid existence in themselves. Even when they are off the stage, their every gesture and phrase is a theatrical pose. They live lives which are sheer surface, sheer cliché, the perpetual substitution of one assumed role for another. They have only a multiple and volatile identity. If there is any unchanged component at all, it is only the anonymous spiritual energy which animates the particular role they have gratuitously chosen to play for the moment. Each role is without depth and without permanence.

But we come to recognize that the other characters in the novel have the same kind of existence, make the same theatrical gestures and speeches, and that the central action of *Nicholas Nickleby* is the elaborate performance of a cheap melodrama, complete with sneering villains, insulted virginity, and a courageous young hero who appears in the nick of time. ". . . you are caught, villains, in your own toils," says Nicholas (*NN,* 54).[2] The scenes of the provincial theater thus act as a parody of the main plot, and of the life of the chief characters in the main story. In spite of himself Dickens reveals the fictive nature of his own novel, and the vacuity of his characters. We come to see the entire novel as an improvised drama which cannot escape the factitiousness of all assumed roles. There is nothing behind each character but the pure spiritual energy which is thwarted by an arbitrary mask and twisted to fit it. The inimitable grotesques who crowd the pages of Dickens' novels have life indeed, but there is no real relation between that life and the way it has been forced to express itself. All of them are, in the end, like Dick Swiveller in *The Old Curiosity Shop.* Dick expresses himself in clichés drawn from music hall songs, clichés which have no real relation to his true situation in the world, or to his true self. He must use these outworn and empty phrases because he knows no other language, just as the characters in Joyce's novels must use an elegant eighteenth-century diction which has no relation to their real condition of life.[3] We come to see all the idiosyncratic characters in Dickens as, like Swiveller, each trapped in his uniqueness and its obsessions, and condemned to be himself without any possibility of escape.

From the point of view of the characters themselves, this

[2] The melodrama is, in fact, enacted twice, once for Kate Nickleby, and once for Madeline Bray.

[3] See, on this point, Hugh Kenner, *Dublin's Joyce* (Bloomington, Ind., 1956), pp. 7–18.

kind of life may be defined in a single word: isolation. Each of these novels, like *Oliver Twist,* has at its center characters who are alienated from society, and the situation of all is to be, like Nell in the midst of the bric-a-brac of the Old Curiosity Shop, surrounded by an inimical world, a world which refuses to support or recognize their existence: ". . . she seemed to exist in a kind of allegory. . . . I had, ever before me, the old dark murky rooms — the gaunt suits of mail with their ghostly silent air — the faces all awry, grinning from wood and stone — the dust, and rust, and worm that lives in wood — and alone in the midst of all this lumber and decay and ugly age, the beautiful child in her gentle slumber, smiling through her light and sunny dreams" (*OCS,* 1).

But it is not merely the protagonists of these novels who have such lives. The chief characters are shown more or less from the inside, enduring their isolation consciously, but, as Dickens says, "most men live in a world of their own" (*NN,* 28), and the few glimpses he allows us into the inner lives of the grotesque characters reveal them also to be living, like Miss La Creevy, in total isolation, as much alone as if they were in the middle of a desert: "The little bustling, active, cheerful creature, existed entirely within herself, talked to herself, made a confidant of herself, was as sarcastic as she could be, on people who offended her, by herself; pleased herself, and did no harm. . . . One of the many to whom . . . London is as complete a solitude as the plains of Syria, the humble artist had pursued her lonely, but contented way for many years . . ." (*NN,* 20). The condition of all the characters in these three novels, then, is to be alone in surroundings which appear as a kind of queer play or spectacle having no relation whatsoever to the character himself: "John stared round at the mass of faces — some grinning, some fierce, some lighted up by torches, some indistinct, some dusky and shadowy: some looking at him, some at his house, some at each other — . . . as if it were some queer play or entertainment, of an astonishing and stupefying nature, but having no reference to himself — that he could make out — at all" (*BR,* 54).

The starting point of *Nicholas Nickleby, The Old Curiosity*

*Shop,* and *Barnaby Rudge* is the same: isolation in the midst of an atomistic milieu, full of a jumble of disorganized objects and people wholly unrelated to the spectator. And each of these novels shows that the unique personage perpetually reënacting himself in an alien environment and in a sealed-in present is not self-sufficient. Alone, he is without substance, hollow. Each novel attempts to transcend this initial condition, but each tries a different road to the same goal. Each seeks something outside the moment and outside the self-enclosed individual, something which will sustain the individual and give him an authentic identity. In one way or another each novel attempts to seize the totality of the spatial and temporal world, and to find in it a structure and a significance to which the individual can relate himself.

In *Nicholas Nickleby* Dickens seeks to avoid the fragmentation of his instinctive atomism by recourse to type characters, conventional plots, and to moral or pseudoreligious judgments which are thick with sentimental clichés. No other novel of Dickens is closer, in plot, characterization, and constantly asserted moral, to the conventions of the decadent drama and the popular novel of Dickens' day. Those characters in *Nicholas Nickleby* who are not true Dickensian grotesques, fresh from the mint of the inimitable Boz, tend to be the merest pasteboard copies of melodramatic type characters: Ralph Nickleby, Sir Mulberry Hawk, Gride, Madeline Bray, Nicholas himself. The very excess of emotion with which Dickens, in a kind of frenzy of false feeling, reiterates the stock commonplaces betrays both their factitiousness and the immense need driving him to accept some traditional or generally accepted framework of judgment and perception: "There are no words which can express nothing with which can be compared, the perfect pallor, the clear transparent whiteness, of the beautiful face which turned towards him when he entered. Her hair was a rich deep brown, but shading that face, and straying upon a neck that rivalled it in whiteness, it seemed by the strong contrast raven black. Something of wildness and restlessness there was in the dark eye, but there was the same patient look, the same expression of gentle mournfulness which he well remembered, and n trace of a single tear. Most beautiful — more beautiful, perhaps than ever — there was something in her face which quite unmanned him, and appeared far more touching than the wildest agony of grief" (*NN,* 53). For Dickens at this time there is no intermediate stage between the affirmation of his true apprehension of the human condition as painful solitude within a kaleidoscopic world, and a wild oscillation to acceptance of the cheapest consolatory sentiments. But these consolations, stock characters and situations and conventional judgments, in the very sentimental excess with which they are asserted, reveal themselves as just what they are: mere human conventions, resting on nothing, and validated by nothing. The frantically affirmed conventions turn out, paradoxically, to be identical with the disconnected fragments from which they seemed to offer an escape. Conventions are the apogee of the all-too-human. Substantiated by nothing which transcends the human, they are nothing. No novel by Dickens more strikingly betrays the vacuity, the insubstantiality, of the merely human, than *Nicholas Nickleby.* For once the speciously theatrical, but for Dickens' great comic genius, would have triumphed.

In *Barnaby Rudge* Dickens treats on a large scale a potential escape from isolation which had a wide significance in his day: revolution, the total destruction of what is, and the substitution, in the future, of an "altered state of society" (*BR,* 39, 51). The real motto of the Gordon rioters is: "Down with everybody, down with everything!" (*BR,* 38). Here Dickens recognized more openly than in *Oliver Twist* the possibility of seizing the goods and status refused by an unjust society frozen in its privileges. And here, as in *Oliver Twist,* his attitude is ambiguous. It is difficult to be sure of the degree of sympathy he extends to the Gordon rioters. He rejects their project of destruction unequivocally, but he cannot help revealing his secret pleasure in the act of destruction itself, and his more open sympathy for the rioters after they fail and are about to be hanged. A single image dominates Dickens' description of the riots, and reveals the almost cosmic significance he gives them. These descriptions reveal in Dickens what one might call a "fire complex." For Dickens the riots were experienced in imagination as the setting fire to the entire world, "as though the last day had come and the whole universe were burning" (*BR*, 68). This transformation of what had been solid, impermeable, and fixed, into the fluidity and penetrability of fire had a special value: what has been transformed into fire is available. In destroying the world by fire, I can identify myself with it: "The more the fire crackled and raged, the wilder and more cruel the men grew; as though moving in that element they became fiends, and changed their earthly nature for the qualities that give delight in hell. . . . There were men who rushed up to the fire, and paddled in it with their hands as if in water; and others who were restrained by force from plunging in, to gratify their deadly longing" (55). But in thus bridging the gap between self and world, far from attaining the identity and status I sought, I merely destroy simultaneously both self and world. Though it reveals the unacknowledged attraction of revolutionary action, *Barnaby Rudge* also shows that for Dickens such action was identical with suicide. Each person must find within the given, within what already is, some recognition of his value.

If *Barnaby Rudge* is oriented toward the future, *The Old Curiosity Shop* is oriented toward the past. Indeed, all three novels have this orientation to some degree. In each, the present moment, seemingly so self-enclosed and exclusive, turns out to be intimately related to the past, determined by its causal action. All three narratives move forward in time to discover the past, and, in each, the discovery of the past reorganizes the present and justifies a new set of relations among the characters. The past sustains the present. What happened in the past is over and done. It *is,* with a solidity always lacking to the present while it is present. So the past, after it is rediscovered, forms a substantial foundation holding up the present, and giving validity to a realignment of the characters.

Though all three novels repeat this pattern, it is the structural axis of *The Old Curiosity Shop.* This novel is organized around an opposition between the city, the prison of the industrial and commercial inferno which is destroying Nell and her grandfather, and the free and pure country which is close to the divine. But the country is also identified, again and again, with the past of barely remembered childhood, and, behind that, with the happy state of preëxistence before birth. The pilgrimage of Nell and her grandfather, as they flee from the city deeper and deeper into the country, forms the central action of the novel. But it is also a pilgrimage toward the past, toward the time of origin. *The Old Curiosity Shop* is Dickens' most dreamlike novel, the only novel of his which reminds one of the dream voyages of the German romantics. And like those prototypes it unequivocally identifies the voyage from the city to the country, from the present to the past, with death:

If the peace of the simple village had moved the child more strongly, because of the dark and troubled ways that lay beyond, and through which she had journeyed with such failing feet, what was the deep impression of finding herself alone in that solemn building, where the very light, coming through sunken windows, seemed old and grey, and the air, redolent of earth and mould, seemed laden with decay, purified by time of all its grosser particles, and sighing through arch and aisle, and clustered pillars, like the breath of ages gone! . . . She . . . thought of the summer days and the bright springtime that would come — of the rays of sun that would fall in aslant, upon the sleeping forms — of the leaves that would flutter at the window, and play in glistening shadows on the pavement — of the songs of birds, and growth of buds and blossoms out of doors — of the sweet air, that would steal in, and gently wave the tattered banners overhead. What if the spot awakened thoughts of death! . . . It would be no pain to sleep amidst [these sights and sounds]. (*OCS*, 53)

One could read the central dramatic action of *The Old Curiosity Shop* in the general perspective of romanticism. As such, it is merely one example among many of a horrified flight from the new industrial, urban, and commercial civilization to the nostalgically remembered rural, agrarian, and "natural" civilization of the past. But Dickens has no illusions about this. He recognizes that the rural paradise no longer really exists, that it is dead, and that to endure on this earth now means to accept life in the city with all its conditions. By showing that escape from the prison of the city to a divinized nature and a divinized past is identical with death, *The Old Curiosity Shop* functions as a radical criticism of *Oliver Twist,* as does the death of Smike in *Nicholas Nickleby.* The escape from alienation which gave *Oliver Twist* a happy ending is shown to be incompatible with continued existence in this world. Henceforth Dickens must seek other solutions to his central problem.

Without doubt the real answer to that problem offered in these three novels is *community,* the establishment in the present of an elaborate network of familial or amicable relations crisscrossing within a large group living in a perpetual holiday of feasts, birthdays, weddings, anniversary celebrations, and christenings. These festivities will be made secure by the benevolent presence of some fatherly figure for whom, since he has money and is a gentleman, none of the problems of alienation arise. The celebration of the qualities and emotions of community is the chief resource of the many Christmas stories which span almost all of Dickens' writing career. Christmas is for him the transformation of selfishness into charity, the reunion of the family group after separation or misunderstanding. With its games and dancing and feasts, it is the very symbol for Dickens, not of the reconciliation of man and God, but of the reintegration of man and man in a close-knit circle of reciprocal glances, handclasps, and kisses. And such are the communities finally presided over by the Cheeryble brothers in *Nicholas Nickleby,* by Mr. Garland in *The Old Curiosity Shop,* and by Mr. Varden in *Barnaby Rudge.* But these communities seem rather to engulf and absorb the personalities of their members than to sustain them, and to transform everyone into a copy of a standard pattern swallowing up all uniqueness, just as Dolly and Joe Willet produce, not individual children, but simply "more small Joes and small Dollys than could be easily counted" (*BR,* 82). The happy endings of these novels do not, at any rate, represent an adequate analysis of the complexities of the theme of direct and intimate relations between man and man in society.

In *Martin Chuzzlewit* Dickens did address himself to that theme, and to the investigation of the kinds of relationship possible between men who, beginning as strangers, seek to establish contact with one another. And in probing this theme he sought always to discover a relationship which would guarantee the uniqueness of each person, that is, would connect him with others in a way enhancing rather than absorbing and destroying his intrinsic identity.

## Chapter IV

# MARTIN CHUZZLEWIT

## I

MR. MOULD was surrounded by his household gods. He was enjoying the sweets of domestic repose, and gazing on them with a calm delight. The day being sultry, and the window open, the legs of Mr. Mould were on the window-seat, and his back reclined against the shutter. Over his shining head a handkerchief was drawn, to guard his baldness from the flies. The room was fragrant with the smell of punch, a tumbler of which grateful compound stood upon a small round table, convenient to the hand of Mr. Mould; so deftly mixed, that as his eye looked down into the cool transparent drink, another eye, peering brightly from behind the crisp lemon-peel, looked up at him, and twinkled like a star. (25)

MR. MOULD is enclosed within his own space. There is nothing around him which is not his world, which does not mirror back to him his own nature, minister to his own comfort of body and mind. Like a marine animal which secretes its own shell, Mr. Mould lives in an environment which contains nothing out of harmony with his character and his way of life. He can enjoy completely a placid, calm repose because nothing whatsoever visible to him is a threat. His peaceful "gaze" is met everywhere by a return look which is not the hostile stare of something alien but is as much his own, himself, as his own face in the mirror. At the center of the scene is Mr. Mould's tumbler of punch in which "another eye," which is yet his own eye, brightly returns his glance. In the room is his family, a further extension of himself. Between Mr. Mould and his family pass reciprocal smiles in a closed circle of domestic affection: "Mr. Mould looked lovingly at Mrs. Mould, who sat hard by, and was a helpmate to him in his punch as in all other

things. Each seraph daughter, too, enjoyed her share of his regards, and smiled upon him in return" (25). But the spatial
extension of his identity does not stop with the walls of his
"harem." Beyond the window, beyond the "rural screen of
scarlet runners" through which Mr. Mould's "moist glance"
wanders "like a sunbeam," as if he were the light source of his
own world, the "wider prospect" reveals only more of the same,
more of Mr. Mould. What he sees is a small shady churchyard
which he regards "with an artist's eye" (25). It is something
he himself has made. And if his glance out the window is like
a sunbeam, it is met by a return of light which is like a human
look, and for the third time, at the limit of his vision and the
edge of his world, Mr. Mould's look is reciprocated: "The light
came sparkling in among the scarlet runners, as if the churchyard winked at Mr. Mould, and said, 'We understand each
other' " (25).

The "household gods" which "surround" Mr. Mould like a
warm cocoon extend to the farthest limits of his view. This
cocoon is made of a series of screens which enclose Mr. Mould:
the handkerchief over his head, the screen of flowers at the
window, and finally the opposite end of the churchyard, beyond which nothing can be seen. And throughout all pervades
the fragrant smell of punch, a sort of symbol of the homogeneity and self-centeredness of Mr. Mould's milieu. What is beyond, the boisterous life of a great city, all the other people living within their own circumscribed worlds, can be detected
only as a barely audible hum. The outside world is wholly unable to penetrate within the successive layers of protection with
which Mr. Mould has surrounded himself. He remains safe,
"deep in the City": "The premises of Mr. Mould were hard of
hearing to the boisterous noises in the great main streets, and
nestled in a quiet corner, where the City strife became a drowsy
hum, that sometimes rose and sometimes fell and sometimes
altogether ceased . . ." (25).

In these passages we are given only what can be seen and
heard, the room, and its objects, the view from the window, the
gestures and speech of Mr. Mould, and the simplest notation
of Mr. Mould's subjective state, his "calm delight." This sub-

jective state is described as belonging to him in the way a property, color or density, belongs to an object. But this does not mean that there is a hidden subjective life masked behind this appearance. Many of the characters in *Martin Chuzzlewit* have no secret interior lives whatever. They exist wholly spread out into their bodies and into their environments. Mr. Mould lives in a world that is so completely himself, he is so completely at home, that he has no possible opportunity to make a withdrawal of his consciousness from what he is conscious of. And in the same way the objects have no separate existence. They exist only as humanized objects, as parts of Mr. Mould. There is thus no distinction here between the realm of consciousness and that of objects. What exists instead is a single homogeneous continuum which stretches without differentiation from Mr. Mould out to the periphery of his vision. The eye which looks at his eye from his punch, the churchyard which winks at him, are as much alive and as little self-conscious as Mr. Mould himself.

The lack of a division into subjective and objective worlds is suggested by the recurrence of an unusual grammatical form. Instead of saying "Mr. Mould's legs," Dickens says "the legs of Mr. Mould." Mr. Mould's legs are not appendages possessed by him, and therefore in a way separate; they are *of* him, within the intimate circle of his existence. Dickens goes on to speak of "the hand of Mr. Mould," and finally uses the locution in a way which strikingly suggests that everything surrounding Mr. Mould has equal status as an extension of himself: he speaks of "the premises of Mr. Mould."

In Balzac's novels, as in *Martin Chuzzlewit,* characters surround themselves with a cocoon or ambience which is their world. But in Balzac we see this happening. It is a result of the subjectivity and imagination, and, above all, of the volition of the character, as he imposes himself on the world of objects. But in Dickens the character does not coerce objects by imagination or will to match his nature. Rather, the objects, like the gesture, appearance, and expression of the character, are from the first moment we see the character perfect clues, for the spectator, to his mentality, and it is impossible to imagine the process by which this situation came into existence.

From the total enclosure of such characters within their own lives it follows that they are so unable to imagine any other kind of life that they are wholly without perspective upon their own lives. It is impossible for them to see themselves or their profession as others see them, and they are thus able to endure what would shock or repel another person. As Pecksniff says, quoting the old proverb, "Use is second nature" (19). Dickens was fascinated by the process of Mithridatean acclimatization whereby a person can become accustomed to an environment which would be intolerable to anyone else. His habit of visiting slums, prisons, and insane asylums was, in one of its aspects, evidence of this obsession. Thus Martin Chuzzlewit is at first disgusted and humiliated by his life of poverty in London, but he soon becomes used to it: "And it was strange, very strange, even to himself, to find, how by quick though almost imperceptible degrees he lost his delicacy and self-respect, and gradually came to do that as a matter of course, without the least compunction, which but a few short days before had galled him to the quick" (13). And so, Mr. Mould and his family have become so gradually "subdued to what they work in" that no element of undertaking has any horror for them. What to another person would seem a sinister and disquieting place is to the Moulds as soothing as a pastoral landscape. There is a rural screen of scarlet runners outside the window, and the sound of coffin-making in the workshop reminds Mr. Mould of "the buzz of insects" and "the woodpecker tapping": "It puts one in mind of the sound of animated nature in the agricultural districts" (25).

So little self-conscious are many characters in *Martin Chuzzlewit* and consequently so little endowed with memory that unless a change within themselves or in the world outside takes place almost instantaneously it will not even be noticed. If such a change takes place "steadily, imperceptibly, and surely" (43), "by the easiest succession of degrees imaginable" (40), it will be to the character as if no change had taken place.

Hence Dickens' need of asserting the swiftness of a metamorphosis in appearance if it is to be recognized as such: "But the
strangest incident in all this strange behaviour was, that of a
sudden, in a moment, so swiftly that it was impossible to trace
how, or to observe any process of change, his features fell into
their old expression . . ." (18).

Since there is no possibility of perceiving progressive change
in this world, it is not possible to enter it by slow transitory
stages, but only by a sudden leap over the impenetrable barriers
which separate it from all the other scenes of the novel. The
description of the Moulds at home opens a chapter and follows
directly after a chapter which involves wholly different characters. Dickens does not give us any means of connecting these
two contiguous chapters. The connection can only be seen
much later when the novel is complete and all the relationships
between the hermetically sealed milieus of the novel can be
seen in a single, retrospective, panoramic glance. In another
passage, at the beginning of a chapter which, again, has nothing to do with the preceding one, Dickens makes explicit the
essential discontinuity of the world of the novel: "The knocking at Mr. Pecksniff's door, though loud enough, bore no resemblance whatever to the noise of an American railway train
at full speed. It may be well to begin the present chapter with
this frank admission, lest the reader should imagine that the
sounds now deafening this history's ears have any connexion
with the knocker on Mr. Pecksniff's door . . ." (21). As in
the cinematic technique of montage, one visual or auditory sensation gives way to another which is like it, but which belongs
to a different place or time. There may turn out to be a multitude of hidden relationships linking all of the apparently disconnected characters and events of the novel in a tight causal
web. But these events are experienced, by the reader and by the
characters, as if they were entirely isolated:

As there are a vast number of people in the huge metropolis of
England who rise up every morning, not knowing where their heads
will rest at night, so there are a multitude who shooting arrows over
houses as their daily business, never know on whom they fall. Mr.
Nadgett might have passed Tom Pinch ten thousand times; might

even have been quite familiar with his face, his name, pursuits, and character; yet never once have dreamed that Tom had any interest in any act or mystery of his. Tom might have done the like by him, of course. But the same private man out of all the men alive, was in the mind of each at the same moment; was prominently connected, though in a different manner, with the day's adventures of both; and formed, when they passed each other in the street, the one absorbing topic of their thoughts. (38)

Two elements may be distinguished here: the actual interdependence of Tom Pinch and Nadgett, and their ignorance, at the time, of this fact. Each of the characters is entirely sealed within his own life, and all the other characters, except those within his own domestic milieu, are entirely a mystery to him.

In *Martin Chuzzlewit,* then, the isolation of Oliver Twist in his underground prison is rediscovered as the essential condition not of outcasts but among people in the free surface world who, unlike Oliver, are perfectly satisfied with their lot. But what is wholly missing in *Martin Chuzzlewit* is the possibility of a rediscovery of the lost past, a recovery of it which will liberate one from the enclosure of the present. The revelations at the end of *Martin Chuzzlewit* illuminate and integrate all that has gone before but this retrospective discovery of meaning does not extend prior to the beginning of the story. Nothing is discovered which is not part of the present time of the action. No meaning reaches out of the past to transform and redefine the present. The difference is radical. The problem which faces the characters of *Martin Chuzzlewit* is Oliver Twist's problem too: how to achieve an authentic self, a self which, while resting solidly on something outside of itself, does not simply submit to a definition imposed from without. But the manner in which this goal was reached in *Oliver Twist* is wholly denied to the characters of *Martin Chuzzlewit.* The arena of *Martin Chuzzlewit* is the present, a present which is irrevocably cut off from the past and in which society in the sense of an integrated community has been replaced by a fragmented collection of isolated self-seeking individuals.

## II

The aim of *Martin Chuzzlewit,* as Dickens himself said, is to show "how selfishness propagates itself; and to what a grim giant it may grow, from small beginnings" (Preface to the first cheap edition, *MC,* p. xi). But selfishness exists in the novel not only as the ethical bent of the characters, but also as the state of isolation in which they live. The novel is full of people who are wholly enclosed in themselves, wholly secret, wholly intent on reflexive ends which are altogether mysterious to those around them. As Sairey Gamp says, in what might serve as an epigraph for the entire novel: ". . . we never knows wot's hidden in each other's hearts; and if we had glass winders there, we'd need keep the shetters up, some on us, I do assure you!" (29). This self-enclosure is explicitly made the predominant trait of some of the characters of *Martin Chuzzlewit:* ". . . the whole object of [Nadgett's] life," says Dickens, "appeared to be, to avoid notice, and preserve his own mystery" (38). The key term for Nadgett is "secret." He represents in a pure state what the characters of *Martin Chuzzlewit* look like not from within their own private worlds, as in the case of our vision of Mr. Mould, but from the outside. Nadgett's behavior, his speech, his action and appearance can be seen and described, but they remain unintelligible, preserving untouched within the secret of what he is: ". . . he was born to be a secret. He was a short, dried-up, withered, old man, who seemed to have secreted his very blood; for nobody would have given him credit for the possession of six ounces of it in his whole body. How he lived was a secret; where he lived was a secret; and even what he was, was a secret" (27). Why does Nadgett remain an unfathomable secret? He is not hidden behind protective screens, like Mr. Mould. He is out in the open where he can be inspected. Even the contents of his pocketbook are no secret. Nevertheless he cannot be known. *What* he is cannot be known, in spite of the evidence, because it is wholly impossible to find out *who* he is. There is no possible direct access to the inner life of Nadgett. What is missing here, and throughout *Martin Chuzzlewit* for the most part, is any inter-subjective world. There is no world of true language, gesture, or expression which would allow the characters entrance to one another's hearts. And Dickens does not permit himself, except on a very few occasions, to employ the convention of the omniscient narrator, able to enter at will the inner consciousnesses of his characters. The world of *Martin Chuzzlewit* is a public world, a world in which what exists is only what could be seen by any detached observer. It is in this sense that it is a fundamentally comic world. For the essential requirement of comedy is an unbridgeable gap between narrator (and reader) and the characters. Far from identifying himself with the subjective experiences of the characters, and realizing them from the inside, the reader of *Martin Chuzzlewit,* like the narrator and the characters themselves, in their relations to one another, remains separated from the personages. He may attribute to the characters the subjective states appropriate to the speech, expression, or gesture which he sees, but the characters actually exist as their appearance and their actions and only as these. They are simply visible, audible, tangible objects, animate, but apparently otherwise exactly like other objects in the world.

For some characters such as Mr. Mould, this presents no problem. Mould exists only as undertaker and as pampered family man. He has no secret. But for certain people, like Nadgett, the manifest data do not hang together and one is forced to assume the existence of something hidden, something which is on principle utterly beyond the reach of mere detached observation. And yet Nadgett is not a special case. He is one example of a large group produced by the peculiar conditions of modern urban life: "he belonged to a class; a race peculiar to the City; who are secrets as profound to one another, as they are to the rest of mankind" (27). The city has brought about this crisis in our knowledge of our neighbor by separating altogether public role and private self. Constant changes of employment, the lack of distinguishing outward characteristics to label members of each profession, the sheer size of the urban community, all these tend to make it more and more impossible to identify a person satisfactorily in terms of his occupation. There is no way to reach Nadgett's secret subjective self. But neither is there any way to define him certainly by his public roles, for he carries in his pocketbook "contradictory cards," which label him as coal merchant, wine merchant, commission agent, collector, and accountant (27). Such are the conditions of city life that it is impossible to know which of these professions he actually practices, if any.

In the end Nadgett exists not as a coherent and intelligible self, either private or public, but as a collection of eccentric and baffling appearances, wholly external appearances which are known to be no true index to that large proportion of his life which remains secret: "He was mildewed, threadbare, shabby; always had flue upon his legs and back; and kept his linen so secret by buttoning up and wrapping over, that he might have had none — perhaps he hadn't. He carried one stained beaver glove, which he dangled before him by the forefinger as he walked or sat; but even its fellow was a secret" (27).

Very many are the cases in *Martin Chuzzlewit* where the visible glove of gesture or expression does not permit us to discover its hidden and invisible fellow, its subjective meaning:

She withdrew into the coach again, and he saw the hand waving towards him for a moment; but whether in reproachfulness or incredulity, or misery, or grief, or sad adieu, or what else, he could not, being so hurried, understand. (40)

Now if Mr. Pecksniff knew, from anything Martin Chuzzlewit had expressed in gestures, that he wanted to speak to him, he could only have found it out on some such principle as prevails in melodramas, and in virtue of which the elderly farmer with the comic son always knows what the dumb-girl means when she takes refuge in his garden, and relates her personal memoirs in incomprehensible pantomime. (3)

Mr. Jobling pulled out his shirt-frill of fine linen, as though he would have said, "This is what I call nature in a medical man, sir." (41)

His very throat was moral. You saw a good deal of it. You looked over a very low fence of white cravat (whereof no man had ever beheld the tie, for he fastened it behind), and there it lay, a valley between two jutting heights of collar, serene and whiskerless before you. It seemed to say, on the part of Mr. Pecksniff, "There is no deception, ladies and gentlemen, all is peace, a holy calm pervades me." (2)

"Seemed to say," "as though he would have said" — the behavior and appearance of the personages seem to be a language, seem to have a meaning, but how is one to know which is the true meaning? There is no possible comparison of outer appearance and inner reality by which the detached spectator or the isolated characters can establish the validity of an interpretation.

The characters of *Martin Chuzzlewit* tend to exist, then, not through the visible expression of a coherent inner life, but as fixed and innate idiosyncrasies behind which one cannot go, because there is apparently nothing behind them. ". . . why does any man entertain his own whimsical taste? Why does Mr. Fips wear shorts and powder, and Mr. Fips's next-door neighbor boots and a wig?" (39). There is no answer. For Dickens the idiosyncrasy of character is an absurd and irreducible fact. Everyone in *Martin Chuzzlewit* resembles the boarders at Todgers', each of whom has a "turn" for something or other, but no one of whom has an existence with any psychological depth or integration: "There was . . . a gentleman of a smoking turn, and a gentleman of a convivial turn; some of the gentlemen had a turn for whist, and a large proportion of the gentlemen had a strong turn for billiards and betting" (9). When there is a party at Todgers', "every man comes out freely in his own character" (9). There is nothing else he can do. The endless repetition by such a character of an eccentricity which is superficial and meaningless and yet is the only identity he possesses is as spontaneous and undeliberate, and as little human, as the putting forth of maple leaves by a maple tree.

But what happens if there is some failure in the mechanism of self-expression? What happens if his environment does not make it possible for such a character to indulge his "turn"?

What can happen is shown in Chevy Slyme, one of the least savory members of the Chuzzlewit family. Slyme has failed utterly to be anyone, to play any recognized social role at all, and the result is, paradoxically, not a sense of his own nonentity, but a sense of his infinite value. Cut off entirely from reality, his self-esteem has swelled to hyperbolic proportions. ". . . he is," says Tigg of Slyme, "without an exception, the highest-minded, the most independent-spirited, most original, spiritual, classical, talented, the most thoroughly Shakspearian, if not Miltonic, and at the same time the most disgustingly-unappreciated dog I know" (4). Chevy Slyme, like Dostoevsky's "underground man," is intensely self-conscious, intensely aware of his freedom and of his uniqueness. Tigg calls him "the American aloe of the human race" (7); "nobody but himself," he says, "can in any way come up to him" (7). And Chevy himself says, "I have an independent spirit. . . . I possess a haughty spirit, and a proud spirit, and have infernally finely-touched chords in my nature, which won't brook patronage. Do you hear? Tell 'em I hate 'em, and that's the way I preserve my self-respect; and tell 'em that no man ever respected himself more than I do!" (7). But Chevy is wholly incapable of bringing into actual existence his magnificent possibilities. Any particular fulfillment of himself in terms of a task undertaken and work done would mean the acceptance of limitation, and the destruction of all the other potentialities of his nature. Slyme feels that he is capable of anything, and this keeps him from being anything. What he wants and expects is that society should accept the possibility for actuality, that he should be recognized for what he is, as if he were a wholly intrinsic and self-sufficient being, like God, not limited by the disgusting necessity of bringing a being into existence through action. His nullity is not his fault, but society's: "I am the wretchedest creature on record. Society is in a conspiracy against me. I'm the most literary man alive. I'm full of scholarship; I'm full of genius; I'm full of information; I'm full of novel views on every subject; yet look at my condition! I'm at this moment obliged to two strangers for a tavern bill! . . . And crowds of impostors, the while, becoming famous: men who are no more on a level with me than — Tigg, I take you to witness that I am the most persecuted hound on the face of the earth" (7).

Chevy had begun by "putting forth his pretensions, boldly, as a man of infinite taste and most undoubted promise" (7). And yet he never does achieve any self at all because there is never anything outside of himself which recognizes and sustains his being. Or if there is anything at all it is only the insubstantial stuff of language, the language which his friend Tigg employs to give their only reality to his unfulfilled possibilities. Slyme, then, exists only in terms of his friend, and only so long as his friend is with him and talking about him. He seems "to have no existence separate or apart from his friend Tigg" (7).

Slyme is proof that, for Dickens, no human being can be sufficient unto himself. A man attains an enduring identity, if at all, only through the establishment of a correspondence between something within and something without.

### III

The characters of *Martin Chuzzlewit,* then, must leave their ambient milieus, the milieus that are so intimately fused with themselves, and seek in the outer world, the world that is alien and unfamiliar, some support for their own beings. Mr. Mould must leave his own "premises" and enter into the "strife" of the city; Tom Pinch must lose his innocent faith in Pecksniff and go down to London; and Martin Chuzzlewit must leave England altogether and go to America.

This exit from himself plunges the individual immediately into a labyrinth. In a moment he loses the way:

Todgers's was in a labyrinth, whereof the mystery was known but to a chosen few. (9)

[Tom Pinch] lost his way. He very soon did that; and in trying to find it again, he lost it more and more. . . . So, on he went, looking up all the streets he came near, and going up half of them; and thus, by dint of not being true to Goswell Street, and filing off into Aldermanbury, and bewildering himself in Barbican, and being constant to the wrong point of the compass in London Wall, and then getting himself crosswise into Thames Street, by an instinct that would have been marvellous if he had had the least desire or reason to go there, he found himself, at last, hard by the Monument. (37)

Mr. Pecksniff, with one of the young ladies under each arm
dived across the street, and then across other streets, and so up the
queerest courts, and down the strangest alleys and under the blind
est archways, in a kind of frenzy: now skipping over a kennel, now
running for his life from a coach and horses; now thinking he had
lost his way, now thinking he had found it; now in a state of the
highest confidence, now despondent to the last degree, but alway
in a great perspiration and flurry. . . . (8)

But in losing his way, the protagonist loses himself. In
*Oliver Twist* the hero began lost, at the center of a labyrinth
seeking through a maze of hostile ways his absent identity
But in *Martin Chuzzlewit* the characters are initially "found,
or so they think, surrounded, like Mr. Mould, with a friendly
and reassuring world which mirrors back themselves. Their
entrance into the labyrinth is the discovery of a world which i
not consubstantial with themselves. It is thus the exact revers
of the labyrinth of *Oliver Twist:* a process of the unintentiona
losing of oneself rather than a frantic attempt to becom
"found."

The state of mind of the person who has thus inadvertentl
entered the maze is one of increasing bewilderment and anx
iety. What had begun as a deliberate and rational attempt t
find his way to a certain goal becomes "frenzy," a perpetua
state of "great perspiration and flurry." At last he realizes th
truth, that he is irrevocably off the track, and an utter state o
resignation and hopelessness ensues. He gives himself up fo
lost: "You couldn't walk about in Todgers's neighborhood, a
you could in any other neighborhood. You groped your way fo
an hour through lanes and bye-ways, and court-yards, and pas
sages; and you never once emerged upon anything that migh
be reasonably called a street. A kind of resigned distractio
came over the stranger as he trod those devious mazes, and
giving himself up for lost, went in and out and round abou
and quietly turned back again when he came to a dead wall o
was stopped by an iron railing, and felt that the means of e
cape might possibly present themselves in their own good time
but that to anticipate them was hopeless" (9). This "resigne
distraction" is something like the catatonic trance of certai

types of insanity. The "stranger" is faced with a world which refuses altogether to yield a sense, to relate itself to his mind. He is both within and without at the same time, within the hostile maze from which he wishes desperately to escape, and outside the hidden meaning behind the "dead walls." In fact he is doubly shut out, estranged now from the comfortable home he has so recently left, and unable to understand the world he has so abruptly entered. Like Martin Chuzzlewit, cast out by his grandfather and alone in London, he has "a pretty strong sense of being shut out, alone, upon the dreary world, without the key of it" (13).

At this halfway point, en route, there are, it seems, two choices. The protagonist can go forward seeking a way out of the maze, or he can run back into the safety of home — like the "people who, being asked to dine at Todgers's had travelled round and round for a weary time, with its very chimney-pots in view; and finding it, at last, impossible of attainment, had gone home again with a gentle melancholy on their spirits, tranquil and uncomplaining" (9). But it is in taking the latter alternative that a person may make an astonishing discovery. The milieu which had seemed so solid and enduring as long as he dwelled monotonously within it has suddenly, through his absence, itself entered the world of vertiginous change: "Change begets change: nothing propagates so fast. If a man habituated to a narrow circle of cares and pleasures, out of which he seldom travels, step beyond it, though for never so brief a space, his departure from the monotonous scene on which he has been an actor of importance, would seem to be the signal for instant confusion. As if, in the gap he had left, the wedge of change were driven to the head, rending what was a solid mass to fragments, things cemented and held together by the usages of years, burst asunder in as many weeks. The mine which Time has slowly dug beneath familiar objects, is sprung in an instant; and what was rock before, becomes but sand and dust" (18). The discovery of sand and dust where there had been solid rock leads inevitably to a shocking deduction: the world which had seemed so perdurable while the individual was within it, such a substantial support for his selfhood, had actually not been constitutive of the self at all. Rather it was the self which, by dwelling permanently at the center of certain objects, had constituted them as an integrated whole. Home is not really a protective cocoon. It is only the presence of the inhabitant which makes it seem so and which makes it keep on seeming so. In actuality, each milieu is only a kind of insubstantial fabric, a psychic rather than an objective phenomenon. The human presence at the center is the creative idea which makes it and holds it together. When that is removed by the inhabitant's own removal the whole scene collapses into fragments and he discovers a world that is everywhere, from the center to the horizon, a mere agglomeration of disconnected things: "Tiers upon tiers of vessels, scores of masts, labyrinths of tackle, idle sails, splashing oars, gliding row-boats, lumbering barges, sunken piles, with ugly lodgings for the water-rat within their mud-discoloured nooks; church steeples, warehouses, house-roofs, arches, bridges, men and women, children, casks, cranes, boxes, horses, coaches, idlers, and hard-labourers: there they were, all jumbled up together, any summer morning, far beyond Tom's power of separation" (40). At first this scene reveals itself as a group of independent objects, each one of which, like the boarders at Todgers', "comes out strongly in [its] own nature." Each noun is matched by an adjective, or rather, not by a mere adjective of static quality, but by a verbal adjective, a participle. Each such form defines its object as existing in a ceaseless and repetitive activity which is the very expression of its nature: "splashing oars, gliding row-boats, lumbering barges, sunken piles." But each of these activities, except for chance collisions, remains wholly isolated, unrelated to the others, like the particles in a Brownian movement. It is not possible to discover a hierarchy among these objects, or a causal chain, or a central principle of organization. In the end the world no longer even seems to be inhabited by active entities. It becomes merely an indefinite number of self-enclosed objects, "all jumbled up together." Men, horses, bridges, it is all the same: even the division into kingdoms of animal, vegetable, or mineral is lost. Finally, as the list is extended, the items even cease to be things and become mere

ames, names which, it is true, correspond to different parts of
ae visual field, but labels which now seem to be increasingly
uperficial. They identify only surface distinctions which cover
ithout depth an undifferentiated mass underneath, a mass
hich is beyond anyone's "power of separation," and is the
aeer pulp or stuff of things.

We may find ourselves at last at the center of the world, at
ae center of the maze. But what we discover there is that the
orld has no center, but is an unimaginable number of plural
ad interchangeable objects, plural because each individual is
aly one among an unlimited supply of the type, and inter-
1angeable because no individual entity has any distinct qual-
y or value of its own: "Then there were steeples, towers, bel-
ies, shining vanes, and masts of ships: a very forest" (9). In
e end we face simply a forest, a wilderness, wilderness upon
ilderness, in which each separate entity is to be defined only
' its hostility, by its implacable resistance to our attempts to
mprehend it, to find ourselves in it: "Gables, housetops, gar-
t-windows, wilderness upon wilderness" (9).

In a world of this sort a person cannot pretend to have a pre-
se object in view. To attend to a certain object or to attend to
other, it is all the same, and in the end such a person reaches
complete state of indifference, of ennui, of passive despair, in
1ich he returns over and over again to the same object be-
use there is absolutely no difference now between one object
d another: "In his first wanderings up and down the weary
eets, he counterfeited the walk of one who had an object in
; view; but, soon there came upon him the sauntering, slip-
od gait of listless idleness and the lounging at street-corners,
d plucking and biting of stray bits of straw, and strolling up
d down the same place, and looking into the same shop-
ndows, with a miserable indifference, fifty times a day" (13).

## IV

There comes a time when this state of mind is radically
anged by a qualitative alteration in the spectator's apprehen-
n of things. The appearance of the world does not change.
t suddenly he feels, he knows, that this spectacle, which re-

fuses so absolutely to respond to the demand for fixity and inte
ligibility, is only the mask for something hidden within. He ca
sense now beyond any possibility of doubt that the extern
world has a significance, but this hidden meaning cannot
perceived except as a kind of atmosphere in the circumambie
world, and as a spontaneous state of fascinated curiosity whic
this atmosphere produces in the spectator: "There was a ghost
air about these uninhabited chambers in the Temple, and a
tending every circumstance of Tom's employment there, whic
had a strange charm in it. Every morning when he shut h
door at Islington, he turned his face towards an atmosphere
unaccountable fascination, as surely as he turned it to the Lo
don smoke; and from that moment, it thickened round ar
round him all day long . . ." (40).

The word "mystery" is Dickens' term for this sense that the
is hidden in the world something alien and yet like oneself
that it would have a personal meaning if that meaning could
discovered. The self-enclosed inhabitants of the London
*Martin Chuzzlewit* live, like the boarders at Todgers', in clc
proximity to other human activities of which they are tota
ignorant. On the other side of the wall of one's own cell in t
beehive there is another cell, and who can tell what is going
there? ". . . the grand mystery of Todgers's was the cellara
approachable only by a little back door and a rusty gratin
which cellarage within the memory of man had had no cc
nexion with the house, but had always been the freehold pr
erty of somebody else, and was reported to be full of wealt
though in what shape — whether in silver, brass, or gold,
butts of wine, or casks of gunpowder — was matter of p
found uncertainty and supreme indifference to Todgers's, a
all its inmates" (9).

The boarders at Todgers' have become accustomed to
proximity of danger and mystery, but not so Tom Pinch. He
haunted by the sense that there is something present behi
each of the opaque appearances which meets his eye. But i
something of which he is totally ignorant. These appearan
contain their mystery and even speak it in their own langua
but he cannot understand this language. It is like being i

strange country in the midst of people whose speech one cannot comprehend: "It seemed to Tom, every morning, that he approached this ghostly mist, and became enveloped in it, by the easiest succession of degrees imaginable. Passing from the roar and rattle of the streets into the quiet court-yards of the Temple, was the first preparation. Every echo of his footsteps sounded to him like a sound from the old walls and pavements, wanting language to relate the histories of the dim, dismal rooms; to tell him what lost documents were decaying in forgotten corners of the shut-up cellars, from whose lattices such mouldy sighs came breathing forth as he went past . . ." (40). This journey is the reverse of the movement from the center of Mould's room out to the noisy city. It is a transition from noise to calm, from the labyrinth to an enclosed home. But it is as if one were entering Mould's premises when Mould and his family were absent and had to infer from the inanimate objects what sort of man he must be. The information is there, but it is indecipherable. And it is impossible to be sure whether the data spring from the objects or from oneself, whether the noise one hears is the sound of one's own footsteps or comes from the old walls and pavements. And yet it is impossible not to deduce from these appearances the presence *somewhere* of another human being, even if such a presence defies common sense: "The mystery and loneliness engendered fancies in Tom's mind, the folly of which his common sense could readily discover, but which his common sense was quite unable to keep away, notwithstanding. . . . Misgivings, undefined, absurd, inexplicable, that there was some one hiding in the inner room — walking softly over head, peeping in through the door-chink, doing something stealthy, anywhere where he was not — came over him a hundred times a day . . ." (40).

A character like Tom, at this stage of his exploration of the external world, has reached a strange impasse. He can no longer rest assured that he is in effect the only person in the world, the only spiritual presence around which things organize themselves. He knows now that someone else exists, and he knows that he cannot remain safely in his self-enclosure. The very continuation of his existence depends on establishing some kind of satisfactory relation to what is outside himself. But this alien world and the people hidden behind its walls remain mysteries. The people especially exist as an inexplicable menace, something behind the door, in the other room, spying on him, hiding wherever he is not, never seen directly, and yet present and active everywhere in the world. How can he come face to face with this incomprehensible and ubiquitous threat, seize it, understand it, and control it?

In *Martin Chuzzlewit,* the apogee of this relation to the world is a striking passage describing the view from the roof of Todgers' boardinghouse.[1] This is a text of capital importance for the entire work of Dickens, since Dickens here most explicitly expresses the dangerous end point to which his characters can be brought by the attitude of passive and detached observation:

After the first glance, there were slight features in the midst of this crowd of objects, which sprung out from the mass without any reason, as it were, and took hold of the attention whether the spectator would or no. Thus, the revolving chimney-pots on one great stack of buildings, seemed to be turning gravely to each other every now and then, and whispering the result of their separate observation of what was going on below. Others, of a crook-backed shape appeared to be maliciously holding themselves askew, that they might shut the prospect out and baffle Todgers's. The man who was mending a pen at an upper window over the way, became of paramount importance in the scene, and made a blank in it, ridiculously disproportionate in its extent, when he retired. The gambols of a piece of cloth upon the dyer's pole had far more interest for the moment than all the changing motion of the crowd. (9)

The observer of this scene knows that there is a spiritual life other than his own present somewhere, but he does not know exactly where it is, and is forced to attribute life indiscriminately to everything he sees. As a result, the spectator perceives a nightmarish animation of what ought to be inanimate objects from the revolving chimney pots which seem to whisper gravel

[1] Dorothy Van Ghent, in an excellent article, "The Dickens World: A View from Todgers's," *The Sewanee Review,* LVIII, 3 (1950), 419–438 uses this passage as her center of focus. Her interpretation, however, differs from mine.

to one another to the piece of cloth which "gambols" with an apparently intrinsic life of its own. And this animation is deliberately and intensely inimical to man. The chimney pots are gossipy spies, or are maliciously hiding the view from the observer on Todgers' roof, or from Todgers' itself, which is here conceived of as an animate being.

Before all this life the observer is absolutely passive. He is at the mercy of these things and especially at the mercy of their motion. There is no stability in the world he sees, but, more astonishingly, he discovers that to this constant metamorphosis of things there corresponds a metamorphosis of himself. When something changes in the scene outside himself, he too changes. The perpetual change in things imposes itself on the spectator until, in the end, he exists as the same person only in the infinitesimal moment of an enduring sensation.

But the spectator on Todgers' roof discovers something even more disquieting. He discovers that the withdrawal of something from the scene produces not simply a blank in his consciousness, a blank which he can easily replace with his own interior life, but an unfillable gap. The exterior and visible void is "ridiculously disproportionate in its extent" because it proves to the observer his own interior nothingness. The removal of the man in the window is the removal of an irreplaceable part of himself, and the observer comes to make the discovery that he is, in one sense, nothing at all, since he is nothing in himself, and, in another sense, is everything, since he can become by turns everything he beholds.

The climax of this experience is a double disintegration of the self. On the one hand, the view from Todgers' brings the spectator a recognition of his aloneness and lack of a stable and substantial self. But, on the other hand, and in the same moment, this alien world, this collection of objects which has no relation to the observer, and no meaning for him, rushes into the inner emptiness, and swamps and obliterates his separate identity. Moreover, this movement of things into the self is matched by a corresponding plunge of the self into things. The ultimate danger is that the looker-on will fall headforemost into the hosts of things, and lose himself altogether:

Yet even while the looker-on felt angry with himself for this, and wondered how it was, the tumult swelled into a roar; the hosts of objects seemed to thicken and expand a hundredfold; and after gazing round him, quite scared, he turned into Todgers's again much more rapidly than he came out; and ten to one he told M Todgers afterwards that if he hadn't done so, he would certainly have come into the street by the shortest cut: that is to say, head foremost. (9)

## V

Mere passive observation, it seems, will not do. Active steps must be taken to escape from the situation of vacillation and nonentity. If the external world merely encountered will yield neither a sense nor a support, the individual must take matters in hand, either build an impregnable defense against the outside world, or cleverly manipulate it, force it to recognize and sustain him.

There are some characters in *Martin Chuzzlewit* who are perfectly aware that there is an alien world outside themselves but who are able to live by a continual manipulation of that world and of other people. Through this manipulation they transform what is alien into an instrument ministering to their own selfish needs. Sairey Gamp is the magnificent dramatization of this way of inhering in the world. It is a way very different from that of Mr. Mould. Mould is present and visible in all that surrounds him as milieu, but what surrounds him is like himself, and therefore is a direct expression of his nature. But Sairey is present in things which are unlike herself and separate from her. She thus is at once present in and absent from her milieu. Presented wholly from the outside, from the point of view of the detached observer, she is Dickens' fullest expression of the paradoxical inherence in a body and in the objective world of a consciousness which always transcends its body and can never be identified with any object.

This presence-absence is strikingly apparent in the animation of objects in the neighborhood of Sairey. Her maltreatment of Tom Pinch is not, apparently, intentional, but is caused by the independent malice of her umbrella: "This tremendous instrument had a hooked handle; and its vicinity was first made

known to him by a painful pressure on the windpipe, consequent upon its having caught him round the throat. Soon after
disengaging himself with perfect good humour, he had a sensation of the ferule in his back; immediately afterwards, of the
hook entangling his ankles; then of the umbrella generally,
wandering about his hat, and flapping at it like a great bird;
and, lastly, of a poke or thrust below the ribs, which gave him
. . . exceeding anguish . . ." (40). Sairey's ignorance of the
malign actions of her umbrella is akin to her complete insensi-
tivity to her patients. ". . . may our next meetin'," she says to
Mrs. Prig, "be at a large family's, where they all takes it reg'lar,
one from another, turn and turn about, and has it business-
like" (29). All things, for Sairey Gamp, including her own
body, and her clothes, are dissociated from her, and yet are
related intimately to her. They are dissociated from her insofar
as she takes no account of them as they are in themselves, the
objects as mere objects, the people as other human beings with
lives of their own. These "realistic" and "objective" elements in
the world disappear altogether for Sairey. She is cut off from
them, and has no idea, for example, of what her patients Lew-
some and Chuffey are suffering or thinking. What does connect
her intimately to the world both of objects and people, so intimately that her mark is apparent everywhere around her, is the
fact that everything is used by her to satisfy her own selfish desires. This dissociation produces the immense comic tension of
her appearances. Everything but her own mind with its selfish
intents is objectified, and so complete is the cleavage between
Sairey and her own body that even her own actions seem to be
performed not by human volition, but by inanimate objects
horribly endowed with life. So it is not Sairey herself who in-
sists that her luggage must be treated in a certain way, but the
luggage itself which has certain human requirements: "every
package belonging to that lady had the inconvenient property
of requiring to be put in a boot by itself, and to have no other
luggage near it, on pain of actions at law for heavy damages
against the proprietors of the coach" (29). It is not Mrs.
Gamp's stipulation, but an "inconvenient property" of the luggage itself, and the language of the rest of the sentence suggests

that not Mrs. Gamp, but the luggage itself, will sue the coach
company. In the next sentence the personification is explicit:
"The umbrella with the circular patch was particularly hard to
be got rid of, and several times thrust out its battered brass noz-
zle from improper crevices and chinks, to the great terror of the
other passengers" (29). There is a hidden human malignity
here acting blindly through insentient objects. It is not simply
the fact that objects appear to be unnaturally human; this fact
itself is the unmistakable evidence that somewhere a human
intelligence exists, a human intelligence which has somehow
got itself magically entangled with inanimate objects and acts
through them, but without full cognizance of what it is doing.
The umbrella is not conscious. It is the sign of consciousness,
an object magically endowed with life by the presence of consciousness. The fact of Sairey's intensely self-centered consciousness makes everything in her neighborhood orient itself
around her like iron filings around a magnet. Thus everything
in her proximity is evidence of her presence — the pattens, the
umbrella, the rearrangement of her patients' rooms (and the
patients) for her comfort, the famous bottle on the chimney
piece — all testify to the existence of Sairey Gamp. But the fact
that she transforms everything, including other people, into
what they are not, does not give us direct access to her subjectivity. The evidence of her subjectivity is a masked evidence.
We do not know it directly, but only through the transformation of things in her neighborhood, the animation of umbrella
and luggage, and the change of people into something which
approaches the status of pure instrumentality. Everywhere we
see signs through which we can directly and intuitively understand Sairey, but we have no direct access to that toward which
the signs point. Sairey herself remains alone, apart, above, and
beyond all her evident inherence in the world, and it is this
ambiguous presence-absence which is the real source of the
brilliant comedy of the scenes in which she appears.

But in the end Sairey fails, fails because she has never ceased
to be alone, selfish. Her way is very firmly rejected by Dickens
when he includes her among the villains exposed in the denouement, and has old Martin Chuzzlewit give her advice "hinting

at the expediency of a little less liquor, and a little more humanity, and a little less regard for herself, and a little more regard
for her patients, and perhaps a trifle of additional honesty"
(52). But more essentially, perhaps, Sairey fails because she
can never bring together the two halves of her contradictory
presence-absence in the world. On the one hand, she remains
wholly alone, isolated in a private world of self-seeking which
is so narrow that it uses even her own body as the instrument of
its gluttonous pleasure. But, on the other hand, whatever outside herself she becomes related to is immediately transformed
into an extension of herself. She never succeeds any more than
did the spectator on the roof of Todgers' in establishing a relation to something which, while remaining other than herself,
is support for herself.

If Sairey dramatizes the cul-de-sac into which total selfishness leads, there are two characters who express the unexpected
theme of the impasse to which total unselfishness leads. One of
these, Tom Pinch, is hardly intended to have this meaning by
Dickens. But it is difficult to see his story except as proof that
the man who is wholly unselfish ends with nothing but the
esteem of those around him, and the privilege of serving them.
Tom's primary loss is Mary, but he actually lacks any real familial or social role. He exists as a sort of supernumerary bach-
elor uncle, affectionately patronized by all his friends and rela-
tives, and their wives and children. His closest relation is to a
member of his own family, his sister, familially the same, rather
than other. This relation is the kind of thing that made it possible for George Orwell to talk about incestuous domestic relationships in Dickens' novels. But the key symbol for Tom is a
striking expression of an even more narrow enclosure: he habit-
ually plays the organ to himself alone in the twilight: "And
that mild figure seated at an organ, who is he? Ah Tom, dear
Tom, old friend! . . . Thy life is tranquil, calm, and happy,
Tom. In the soft strain which ever and again comes stealing
back upon the ear, the memory of thine old love may find a
voice perhaps; but it is a pleasant, softened, whispering mem-
ry, like that in which we sometimes hold the dead, and does
not pain or grieve thee, God be thanked!" (54). The sentimen-

tality of this passage is itself a sign of Dickens' uneasiness. He wants to present Tom as an attractive figure, but he cannot help betraying by his patronizing tone the fact that he would rather sympathize at some distance from such a character, than actually be such a person. Indeed, Tom is shown throughout the novel as something of a fool. His name recalls "Poor Tom's a-cold," and "Tom Fool"; it is the stock name for a harmless lunatic. Tom is more to be admired from the safe standpoint of worldliness, than actually to be imitated. He may, like the innocent good fool of Erasmus, be rewarded in heaven (though little is made of this), but from the point of view of life in this world, the real arena of Dickens' novels, his life is, after all, a negative affair.

The case of Mark Tapley is more explicit. Mark's selfishness is to want "credit" for being "jolly," that is, cheerful and unselfishly helpful in all situations. "My constitution is," he says, "to be jolly; and my weakness is, to wish to find a credit in it" (48). Mark can only get "credit" for his jollity if he is jolly in a situation which is so hopelessly unpleasant that not one element of his jollity derives from anything outside himself. But over and over again he discovers that his mere presence transforms a scene and the people in it from being disagreeable to being themselves jolly, and thus a source of Mark's own jollity. We come to recognize that there is a lack of generosity in the desire to be wholly alone in one's unselfishness. It means being among people wholly selfish themselves, so that there is no "income" of charity for one's own generosity and kindliness. Mark takes a perverse pleasure in finding himself among selfish people, and this is very close to taking pleasure in contemning human beings, not in loving them. The only healthy unselfishness Mark discovers, takes pleasure in the return of the gift to the giver. Mark finds that unselfishness always must be a reciprocal relation, and wisely abandons his selfish attempt to get "credit" for it: "findin' that there ain't no credit for me nowhere; I abandons myself to despair, and says, 'Let me do that as has the least credit in it, of all; marry a dear, sweet creetur as is wery fond of me: me being, at the same time, wery fond of her: lead a happy life, and struggle no more again' the bligh-

which settles on my prospects' " (48). Mark has to reconcile himself to getting pleasure (that is, being, paradoxically, selfish) in the very process of giving pleasure.

But most of the characters are unwilling to consider such reciprocity, and instinctively try every means they can find to do without other people. One of these instinctive evasions is the attempt to establish within the self a reflexive relation. This means dividing the self up into two parts, a self-division which may take several forms.

It is possible to divide the self into a self which serves and a self which is served, as, for example, does Martin Chuzzlewit, who "is his own great coat and cloak, and is always a-wrapping himself up in himself" (33). Such a splitting will allow a person to perform selfish acts as though they were acts of public service and generosity. Thus, Pecksniff is shown "drawing off his gloves and warming his hands before the fire, as benevolently as if they were somebody else's, not his" (3), and he is even able to divide himself from his digestion, and look upon that process as a wonderful piece of machinery of general utility to mankind: "I really feel at such times as if I was doing a public service" (8). The subterfuge here is the simple one of treating oneself impersonally as if one were another person. It is not the self-seeking consciousness which is enjoying the meal or the warm fire, but an objective body which is separate from consciousness, and toward which one should feel the same sort of altruism one owes the human race in general.

But there can be an even more radical schism in the self, not simply a splitting up into what Dorothy Van Ghent calls "a me-half and an it-half," [2] but a division into two subjectivities, a self which exists and a self which recognizes and justifies that existence. One sign of the complete isolation and secrecy of Nadgett's life is the fact that he sends letters to himself (27). His communication is entirely internal; the only I-thou dialogue he takes part in is within himself. The most fully developed form of such an internal dialogue, however, is the relation between Sairey Gamp and the nonexistent Mrs. Harris. Like a child whose imaginary playmate will take the blame for

[2] "The Dickens World," p. 421.

her misdeeds, praise her for her good, and provide an escape from her new awareness of her separate identity, Sairey creates in Mrs. Harris a justification for her existence: " 'Mrs. Harris,' I says, . . . 'leave the bottle on the chimley-piece, and don't ask me to take none, but let me put my lips to it when I am so dispoged, and then I will do what I'm engaged to do, according to the best of my ability.' 'Mrs. Gamp,' she says, in answer, 'if ever there was a sober creetur to be got at eighteen pence a day for working people, and three and six for gentlefolks — night watching,' " said Mrs. Gamp, with emphasis, " 'being a extra charge — you are that inwallable person' " (19). Mrs. Harris is justification for Sairey both in the sense of offering an apparently independent definition of her nature, and in the sense of upholding that definition against all those who doubt her honesty. And yet, being unreal, existing only in Sairey's mind, Mrs. Harris is entirely within Sairey's control. She has remained true to her nature as selfish. She depends on nothing outside of herself. It is no wonder that Betsy Prig's doubting of the existence of Mrs. Harris produces such a violent quarrel, and leaves the shattered Sairey "murmuring the well remembered name which Mrs. Prig had challenged — as if it were a talisman against all earthly sorrows . . ." (49). Mrs. Harris is indeed Sairey's fundamental support and self-defense. Without Mrs. Harris, Sairey Gamp would not exist as herself.

Another form of self-division reveals the secret bad faith which undermines all such attempts to find within the self a substitute for the outside world and for other people. A character may separate himself into a false self which is exposed to the public gaze and a real self which remains safely hidden within. The external self forms a hard opaque surface which other people cannot pierce. Such a person manipulates the self he is for others while keeping the authentic self beyond their reach, like Nadgett, who remains a secret by keeping himself "wrapped up in himself" (38), and like Pecksniff, who tries "to hide himself within himself" (30). This strategy is, like the invention of an imaginary friend, a technique of disguised self-creation, but there is something ominous in the fact that it is an external, public self which is created, a self which the character disengages from himself in the very motion of creating it. Nevertheless, it has the inestimable advantage of keeping his actual thoughts and intentions a secret, and very many are the characters in *Martin Chuzzlewit* who survive by delivering over to the public as hostage a false image of themselves. Sometimes both selves may have objective expression, one that is open to the public, and another that must be deliberately hidden. Such a person is Mrs. Todgers, who has "affection beaming in one eye, and calculation shining out of the other" (8). This self-division can even be manifested in a permanent dissociation of a person's face into two distinct and incongruous profiles: "Two gray eyes lurked deep within this agent's head, but one of them had no sight in it, and stood stock still. With that side of his face he seemed to listen to what the other side was doing. Thus each profile had a distinct expression; and when the movable side was most in action, the rigid one was in its coldest state of watchfulness. It was like turning the man inside out, to pass to that view of his features in his liveliest mood, and see how calculating and intent they were" (21). The paradox here is that the sightless, expressionless profile accurately externalizes Scadder's inner nature. By a physical accident the hidden self is betrayed at a surface area which is not under the control of the will, and Scadder is, without being able to help it, "turned inside out."

At the limit, the two profiles separate altogether, become two people, and we have the motif of the *Doppelgänger*. Thus, Jonas Chuzzlewit disguises himself, and sneaks out of his bedroom by a back entrance to murder Tigg. Everyone in the house thinks he is still in his room. While acting out the evil intention of his inner self, he has left behind the appearances of the self other people think he is. But this other self takes on a life of its own, and haunts the murderer: "He was so horribly afraid of that infernal room at home. This made him, in a gloomy, murderous, mad way, not only fearful *for* himself but *of* himself; for being, as it were, a part of the room: a something supposed to be there, yet missing from it: he invested himself with its mysterious terrors; and when he pictured in his mind the ugly chamber, false and quiet, false and quiet, through the dark hours of two nights; and the tumbled bed, and he not in it, though believed to be; he became in a manner his own ghost and phantom, and was at once the haunting spirit and the haunted man" (47). Jonas is, one may believe, afraid of the public self for two reasons. It is the avenue through which the hidden self may be discovered. Someone may break open the locked door of his bedroom and discover that he is not there. But, more subtly, the horror of his apprehension of himself as murderer, completely cut off now from all honest social relations, is expressed in a fear of the very solidity of his other self. In a way, the self other people think he is has no existence at all, but in another way it has a much more substantial existence than his interior self, since it is at least recognized and believed in by other people. So great is the distance between the two selves that they are wholly irreconcilable and cancel one another out. What had started as an attempt to create and sustain the self by an internal reciprocal relation ends as a process of self-destruction.

It is self-destructive in a very special way. All the attempts to form a reflexive relation have the strange result of testifying indubitably to the existence of other consciousnesses, and to each man's unwilling dependence on other people. Such strategies set at war the individual's private self and the self he is for others, and in the end prove that the very attempt to be self-sufficient has had as a hidden premise the existence of other minds. Gazing into a mirror, archetypal image of a reflexive relation, turns out to be gazing not at one's secret self, but at the way one looks to others. It turns out to be a confession that one *is* what one appears in the eyes of others. Thus Jonas, after the murder, "looking in the glass, imagined that his deed was broadly written in his face" (47). Or there is Pecksniff, who, after Tom Pinch's belief in him has been shattered, "look[s] at himself in the parson's little glass that hung within the door" (31), as if to reassure himself that he still exists! And finally there is Mr. Mould at a funeral, "glancing at himself in the little shaving-glass, that he might be sure his face had the right expression on it" (19). But all these characters, far from creating themselves in their own mirror image, are actually accepting as the essential definitions of themselves what they look like to other people, or are at least taking great trouble to manufacture a public self. They are all like the Honourable Elijah Pogram, who "composed his hair and features after the Pogram statue, so that any one with half an eye might cry out, 'There he is! as he delivered the Defiance!' " (34).

The characters of *Martin Chuzzlewit* are doubly at the mercy of others: on the one hand, another person may at any time pierce the carefully constructed social shell, and, on the other, even if this does not happen, each person depends absolutely on the others, since it is only in their eyes that the public self exists at all.

And there is no longer any illusory belief in the existence of any area of safety. The portentous figure of the spy haunts *Martin Chuzzlewit* as he does Dickens' other novels. A man may think he is alone, but the spy is there all the time, in the most unlikely avatars, secretly looking on. Apparently Nadgett wants nothing but to protect himself from others and to avoid human contact altogether: "The secret manner of the man disarmed suspicion . . . ; suggesting, not that he was watching any one, but that he thought some other man was watching him" (38). But, seemingly so secret, Nadgett is actually engaged in a very intense one-way human relationship, as Jonas discovers too late: "This man, of all men in the world, a spy upon him; this man, changing his identity: casting off his shrinking, purblind, unobservant character, and springing up into a watchful enemy!" (51).

There is no help for it. Each man must seek some kind of direct relationship to other people, a relationship which recognizes the fact of their consciousness, and makes it an integral part of the structure of his own inherence in the world.

## VI

Perhaps man's most primitive, instinctive reaction to other people is the attempt to coerce them by brute force to act toward him in the way he wishes. This is the temptation of sadism. There are many sadists in Dickens' novels, but no character in Dickens, except, perhaps, Quilp, is more purely and undilutedly a sadist than Jonas Chuzzlewit. Jonas marries Mercy Pecksniff entirely for revenge. He wishes to escape from the image of himself which Mercy has freely formed by destroying that freedom itself. Before their marriage Mercy treats Jonas as if he were no threat to her at all, as if she could safely call him anything she likes, as if she could safely "hate and tease" (20) Jonas all her life. Jonas marries Mercy in order to destroy in her this power over him: "You made me bear your pretty humours once," he says, "and ecod I'll make you bear mine now. I always promised myself I would. I married you that I might. I'll know who's master, and who's slave!" (28). The only human relationship Jonas can imagine is the relationship of master and slave. If he is not master he is slave, and he has felt himself enslaved by Mercy's words and by her attitude toward him. His method of retaliation is to coerce Mercy by physical force into the attitude toward him he wants. Or rather, since he hardly reaches this sort of sophistication, he attempts to destroy in Mercy the power to form any image of him at all. He is "determined to conquer his wife, break her spirit, bend her temper, crush all her humours like so many nut-shells — kill her, for aught I know" (28). But, as the sequence of planned acts in this passage reveals, Jonas can only destroy all "spirit" in Mercy by destroying Mercy herself. As long as there is any consciousness in Mercy at all she will be able to reassert with a single look her power to form an opinion of him.

And Jonas is indeed led to murder by just such an attempt to remain independent, to escape the power of another over him. Tigg is, he thinks, the only man who knows he has murdered his father, the only man who sees beneath what he apparently is to what he really is. But paradoxically it is in the very attempt to keep his secret and remain on the surface what he has always been that Jonas inexorably becomes what Tigg thinks he is. He has not really killed his father at all, though he thinks he has, but he does kill Tigg in the attempt to keep his crime (which existed only in intention) and his real nature (which has remained until now only potential) hidden from public knowledge. He thus becomes in reality what he has heretofore been only in possibility. But, more startlingly and dramatically, Dickens describes a progressive change in Jonas' outward appearance which modulates him from what he is early in the story, a comic figure, a blustering braggart and coward, to a melodramatic personification of pure evil. This metamorphosis begins at the moment Tigg tells him he has found out his supposed secret (38), and crystallizes when he attempts to flee the country, is stopped by Tigg, and forms a settled intention to escape Tigg by murdering him: "He had the aspect of a man found out, and held at bay; of being baffled, hunted, and beset; but there was now a dawning and increasing purpose in his face, which changed it very much. It was gloomy, distrustful, lowering; pale with anger, and defeat; it still was humbled, abject, cowardly, and mean; but, let the conflict go on as it would, there was one strong purpose wrestling with every emotion of his mind, and casting the whole series down as they arose" (41). The "whole series" of other possible moods and accompanying selves is giving way here to a single dominant self, the self Jonas will permanently become when he actually kills Tigg. When the murder is discovered the transmutation is complete, and we see Jonas last, just before he poisons himself, writhing in anguish on the floor, like "some obscene and filthy animal, repugnant to the sight" (51). Jonas has become altogether, inside and out, what Tigg took him for. The sadist, far from controlling his identity by controlling others, has ended entirely at the mercy of others and of their freedom to control him.

It is useless, then, to attempt to coerce another person overtly. He is not so easily or safely controlled. But perhaps it is possible to choose willingly to be slave rather than master. Such a person will simply let other people make him whatever they wish, live in pure passivity. Forgetting altogether the possibility of a valid inner life, he will accept the public self as the real and only self and live as sheer appearance. A man who does this may not be certain what sort of self he will have, but such is the power of surface that by the mere passive activity of displaying himself a being of sorts will spring into existence. This is apparently the technique of the porter of the Anglo-Bengalee Disinterested Loan and Life Assurance Company.

This man lives so completely on the surface that Dickens calls him simply "the waistcoat": "there was a porter on the premises — a wonderful creature, in a vast red waistcoast and a short-tailed pepper-and-salt coat — who carried more conviction to the minds of sceptics than the whole establishment without him. No confidences existed between him and the Directorship; nobody knew where he had served last; no character or explanation had been given or required. No questions had been asked on either side. This mysterious being, relying solely on his figure, had applied for the situation, and had been instantly engaged on his own terms" (27). Like the Anglo-Bengalee itself the porter exists entirely as appearance, an appearance behind which, it may be, there is nothing at all.

Dickens' America is an entire society which lives as pure surface, a surface which hides a profound void. Dickens acutely saw that America, the country where all conventions and traditions had been destroyed for the sake of the free development of the individual, could for that very reason become, and was indeed becoming, a country where authentic individuality was impossible. Dickens' Americans are already, in David Riesman's phrase, "other-directed." They have no inner life; they exist only in public. This means, in the end, that they exist only as language. Dickens' Americans are characterized by their inexhaustible flow of talk. But a person who exists only as language will depend absolutely on the presence of some other person in whose mind that language will have meaning. Alone he will be nothing. Moreover, the words he speaks and exists in may be arbitrary. They may have no integral relation to anything within himself. Such a person can by a mere act of will transform himself by transforming what he says. America is for Dickens primarily the place of double-talk and of double-think, the place where theft is called "independence," a violent vagabond is called "a splendid sample of our na-tive raw material sir" (33), and the tarring and feathering of an opponent "planting the standard of civilisation in the wilder gardens of My country" (33). The Americans are unable to carry on any dialogue or conversation. They can only make speeches, speeches in which reality is utterly buried beneath vaporous clouds of words. As is shown by authentic examples of the kind of language Dickens was parodying, metaphor or personification cut loose from any tradition of substantial analogy was the habitual trope of even the most distinguished American orators of the middle nineteenth century.[3] In Dickens' parodies of American parliamentary and journalistic language hyperbolic metaphor is the chief means of leaving reality behind:

Verdant as the mountains of our country; bright and flowing as our mineral Licks; unspiled by withering conventionalities as air our broad and boundless Perearers! Rough he may be. So air our Barrs. Wild he may be. So air our Buffalers. But he is a child of Natur', and a child of Freedom; and his boastful answer to the Despot and the Tyrant is, that his bright home is in the Settin' Sun. (34)

. . . may the British Lion have his talons eradicated by the noble bill of the American Eagle, and be taught to play upon the Irish Harp and the Scotch Fiddle that music which is breathed in every empty shell that lies upon the shores of green Co-lumbia! (21)

But America is not the only institution which exists entirely in a hyperbolic language having no foundation whatsoever in reality. The Anglo-Bengalee exists chiefly as words, as the name of the company "repeated at every turn until the eyes are dazzled with it, and the head is giddy" (27). Nor are Scadder, Pogram, and Chollop the only characters who use a language which is mere modulated air, referring to nothing real. "We shall go forth to-night by the heavy coach — ," says Mr. Pecksniff, "like the dove of old, my dear Martin — and it will be a week before we again deposit our olive-branches in the passage. When I say olive-branches, . . . I mean, our unpretending luggage" (6).

In the end such language and the people who use it cease

[3] See F. O. Matthiessen's discussion of this in *American Renaissance* (New York, 1941), pp. 14–24, esp. 19–22. Matthiessen quotes the following passage from Edward Everett's address for Washington's birthday: ". . . the name and memory of Washington on that gracious night will travel with the silver queen of heaven through sixty degrees of longitude, nor part company with her till she walks in her brightness through the golden gate of California, and passes serenely on to hold midnight court with her Australian stars" (p. 20).

altogether to be meaningful or human. "Mind and matter," says one of the "Literary Ladies" Martin meets in America, "glide swift into the vortex of immensity. Howls the sublime, and softly sleeps the calm Ideal, in the whispering chambers of Imagination" (34). This is pure poetry, but pure poetry reduces itself for Dickens to pure lie, since it has dissociated itself altogether from the objective world, and no longer has any self-subsistent transcendent world on which to depend. Tigg has created the Anglo-Bengalee out of nothing, made it "[start] into existence one morning, not an Infant Institution, but a Grown-up Company running alone at a great pace, and doing business right and left" (27). He has done so as director of the "ornamental department," "the inventive and poetical department" of the company (27).

There is, then, a convergence of the themes of selfishness, of money, of false language, and of "other-direction" in Dickens' novel. The selfishness of many characters is dramatized in their greed for money (Jonas, Anthony, Pecksniff, Tigg, the Americans), and the novel could be defined as Dickens' first elaborate attack on the money worship of commercialized man. His characterization of the Americans applies equally well to many of the Englishmen in the novel: "All their cares, hopes, joys, affections, virtues, and associations, seemed to be melted down into dollars. Whatever the chance contributions that fell into the slow cauldron of their talk, they made the gruel thick and slab with dollars. Men were weighed by their dollars, measures gauged by their dollars; life was auctioneered, appraised, put up, and knocked down for its dollars" (16). But love of money is more than a symbol of the inturned selfishness which cuts the characters off from one another, or, rather, relates them to one another only through the impersonal bond of the "cash-nexus." It is because these people have submitted to money as the sole yardstick of value that they have only superficial and inauthentic identities. In *Martin Chuzzlewit* people are at once wholly turned in upon themselves and wholly dependent upon the value they have in other people's eyes. Like Anthony Chuzzlewit, they want to hoard more and more money, miser-like, and make it an expression of their self-contained value and substantiality. When they have amassed a great fortune, they can be independent of other people and sit in secret gloating over their gold. But at the same time they must recognize, even if only implicitly, that money has no value in itself. Its value lies only in the conventional ascription of worth agreed upon by society. The miser cannot, then, exist in secret, self-sufficiently. He has just that amount of value which society ascribes to the money he possesses, or is thought to possess. The founders of the Anglo-Bengalee recognize the factitiousness of money, and see that since money has no real substance in itself the appearance of wealth is exactly the equivalent of its real possession, so long as the fraud is not discovered. But here the theme of money approaches and merges into the theme of false language. Public language is a kind of paper currency. As long as people are willing to accept it as real, they will ascribe to the speaker the reality which ought to lie behind his language. The Anglo-Bengalee is created out of nothing through the prestidigitations of language, but this is only possible because the words are employed in a public realm where all measurement of value in terms of real substance has been replaced by the universal gauge of money. In a world where nothing is real, or in which everything has only the impalpable reality of money, the linguistic façade of the Anglo-Bengalee is as good as the real thing.

Moreover, the measurement of everything by its cash value tends to reduce all things and persons to anonymity. The uniqueness of personality is erased, and each person *is* whatever money he has. The use of debased language and the measurement of everything by money operate together to deprive the Americans of individuality. They have become like standardized and interchangeable coins. So Dickens can say that the ladies of America "were strangely devoid of individual traits of character, insomuch that any one of them might have changed minds with the other, and nobody would have found it out" (16). If the minds of these ladies could be changed without discovery, it is really because they have no separate minds at all, but only a kind of mechanism of clichés. Their exterior appearances are interchangeable too. Each individual belongs to a certain conventional type, and, like the objects which appeared from the roof of Todgers' or to Tom Pinch in London, no individual has any separate value or identity. If one were to disappear, there would always be another to take his place, and nothing would be lost. It is a collective world, where any group is never a society, but merely another agglutinative compound of the same universal stuff: "Here and there, some yawning gentlemen lounged up and down with their hands in their pockets; but within the house and without, wherever half a dozen people were collected together, there, in their looks, dress, morals, manners, habits, intellect, and conversation, were Mr. Jefferson Brick, Colonel Diver, Major Pawkins, General Choke, and Mr. La Fayette Kettle, over, and over, and over again. They did the same things; said the same things; judged all subjects by, and reduced all subjects to, the same standard" (21).

Dickens' comic vision of America culminates in a world of puppets who are reduced to their gestures, their grimaces, their imitations of one another. These puppets exist entirely as appearance, as a surface which rigidly and mechanically imitates life. Beneath the superficial façade which they have attained by submitting passively to a wholly public life there is nothing at all, an emptiness and silence of which the characters themselves are not even aware.

## VII

Sometimes, however, such a character discovers his nonentity. This is most likely to happen if he finds that he is not even remaining the same public self from one day to the next. For if he depends altogether on other people in order to be, then other people can remake him as they will, and he may find himself undergoing a dizzying series of metamorphoses within which there is no continuity, no persistence of anything which is the same. If he finds himself constantly in danger of becoming other, how can he believe in himself? Thus the boarders at Todgers' name and rename the servant boy at their pleasure. He is forced to become one after another a series of inconsistent avatars no one of which has any relation to what he is for himself: "Benjamin was supposed to be the real name of this young retainer, but he was known by a great variety of names. Benjamin, for instance, had been converted into Uncle Ben, and that again had been corrupted into Uncle; which, by an easy transition, had again passed into Barnwell, in memory of the celebrated relative in that degree who was shot by his nephew George, while meditating in his garden at Camberwell. The gentlemen at Todgers's had a merry habit, too, of bestowing upon him, for the time being, the name of any notorious malefactor or minister; and sometimes when current events were flat, they even sought the pages of history for these distinctions; as Mr. Pitt, Young Brownrigg, and the like" (9). Each of these "selves" lasts only "for the time being," and there is no predictable rationale in the transitions. Young Bailey is in the position of one who, when he goes to bed at night, does not know who he will find himself to be in the morning. No doubt the joke lies in the inappropriateness of all these names, the dissimilarity of each to the others, and more especially to Bailey himself. But can we not see a connection between Bailey's experience of an externally imposed transformation, and his decision to take matters into his own hands and be himself the source of an entirely new identity? It is no longer a question, when he does this, of creating a false protective surface behind which one hides, but of accepting the fact that he is what other people see, and of controlling and creating that self by an act of will. Having been passively a constant succession of different names, of different selves, he becomes himself the source of a new self and forces others to accept him, just as the earlier metamorphoses had been forced on him. He takes his revenge by appearing one day with a new job, new clothes, and a new self: "Paul Sweedlepipe, the meek, was so perfectly confounded by his precocious self-possession, and his patronising manner, as well as by his boots, cockade, and livery, that a mist swam before his eyes, and he saw — not the Bailey of acknowledged juvenility, from Todgers's Commercial Boarding House, who had made his acquaintance within a twelvemonth, by purchasing, at sundry times, small birds at twopence each — but a highly-condensed embodiment of all the sporting grooms in London;

an abstract of all the stable-knowledge of the time; a something at a high-pressure that must have had existence many years, and was fraught with terrible experiences" (26). Bailey has produced such a convincing façade that it is impossible not to believe that there is a corresponding reality within. The alternatives are "to take Bailey for granted" or "to go distracted" (26), go distracted because the whole technique by which one infers reality from the data of sensation is put in question. By a sheer effort of will, the "high-pressure" of his inexhaustible vitality — "And what a Life Young Bailey's was!" (49) says Sweedlepipe later — Bailey has "eclipsed both time and space, cheated beholders of their senses, and worked on their belief in defiance of all natural laws" (26).

Bailey seems to have succeeded completely in controlling himself by controlling the vacillation of the self he is for others. But another similar transmogrification does not succeed so well. Montague Tigg becomes Tigg Montague and changes himself from a shabby beggar to the splendidly arrayed chairman of the Anglo-Bengalee: "Flowers of gold and blue, and green and blushing red, were on his waistcoat; precious chains and jewels sparkled on his breast; his fingers, clogged with brilliant rings, were as unwieldy as summer flies but newly rescued from a honey-pot. The daylight mantled in his gleaming hat and boots as in a polished glass" (27). Tigg is the triumph of a multiple and dazzling surface, forbidding any access to the interior. And yet the deception does not work, or, rather, the façade, however changed it may be, is still recognizably a projection of the same false interior, still only a remodeling of the same substance: ". . . though changed his name, and changed his outward surface, it was Tigg. Though turned and twisted upside down, and inside out, as great men have been sometimes known to be; though no longer Montague Tigg, but Tigg Montague; still it was Tigg; the same Satanic, gallant, military Tigg. The brass was burnished, lacquered, newly-stamped: yet it was the true Tigg metal notwithstanding" (27). Doubtless this is a way of asserting the comfortable doctrine of the impossibility of substantial change in character. Dickens, as we have seen in *Oliver Twist*, holds firmly to the idea that each human being has an essence, a permanent nature which is born with him and persists through all the vicissitudes of his experience. In spite of the discovery of a subjective nothingness in the view from Todgers', Dickens believes that Tigg cannot cease to be himself however much he changes himself, any more than Oliver can cease to be virtuous and gentle whatever his experience. Indeed, since the public self which coerces belief from beholders has been chosen and created by Tigg himself, it cannot help but be an extension of himself, a new shape given to his own metal, arbitrary and unjustified, and depending on the subjective energy of the inner self for its existence.

Two extreme dangers, then, face the character who attempts to achieve an authentic self by accepting the necessity of being related to others. He may live in a constant state of inner tension resulting from the strain of sustaining an assumed identity in the eyes of those around him. Martin observes in Major Pawkins, as in other Americans, "a peculiar air of quiet weariness, like [that of] a man who had been up all night" (16). What is this "listlessness and languor" (16) if not spiritual exhaustion, consequence of a continually repeated act of self-creation?

Or, at the other extreme, a passive submission to other people will lead to complete spiritual paralysis. To let other people choose what one will be and to let them do all the work of bringing that identity into being is, in the end, to be nothing at all. Thus poor old Chuffey, the Chuzzlewit clerk, only lights up into a "sentient human creature" when he is spoken to by old Anthony Chuzzlewit. If that does not happen, or if it ceases to happen, he relapses into total nothingness: ". . . being spoken to no more, the light forsook his face by little and little, until he was nothing again" (11); ". . . breathing on his shrivelled hands to warm them, [he] remained with his poor blue nose immoveable about his plate, looking at nothing, with eyes that saw nothing, and a face that meant nothing. Take him in that state, and he was an embodiment of nothing. Nothing else" (11).

This collapse into nothing can take two forms. A loss of faith in someone other than oneself can cause the disintegration not only of that person, but of the entire world itself. Just as a person's removal from the center of a long-abiding world causes it to fall into fragments, so, for Tom Pinch, the loss of faith in Pecksniff, who had been, so to speak, the Platonic idea of his world, its organizing principle, causes a substantial change not only in his apprehension of Pecksniff, but in his apprehension of the whole world: "But there was no Pecksniff; there never had been a Pecksniff, and the unreality of Pecksniff extended itself to the chamber, in which, sitting on one particular bed, the thing supposed to be that Great Abstraction had often preached morality with such effect, that Tom had felt a moisture in his eyes . . ." (31); "Oh! what a different town Salisbury was in Tom Pinch's eyes to be sure, when the substantial Pecksniff of his heart melted away into an idle dream!" (36).

Or, the collapse may be of the character himself, an evaporation into the utter nonentity he has never really ceased to be. Like Chuffey, Pecksniff loses his positive existence when he is alone: "But Mr. Pecksniff . . . certainly did not appear to any unusual advantage, now that he was left alone. On the contrary, he seemed to be shrunk and reduced; to be trying to hide himself within himself; and to be wretched at not having the power to do it. His shoes looked too large; his sleeve looked too long; his hair looked too limp; his features looked too mean . . ." (30). And when he is denounced by old Martin at the end of the novel he collapses publicly and for good, like a deflated balloon: "Not only did his figure appear to have shrunk, but his discomfiture seemed to have extended itself, even to his dress. His clothes seemed to have grown shabbier, his linen to have turned yellow, his hair to have become lank and frowsy; his very boots looked villainous and dim, as if their gloss had departed with his own" (52). Various critics have reproached Dickens for transforming Pecksniff into "a drunken, squalid, begging-letter-writing man" (54), but it is only the permanent deflation of Pecksniff which will allow Dickens to make his point dramatically. Even in his greatest success and glory, as in the scene of the laying of the cornerstone of the building whose design he has stolen from Martin, Pecksniff has never possessed real substance. Like other characters in *Martin*

*Chuzzlewit,* he struggles unsuccessfully to reconcile two radically incompatible needs.

There is no way, it seems, to combine simultaneously the two necessities of authentic individuality. If a person is simply what he is in the eyes of other people he is, in the end, something which has nothing to do with himself; hence he is nothing. But if he is something which derives wholly from himself he will rest on nothing outside himself, and, such is the unique peculiarity of the human condition, he will be nothing. However much Dickens believes that each person has an essence, a permanent intrinsic nature, he still also believes that he has a satisfactory identity only when that essence is recognized and accepted by something outside himself. Only if a man could be simultaneously independent *and* completely justified by something external could the void be filled and a stable identity attained. But whichever way they turn, whether by rejecting the existence of other people or by accepting it, the characters of *Martin Chuzzlewit* find themselves, at last, back in the same state of nonentity.

VIII

Everywhere in *Martin Chuzzlewit,* then, we find in the characters a vacillation between the desire to be wholly autonomous, and the even more intense desire to discover something outside themselves which will recognize their being.

The dramatic action of *Martin Chuzzlewit* is disentangled through a human relationship which represents an escape from this vacillation, the only escape which Dickens can discover at this time. The escape is *love,* the joining together of heroes and heroines which ends the novel, and sends the protagonists off to live happily ever after. Love is for Dickens that human relationship in which each partner, by giving himself unselfishly to the other, becomes the foundation and justification of the other's selfhood. But at this stage of Dickens' career love is shown from the outside, as a mystery. It brings the story happily to a close, but Dickens cannot really show how that happens. Love makes the Temple fountain sparkle and smile for John and Ruth, but not for Dickens. Nowhere is Dickens' self-betraying sentimentality more present here than in the treatment of the love affairs of his characters. All Dickens' attempts to get inside these relationships and show their reciprocity only move him (and the reader!) further and further away into the isolation of a self-generated emotion.

Furthermore, there is a very acute analysis, within the novel, of the way lovers are selfish in their relationship to other people. We remember how Tigg, speaking of commercial corporations, had said, "We companies are all birds of prey" (27), and how Anthony Chuzzlewit had spoken of selfish cooperation as a way to escape impotent isolation: "We are the two halves of a pair of scissors, when apart, Pecksniff; but together we are something. Eh?" (11). The intensely exclusive partnership of lovers is an unexpected repetition of this. The marriage of Mary and Martin means necessarily the eternal unfulfillment of Tom Pinch's love for Mary, and it was the fact that Mary and Martin had secretly and selfishly chosen one another which originally led old Martin to repudiate his grandson: "he tortured himself with the reflection that they, so young, to whom he had been so kind a benefactor, were already like the world, and bent on their own selfish, stealthy ends" (52). Just as Martin's social sin was to attempt to be entirely self-sufficient in America, and to make his fortune independently, so his sin within the world of personal relations was to choose Mary for himself.

No doubt Dickens' intention, in this as in the treatment of Mark Tapley's unsuccessful and immoral attempt to find "credit" in being jolly, was to show that there is a necessarily selfish element in all unselfishness, an element which must be accepted as in the nature of the moral life. But the problem cannot be so easily solved for his protagonists, since such a resolution would leave them still isolated from the human community. The solution offered brings the story to a close. It intertwines the social and personal issues, and reduces them both to the fundamental problem in Dickens' imaginative universe: How can the outcast find his way justifiably back into the human world?

Martin Chuzzlewit, like Pip, has "great expectations": "I have," he says, "been bred up from childhood with great expectations, and have always been taught to believe that I should be, one day, very rich" (6). Again in *Martin Chuzzlewit,* as in *Oliver Twist,* we find centrally operative in the eventual fulfillment of these expectations the theme of the secret manipulation of the hero's life, the theme of a benevolent human providence. Apparently Martin is all alone. Throughout most of the story he has a consciousness of his isolation, of the fact that he must make his own way in the world. But his experiences in America portray the frustration of his attempt, both in his own total failure and in his discovery of the full implications of such aloneness. Dickens' Americans are a people without a past, a people who have made a code of going it alone after having made a clean sweep of all past institutions and beliefs. They are a people who have and are only what they have taken and made for themselves. Martin, disinherited by old Martin after he has chosen for himself the girl his grandfather wanted him to marry, is thrust into a world like that inhabited by the thieves of *Oliver Twist,* and when he goes to America he enters a whole nation full of people living in the isolation of the lonely crowd. But there is, it seems, no way out of this situation, once one is really in it, as the unhappy fates of the thieves in *Oliver Twist,* as well as the treatment of selfishness in *Martin Chuzzlewit,* show. The Americans cannot in any way escape from their isolation and from the fact that their every word and act is dishonest. They can never escape from the isolation of each man from all the others which makes society in America a game of subterfuge and a masquerade of false appearances. And they have no way to get even the necessities of life and a minimal identity without taking the one, and creating the other — and therefore possessing them illegitimately. Dickens' Americans are condemned to isolation and guilt.

Dickens devises for his hero an escape from this intolerable condition which is a variation of the resolution he used in *Oliver Twist.* Just as Oliver was in reality all along that which he tried to make himself by resisting the thieves, so Martin is all along secretly loved by old Martin. In the end Martin does not win a place for himself in the world, but has his original great expectations fulfilled from the outside by his grandfather. Old Martin, with unselfish abnegation, gives him Mary and a fortune. The handclasp which is to be in *Great Expectations* the symbol of human interrelationship and mutual responsibility appears already here, but it expresses not the free and unjustified choice of two lovers for one another, but rather the place of old Martin as a human providence who is the source and guarantee of human community: "Martin took him [Tom Pinch] by the hand, and Mary too, and John, his old friend, stoutly too: and Mark, and Mrs. Lupin, and his [Tom's] sister, little Ruth" (52). Only when old Martin gives his permission can this tableau give way to a handclasp and embrace between Martin and Mary.

Nevertheless, here again, just as Oliver only became himself, that is, the son of his real parents, because he was able to be himself without any external evidence of who he was, so Martin can be rewarded by old Martin and given a place in society only after he has learned the hard lesson of unselfishness in the isolation of an American swamp. This isolation is precisely to be defined by the fact that during that time he had no knowledge of anything outside himself on which he could depend to help him, reward him, or recognize him. Again Dickens contrives to have it both ways, to have his hero both responsible for what he is, and not guilty of creating himself. Like Oliver, Martin can only win so much because he has lost so much. Here too, there is an intervening testing period of isolation in which the hero makes himself by his own efforts what he is later constituted as being by some outside authority. The "good" characters in Dickens' novels, at this stage of his career, are never left permanently in their condition of self-reliant isolation. Dickens does not yet have the courage to face the real implications of his view of human existence, and contrives a release for his hero which is only a sidestepping of the problems of his basic theme. Martin does not extricate himself; he is rescued by outside forces. And yet the whole bent of Dickens' nature drove him to discover a way in which the outcast could justifiably escape through his own efforts. In the novels which follow *Martin Chuzzlewit* we can see Dickens moving toward more unequivocal dramatizations of his sense of the world.

*Chapter V*

# DOMBEY AND SON
# DAVID COPPERFIELD

I

N *Dombey and Son,* as Kathleen Tillotson has shown,[1] Dick-
s consciously attempted to curb his exuberant proliferation
characters and scenes, and to concentrate his novel around a
gle unifying theme. And, indeed, though it is no more the
hole truth to say that the theme of *Dombey and Son* is pride
an it is to say that the theme of *Martin Chuzzlewit* is selfish-
ss, the reader is conscious in the former of a single steady
rrent of duration which follows with a slow and stately curve
e relations of a proud father and his daughter from their be-
nning to their end. *Dombey and Son* has a temporal coher-
ce which was entirely lacking in *Pickwick Papers,* though
t altogether in *Oliver Twist* or in *The Old Curiosity Shop.*
t perhaps for that very reason we are all the more conscious
the temporal and spatial gaps between chapters. Each scene
represented in such elaborate detail and completeness as a
f-enclosed place and time that we become intensely aware of
at has been left out between chapters and not represented at
. The novel is really not so much a continuous curve as a se-
s of short, nearly straight lines, each of which advances the
tion a little way. Seen from a distance as we view the totality
the novel these lines organize themselves into a single curve.
always in Dickens there is a conflict between the comic or

[1] See *Novels of the Eighteen-Forties* (Oxford, 1954), pp. 157–201.

pathetic moment, presented with intense immediacy, for i
own sake, and the organization of these moments into a whol

In the same way, Dickens' deliberate effort to achieve uni
of action and theme makes us more aware of the mutual excl
sion of diverse milieus in *Dombey and Son,* the milieu of M
Dombey's somber mansion and the milieu of Sol Gills' shop
the sign of the wooden midshipman. A character like Floren
Dombey who moves between them becomes in a way a diffe
ent person as she moves from one milieu to another. At lea
she moves in each case within the circuit of different radiatio
and influences which make it seem as if the other ambien
could hardly exist. Each milieu represents a different soci
class, and one of the central purposes of *Dombey and Son* is
confront the pride, falsity, and isolation of the upper class, i
mured in its riches, living in a perpetual masquerade of pi
tense, and the lower class, with its warmth of generosity an
sentiment, breaking down all barriers between person an
person.

But another theme of *Dombey and Son* is the exact oppos:
of this: it asserts that though upper and lower classes are i
deed mutually exclusive circles, they nonetheless repeat o
another without knowing it, as the "sale" of Edith Domb
is repeated in the lower class by the sale of Alice, her cousi
"Were this miserable mother, and this miserable daughter, or
the reduction to their lowest grade, of certain social vices son
times prevailing higher up? In this round world of many c
cles within circles, do we make a weary journey from the hi
grade to the low, to find at last that they lie close together, th
the two extremes touch, and that our journey's end is but o
starting-place? Allowing for great difference of stuff and te
ture, was the pattern of this woof repeated among gentle blo
at all?" (34). Yes, upper class repeats lower, and the sai
moral and psychological laws prevail throughout the hum
world.

One of the most striking proofs of this is our recognition th
both upper- and lower-class people, both the "serious" ch
acters and the comic grotesques, live in the same isolation. I
the incompatible milieus are made, here as in other Dicke

ovels, by the lives that are lived within them, and the exclu-
veness of scene is determined by the exclusiveness of each per-
n. Of all the characters it would be true to say, as Dickens
ys of Carker: "with the daily breath of that original and mas-
r of all here [in his house], there issues forth some subtle por-
on of himself, which gives a vague expression of himself to
erything about him" (33). Dickens here finds a term to de-
ne the enclosure of personality within itself and within the
ings it has transformed into a mirror of itself: *habit,* the un-
nscious repetition of the same narrow judgments, feelings,
d view of things, a repetition which eventually blinds one to
l the world, even to the world of habit itself: "I have good
ason to believe that a jog-trot life, the same from day to day,
ould reconcile one to anything. One don't see anything, one
n't hear anything, one don't know anything; that's the fact.
e go on taking everything for granted, and so we go on, un-
whatever we do, good, bad, or indifferent, we do from
bit. . . . I [am] deaf, dumb, blind, and paralytic, to a mil-
n things, from habit" (33). So, Florence lives "within the
rcle of her innocent pursuits and thoughts"·(23), as if "in a
eam wherein the overflowing love of her young heart ex-
nded itself on airy forms, and in a real world where she had
perienced little but the rolling back of that strong tide upon
elf" (47); and so little Paul "saw things that no one else saw
the patterns [of the wallpaper]; found out miniature tigers
d lions running up the bedroom walls, and squinting faces
ring in the squares and diamonds of the floor-cloth," and
ved on, surrounded by this arabesque work of his musing
ncy, and no one understood him" (12); and so Captain Cut-
's mental world is "an odd sort of romance, perfectly unimag-
ative, yet perfectly unreal" (49). Such characters define
emselves by negation, by their power to say "no" to every-
ng which is not themselves. Thus Susan Nipper sets herself
ainst everyone with the negations of her characteristic form
expression: "I may be very fond of pennywinkles, . . . but
lon't follow that I'm to have 'em for tea" (3). If Miss Tox,
ss Pipchin, Major Bagstock, and Mrs. Skewton are upper-
ss grotesques, walling out other people with their peculiar

eccentricities and their obedience to stale conventions, and
Mr. Dombey "shut[s] out all the world as with a double do
of gold" (20), Captain Cuttle is no less isolated within his i
penetrable linguistic wall of clichés and inapt quotatio
madly askew, and Captain Bunsby is a striking example of
comic disjunction between spirit and body. The subjective li
of Bunsby is hidden behind a face and a body which are st
idly inexpressive and opaque. His gaze is never directed at t
people around him, and his speech is accompanied by
change of expression. His gestures seem to have no relation
any conscious intention, but to be made of their own accord
limbs which are animated by a mysterious and unconscious li
of their own: "A deep, gruff, husky utterance, which seem
to have no connection with Bunsby, and certainly had not t
least effect upon his face, replied, 'Ay, ay, shipmet, how gc
it!' At the same time Bunsby's right hand and arm, emergi
from a pocket, shook the Captain's, and went back again. .
The stolid commander appeared, by a very slight vibration
his elbows, to express some satisfaction . . . ; but if his fa
had been as distant as his gaze was, it could hardly have e
lightened the beholders less in reference to anything that w
passing in his thoughts" (23).

The central problem of *Dombey and Son,* a problem fac
by all the characters, is how to break through the barriers se
rating one from the world and from other people. For he
what is outside each person is alien and unfriendly; the p
tagonists differ from the other characters only in the comple
ness of their isolation. So little Paul lives "with an aching vc
in his young heart, and all outside so cold, and bare, a
strange" (11), and so Florence "live[s] alone in the great drea
house, . . . and the blank walls [look] down upon her with
vacant stare, as if they had a Gorgon-like mind to stare h
youth and beauty into stone" (23).

But this novel is in one way far more open than its predece
sors, in spite of the isolation of each character and each scer
For all these characters expand outward from their priva
centers, and come into collisions with other characters a
other milieus: "Like a heavy body dropped into water . . .

was in the nature of things that Sir Barnet must spread an ever-widening circle about him, until there was no room left. Or, like a sound in air, the vibration of which, according to the speculation of an ingenious modern philosopher, may go on travelling for ever through the interminable fields of space, nothing but coming to the end of his moral tether could stop Sir Barnet Skettles in his voyage of discovery through the social system" (24). Not merely do characters from widely different social levels continually meet and interact; the contact between characters is much more immediate and intimate than it was in *Martin Chuzzlewit*. *Dombey and Son* contains a much more elaborate and subtle treatment of direct psychological conflicts. Here other people no longer exist either as comic spectacle, beheld at a distance, or as directly possessed in the naïve immediacy of festival celebrations within the family circle. We have rather the long evolution of relationships between people who are opposed, but nevertheless deeply implicated in one another's lives. There is a movement from mere passive perception to psychological interaction. This is strikingly apparent in the central action itself, the relations of Florence, her father, Edith, and Mr. Carker. The relations between Edith and Mr. Dombey dramatize a bitter conflict of two personalities, each determined to dominate the other, and finding in the other a solid resistant object which altogether escapes his will. Mr. Dombey, whose pride centers on his "power of bending and binding human wills" (5), finds that "a marble rock could not have stood more obdurately in his way than [Edith]" (47), as she sets herself against his boast that he "will have submission" (42), that his "will is law" (42). She takes the extreme step of asserting the freedom of her spirit by letting him believe she has dishonored herself and him by running away with Mr. Carker. And in the treatment of the relations between Carker and Edith, one might add, we find a new delicacy, for Dickens, in the perception of nuances of intersubjectivity.

The real center of the novel, however, is parent-child relations, a theme which connects *Dombey and Son*, back through *The Old Curiosity Shop*, with *Oliver Twist*. This is the last of Dickens' novels in which the establishment of satisfactory relations with one's parents can be an escape from isolation. But here again there is a shift toward the direct representation of relations between person and person. For Oliver it was enough to find his parents or substitutes for them, and to enter into a paradisiacal state recalling the unity of child and parent in earliest infancy. But the tragedy of the lives of little Paul and Florence is that they have a parent, possess him in flesh and blood, and yet are, for different reasons, infinitely divided from him. The central passage of *Dombey and Son* is that in which Dickens asserts that "not an orphan in the wide world can be so deserted as the child who is an outcast from a living parent's love" (24). *Dombey and Son* shows us people apparently living with all that Oliver wanted — money, family, and status — and yet enduring exactly Oliver's state of forlorn alienation from all about them. The death of little Paul reiterates the deaths of Oliver's avatars in *Oliver Twist* and the death of Nell in *The Old Curiosity Shop,* but Paul is inexorably destroyed by a mistaken, selfish, and all-devouring love rather than by the complete absence of love. And Florence wins her father's love only when his selfish pride has been subdued and the barriers between them have been broken down at last.

But how can the walls of pride, or simply of the innate uniqueness of each character, be demolished, and direct contact between persons be established? What is the concept of love in *Dombey and Son?*

Here we must recognize an authentic religious motif in the novel, the apprehension of a transcendent spirit, present in nature and reached through death, but apparently unattainable in this world. If the everyday social world of *Dombey and Son* is a realm of self-enclosed milieus, of the impossibility of communication between people, of triumphant solitude, the sea of death, with its "wild waves" (which have caused so much unnecessary embarrassment to Dickens' readers), is the authentic symbol of a nonhuman power whose chief characteristics are reconciliation and continuity. The sea is a place of the incessant repetition of a murmuring speech which no human ears can understand: "The sea, Floy, what is it that it keeps on saying?" (8); "always saying — always saying!" (12). The sea is the place of origin and ending, the place from which all things come and to which they go, "[w]here those wild birds lived, that were always hovering out at sea in troubled weather; where the clouds rose and first began; whence the wind issued on its rushing flight, and where it stopped" (14). Toward this sea the rushing river carries Paul when he dies. But, most important, the sea is the symbol of that realm beyond this earth where the seemingly inescapable separation between people will be transcended and the reciprocity of love will be possible: "The golden water she remembered on the wall, appeared to Florence, in the light of such reflections, only as a current flowing on to rest, and to a region where the dear ones, gone before, were waiting, hand in hand; and often when she looked upon the darker river rippling at her feet, she thought with awful wonder, but not terror, of that river which her brother had so often said was bearing him away" (24). But the ocean is, precisely, transcendent. Its message cannot be understood by mortal ears, and its fluidity, breaking up the solid and enclosed and putting every thing and person in contact with every other thing and person, cannot, it seems, be attained in this world. And yet it is satisfactory existence within this world which Dickens' characters always seek.

There is, though, an immediate, immanent form of this fluidity: human feeling, an undifferentiated current of sympathy, potentially existing in anyone's heart as the same presence, and flowing out through the prisons of language and inalterable peculiarities to bathe all those around in a warm glow of love. This unintellectualized feeling derives from the divine sea, and makes its qualities available in the human world: "And the voices in the waves are always whispering to Florence, in their ceaseless murmuring, of love — of love, eternal and illimitable, not bounded by the confines of this world, or by the end of time, but ranging still, beyond the sea, beyond the sky, to the invisible country far away!" (57). The human form of this ubiquitous spiritual force is spontaneous and nonrational feeling, everywhere the same. When it is shared in a reciprocal interchange, this outgoing feeling puts the characters of *Dombey and Son* in contact with one another, in spite of the apparently unbreakable barriers between them, and solves the fundamental problem of the novel:

> . . . he fairly overflowed with compassion and gentleness. (48)

> There was a glory and delight within the Captain that spread itself over his whole visage, and made a perfect illumination there. . . . But the fulness of the glow he shed around him could only have been engendered in his contemplation of the two together, and in all the fancies springing out of that association, that came sparkling and beaming into his head, and danced about it. (49)

> In the beating of that heart for her, and in the beating of her own for him, all harsher music was unheard, all stern unloving hearts forgotten. Fragile and delicate she was, but with a might of love within her that could, and did, create a world to fly to, and to rest in, out of his one image. (56)

## II

If *Dombey and Son* is Dickens' most mature treatment of the child-parent relationship, *David Copperfield* is the first of his novels to organize itself around the complexities of romantic love. For the first time marriage, in a more than conventional way, is seen as offering a solution to the problem of solitude and dispossession. And if earlier novels contained many varied examples of good or bad parents or children, *David Copperfield* repeats in several minor stories the theme of marriage (Annie and Dr. Strong; Traddles and Sophy; the bad marriage of Betsey Trotwood — which has made her, like Miss Havisham, already overshadowed when we meet her by a definitive event in her past).

But one must mention here, even if only digressively, one of the great triumphs of Dickens' genius: Mr. Micawber. Most of Dickens' comic eccentrics achieve only a hollow or superficial identity, and are either destroyed by their situations, move from them into the nothingness of pure façade, or, like Captain Cuttle, really cease to be comic grotesques, and become more or less serious characters. But Micawber escapes either alternative by carrying to its very limit the strategy of the assumed role. For once the comedian is supremely successful, or at least a magnificent failure. Such is "the latent power of Mr. Micawber" (57) that he can always completely spiritualize his situation and thus escape it. Even when he is literally caught and imprisoned, he can spring out in a moment by a mere redefinition of what has happened: "You find me, fallen back, *for* a spring" (27). This perpetual transcendence of spirit over concrete reality takes a special form: it is transcendence through language. If the manipulation of words is a fundamental expression of human freedom, Micawber must be said to tax this resource to the utmost. He throws forth a perpetual stream of metaphors, clichés, and hyperboles. He writes letters on every possible occasion, letters which, even if they assert his acceptance of his doom ("The fair land of promise lately looming on the horizon is again enveloped in impenetrable mists, and for ever withdrawn from the eyes of a drifting wretch whose Doom is sealed!" (54)), effectually escape from reality by transcending it linguistically. "Mr. Micawber's enjoyment of his epistolary powers," as David says, ". . . really seemed to outweigh any pain or anxiety that the reality could have caused him" (52).

Perhaps, indeed, there is a secret identity between the linguistic enterprise of Micawber and that of Dickens himself, as it is transposed into the attempt by David Copperfield to tell all that he remembers about himself and about his experience. For *David Copperfield,* as everyone knows, is Dickens' most personal book. Its point of genesis is the autobiographical fragment (published in Forster's *Life*) which describes Dickens' early life and his painful experiences as a blacking factory drudge. But, more than this, the narrative of *David Copperfield* is the clearest account we have anywhere of the secret springs of Dickens' imagination, of the mixture in his creative impulse of "childish recollections and later fancies, the ghosts of half-formed hopes, the broken shadows of disappointments dimly seen and understood, the blending of experience and imagination" (46). Here we can find directly asserted the link between the gift of creative imagination and the point of view of the alienated child: "When my thoughts go back now, to that slow agony of my youth, I wonder how much of the histories I invented for such people hangs like a mist of fancy over well-remembered facts! When I tread the old ground, I do not wonder that I seem to see and pity, going on before me, an innocent romantic boy, making his imaginative world out of such strange experiences and sordid things" (11).

The "mists of fancy," then, are inseparable from "well-remembered facts," and we must define Dickens' creative genius as not so much a brilliantly distorted view of reality in the present as the continuing memory of the way he once saw things long ago — as a child. Here is a way to account for the omnipresence of the locution "as if" in Dickens' most brilliant metaphorical transformations. The "as if" admits the fictitious nature of a surrealist view of persons or things. It testifies to the copresence of Dickens' childish view and his mature, disillusioned view, and points to the persistence of the former as the source of what we think of as the distinctively Dickensian imagination. Like many another Victorian, Dickens continued to possess his creative power only by keeping what William Empson, speaking of nineteenth-century poetry generally, has called a "tap-root" to childhood.[2] But here, strangely enough, it is a childhood of separation and distance from all people and things, rather than of a Wordsworthian unity with nature.

*David Copperfield,* at any rate, is before everything a novel of memory, a *Bildungsroman* recollecting from the point of view of a later time the slow formation of an identity through many experiences and sufferings. As David says: "this narrative is my written memory" (58).

The novel is full of references to memory and to its operations, reminding us again and again that these are reminiscences drawn up from what David calls "the sea of my remembrance" (53), and haloed with "a softened glory of the Past, which nothing could have thrown upon the present time" (44).

There are first of all passages which assert the pictorial vividness of memory, the way certain remembered scenes start up bidden or unbidden from the past and are relived in imagination in all their concrete and sensuous immediacy:

[2] See *Some Versions of Pastoral* (Norfolk, Conn., n.d.), p. 261.

Can I say of her face — altered as I have reason to remember it, perished as I know it is — that it is gone, when here it comes before me at this instant, as distinct as any face that I may choose to look on in the crowded street? (2)

All this, I say, is yesterday's event. Events of later date have floated from me to the shore where all forgotten things will reappear, but this stands like a high rock in the ocean. (9)

I do not recall it, but see it done; for it happens again before me. (55)

But we also find the experience of a superimposition of past and present via the associative link of some specific sensation in the present. For David, as for Marcel in À la Recherche du temps perdu, a smell or a sound in the present can be a signe mémoratif producing the miracle of affective memory:

There were two great aloes, in tubs, on the turf outside the windows; the broad hard leaves of which plant . . . have ever since, by association, been symbolical to me of silence and retirement. (16)

The feeling with which I used to watch the tramps, as they came into the town on those wet evenings, at dusk, . . . came freshly back to me; fraught, as then, with the smell of damp earth, and wet leaves and briar, and the sensation of the very airs that blew upon me in my own toilsome journey. (60)

The scent of a geranium leaf, at this day, strikes me with a half comical, half serious wonder as to what change has come over me in a moment; and then I see a straw hat and blue ribbons, and a quantity of curls, and a little black dog being held up, in two slender arms, against a bank of blossoms and bright leaves. (26)

But this mode of memory is not, for David, a difficult or rare occurrence, as it is for Marcel. Memories come easily, touched off by the slightest voluntary or involuntary associative stimulus, and crowd into the mind of the autobiographer:

I don't know why one slight set of impressions should be more particularly associated with a place than another, though I believe this obtains with most people, in reference especially to the associations of their childhood. I never hear the name, or read the name, of Yarmouth, but I am reminded of a certain Sunday morning on the beach, the bells ringing for church, little Em'ly leaning on my shoulder, Ham lazily dropping stones into the water, and the sun, away at sea, just breaking through the heavy mist, and showing us the ships, like their own shadows. (3)

I now approach a period of my life, which I can never lose the remembrance of, while I remember anything; and the recollection of which has often, without my invocation, come before me like a ghost, and haunted happier times. (10)

The present for the grown-up David is no desiccated emptiness watered occasionally and fortuitiously by the sudden rains of memory. The multitudinous past, as in the case of Henry James, is in danger of swamping, engulfing, the present, and overrunning all its attempts to put the past or the present in coherent order: "There was that jumble in my thoughts and recollections, that I had lost the clear arrangement of time and distance. Thus, if I had gone out into the town, I should not have been surprised, I think, to encounter some one who I knew must be then in London. So to speak, there was in these respects a curious inattention in my mind. Yet it was busy, too, with all the remembrances the place naturally awakened; and they were particularly distinct and vivid. . . . Something within me, faintly answering to the storm without, tossed up the depths of my memory, and made a tumult in them" (55). But this tendency to be, in certain states of excitement, thrown into tumultuous confusion by memory is countered by a distance one usually feels between David and even the most intensely relived of his memories. He separates himself from them, and holds them at arm's length, even while reliving them. There is no Proustian doctrine of the transcendence of time through a merger of past and present: "I have stood aside," says David, "to see the phantoms of those days go by me" (43). The past is, for Dickens, definitively past, and lost in the ocean of things that once were, and are no longer: "Yet the bells . . . told me . . . of the many, never old, who had lived and loved and died, while the reverberations of the bells . . . , motes upon the deep of Time, had lost themselves in air, as circles do in water" (52).

But, though the past can never be fully recaptured, nevertheless all David's memories hang together to form a whole, the integrated continuum of his past life as it has led by stages up to his present condition. All David's memories are linked to one another. Any one point radiates backward and forward in a multitudinous web connecting it to past and future:

I was so filled with the play, and with the past — for it was, in a manner, like a shining transparency, through which I saw my earlier life moving along . . . . (19)

. . . I had reason to remember it thereafter, when all the irremediable past was rendered plain. (29)

I now approach an event in my life, so indelible, so awful, so bound by an infinite variety of ties to all that has preceded it, in these pages, that, from the beginning of my narrative, I have seen it growing larger and larger as I advanced, like a great tower in a plain, and throwing its forecast shadow even on the incidents of my childish days. (55)

We recognize eventually that this novel has a duration and a coherence denied to all the third-person narratives among Dickens' novels. The spiritual presence of the hero organizes all these recollected events, through the powerful operation of association, into a single unified pattern which forms his destiny. At first David, as a child, can only experience isolated fragments of sensation, without possessing any power to put these together to form a coherent whole: "I could observe, in little pieces, as it were; but as to making a net of a number of these pieces, and catching anybody in it, that was, as yet, beyond me" (2). But in the end the protagonist can boast that he has fabricated his own destiny by living through these experiences, and holding them together with the magnetic field of his mind. Without his organizing presence the world might fall back into disconnected fragments.

However, there are also throughout the novel repeated references to a very different kind of unifying presence, a presence external to the hero, guiding his life, and casting into any moment of time foreshadowings, presentiments, of the future, and echoes of the past. This providential spirit has determined the cohesion of events and their inalterable necessity. The hero has not made his own life and given himself a developing identity through the psychological power of memory; his destiny and identity and those of other people have been made by a metaphysical power, the power of divine Providence:

Is it possible, among the possibilities of hidden things, that in the sudden rashness of the child and her wild look so far off, there was any merciful attraction of her into danger, any tempting her towards him permitted on the part of her dead father, that her life might have a chance of ending that day. (3)

. . . from the greater part of the broad valley interposed, a mist was rising like a sea, which, mingling with the darkness, made it seem as if the gathering waters would encompass them. I have reason to remember this, and think of it with awe; for before I looked upon those two again, a stormy sea had risen to their feet. (46)

"Ay, Mas'r Davy. I doen't rightly know how 'tis, but from over yon there semed to me to come — the end of it like;" . . . . The remembrance of this . . . haunted me at intervals, even until the inexorable end came at its appointed time. (32)

Which of these interpretations is the correct one? Or is there some way they can be reconciled? To do so would be to allow David to have his cake and eat it, to be both self-determining *and* justified and determined from the outside. To see how the novel escapes from its dilemma will be to reach the very heart of its central dramatic action: the developing relationship between David and Agnes.

David has, during his childhood of neglect and misuse, been acutely aware of himself as a gap in being. He has seemed to himself to be "a blank space . . . , which everybody overlooked, and yet was in everybody's way" (8), "cast away among creatures with whom I had no community of nature" (9), "a somebody too many" (8). Even after his marriage to Dora he has felt, in a phrase which is repeated again and again in the novel, an "old unhappy loss or want of something never to be realised" (58). After he is married to Dora, he wishes that his child-wife "had had more character and purpose, to sustain me, and improve me by; had been endowed with power to fill up the void which somewhere seemed to be about me" (44). The center of David's life, then, is the search for some relationship to another person which will support his life, fill up the emptiness within him, and give him a substantial identity. And the turning point of his destiny is his recognition that it is Agnes who stands in that relation to him: ". . . without her I was not, and I never had been, what she thought me" (58); "What I am, you have made me, Agnes" (60). After this recognition, he must "discipline" his "undisciplined heart" (48) [3] by renouncing any claim on Agnes, and, through that renunciation, become worthy of possessing her at last as his wife. David in the end has altogether escaped from his initial condition of emptiness and nonbeing, when his life was "a ruined blank and waste" (58). He stands in an unmediated relation to that which is the source of his being and the guarantee of the solidity of his selfhood: "Clasped in my embrace, I held the source of every worthy aspiration I had ever had; the centre of myself, the circle of my life, my own, my wife; my love of whom was founded on a rock!" (62). David's relation to Agnes is a late example of that transposition of religious language into the realm of romantic love which began with the poets of courtly love, and which finds its most elaborate Victorian expression in *Wuthering Heights*. David has that relation to Agnes which a devout Christian has to God, the creator of his selfhood, without whom he would be nothing.

But has David chosen these roles for Agnes and himself, or has he simply assented to them passively? If the former is the case, then David's existence is returned in a way to the same emptiness, since he has no power in himself to validate Agnes as his human goddess. And if the latter possibility is the case, then David is a mere puppet, manipulated by his destiny. Dickens contrives to have it both ways for David, and in having it both ways he achieves the only satisfactory solution to his problem. On the one hand, since David has been for so long ignorant of the place Agnes has in his life, and has finally discovered it for himself, he can say truthfully: "I . . . had

[3] Another phrase which is repeated again and again. See Gwendolyn Needham, "The Undisciplined Heart of David Copperfield," *Nineteenth-Century Fiction*, IX (1954), 81–107.

worked out my own destiny" (62). And, on the other hand, two striking passages assert covertly that Agnes has been all along secretly destined for him by a benign Providence:

He seemed to swell and grow before my eyes; the room seemed full of the echoes of his voice; and the strange feeling (to which, perhaps, no one is quite a stranger) that all this had occurred before, at some indefinite time, and that I knew what he was going to say next, took possession of me. (25)

"If you had not assured us, my dear Copperfield, on the occasion of that agreeable afternoon we had the happiness of passing with you, that D. was your favourite letter," said Mr. Micawber, "I should unquestionably have supposed that A. had been so."

We have all some experience of a feeling, that comes over us occasionally, of what we are saying and doing having been said and done before, in a remote time — of our having been surrounded, dim ages ago, by the same faces, objects, and circumstances — of our knowing perfectly what will be said next, as if we suddenly remembered it! I never had this mysterious impression more strongly in my life, than before he uttered those words. (39)

Both of these passages describe experiences of *déjà vu,* the strange sensation of autohypnosis in which one feels oneself to be reënacting a scene which has occurred before, long ago in the past, or in another life. Both are connected with Agnes. And both have a peculiar characteristic: in each case David not only feels that it has all happened before, but also that he knows what is about to happen. In other words, both experiences are oriented toward the future, and seem to indicate that the future is already mapped out and fated to happen in a certain way. Both experiences are covert premonitions of the place Agnes is to have in David's life. But at the time David cannot understand the divine hints, and is left to work out his own destiny. It is only long afterward, in the perspective of his total recollection of his life, that David can understand these moments and give them their true value. Only then can he see that it is not so much his own mind as the central presence of Agnes which organizes his memories and makes them a whole: "With the unerring instinct of her noble heart, she touched the chords of my memory so softly and harmoniously, that not one jarred within me; I could listen to the sorrowful, distant music, and desire to shrink from nothing it awoke. How could I, when, blended with it all, was her dear self, the better angel of my life?" (60). David, then, has both made himself and escaped the guilt which always hovers, for Dickens, over the man who takes matters into his own hands.

Years later, *Great Expectations* was to be a radical revaluation of this solution of Dickens' central problem, but the next novel, *Bleak House,* reopens the issue in a different way by questioning the compatibility of the psychological and metaphysical ways of putting a fragmented world together and organizing it into a coherent whole. *Bleak House* represents in a way the watershed peak of Dickens' career. Here, in a novel in which, as Dickens said, he "purposely dwelt upon the romantic side of familiar things" (Preface to the first edition, *BH,* p. xi), he makes the first of his large-scale attempts to synthesize in a single complex whole the familiar and the romantic, the objective facts of all the life of his age, and his own dreamlike apprehension of those facts as they appeared when transposed within the interior regions of his imagination.

## Chapter VI

## BLEAK HOUSE

### I

LONDON. Michaelmas Term lately over, and the Lord Chancellor sitting in Lincoln's Inn Hall. Implacable November weather. As much mud in the streets, as if the waters had but newly retired from the face of the earth. . . .

Fog everywhere. Fog up the river, where it flows among green aits and meadows; fog down the river, where it rolls defiled among the tiers of shipping, and the waterside pollutions of a great (and dirty) city. Fog on the Essex marshes, fog on the Kentish heights. (1)

AT the beginning of *Bleak House* the reader is immediately located in a certain place at a certain time. And this space-time has a center: "at the very heart of the fog, sits the Lord High Chancellor in his High Court of Chancery" (1). But the spectator's place, as he shares the narrator's vision, is indefinite. He is, it seems, simultaneously everywhere in London and its environs, able to move instantaneously from the Essex marshes to the Kentish heights, and anywhere between. The spectator is granted a kind of omnipresence, rather like that in T. S. Eliot's "Preludes," where the consciousness of the speaker of the poem is really the consciousness of all the city, of all the "masquerades/That time resumes."

The world which is revealed to this omnipresence is not, it seems, a world of multiplicity. Prior to any individual entities are the fog and mud. They are everywhere, dissolving all solid form, like the shimmering atmosphere of an impressionist painting. We seem to be in a world near the beginning of time, when the primal flood, a flood whose context is Victorian geology rather than the Bible, has "but newly retired from the face of the earth": "it would not be wonderful to meet a Megalosaurus, forty feet long or so, waddling like an elephantine lizard up Holborn Hill" (1). All the later heterogeneity has scarcely begun to detach itself from the two primary elements of water and earth. The mud, compound of the two, has drowned all distinct entities: "Dogs, undistinguishable in mire. Horses, scarcely better; splashed to their very blinkers" (1). And the fog is everywhere, flowing as a vaporous form of the river over everything solid, penetrating everything, becoming defiled by what it touches, the earth, but transforming everything, even the earth, into a form of itself, the fluid and shapeless mud. Initially, the spectator, wherever he looks, sees nothing whatever but fog: "Chance people on the bridges peeping over the parapets into a nether sky of fog, with fog all round them, as if they were up in a balloon, and hanging in the misty clouds" (1).

In *The Social History of Art* Arnold Hauser defines impressionism as: ". . . an urban art, not only because it discovers the landscape quality of the city and brings painting back from the country to the town, but because it sees the world through the eyes of the townsman and reacts to external impressions with the over-strained nerves of modern technical man. It is an urban style, because it describes the changeability, the nervous rhythm, the sudden sharp but always ephemeral impressions of the city." [1] The opening paragraphs of *Bleak House,* with their evocations of a single atmosphere unifying a complex urban scene and their sudden leaps from one element in the scene to another, are perfectly described by Hauser's words. In his recent book on "the crisis of the hero in the Victorian novel," Mario Praz, however, comes to a very different conclusion. He bases an interpretation of the nineteenth-century English novelists, including Dickens, on a comparison with the genre painting of Frith and Landseer. The work of these painters presents a comfortable world of middle-class domesticity or peaceful rural landscape. Dickens' work, says Praz, is redeemed from sensationalism and sentimentality only by the numerous picturesque descriptions, comic, grotesque, or pathetic, which

[1] Arnold Hauser, *The Social History of Art* (London, 1952), II, 871.

punctuate his novels. These can be called genre paintings in prose.[2] In my opinion, the initial paragraphs of *Bleak House,* and indeed the characteristic "atmosphere" throughout Dickens' work, can by no means be accounted for by this analogy, however apt it may be for certain scenes in Dickens. The comparison with painting of whatever sort remains, of course, a parallelism of limited validity. The link between two forms of art is usually made via abstract concepts which apply in different ways to each. But Dickens' descriptive art is much more accurately described as impressionist painting in prose than as analogous to genre painting. Dickens substitutes for the impressionist painters' use of a single color the recurrence of symbolic motifs, but in both there is the same sense of a pervasive space which destroys the self-enclosed solidity of all separate things. The discrete elements of Dickens' scene are held together only by their common submission to the atmospheric qualities of fog and mud. These pervading presences cause the distinct elements to blur, to interpenetrate and merge into one another. The world in a painting by Turner or Monet is melted into a single shimmering atmospheric surface which seems to be the mask for an unattainable reality just beyond appearance. In the same way, the fog in *Bleak House* transmutes the banal presences of a November day into signs of an impalpable extrasensible reality which they seem obscurely to reveal.

But within the fog, surrounded by fog, separated from one another by fog, and threatened with dissolution by it, certain distinct objects may nevertheless be detected: "Fog creeping into the cabooses of collier-brigs; fog lying out on the yards, and hovering in the rigging of great ships; fog drooping on the gunwales of barges and small boats. Fog in the eyes and throats of ancient Greenwich pensioners, wheezing by the firesides of their wards; fog in the stem and bowl of the afternoon pipe of the wrathful skipper, down in his close cabin; fog cruelly pinching the toes and fingers of his shivering little 'prentice boy on

---

[2] See *La Crisi dell'Eroe nel Romanzo Vittoriano* (Florence, 1952), the translation by Angus Davidson: *The Hero in Eclipse in Victorian Fiction* (New York, 1956), and the review by Roland Ball in *Comparative Literature,* VI (1954), 79–82.

deck" (1). These objects and people are more separated by the fog than linked by it. The fog, a fog that is both a physical mist and a spiritual blindness, forms an opaque barrier between any one place and any other. The wrathful skipper is indifferent to the suffering of the 'prentice boy on deck; neither of them is aware of the ancient Greenwich pensioners; and the narrator too is at a distance from any of these people or objects. They are seen from the outside. What is seen forms a tableau in which everything is present at once in a pell-mell disorder, like the cows and people in a painting by Chagall. Things are visible, outlined in the fog, but nothing is related to anything else. Each new object is simply added to the others in a succession which makes more and more obvious their disconnection. Each fragmentary glimpse is like a momentary illumination from one direction of an unknown object. The sum of all these glimpses cannot be added up to make a coherent three-dimensional shape. They are spatial perspectives from different viewpoints of a condition of reality too complex to be seen from any one perspective. Confronted with a complexity which exceeds the senses and the mind, the spectator ends, it may be, like Baudelaire at the sight of seven identical old men appearing one by one out of the fog, *"blessé par le mystère et par l'absurdité."* Is it a "mystery," or is it merely an "absurdity"? Do these appearances hide a secret order and meaning or are they indeed a chaos? At first there is no way to tell.

For Dickens, as for Baudelaire, the disorder of the outward particulars of the city world corresponds to a human condition of hallucinatory incoherence. "Never can there come fog too thick," says Dickens, "never can there come mud and mire too deep, to assort with the groping and floundering condition which this High Court of Chancery, most pestilent of hoary sinners, holds, this day, in the sight of heaven and earth. . . . On such an afternoon, some score of members of the High Court of Chancery bar ought to be — as here they are — mistly engaged in one of the ten thousand stages of an endless cause, tripping one another up on slippery precedents, groping knee-deep in technicalities, running their goat-hair and horse-hair warded heads against walls of words, and making a pretence of equity with serious faces, as players might" (1). Just as inanimate objects are a kaleidoscopic spectacle seen dimly through the fog, so human actions are an absurd vaudeville, solemnly performed, but apparently empty of inner meaning.

At the beginning of *Bleak House,* then, we see things through the eyes of a narrator who testifies passively to the existence of the various segments of a world which is split up into innumerable atomically isolated pieces. A technique analogous to this on a larger scale is employed throughout the novel. The narrative line of *Bleak House* shifts continually from one space-time to another apparently simultaneous with it but otherwise unconnected. It is not until we are far into the novel that relations between widely separated actions and milieus begin to appear. At first it seems that Dickens, inexplicably, has chosen to write two or three novels at once, and to alternate with no apparent rhyme or reason from portraits of the aristocratic world of Lady Dedlock at Chesney Wold to the very different stories of Esther Summerson and the wards in Jarndyce. Moreover, a great number of minor characters are presented who have no obvious relation to the major stories. The discontinuous narrative technique of Dos Passos, Faulkner, and other twentieth-century novelists is strikingly anticipated. Even if we can expect, knowing Dickens, that everything will turn out to be related to everything else, neither the narrator nor the characters are aware of this at the time. What we experience is the successive presentation of events which apparently have no connection whatever with one another.

Moreover, in spite of the necessary discursiveness of language, the mode of description in the opening paragraphs implies that these atomic particles are all present at once. They exist not "one by one," but simultaneously. There are, one observes, no verbs at all in the main clauses of the sentences until the fourth paragraph. The effect of this absence is to suggest that all of these events are occurring in the same instant. They exist substantivally, as present facts ("mud," "smoke," "flake of soot," "dogs," "horses," "foot passengers," "fog"). And, since participles are substituted for the absent verbs, these substantives are asserted to exist in the immediate fulfillment of their present activity: the Lord Chancellor is "sitting," the smoke "lowering," the foot passengers "jostling," the fog "creeping." These activities form a continuous nonprogressive present time. When we first see them they are already energetically being themselves, or, rather, "doing" themselves, and as long as we watch them they continue this action without cessation or change. The fog forms a paradoxical spatial continuum, paradoxical since it must be said to isolate objects from one another rather than to relate them. Matching this spatial continuum, there is a temporal one, formed by the prolongation through time of activities located in isolated centers, separated from one another by the fog. But if they do not affect one another, all of them act together to give a continuous forward temporal motion to the entire scene. This motion is, like the spatial continuum, paradoxical: it is a motion which does not move anywhere. It is made up of the perpetual repetition of activities, each of which exists isolated in its own always present happening. These activities are plunged into a homogeneous time just as they are plunged into the homogeneous space of fog. The foggy space-time taken as a whole constitutes an indeterminate continuum. Within this continuum there are human beings or objects, but each of these is isolated from all the others, and swallowed up in the ubiquitous and persistent fog.

But the substitution of participles for verbs in the first three paragraphs of the novel has a further effect: it removes the spectator and narrator from the scene, or at least it seems to reduce him to an anonymous and detached observer, a neutral seeing eye. To say "the fog creeps" much more actively involves the spectator in perception and judgment than to say "fog creeping." The latter expression suggests that the activity is happening, but somewhere outside the immediate area of sensation. I know that the fog is creeping, but I do not directly and intimately know it. I dissociate myself from the activity and contemplate it from a distance.

This paradoxical combination of detachment and immediacy exists throughout the novel, for when Dickens finally uses verbs they are in the present tense, and the historical present is used throughout the novel in the third-person narration. If the use of participles rather than full verb forms withdraws the narrator from his world, the present tense narration is still far more detached than narration in the more usual past tense. The present tense describes a world which seems to come into existence from moment to moment under the eyes of the passive spectator as he finds, from moment to moment, the language to describe it: "On the morrow, in the dusk of evening, Mr. Weevle modestly appears at Krook's, . . . and establishes himself in his new lodging; where the two eyes in the shutters stare at him in his sleep, as if they were full of wonder. On the following day Mr. Weevle, who is a handy good-for-nothing kind of young fellow, borrows a needle and thread of Miss Flite, and a hammer of his landlord, and goes to work devising apologies for window-curtains, and knocking up apologies for shelves, and hanging up his two teacups, milkpot, and crockery sundries on a pennyworth of little hooks, like a shipwrecked sailor making the best of it" (20). The special tone of this passage is given by the fact that it is in the present tense. In ordinary past-tense narration events are recounted in chronological sequence, but they all exist at the very beginning of the narration in the mode of already having happened. Here, at any moment of the narration, certain events have just happened, another is happening, and others have not yet come into existence. The actual manner of human existence in time is here represented in language in a way that it never can be in the past-tense form of narration. We are here in a world which has a nondetermined future. There is apparently but one constant the consciousness of the narrator. He watches things come one by one into existence in the present and fall into the nonexistence of the past, to be succeeded by new events which have no necessary connection with what preceded them. Even the clairvoyant detective, Mr. Bucket, must testify to this unpredictability. He speaks for all the characters and for the mode of existence of the entire universe of *Bleak House* when he says: "You don't know what I'm going to say and do, five minutes from this present time . . ." (54).

If the real world is made up of isolated and momentary atoms of perception following one another in no authentic causal succession, any attempt to find an intelligible order in the universe is doomed to failure. Worse, it may lead to the invention of a factitious order. Any construction of what is actually disconnected fragments into a coherent whole, a "train of circumstances" (54), will be the projection outward from the mind of something subjective rather than the description of something which exists independently of man. It will be the creation out of self-enclosed fragments of an order which exists nowhere but in the mind.

And yet everywhere in *Bleak House* we see characters who are engaged in an attempt to vanquish the chaos of a merely phenomenal world. These characters, in one way or another, try to discover in the world an intelligible order, an authentic relationship between events. And this will happen, they know, only if they can find in the world patterns of events which are meaningful for them, either in the sense that the world will yield its secret to them and can thus be manipulated by them, or in the sense that the world will reveal to them their own secret. But, in either case, the assumption is that the world in itself has a secret order and meaning, an order independent of the patterning spirit of the inquiring spectator. Within the merely perceptual, momentary, and fragmented world is hidden a historical continuity, a story, a human significance.

At certain moments the characters in *Bleak House* do seem to reveal themselves as having a historical existence, even though it may be one of which they are not themselves aware. Their present state, visible in gesture, appearance, or speech, reveals and hides their pasts. Thus George Rouncewell's military past is still obscurely present in his demeanor: "What is curious about him is, that he sits forward on his chair as if he were, from long habit, allowing space for some dress or accoutrements that he has altogether laid aside. His step too is measured and heavy, and would go well with a weighty clash and jingle of spurs. He is close-shaved now, but his mouth is set as if his upper lip had been for years familiar with a great moustache. . . . Altogether, one might guess Mr. George to have been a trooper once upon a time" (21). And in the same way Esther intuitively perceives from her first glimpse of

Prince Turveydrop the appearance and way of life of his dead mother: ". . . he had a little innocent, feminine manner, which . . . made this singular effect upon me: that I received the impression that he was like his mother, and that his mother had not been much considered or well used" (14).

But sometimes the relation of the present to the past does not reveal itself so clearly as this. A present perception simply coincides with a spontaneous and wholly inexplicable revivification of something from the past: "And, very strangely," says Esther, "there was something quickened within me, associated with the lonely days at my godmother's; yes, away even to the days when I had stood on tiptoe to dress myself at my little glass, after dressing my doll" (18). Even this mystery or secret hidden behind the opaque surfaces of things can perhaps be forced to reveal itself. Careful observation and the delicate exercise of intelligence can wrest from things their meaning. The human mind can remember past events and relate them to the present. Using this power, it can force objects to show forth the significance and coherence which would otherwise remain hidden.

Krook, Snagsby, Mrs. Snagsby, Guppy, Esther Summerson, Tulkinghorn, Inspector Bucket, Hortense, Lady Dedlock, all of these characters seek or fear some kind of clarity, some knowledge about themselves or about one another, some revelation of a mystery. And *Bleak House* as a totality is a "mystery story." The forward movement of the novel coincides with the slow discovery of a truth which at first remains enigmatically hidden behind appearances. The entire novel seeks to explain, by a retrospective reconstruction going counter to the forward movement of the novel, how the world came to be in the befogged, mud-soaked, fragmented, and decomposed state presented in the initial paragraphs. In a sense all the novel is present in the initial moment and is only explicated or pieced together by the events which follow. The entire novel dramatizes the full meaning of the situations of the man from Shropshire, Miss Flite, and the wards in Jarndyce, of whom we catch a glimpse in the first chapter, and of the icy boredom of Lady Dedlock, whom we meet in the second chapter. This method parallels that of a mystery story,[3] and indeed *Bleak House,* like most of Dickens' novels, has at its center a family mystery which is slowly revealed as the novel progresses. But Lady Dedlock's past is only one aspect of a greater mystery. In the opening paragraphs the novel presents the corpse of a dead society, smothered in fog, immobilized in mud, paralyzed by the injustices of an outmoded social structure frozen in its stratifications, and enmeshed in the nets of inextricably tangled legal procedures. The rest of the novel initiates us into the nature and causes of this general paralysis.

The first stage in this process of uncovering is the mere sense that there is more in the immediate scene than meets the eye. Very many characters in *Bleak House* are seized with a strange sense that something is hidden in what they see. They feel that in some unfathomable way they are involved in a mystery, the secrets of someone else's life or of their own:

. . . the more I think of that picture the better I know it, without knowing how I know it! (7)

. . . I find myself wrapped round with secrecy and mystery, till my life is a burden to me. (47)

This sense of mystery is experienced as an intuition that what are apparently disconnected fragments of experience could actually be made to fit together into an intelligible whole, like the pieces of a puzzle. This sense of "broken thoughts" (24) which do not quite fit into a whole most often involves the connection of the present moment with past moments to which it seems in some inexplicable way related: ". . . why her face should be, in a confused way, like a broken glass to me, in which I saw scraps of old remembrances; . . . I could not think" (18). But the sense that what is immediately perceived hides, in a confused way, an enigma which is the involvement of the present in what is outside the present may also take the form of premonition. One feels that something catastrophic is about to happen, something which will be a clarification, but a

[3] It might also be compared to the built-up compositions of cubist painting. A relationship between the method of cubism and the technique of the mystery story has been suggested by H. M. McLuhan in *The Mechanical Bride* (New York, 1951), pp. 106–110.

destructive clarification, an explosion of the present settled order of things into some wholly different form. It will be, in the
phrase Dickens uses for a chapter title, the "springing [of] a
mine" (54): "Mr. Snagsby cannot make out what it is that he
has had to do with. Something is wrong, somewhere; but what
something, what may come of it, to whom, when, and from
which unthought of and unheard of quarter, is the puzzle of his
life. . . . [H]e is a party to some dangerous secret, without
knowing what it is. And it is the fearful peculiarity of this condition that, at any hour of his daily life, . . . the secret may
take air and fire, explode, and blow up . . ." (25).

Some characters in *Bleak House* have a kind of holy dread of
the revelation of the mystery in which they find themselves involved. Thus Esther tells us that she was "fearful of the light
that dimly broke upon [her]" (43) when part of the secret of
her past was about to be revealed. She did nothing overtly to
deduce from the data at her disposal the secret they hid, just as
John Jarndyce makes no attempt to disentangle the facts of his
case in Chancery.

But other characters have no such dread. They willingly and
eagerly engage in an activity of hypothesis and analysis. This
activity is essentially an attempt to put together the fragments
of the world into a coherent whole, and thus to make these
fragments reveal the hidden motivating principles which are
their explanation and their law.

So, Krook attempts to find in the chaotic documents of his
rag-and-bottle shop some valuable document which will bring
him a fortune, just as the Smallweeds carry on Krook's research
after his death, "rummaging and searching, digging, delving,
and diving among the treasures of the late lamented" (39).
And so the original owner of Bleak House "lived [there] shut
up: day and night poring over the wicked heaps of papers in
the suit, and hoping against hope to disentangle it from its mys-
tification and bring it to a close" (8), just as Mrs. Snagsby
lives in "her own dense atmosphere of dust, arising from the
ceaseless working of her mill of jealousy" (54). The one occupation of her jealous mind is "to piece suspicious circumstances
together" (54), just as Sir Leicester, confronted with the story

of an aristocratic wife unfaithful to her husband, "arranges a sequence of events on a plan of his own" (40). We even find Esther engaged in this activity of reconstruction, not, however, in connection with her own life: ". . . I observed it in many slight particulars, which were nothing in themselves, and only became something when they were pieced together" (50).

This attempt to triumph over mystery by the exercise of intelligence may fail. The pattern put together with such care may be simply mistaken. It may exist nowhere but in the mind of the detective, and the world may keep its secret unviolated even after the most prodigious activities of hypothesis and analysis of data. To Mrs. Snagsby it seems "as clear as crystal that Mr. Snagsby is [Jo's] father" (25), but she is altogether mistaken. This not merely parodies the main plot; it also gives us a striking case of the failure of intelligence — or at least of a certain low form of intelligence. Mrs. Snagsby ends in possession of her own dense atmosphere of dust. She remains enclosed in herself, cut off from the truth behind the data she has so carefully arranged.

A more important case of the same kind of false reconstruction is given by the murder of Tulkinghorn. Using the technique of the detective story, Dickens presents the events in such a way that he hopes the reader will be beguiled into assuming that Lady Dedlock is the murderess. All appearances and also our knowledge of her motives lead to this conclusion. And yet, as it turns out, Lady Dedlock is not guilty. There is another interpretation of the appearances which integrates them just as well, and is, in fact, the correct one. For a moment, when the truth is revealed, the narrative seems like one of those Gestaltist diagrams which can be interpreted in either of two ways, and alternates between one apparent pattern and another as the mind projects one or another structure to unify the dispersed fragments. The reader glimpses the possibility that the dispersed fragments are the true reality. Behind the value of the murder of Tulkinghorn as melodramatic plot there is a thematic relevance which goes to the heart of the novel. Does the intelligible structure seen in discursive events by the narrator, by Esther, or by the reader discover something which is the essence organizing them, or is this coherence a kind of filmy mirage of order projected by the mind over what is radically heterogeneous and disconnected?

Sometimes a secret is truly discovered. At least certain incontestable facts about the world are uncovered from their hiding places in the past or in the closely guarded hearts of those who seek to protect them. *Bleak House* presents many characters who make it their business to spy on other characters, who try to ferret out the secrets which are hidden behind an impenetrable reserve. Thus Hortense, Lady Dedlock's maid, is "maliciously watchful . . . of every one and everything" (18), and Guppy sets himself up as a detective. He slowly pieces together the facts about Esther's birth. "It's going on," he says of his "case," "and I shall gather it up closer and closer as it goes on" (29).

Tulkinghorn and Bucket exemplify this theme most elaborately. Mr. Tulkinghorn's business is to be a silent and inscrutable depositary of family secrets: "He is surrounded by a mysterious halo of family confidences; of which he is known to be the silent depository. There are noble Mausoleums rooted for centuries in retired glades of parks, among the growing timber and the fern, which perhaps hold fewer noble secrets than walk abroad among men, shut up in the breast of Mr. Tulkinghorn" (2). Tulkinghorn is an excellent example of Dickens' conception of the spy. Enclosed in himself, he is secretly intent on everything which is going on around him. He is "in face, watchful behind a blind" (27). Apparently always "the same speechless repository of noble confidences" (12), "the same dark, cold object, at the same distance, which nothing has ever diminished" (41), he is actually engaged in a slow, relentless uncovering of Lady Dedlock's secret. Tulkinghorn's motivation is simple and all-inclusive. He has no desire to form human contact with other people through his knowledge of them. He wants solely the power over other people which his knowledge of their secrets will give him: "His calling is the acquisition of secrets, and the holding possession of such power as they give him, with no sharer or opponent in it" (36). If he can discover the secret truths and forces behind appearances, Tulkinghorn believes, he will be able to manipulate the world at his pleasure. When once he has complete knowledge, in the limited world of aristocratic families, he will be omnipotent there too. And this omnipotence will have been gained, like that of Balzac's detective types, through a prodigious operation of inductive logic, working backward from effects to causes. But in Balzac's novels, we are shown this process from the inside. We follow it step by step as the supremely intelligent detective or spy mounts toward the first cause which initiated and will explain a long series of events. Dickens, on the other hand, never shows the process, and indeed we almost never enter the subjectivity of the detective at all. We see him from the outside as he collects data and as he calculates, and we see his results. We know that a complex process of thought must exist, but it remains, to us, like the mental operations of most of Dickens' characters, a mystery.

But does Tulkinghorn succeed in knowing the world and therefore in commanding it? Tulkinghorn is, in fact, never able to use his knowledge, never able, before his death, to reveal what he knows about Lady Dedlock. He is not even able to coerce Lady Dedlock into acting as he desires. Moreover, his own nemesis, imaged in the "pointing allegory" on the ceiling of his room, catches him unawares. All his knowledge, and all the elaborate care with which he has tried to make the world around him yield to his intelligence, do not permit him to see prophetically into the future or to protect himself from an unpredictable fate: "He is in the confidence of the very bricks and mortar. The high chimney-stacks telegraph family secrets to him. Yet there is not a voice in a mile of them to whisper 'Don't go home!'" (48). In death Tulkinghorn's secrets are of no use to him. "Where are all those secrets now?" asks Dickens. "Does he keep them yet? Did they fly with him on that sudden journey?" (53). Moreover, his secrets never did him any good when he was alive. Forcing the world to yield to his detective skill, he simply transformed the world into his abstract knowledge of it. And he remained himself cut off from the world, isolated within his own secret life. The more completely he knew the world, the more completely he was separated from it, forced to dwell entirely without intimate contact with a single other human being. However total his possession of his world by intellectual comprehension, he remained in the same inhuman solitude: ". . . smoke-dried and faded, dwelling among mankind but not consorting with them, aged without experience of genial youth, and so long used to make his cramped nest in holes and corners of human nature that he has forgotten its broader and better range . . ." (42).

If Tulkinghorn fails to triumph over the world through detective intelligence, there is another character who comes much closer to success. Whereas Tulkinghorn worked retrospectively, piecing together some past event from data uncovered in the present, Bucket, the master detective, is able to act, by a kind of superb logic which works like intuition, in the present. He is able to translate the data of immediate sensation into their corresponding inner realities, as when "in a moment's hesitation on the part of Mr. Snagsby, [he] dips down to the bottom of [Snagsby's] mind" (22), or as when he sees "through the transparency of Mrs. Snagsby's vinegar at a glance" (54). In his solution of the murder of Tulkinghorn he is not only able to discover that Hortense has committed the crime, but is also able to coincide with her movements in the present and thus to collect the evidence necessary to convict her. Since he does not, like Tulkinghorn, seek power through his knowledge, he is even less vulnerable than the lawyer to the distortions of selfish desire. He is detached and objective, and prepares and springs his traps with the exemplary coolness of a great gamester: "From the expression of his face, he might be a famous whist-player for a large stake — say a hundred guineas certain — with the game in his hand, but with a high reputation involved in his playing his hand out to the last card, in a masterly way" (54). In the completeness with which he possesses the secret motions of things in the very moment in which they occur he is much closer than Tulkinghorn to being a human version of Providence, omnipresent and omniscient. His possession of the entire spatial expanse of the world around him is suggested in the way, when he is leading Mr. Snagsby into the infernal depths of Tom-all-Alone's or when he is taking Esther through the labyrinth of London, a flash of his policeman's lantern always receives an answering flash from an apparently inexhaustible number of hidden accomplices (59). Bucket's power over the world around him is apparently magical. If he is not omnific, he at least has a kind of power of annihilation: "In a few instances, Mr. Bucket, coming behind some undersized young man with a shining hat on, and his sleek hair twisted into one flat curl on each side of his head, almost without glancing at him touches him with his stick; upon which the young man, looking round, instantly evaporates" (22). And Bucket is omnipresent too. Dickens describes him in language which reminds us of that used to define an immanent deity:

Otherwise mildly studious in his observation of human nature, on the whole a benignant philosopher not disposed to be severe upon the follies of mankind, Mr. Bucket pervades a vast number of houses, and strolls about an infinity of streets. . . . Time and place cannot bind Mr. Bucket. (53)

"He's in all manner of places, all at wanst." (46)

. . . he mounts a high tower in his mind, and looks out far and wide. (56)

The masterpiece of Bucket's art is his tracking down of Lady Dedlock after she has run away and is seeking to lose herself. Before, he had at least the fact of the murder to build upon and to extrapolate through a series of acts and motivations to the present. Now he seeks to follow the very movement by which an apparently fortuitous action comes into being. Nevertheless, he succeeds, like a great whist player, in outwitting his opponent, in reading her mind and in circumventing the strategy by which she attempts to lead him in the wrong direction.

And yet he fails. However rapid his intuitions and deductions, however omniscient his clairvoyance, he is always a moment or two behind the event itself. He is not able to prevent Lady Dedlock from reaching the entrance to the pauper graveyard and dying there. He brings Esther to her mother at the very moment when she has just died. However superhuman his prodigies of deduction, he can only reconstruct the past, even though it may be a past which has just happened. He is unable to anticipate the future, and he is thus, in the end, immensely inferior to the divine Providence.

Moreover, as in the case of Tulkinghorn, Bucket's triumph does not bring him a specifically human inherence in the world. In transforming the world into a complex game of whist Bucket transforms it into an abstract and desiccated diagram of itself. Bucket, like Tulkinghorn, is cut off from real experience. And along with this isolation from the real substance of experience goes a corresponding dehumanization and emptying of the calculator himself. Transforming everything into the rarefied substance of his own thought, Bucket becomes progressively more isolated. Or, rather, his human reality, his compassion for Sir Leicester or his kindness to Esther, does not seem related to his professional character as a detective. And indeed Dickens, though he may admire Bucket as a model detective, has given us his character in his name. "Bucket" suggests not only that the detective is, like Tulkinghorn, a repository for evidence, but that he is, after all, hollow.

But perhaps the real detective is the narrator himself, attempting through mere passive perception and the exercise of constructive intelligence to discover the laws of the world he sees. If he succeeds, he will be able to understand how the world came to be as it appears to him on the first foggy afternoon in London. He finds, however, that things, however earnestly he inspects them, still remain merely disconnected facts, happening one after the other in an eternal present formed out of the instantaneous annihilation of what has just occurred. He finds that he must seek the help of an *involved* spectator in order to wrest its secret from the world. Throughout *Bleak House* the narration of the third-person anonymous spectator telling his story in the vivid immediacy of the historical present alternates with the narration of Esther Summerson, telling her story in the first person, in retrospect, after a lapse of eight years. The complex interaction of the two narrations is most directly before the reader at the juncture of one form of narration with another. To give one example: At the end of the thirty-first chapter, Esther tells how she fell ill of the disease which temporarily blinded her and permanently disfigured her face. She recalls how she broke the news to her servant Charley: ". . . I cannot see you, Charley; I am blind" (31). The next moment, at the beginning of the next chapter, we are given an impressionist description of Lincoln's Inn by the third-person narrator. It is with something of a shock that we realize it repeats the motif of eyesight: "From tiers of staircase windows, clogged lamps like the eyes of Equity, bleared Argus with a fathomless pocket for every eye and an eye upon it, dimly blink at the stars" (32). The effect of this juxtaposition is a strange sense of double vision. At one moment we are going through the anguish of Esther's subjective experience, tempered only by being given in the form of reminiscence, and at the next we are plunged back into the past, and are directly present at a scene evidently contemporaneous with Esther's suffering, but seen now objectively, dispassionately, through the anonymous "camera eye" of the third-person narrator.[4]

The use of Esther Summerson as secondary narrator is an important admission of the failure of Dickens' habitual point of

[4] It might be objected that since the two chapters stand at the juncture of two monthly parts they were not read together when the novel first appeared. The following passage from the preface to the first edition of *Little Dorrit* is, I think, full justification for reading them as juxtaposed: "I have been occupied with this story, during many working hours of two years. I must have been very ill employed, if I could not leave its merits and demerits as a whole, to express themselves on its being read as a whole. But, as it is not unreasonable to suppose that I may have held its various threads with a more continuous attention than any one else can have given to them during its desultory publication, it is not unreasonable to ask that the weaving may be looked at in its completed state, and with the pattern finished" (*LD*, p. ix). The principle here stated can surely be applied to all Dickens' novels, with the possible exception of *Pickwick Papers*. It seems to rule out definitively the notion that he looked upon the serial publication of his novels as seriously affecting their structure. His novels, Dickens is saying, are meant to be read as a single harmonious whole. They have the kind of unity in multiplicity possessed by a patterned fabric. Like a tapestry, each of Dickens' novels is woven bit by bit over a long period of time, but forms a single design when it is complete. To put it another way, the fact that Dickens carried the motif of eyesight over from the end of one monthly part to the beginning of the next, even though the latter was in the alternate narrative form, is itself an excellent indication that he was as much interested in subtly linking one part with another as he was in ending each monthly part with a dramatic climax.

view, the detachment of the spectator from the roof of Todgers'. Against the succession of disconnected moments experienced by the third-person narrator, *Bleak House* juxtaposes the vision of a person for whom events are seen in retrospect to have a continuity because the person was herself involved in them. She recognizes them, now that the immediate experience is over, as the unfolding of her destiny. This may suggest that although from the limited perspective of the present events appear opaque and mysterious, they will actually turn out in the future to have been part of an unbreakable and intelligible chain of causes and effects which will form the "fates" of the characters.

But, once again, who is to say that this synthetic and a posteriori structuring is not a mental rather than an objective reality? The vividness and immediacy of the sections in the present tense gives them a kind of priority, and suggests that the structuring of events into a "destiny" is a falsification, an intellectual deformation. Or, to put it another way, since this order in events can be perceived only when they have entered the nonexistence of the past, perhaps it exists only when, so to speak, it no longer exists, only when it is part of the shadowy limbo of history. Perhaps people do not really have "fates" until they are dead, or until the adventures of their lives are over, and can be seen in retrospect. The true reality, it may be, is the mysterious and threatening present plunging blindly into an unpredictable future. Intimate contact with reality may be gained only through immediate sensation. The real world, then, would be the world that appears to Jo the crossing sweeper: atomic moments of sensation which have no connection with one another and no meaning in themselves, appearances which hide, perhaps, a transcendence whose mere presence cannot even be detected in things by blind and ignorant man: "And there he sits, munching and gnawing, and looking up at the great Cross on the summit of St. Paul's Cathedral, glittering above a red and violet-tinted cloud of smoke. From the boy's face one might suppose that sacred emblem to be, in his eyes, the crowning confusion of the great, confused city; so golden, so high up, so far out of his reach. There he sits, the sun going down, the river running fast, the crowd flowing by him in two streams — everything moving on to some purpose and to one end — until he is stirred up, and told to 'move on' too" (19). If the world contains a principle of order and meaning, it is wholly unintelligible to man, wholly "out of reach." There is no true historical continuity in the world. There is nothing but a confused flowing, a random series of unrelated motions. These motions share only one factor in common, a factor which equally negates them all: they are all motions toward death, toward the cessation of all motion.

But perhaps the juxtaposition of many different points of view will at least not mislead us into thinking that the world is what it appears from any single perspective. And the more points of view are presented, the closer we will approach to an ideal point where, if all of the possible points of view were presented simultaneously, our view of the world and the world itself would coincide. But even at this point the world would remain at a distance from the spectator, merely present to him in its unintelligible opacity. There would still be an unbridgeable gap between subjective awareness and its hunger for an authentic relation to the world and to its contents. These contents would remain mere brute existences, impenetrable in their solidity, truncated fragments which would refuse to form themselves into a whole.

If such is the case, the mind should abandon as hopeless its attempt to master and to understand the world, since any order it finds will necessarily be the product of its own invention and not part of the intrinsic structure of things. The real world may be, then, like the landscape of which Dickens gives us a glimpse late in the novel. It is a world of fragmentariness, of the total absence of connection:

Bridges are begun, and their not yet united piers desolately look at one another over roads and streams, like brick and mortar couples with an obstacle to their union; fragments of embankments are thrown up, and left as precipices with torrents of rusty carts and barrows tumbling over them; tripods of tall poles appear on hilltops, where there are rumours of tunnels; everything looks chaotic, and abandoned in full hopelessness. (55)

## II

The whole race he represented as having evidently been, in life, what he called "stuffed people," — a large collection, glassy eyed, set up in the most approved manner on their various twigs and perches, very correct, perfectly free from animation, and always in glass cases. (37)

There is, however, one form of real duration for the characters of *Bleak House,* if not for the narration as a whole. Many characters endure as themselves through the reiteration from one time to another of an identity which remains exactly the same. These characters dissociate themselves from the permanent background of fog, and enact before us their brief pantomimes, only to disappear and to be replaced by others. And, like the existences defined by the present participles in the opening paragraphs of the novel, as long as they are before us, they remain continuously the same. Moreover, we notice that when they return, after what may be a long intervening time during which our attention is turned to other, unrelated, characters, they return as still the same. Even when they are out of our immediate focus of vision, they do not change, and apparently they have gone on being themselves without any break in the continuity of their lives. On the one hand, then, the reader's experience of the world of *Bleak House* is discontinuous. It is made up of sudden jumps, without transition, from one self-enclosed space-time, filled up with characters in action, to another unrelated one. Together, all these space-times make up a conglomeration of fragmentary human bric-a-brac which does not cohere into a significant totality. But, on the other hand, each of these enclosed space-times, organizing itself around a single character or group of characters, is itself homogeneous and continuous. Whenever we come back to it, we may be sure of finding it still obeying its own laws. The world as a whole is a kind of chaos, whose only pervasive factor is the undifferentiated fog. But within this chaos, isolated and sealed bubbles exist which are unified totalities, with constant properties. They are endowed with a permanent stability by the persistence within them of characters who endure through time as continuously the same. These characters, indeed, create their own ambience around themselves, and carry it with them wherever they go. Their ambience-bubbles are like Leibnizian monads. Each mirrors the universe and organizes it into a whole surrounding a center. It is a center of consciousness, but not of self-consciousness. Dickens cannot, therefore, show these bubbles from the inside. He must show them as they appear to some spectator. Each one manifests itself in the harmonious animation of everything surrounding its center. Everything around the person, his body, his gestures and expression, and his domestic belongings, testifies to the presence of an organizing and transforming principle which can never be directly shown. But if the mode of existence of these sealed bubbles reminds us of Leibnizian monads, there is, of course, a radical difference. The various monads are mutually exclusive, as in Leibniz, but here there is apparently no notion of a grand interlocking totality, a general harmony. The monads are not in fact in contact with one another at all, not even via the material which each organizes differently. They are contradictory perspectives on the universe. And each can persist only through ignorance of the existence of all the others. Much of the comedy of Dickens' self-centered grotesques derives from the confrontation of several such characters whose worlds are mutually contradictory, but who go on blindly being themselves even in the presence of forces which should, the spectator can see, prick their bubble worlds and annihilate them.

For the characters themselves, however, their spatial surroundings are a homogeneous whole, and time too is. a continuum. For them, any present state is the reaffirmation of what they were and a new version of what they will be. If they do not have a historical existence in the sense of a progressive realization of their destinies, at least they have escaped a temporal existence which is the mere succession of moments wholly unconnected with one another. It is only the narrator and the reader, it may be, who are in danger of experiencing a decomposition of time into an anarchic series of subjective states. The characters in *Bleak House* can escape this disintegration by a continual reduplication of themselves.

So Mrs. Bagnet affirms herself as the same person through all the diversity of her experience as a soldier's wife: "She's as usual, washing greens. I never saw her, except upon a baggage-waggon, when she wasn't washing greens!" (27). And so Mrs. Badger continually relives her life with her three husbands, "speaking of [them] as if they were parts of a charade" (17). And Sir Leicester Dedlock is concentrated permanently on making his own life the reduplication of all the generations of his ancestors whose portraits adorn the walls of Chesney Wold, just as Mrs. Woodcourt is fixed in her pride on her great ancestor, Morgan ap-Kerrig (17). Such characters exemplify perfectly the monomaniac purity of Dickens' comic personages. Entirely concentrated upon themselves and upon their single obsession, they could change only through a change in their relation to their *idée fixe*. They exist entirely as their obsession and as the eternal repetition of the feelings which are appropriate to it. This existence is at the opposite extreme from that of the eighteenth-century human type who was made only of his momentary and fleeting sensations, sensations which were immediately dissolved and forgotten as they were succeeded by others. The latter kind of being, the kind we meet, say, in Marivaux's novels and plays, was never the same person from one moment to another, but the nature of Dickens' self-centered monomaniacs is at the opposite pole. They are never anything but exactly identical with themselves. They do not need to wait for death to give them permanence. They have already, like the aristocratic world in Dickens' view of it, "found out the perpetual stoppage" (12).

This means that they can ignore the fact of their own future death. In finding out the secret of perpetual stoppage they have found out the secret of eternal youth. Many characters in *Bleak House* have in one way or another succeeded in evading the normal process of growth from childhood to maturity. Old in years, they remain young in spirit and attitude. Thus Harold Skimpole says, "I have no idea of time" (18), and as a result of the hard and deliberate selfishness of his hypocritical pose he has been able to remain, as he and Jarndyce say repeatedly, "a child" (6). By a complete refusal to take responsibility for "the

ities and accountabilities of life" (6), Skimpole has escaped
from time and its destructiveness. The latter is visible only in a
kind of "depreciation" which gives him "more the appearance
. . . of a damaged young man, than a well-preserved elderly
one." Skimpole changes through time not by the normal growth
and maturing of a human being, but by a scarcely perceptible
decay. It is as though he were an inanimate object which has
retained its original form and appearance even when old and
secretly mined with age. Skimpole has evaded the constant metamorphosis of ordinary human temporality by not having any
object in life, by refusing to choose a project and carry it out by
voluntary action through time. He has thus avoided that using
up of his forces which is, for Dickens as for Balzac, the tragedy
of passion and effort. By remaining perpetually uncommitted
Skimpole remains perpetually young and fresh, perpetually
ready for the life he never has.

Other young-old characters in the novel, however, show that
Skimpole's escape from time is not necessarily identified with
his passivity. Boythorn, modeled on Landor as Skimpole is modeled on Leigh Hunt, has maintained the inexhaustible vitality
of his youth in a way directly opposite to that of Skimpole. His
name suggests his youthfulness as well as his aggressive nature.
Full of a great reservoir of energy which is always in excess of
its object, he has remained young and vigorous. If Skimpole
avoids destructive contact with the world by passivity and
dreaming, Boythorn leaps beyond or over any situation in
which he finds himself by an instantaneous act of violence
which is actually a mere violence of words. "His language is as
sounding as his voice. He is always in extremes; perpetually in
the superlative degree. In his condemnation he is all ferocity"
(9). But in the end Boythorn, like Skimpole, accomplishes
nothing: "the very fury of his superlatives . . . seemed to go
off like blank cannons and hurt nothing" (9). Boythorn's reward for a relation to time and to the world which is in its way
as abstract and ineffectual as Skimpole's, is to be, like Skimpole,
eternally young, eternally in possession of unused forces.

But the full implications of this stoppage of time are revealed in the characters who are old-young rather than young-

old. Far from being a perpetuation of life, it is a choice
death, the choice of a life which is neither youth nor age, b
a horrible semblance of life, mechanical, false, a living deat
The Smallweed family, for example, "has had no child born
it," only "complete little men and women" who "have been o
served to bear a likeness to old monkeys with something d
pressing on their minds" (21). Young Smallweed "is a wei
changeling, to whom years are nothing. He stands precocious
possessed of centuries of owlish wisdom. If he ever lay in
cradle, it seems as if he must have lain there in a tail-coat. F
has an old, old eye, has Smallweed . . ." (20). And Volun
nia, the ancient aristocratic parasite of Sir Leicester Dedlock,
a grisly and macabre imitation of girlish youth and life (66
She is like those other aristocratic ladies of *Bleak Hous*
"ancient charmers with skeleton throats, and peachy chee
that have a rather ghastly bloom upon them seen by dayligh
when indeed these fascinating creatures look like Death ar
the Lady fused together" (56). Volumnia and the Smallwee
have cheated death, as Skimpole has, but only by choosing
death-in-life which is repulsive in its grotesque imitation
youthful vitality. They are like Poe's mesmerized man who sti
lived on at the point of death, but who lived only because h
existence had been frozen in a life that was really death. Lil
Poe's M. Vlademar, the Smallweeds could say: "I am dead."

But the most striking portrait of the gruesome permanenc
of an anachronistic and static existence is old Mr. Turveydro
the "model of Deportment": "He was a fat old gentleman wit
a false complexion, false teeth, false whiskers, and a wig. . .
He was pinched in, and swelled out, and got up, and strappe
down, as much as he could possibly bear. He had such a necl
cloth on (puffing his very eyes out of their natural shape), an
his chin and even his ears so sunk into it, that it seemed a
though he must inevitably double up, if it were cast loose. . .
He had a cane, he had an eye-glass, he had a snuff-box, he ha
rings, he had wristbands, he had everything but any touch c
nature; he was not like youth, he was not like age, he was no
like anything in the world but a model of Deportment" (14
In his attempt to maintain a rigid standard of deportment, th

tificial stylishness of a Regency dandy, long after such a
yle is out of fashion, Turveydrop has destroyed every bit of
ature in himself. He is in a way even more useless and deca-
ent than his models, the dandies whose own "model" was the
otorious Beau Brummell.[5] At least Brummell employed his
tificiality to conquer the society of his day, triumphing even
ver the Prince Regent himself. But Turveydrop is utterly out-
oded and utterly unrelated to contemporary society. He ex-
ts in a total vacuum. "A levelling age," as he says, "is not fa-
ourable to Deportment" (14). Turveydrop has triumphed
ver time, being neither old nor young, but he has triumphed
aly by ceasing to be human, by becoming a kind of window
esser's dummy. Everything about him is false, and we suspect
aat the reality underneath is only a kind of soft pulp or clay
hich would collapse into a formless mass if the rigid outer
ust were removed. He is a triumph of will, but of a will
hich, in constructing a fixed and enduring surface, has not
en able to prevent what is beneath the surface from becom-
g more and more inauthentic and inhuman. He exists interi-
ly only as his static volition and as the parasitic greediness
hich is its analogue. As in the case of Skimpole, his reiteration
' himself is a form of selfish inactivity: Prince Turveydrop's
distinguished father did nothing whatever, but stand before
e fire, a model of Deportment" (14).

The escape from time of all these characters can only be
chieved by a hermetic enclosure which does not allow any-
ing whatever of novelty or change to come in from the out-
de. The enclosure which we found in *Martin Chuzzlewit* as
e mode of existence of Mr. Mould, reappears as the condition
' many characters in *Bleak House*. Tulkinghorn lives in a
uilding where "lawyers lie like maggots in nuts" (10). Rich-

[5] See Captain Jesse's *The Life of George Brummell, Esq.* (London,
44) for a possible source of Dickens' Turveydrop. Thackeray reviewed
sse's book in *The Morning Chronicle* on May 6, 1844. (See William
akepeace Thackeray, *Contributions to the Morning Chronicle*, ed. G. N.
ay (Urbana, Ill., 1955), pp. 31–39.) Many details of Brummell's dress
id appearance as described in Jesse's book match Turveydrop. Like Turvey-
op, Brummell was not actually a member of the aristocratic society he
ed, and Turveydrop too is, as Thackeray calls Brummell, "heartless, and
swindler, a fool, a glutton, and a liar" (*Contributions*, p. 36).

ard and Ada live after their marriage in a "dull dark corne[r]
(60), and their apartment is near their lawyer's office, which [is]
"in disposition retiring and in situation retired, . . . squeeze[d]
up in a corner, and blink[ing] at a dead wall" (39). Th[e]
Smallweeds dwell "in a little narrow street, always solitar[y,]
shady, and sad, closely bricked in on all sides like a tomb" (21[).]
Their parlor is "certain feet below the level of the street" (21[).]

But the self-enclosure of these characters is not a comic an[d]
comfortable insulation, as was Mould's. It is rather a sombe[r]
interment. It is accompanied, even in the case of unself-co[n-]
scious people like the Smallweeds, by evident spiritual pai[n.]
This suffering is visible rather in Dickens' descriptions of th[e]
environment of these characters than in direct presentations [of]
their subjective states, but it is nonetheless unmistakably ther[e,]
as a kind of pervasive atmosphere of staleness and immobilit[y.]
And the life that is lived in this enclosure may be a physic[al]
or spiritual paralysis, like that of Grandfather Smallweed, [or]
that of Sir Leicester, who is "like one of a race of eight-d[ay]
clocks in gorgeous cases that never go and never went" (18[),]
or like that of the world of fashion and the Court of Chancer[y,]
which are "things of precedent and usage; over-sleeping Ri[p]
Van Winkles, who have played at strange games through a de[al]
of thundery weather; sleeping beauties, whom the Knight wi[ll]
wake one day, when all the stopped spits in the kitchen sha[ll]
begin to turn prodigiously!" (2). The evil of such a seale[d]
world is, as Dickens sees it, that it refuses to "receive any im[-]
press from the moving age" (12): ". . . it is a world wrappe[d]
up in too much jeweller's cotton and fine wool, and cann[ot]
hear the rushing of the larger worlds, and cannot see them [as]
they circle round the sun. It is a deadened world, and its growt[h]
is sometimes unhealthy for want of air" (2). And so Georg[e]
Rouncewell says of the Smallweed household: "It wants a bit [of]
youth as much as it wants fresh air" (21). Inside such pr[o-]
tected circles things remain exactly the same, while outside th[e]
world is moving on toward situations which are more and mo[re]
different from their origin. As this happens, what is inside th[e]
closed circle becomes more and more inappropriate and fals[e,]
like the cant made up of Old Testament phrases which Chad[-]

band so ludicrously misapplies to contemporary reality, or like the outmoded language of sentiment which has Guppy locked in its enchanted circle, or like the political world, with its circling substitutions in which Lord Coodle, Sir Thomas Doodle, the Duke of Foodle and so on down to Quoodle are replaced by Buffy, Cuffy, Duffy, and Puffy, and they in turn by the Doodle faction again. The "perpetual stoppage" really means "putting back the hands upon the Clock of Time, and cancelling a few hundred years of history" (12).

These enclosed worlds remain precariously safe inside their unpierceable walls, existing as an eternally repeated circular motion which is constantly beginning over and over again and never accomplishing anything. Such a circular repetition occurs again and again in *Bleak House:*

The fashionable world — tremendous orb, nearly five miles round — is in full swing, and the solar system works respectfully at its appointed distances. (48)

The town awakes; the great tee-totum is set up for its daily spin and whirl . . . . (16)

So the little boy you saw just now waltzes by himself in the empty kitchen . . . . (38)

We are always appearing, and disappearing, and swearing, and interrogating, and filing, and cross-filing, and arguing, and sealing, and motioning, and referring, and reporting, and revolving about the Lord Chancellor and all his satellites . . . . [E]verybody . . . must go down the middle and up again, through such an infernal country-dance of costs and fees and nonsense and corruption, as was never dreamed of in the wildest visions of a Witch's Sabbath. . . . And thus, through years and years, and lives and lives, everything goes on, constantly beginning over and over again, and nothing ever ends. (8)

Like the succession of generations in the Dedlock family, such a circular motion is an endless process of palingenesis. Each new Sir Leicester is exactly like all the others, and will soon be, like the others, what he has really been in life, a forgotten portrait on the walls (16). In the end, each sealed world of repetition is seen to be a place where the present, far from gaining authenticity through its relation to the past, melts into total unreality. The present is already a thing of memory. It is dissolved and negated precisely because it is an exact reiteration of the past.

For the repetitive characters themselves, this nothingness exists either veiled in a total unself-consciousness, or as a present state of prolonged self-absorbed suffering. For most such characters in *Bleak House,* the continuity given to their lives by their reiteration of themselves only exists and is perceived by the narrator and the reader. It does not exist at all for the characters themselves. The Smallweeds, Sir Leicester, Volumnia, or Skimpole are shown as hardly self-conscious, or, if aware of themselves at all, as conscious only of their present states and hardly ever casting a retrospective eye into the past or a prophetic eye into the future. And indeed how could they be aware of the temporal continuity of their lives? For them, the present moment cannot be differentiated from any of the others because it is in fact not different. And without differentiation the movement of withdrawal and comparison necessary to self-consciousness is impossible. Ignorant of the future, such characters are forgetful of the past, and live entirely locked in the present. Such a repetition is not a meaningful reiteration of themselves, like the Kierkegaardian repetition, because it is necessarily unconscious. There is a moment of forgetting which separates each successive identical moment, like the fog which surrounds each perceptible object for the spectator in the opening scene of the novel. The repetition of these characters turns out to be the constant renewal of a division from themselves rather than the continued affirmation of themselves. Like Jo the crossing sweeper, all these characters live entirely without "awakened association, aspiration or regret, melancholy or joyful reference to things beyond the senses" (16). Such repetition is in the end identical with the world of temporal division from which self-duplication seemed at first to escape.

But for some characters the endless reëxperiencing of the same state is accompanied by exacerbated self-consciousness, a self-consciousness which is precisely to be defined as the heightened awareness of their spiritual paralysis. So, Lady Dedlock's state is the perfectly lucid and deliberate prolonging from moment to moment of the same frozen state. She lives as the desperate attempt to cease to be her real self, the mistress of Captain Hawdon and the mother of Esther, and to become a false self, the unstained wife of Sir Leicester and the leader of fashionable society. This false self is kept in being only by the endless reiteration of the act of will which creates her false surface: ". . . having conquered *her* world, [Lady Dedlock] fell, not into the melting, but rather into the freezing mood" (2). Before and behind her lie only the reduplication of this despairing act of self-negation, eternally renewed, eternally unsuccessful. This despair is visible on the surface only as a fashionable ennui. Lady Dedlock is "in the desolation of Boredom and the clutch of Giant Despair . . . Weariness of soul lies before her, as it lies behind — her Ariel has put a girdle of it round the whole earth . . ." (12). "Conscience-stricken, underneath that mask" (36), Lady Dedlock is entirely enclosed within her own suffering. Even in the midst of all the light and glitter of fashionable society she is alone, traveling her own isolated road as if she were in the middle of a desert: "Through the desert that lay before her, she must go alone" (36).

The repetition of Lady Dedlock, then, is the self-conscious reaffirmation of an act of repression or of self-denial, an act which was first performed long ago in the past. Her present is a frozen and solid form of that past. For other characters, however, the orientation of the repetition is toward the future. It is the repetition of eternal expectation. Such characters are forever awaiting the occurrence of some definitive event which will fill their emptiness and give them a positive existence. Whereas Sir Leicester, Turveydrop, and Lady Dedlock live in a present which is too fixed and inflexible, too filled with a predetermined content, other characters live as a perpetual not-yet, the perpetual anticipation of something which is evermore about to happen. Such is the state of the suitors in Chancery, who put their hope in the eventual settlement of their cases. Thus, Richard Carstone can say of his life, ". . . it's monotonous, and to-day is too like yesterday, and to-morrow is too like to-day" (17). And so lived the original owner of Bleak House:

"He gave it its present name, and lived here shut up: day and night poring over the wicked heaps of papers in the suit, and hoping against hope to . . . bring it to a close" (8). And so poor crazy Miss Flite lives in the continual expectation of "a judgment. Shortly. On the Day of Judgment"(3).

Repetition, of whatever sort, whether conscious or unconscious, far from being superior to a momentary and disconnected existence, leads to a life which is simply a death in life. A monotonous reaffirmation of the same identity is exactly the same mode of existence as a frozen immobility:

. . . the clay and water are hard frozen, and the mill in which the gaunt blind horse goes round all day, looks like an instrument of human torture. (56)

### III

It is a dull street under the best conditions; where the two long rows of houses stare at each other with that severity, that half-a-dozen of its greatest mansions seem to have been slowly stared into stone, rather than originally built in that material. (48)

The Temple, Chancery Lane, Serjeants' Inn, and Lincoln's Inn even unto the Fields, are like tidal harbours at low water; where stranded proceedings, offices at anchor, idle clerks lounging on lop-sided stools that will not recover their perpendicular until the current of Term sets in, lie high and dry upon the ooze of the long vacation. (19)

Though the world of *Bleak House* is not, we discover, the sheer atomistic chaos it at first appears to be, the connection, by repetition, of successive moments in isolated locations does not organize this chaos. It does not seem that a truly human existence is possible here — no organization of time into a lived duration, no relation between people making possible significant communication. But we come to see that the inhuman fixity and paralysis which seems to possess things and men in *Bleak House* is not a permanent condition. It is not now in the same stasis it has always maintained. The houses were not originally stone. They were "slowly stared into stone." And the ooze and idleness of the long vacation is merely the motionless end point of a progressive withdrawal of the tide of human action and life. Prior to the timeless paralysis of things there was a long process of deceleration and decay. It is impossible to stop the forward movement of things in time. Both an attempt to freeze the present as a repetition of a past time and the eternally repeated moment of expectation which awaits some definitive event in the future are essentially a denial of the proper human relation to time and to the objective world. Both are cut off from the "moving age." But man cannot cut himself off from time and the world. If he is not related authentically to them, if he does not command them, they will command him. He will be assimilated into the inhuman world and become part of a mechanical concatenation of causes and effects which is a horrible parody of historical continuity. In the absence of human intervention things will take matters into their own hands, and initiate a long natural process of decay and disintegration in which man will become unwittingly involved. The world possesses an immanent tendency toward decomposition which only the most delicately and resolutely applied constructive force can counteract. And it is just this force which is almost totally absent in *Bleak House*.

The world of the novel is already, when the story begins, a kind of junk heap of broken things. This is especially apparent in the great number of disorderly, dirty, broken-down interiors in the novel. The Jellyby household is "nothing but bills, dirt, waste, noise, tumbles down-stairs, confusion, and wretchedness" (14). At the time of the preparations for Caddy Jellyby's marriage "nothing belonging to the family, which it had been possible to break, was unbroken . . . ; nothing which it had been possible to spoil in any way, was unspoilt; . . . no domestic object which was capable of collecting dirt, from a dear child's knee to the door-plate, was without as much dirt as could well accumulate upon it" (30). The Jellyby house is perhaps the extreme case, but Skimpole's home too is "in a state of dilapidation" (43), Symond's Inn, where Richard Carstone's lawyer, Vholes, lives, has been made "of old building materials, which took kindly to the dry rot and to dirt and all things decaying and dismal" (39), and Richard himself lives in a room which is full of "a great confusion of clothes, tin cases, books,

boots, brushes, and portmanteaus, strewn all about the floor"
(45). The "dusty bundles of papers" in his room seem to
Esther "like dusty mirrors reflecting his own mind" (51).

These present states of disorder are not simply inorganic
formlessness; they are the terminal point of an organically interconnected series of stages which led naturally and inevitably from one to another. The present stage of rottenness is the
result of an inverted process of growth, "like [that] of fungus or
any unwholesome excrescence produced . . . in neglect and
impurity" (46). Such a process escapes from the discontinuous, but only to replace it with a mode of continuity which is
apparently an irreversible growth toward death. This death will
be defined as the putrefaction of every organic form and as the
pulverization of every structured inorganic thing. There is here
no Spencerian constructive law immanent in nature and guar-
anteeing, through the impersonal operation of causality, the
creation of ever finer and more discriminated forms of life.
Rather, it is as though the generative cause and immanent principle of growth had been withdrawn altogether, leaving things
to fall back to their primal disorder.

Sometimes this process appears, not as a certain stage which
it has now reached, but in the very midst of its happening. Although the participles in the opening paragraphs of the novel
suggested the present activity of inanimate objects, participial
forms can also express the falling away and disintegration from
moment to moment of things which are collapsing into chaos.
Thus, Esther is painfully aware of "the musty *rotting* silence of
the house" where Ada and Richard are living (51), and in
Nemo's room, "one old mat, trodden to shreds of rope-yarn, lies
*perishing* upon the hearth" (10). A description of the beach at
Deal shows it as a kind of wasteland of disunity, and ends with
the apparent metamorphosis of the inhabitants into a lower
form of existence. The heterogeneity gives way at last to a single substance into which the men seem to be transforming
themselves, just as the litter of the beach dissolves into the sea
and the fog: "The long flat beach, with its little irregular
houses, wooden and brick, and its litter of capstans, and great
boats, and sheds, and bare upright poles with tackle and blocks

and loose gravelly waste places overgrown with grass and weeds, wore as dull an appearance as any place I ever saw. The sea was heaving under a thick white fog; and nothing else was moving but a few early ropemakers, who, with the yarn twisted round their bodies, looked as if, tired of their present state of existence, they were spinning themselves into cordage" (45). Perhaps the best example of this disintegration is the initial description of Tom-all-Alone's, which makes an elaborate use of present participles to express an active process of decomposition matching the forward movement of time: "It is a street of perishing blind houses, with their eyes stoned out; without a pane of glass, without so much as a window-frame, with the bare blank shutters tumbling from their hinges and falling asunder; the iron rails peeling away in flakes of rust; the chimneys sinking in; the stone steps to every door (and every door might be Death's Door) turning stagnant green; the very crutches on which the ruins are propped, decaying" (8).

One might plot the curve of this approach to maximum entropy by a series of crucial points. There was once evidently, long ago in the past, a time when things were orderly, when everything fitted into its place in an organic structure, and when each individual object was itself a formal unity. From that point things passed eventually to a stage in which they were simply collections of broken objects thrown pell-mell together. Things are then like the wreckage left behind after the destruction of a civilization. Each fragmentary form once had a use and a purpose, but is now merely debris. Such collections form the contents of Krook's rag and bottle shop or of the closets of the Jellyby house:

In all parts of the window, were quantities of dirty bottles: blacking bottles, medicine bottles, ginger-beer and soda-water bottles, pickle bottles, wine bottles, ink bottles . . . . A little way within the shop-door, lay heaps of old crackled parchment scrolls, and discoloured and dog's-eared law-papers. I could have fancied that all the rusty keys, of which there must have been hundreds huddled together as old iron, had once belonged to doors of rooms or strong chests in lawyers' offices. The litter of rags . . . might have been counsellors' bands and gowns torn up. One had only to fancy . . .

that yonder bones in a corner, piled together and picked very clean, were the bones of clients, to make the picture complete. (5)

But such wonderful things came tumbling out of the closets when they were opened — bits of mouldy pie, sour bottles, Mrs. Jellyby's caps, letters, tea, forks, odd boots and shoes of children, firewood, wafers, saucepan-lids, damp sugar in odds and ends of paper bags, footstools, blacklead brushes, bread, Mrs. Jellyby's bonnets, books with butter sticking to the binding, guttered candle-ends put out by being turned upside down in broken candlesticks, nutshells, heads and tails of shrimps, dinner-mats, gloves, coffee-grounds, umbrellas . . . . (30)

Not only are things moving in the direction of increasing disorder, they are also moving further and further beyond the limits of human intelligence. Whatever human meaning and order there may have been originally is now obliterated in complexity which defies comprehension: "This scarecrow of a suit has, in course of time, become so complicated, that no man alive knows what it means" (1). Even if there were some intelligible purpose in the original impetus which set the case in motion, that purpose has been utterly lost in its own self-proliferating complexity. Now the case runs automatically, without any direction from the thousands of people, suitors and lawyers, who are mere parties to it, mere instruments of its autonomous activity: "It's about a Will, and the trusts under a Will — or it was, once. It's about nothing but Costs, now. We are . . . equitably waltzing ourselves off to dusty death, about Costs. That's the great question. All the rest, by some extraordinary means, has melted away" (8).

But in the end even this kind of structure, a structure so elaborate that it cannot be understood by the human mind, yields to complete heterogeneity. And a world of complete heterogeneity is, paradoxically, a world of complete homogeneity. Since nothing has any relation to anything else and cannot therefore be understood in terms of a contrast to anything else, everything is, finally, the equivalent of everything else. The contents of Krook's rag and bone shop, like everything involved in Chancery, are transformed at last to mere undifferentiated dust, another form of the fog and mud which dominate the opening scene of the novel. Everything there is "wasting away and going to rack and ruin," turning into "rust and must and cobwebs" (5). The final product is made up of thousands of distinct particles, but each particle is, in the end, no more than another example of the general pulverization. So Tom-all-Alone's is at one stage of its decay like the ruined body of a man half dead and crawling with vermin: "these tumbling tenements contain, by night, a swarm of misery. As, on the ruined human wretch, vermin parasites appear, so, these ruined shelters have bred a crowd of foul existence that crawls in and out of gaps in walls and boards; and coils itself to sleep, in maggot numbers, where the rain drips in . . ." (16). But later on even this semblance of life disappears from the scene and Tom-all-Alone's is like the cold and lifeless moon, a "desert region unfit for life and blasted by volcanic fires" (46), with a "stagnant channel of mud" for a main street (46). In the end, any organic entity, whether human or material, which gets caught up in the process of decomposition becomes nothing but a powdery or pasty substance, without form or life. This process can be either a physical or a spiritual disintegration, either the destruction of the individual through his absorption in the impersonal institution of "law and equity," or the dissolution of all solid material form in "that kindred mystery, the street mud, which is made of nobody knows what, and collects about us nobody knows whence or how" (10). One of the basic symbolic equations of the novel is the suggested parallel between these two forms of disintegration.

The mud and fog of the opening paragraphs of the novel are not, we can see now, the primeval stuff out of which all highly developed forms evolve. They are the symptoms of a general return to the primal slime, a return to chaos which is going on everywhere in the novel and is already nearing its final end when the novel begins.

The human condition of the characters of *Bleak House* is, then, to be thrown into a world which is neither fresh and new nor already highly organized, but is a world which has already gone bad. From the very first moment in which they are aware of themselves at all, the characters find themselves involved in this world. Their dereliction is to be already a suitor in a case which began long before they were born, or already tainted with the quasi-sin of illegitimacy. Their mode of being in the world is to be already committed to a situation which they have not chosen.

This dereliction will never end, as long as the character is alive. It is the permanent condition of human existence in *Bleak House*. The fact that almost all of the characters in the novel are in one way or another engaged in an endless suit in Chancery is much more than a mere device of narrative unity. To be involved in an endless case, a case which can only be concluded by the total using up of both suit and suitor, becomes a symbol in the novel of what it is to be in the world at all. It is because a person is part of a process, because he is born into a case which is going on at his birth and remains unfinished throughout his life, that he cannot settle down, cannot find some definitive formulation of his identity and of his place in the world. But to be unfinished, to be open toward the future, to be evermore about to be, is, for Dickens, to be human. Richard suffers the human situation itself and defines the state of all the characters when he describes himself as living permanently in a "temporary condition" (23): ". . . I am a very unfortunate dog not to be more settled, but how *can* I be more settled? If you lived in an unfinished house, you couldn't settle down in it; if you were condemned to leave everything you undertook, unfinished, you would find it hard to apply yourself to anything; and yet that's my unhappy case. I was born into this unfinished contention with all its chances and changes, and it began to unsettle me before I quite knew the difference between a suit at law and a suit of clothes; and it has gone on unsettling me ever since" (23). Richard's error is not to understand that his case can never be finished, to live in the expectation of an end which will settle his life in a permanent form: "it can't last for ever. We shall come on for a final hearing, and get judgment in our favour . . . . These proceedings will come to a termination, and then I am provided for" (23). But the nature of these proceedings is precisely to be interminable as long as the character is alive.

For many of the characters the determining cause which has made of their situations what they irrevocably are, occurred so long before their birth that it assumes a quasi-mythical character. They attempt to trace the series of effects and causes from the present moment back retrogressively to the first cause, only to be lost in the mists and confusions of the past. Long, long ago in the past, so long ago that no one now has any direct contact with what happened then, the chain of causes and effects which has brought things to their present pass was initiated. Such characters seem to be involved in a kind of original sin for which they must innocently suffer: "How mankind ever came to be afflicted with Wiglomeration, or for whose sins these young people ever fell into a pit of it, I don't know; so it is" (8).

But for other characters the definitive event which has determined their lives is prior to the beginning of the novel but not prior to their birth. As in Faulkner's novels, we are presented with characters who are when we first meet them already doomed by something which happened long ago in their own lives, something which they hide carefully from the world, but on which their conscious attention is permanently fixed in a kind of retrospective fascination. All their lives are spent attempting unsuccessfully to escape from this determining moment. It is a constantly reënacted failure which only makes their lives all the more permanently attached to a past from which they cannot separate themselves, and which irrevocably defines them as what they are. The secretly obsessed quality of many of the characters in *Bleak House* makes this novel very different from *Martin Chuzzlewit*. In the earlier novel the characters either had no inner lives at all as distinct from their environments, or had subjectivities which were anonymous and empty, mere pure and vivid vision, existing only in the present. In *Bleak House,* some characters are seen as possessing, not this anonymous lucidity, but a concentrated awareness of their pasts and of their destinies. Such consciousnesses are not yet shown from the inside, as they will be in *Little Dorrit,* but their presence is unmistakably implied by the actions of the characters and revealed in occasional glimpses of their interior worlds. Of the tragedy of Boythorn's projected marriage, Jarndyce says: "That time has had its influence on all his later life" (9, and see 43). And Nemo was living, we realize, in the constant suffering of the tragedy of his relations to Lady Dedlock, just as George Rouncewell's bluff exterior hides a secret remorse for having run away from home, and just as Tulkinghorn lives in a state of quiet desperation. He is shown for one moment as he is for himself, remembering a friend of his, obviously a surrogate for himself, a "man of the same mould," who "lived the same kind of life until he was seventy-five years old," and then hanged himself (22). But Lady Dedlock is, of course, the chief example of this theme. Her boredom hides an intense concentration on her own past, and all her attempts to cease to be the lover of Captain Hawdon only carry her more irresistibly toward her final reaffirmation of her past self. Her tragedy, like that of Racine's characters, of Hardy's, or of Faulkner's, is the tragedy of the irrevocable. Her fate is to be the doomed victim of her own past, a past which continues itself ineluctably into her present state as long as she lives.

But the determining cause which makes impotent victims of all these characters does not exist solely as a kind of mythical event occurring so long ago that no direct contact with it is possible, nor does it exist solely as an impersonal force which imposes itself from the outside on people and warps or destroys them. It may be both of these, but in its most powerful form it is immanent, present in the contemporary spiritual condition of the characters, although they may not even be consciously aware of it. It is able to get inside its victims, and inhabit them as a destructive force. It then no longer needs to exist as an exterior power, and can withdraw and disappear, leaving the possessed character to his isolated doom. Everywhere in *Bleak House* we can see the intrusion into the present of a fatally determining past from which the characters can in no way free themselves because it has become part of the very substance of their beings. In *Bleak House* the present is not really something isolated and without engagement in the past, but is the preservation of the past and its continuation in the present. Inhabited by immanent determining forces tending irreversibly toward their dissolution the characters disintegrate, just as

Grandfather Smallweed collapses "like some wound-up instrument running down" (39), and just as his daughter "dwindled away like touchwood" (21).

The self-enclosed life of the characters of *Bleak House* is, then, not a mechanical repetition. It is a clock that runs down, something organic which has died and decays, the entropy of an enclosed system approaching the maximum equilibrium of its forces. As in the "circumscribed universe" of Poe,[6] since there is no influx of life, energy, air, or novelty from the outside, there is a gradual exhaustion of the forces inside, a disaggregation of all solid forms, as all diversity is slowly transformed into a bland and motionless homogeneity. Such an enclosed system will, like a case in Chancery, eventually "die out of its own vapidity" (24), or "lapse and melt away" (65). Beneath a carapace of solitude the will, the strength, the life of these characters exhausts itself, consumes itself in its own internal activity. So Richard, "the good consuming and consumed, the life turned sour," is slowly transformed into "the one subject that is resolving his existence into itself" (39). Wholly enclosed within his own obsession, such a character experiences a steady decomposition of his life, an acceleration toward the ultimate disorder and lifelessness of dust and mud:

My whole estate . . . has gone in costs. The suit, still undecided, has fallen into rack, and ruin, and despair, with everything else . . . (15)

In the meantime [while Tom Jarndyce became absorbed in his suit], the place became dilapidated, the wind whistled through the cracked walls, the rain fell through the broken roof, the weeds choked the passage to the rotting door. (8)

His voice had faded, with the old expression of his face, with his strength, with his anger, with his resistance to the wrongs that had at last subdued him. The faintest shadow of an object full of form and colour, is such a picture of it, as he was of the man from Shropshire whom we had spoken with before. (24)

. . . it is the same death eternally — inborn, inbred, engendered in the corrupted humours of the vicious body itself, and that

[6] See Georges Poulet, "L'Univers circonscrit d'Edgar Poe," *Les Temps Modernes*, CXIV, CXV (1955), 2179–2204.

only — Spontaneous Combustion, and none other of all the deaths that can be died. (32)

Krook's death by spontaneous combustion, described in the last quotation, is of course the most notorious example of this return to homogeneity in *Bleak House*. Krook is transformed into the basic elements of the world of the novel, fog and mud. The heavy odor in the air, as if bad pork chops were frying, and the "thick yellow liquor" which forms on the window sill as Krook burns into the circumambient atmosphere, are particularly horrible versions of these elements.

But if the deterioration of the characters in *Bleak House* can appear as the inescapable fulfillment of an inner principle of corruption, it can also appear as a destiny which draws the characters from some prospective point toward their doom. Instead of being pushed from behind or from within, the characters may be attracted from the future. This may appear in the sudden collapse or dissolution of some object or person which has long been secretly mined from within by decay, and goes to pieces in a moment when some artificial foundation or sustaining principle gives way. So the houses in Tom-all-Alone's collapse (16); so the man from Shropshire "break[s] down in an hour" (24); and so the death of Tulkinghorn seems to Lady Dedlock "but the key-stone of a gloomy arch removed, and now the arch begins to fall in a thousand fragments, each crushing and mangling piecemeal!" (55). "It was right," she says, "that all that had sustained me should give way at once, and that I should die of terror and my conscience" (59). Indeed the spontaneous combustion of Krook is just such a rapid fulfillment of a process which has been preparing itself invisibly for a long time, just as the stroke which paralyzes Sir Leicester makes him physically what he spiritually has been all along, a frozen and outmoded form of life, speaking "mere jumble and jargon" (56).

In all these cases, it is as though a hidden orientation suddenly revealed itself when, all restraint gone, the character yields at last to a destiny which has been attracting him with ever-increasing intensity. As Bucket says, "the frost breaks up, and the water runs" (54). It does not run randomly, however, but toward a center which has all along been exerting its gravitational pull. This pull does not now commence, but only now manifests itself. And so Miss Flite can speak of the Court of Chancery not as a first cause, but as a final cause drawing men to their ruin by means of its irresistible magnetic attraction:

"There's a cruel attraction in the place. You *can't* leave it. And you *must* expect. . . . It's the Mace and Seal upon the table."
What could they do, did she think? I mildly asked her.
"Draw," returned Miss Flite. "Draw people on, my dear. Draw peace out of them. Sense out of them. Good looks out of them. Good qualities out of them. I have felt them even drawing my rest away in the night. Cold and glittering devils!" (35)

For many characters their disintegration is not so much the working out of a chain of causes and effects begun long in the past as it is the fatal convergence of their inner lives and their external situations toward a point where both will coincide at their death. Richard had mistakenly believed that "either the suit must be ended, . . . or the suitor" (51). But he is slowly consumed by his vampire-like lawyer, Vholes, just as the case of Jarndyce and Jarndyce is entirely consumed in costs. When both processes are finally complete, Vholes gives "one gasp as if he had swallowed the last morsel of his client" (65). The termination of the interminable case coincides necessarily with the exhaustion of all the money involved in it, and with the simultaneous death of Richard. All of these events inevitably occur together as the vanishing point toward which all the parallel motions have been converging, as toward their final cause. This temporal progression is glimpsed by Esther in a momentary scene which prognosticates Richard's fate. It is a good example of the way scenes in Dickens which are initially merely narrative realism are transformed into symbolic expressions of the entire destiny of a character: "I shall never forget those two seated side by side in the lantern's light; Richard, all flush and fire and laughter, with the reins in his hand; Mr. Vholes, quite still, black-gloved, and buttoned up, looking at him as if he were looking at his prey and charming it. I have before me

the whole picture of the warm dark night, the summer light-
ning, the dusty track of road closed in by hedgerows and high
trees, the gaunt pale horse with his ears pricked up, and the
driving away at speed to Jarndyce and Jarndyce" (37).

In the same way the life and death of Jo the crossing sweeper
are made symbolic. During his life Jo has been continually
forced to "move on." His death is imaged as the "breaking
down" of a cart that as it disintegrates approaches closer and
closer to an end point which will be its total fragmentation:
"For the cart so hard to draw, is near its journey's end, and
drags over stony ground. All round the clock it labours up the
broken steps, shattered and worn. Not many times can the sun
rise, and behold it still upon its weary road" (47). And so the
death of Lady Dedlock is described as a journey which is the
slow closing in of her destiny: "When I saw my Lady yesterday, . . . she looked to me . . . as if the step on the Ghost's
Walk had almost walked her down" (58). Like Richard's future, the prospect before and beside the road which she is journeying is getting narrower and narrower. The end point will be
her death, the complete extinction of all possibility of choice or
movement: "The dark road I have trodden for so many years
will end where it will. I follow it alone to the end, whatever
the end be. . . . [Danger] has closed around me, almost as
awfully as if these woods of Chesney Wold had closed around
the house; but my course through it is the same" (36).

But this sudden break-up of things when the keystone of the
arch has been removed may be imaged not as a narrowing, but
as a descent deeper and deeper into the pit of the dark and unformed. When the fragile foundations which have been precariously upholding things give way, there is a sudden drop
vertically into infernal depths. The Chancery suit is a "dead
sea" (37), and Richard "sink[s] deeper and deeper into difficulty every day, continually hoping and continually disap-
pointed, conscious of change upon change for the worse in
[himself]" (39). Mr. Snagsby, being led by Bucket and his col-
leagues into the heart of Tom-all-Alone's, "feels as if he were
going, every moment deeper and deeper down, into the infernal gulf" (22). What he sees is like a vision of hell itself.

Not the least horrible part of this visionary experience is the way the human dwellers in Tom-all-Alone's seem to have been transformed into the elements they live in, the fog and mud: ". . . Mr. Snagsby passes along the middle of a villainous street, undrained, unventilated, deep in black mud and corrupt water . . . . [T]he crowd flows round, and from its squalid depths obsequious advice heaves up to Mr. Bucket. Whenever they move, and the angry bull's-eyes glare, it fades away, and flits about them up the alleys, and in the ruins, and behind the walls . . ." (22).

But it is Lady Dedlock's journey to death, after the murder of Tulkinghorn has revealed her secret, which is the most elaborate dramatization of this kind of disintegration. The chase after Lady Dedlock by Bucket and Esther is not simply a Victorian melodrama. It is a subtly symbolic dramatization of the destiny of Lady Dedlock and of her relation to her daughter. Once her "freezing mood" is melted, she rapidly becomes, like Poe's mesmerized man when his trance is broken, what she has really been all along: dead. The thawing snow, the change of direction from a centrifugal flight outward from the city to a return to the center of disintegration and corruption where her dead lover lies buried, her disguise in the dress of a brickmaker's wife whose baby has died, all these function symbolically. Here, more intensely than for any other character, we experience the descent into formlessness which follows inevitably the failure to achieve a proper relation to the onward motion of time.

Bucket's chase after Lady Dedlock is presented through Esther's eyes. All that happens has for her a visionary, dreamlike quality: "I was far from sure that I was not in a dream" (57); ". . . the stained house fronts put on human shapes and looked at me; . . . great water-gates seemed to be opening and closing in my head, or in the air; . . . the unreal things were more substantial than the real" (59). The dominant symbol of the whole sequence is contained here in the image of water-gates opening and closing. The process of Lady Dedlock's dying after her freezing mood has broken is mirrored in nature itself in the melting snow which lies everywhere that night: "From the portico, from the eaves, from the parapet, from every ledge and post and pillar, drips the thawed snow. It has crept, as if for shelter, into the lintels of the great door — under it, into the corners of the windows, into every chink and crevice of retreat, and there wastes and dies" (58).

At the center of all this melting is perhaps the river, which is reached by a "labyrinth of streets" (57). There, Bucket fears, Lady Dedlock may be found: ". . . he gazed into the profound black pit of water, with a face that made my heart die within me. The river had a fearful look, so overcast and secret, creeping away so fast between the low flat lines of shore: so heavy with indistinct and awful shapes, both of substance and shadow: so deathlike and mysterious" (57). But the real center, reached by "descending into a deeper complication of such streets" (59), is the pauper graveyard, the low point into which all things are resolving, the center of anonymity, putrefaction, and formlessness, the point at which Lady Dedlock at last becomes herself at the very moment of her death: "The gate was closed. Beyond it, was a burial-ground — a dreadful spot in which the night was very slowly stirring; but where I could dimly see heaps of dishonoured graves and stones, hemmed in by filthy houses, with a few dull lights in their windows, and on whose walls a thick humidity broke out like a disease. On the step at the gate, drenched in the fearful wet of such a place, which oozed and splashed down everywhere, I saw, with a cry of pity and horror, a woman lying — Jenny, the mother of the dead child" (59). But the woman is, of course, really Lady Dedlock, herself the mother of a dead child, the child Esther might have been. That Lady Dedlock's death is in a way a liberation is suggested by her contrary movements during her flight out from the city and then back toward its dark center. At the extremity of her outward flight she sends her surrogate, the brickmaker's wife, on out into the open country to lead her pursuers astray. This woman, in her movement toward freedom and openness, is Lady Dedlock's representative only because Lady Dedlock herself voluntarily chooses to return to her destined death at Nemo's grave, or, rather, to her death at a place where she is still shut off by one final symbolic barrier, the closed gate, from union with her dead lover. In assuming at last the self she has been fleeing for so long, Lady Dedlock achieves the only kind of freedom possible in Dickens' world, the freedom to be one's destined self, the Kierkegaardian freedom to will to accept oneself as what one already irrevocably is.

But for most of the characters, even such a narrow freedom is not possible. Their decomposition happens to them, rather than being chosen, and the image for their final end is not even permitted the hint of life-giving regeneration suggested by Lady Dedlock's melting from her frozen state. Their lives are single cases of a vast process of disintegration into dust, and the entire world of the novel is being transformed into "ashes . . . falling on ashes, and dust on dust" (39):

In his lowering magazine of dust, the universal article into which his papers and himself, and all his clients, and all things of earth, animate and inanimate, are resolving, Mr. Tulkinghorn sits at one of the open windows . . . . (22)

## IV

I think the business of art is to lay all that ground carefully, not with the care that conceals itself — to show, by a backward light, what everything has been working to — but only to *suggest,* until the fulfilment comes. These are the ways of Providence, of which ways all art is but a little imitation.

(Letter to Collins, *Let.,* III, 125)

The world of *Bleak House* at first seemed to be a collection of unrelated fragments plunged into an ubiquitous fog. Then we recognized the presence, in isolated centers, of repetitive sameness. Now both recognitions have been replaced by the vision of an omnipresent decomposition, going forward steadily, and, it seems, irreversibly, everywhere in the world. Is there any "open window"? Is there any possibility of escape from this universal process, or are all the characters, without exception, doomed to experience no other life but the slow, steady moldering away of their existences, as they helplessly drift toward a final dissolution?

This process of dissolution is not really, we come to see, the result of the self-enclosure of each individual life or each isolated circle of society. It comes rather from the absence of moral relationship between people in the novel. In one sense this absence leaves the characters isolated in the self-destructive depreciation of their beings, but in another sense it leaves them at the mercy of impersonal, unintentional contact with one another. For Dickens, the world is one unified whole, and if the relations between one man and another and between man and the world are not beneficent, they will be harmful. No man can cut himself off from the world and from other people. At first apparently a world of truncated fragments, *Bleak House* turns out to be a world in which everything is intimately connected with everything else, both temporally and spatially. Even people who seem to be separated by great gulfs of space, time, or social status actually have the most decisive effect on one another's lives. The world of *Bleak House* is a vast interlocking system in which any action or change in one place will have a corresponding and reciprocal effect on every other place:

On the coincidences, resemblances, and surprises of life, Dickens liked especially to dwell, and few things moved his fancy so pleasantly. The world, he would say, was so much smaller than we thought it; we were all so connected by fate without knowing it; people supposed to be far apart were so constantly elbowing each other; and to-morrow bore so close a resemblance to nothing half so much as to yesterday.[7]

". . . the whole bileing of people was mixed up in the same business, and no other." (59)

What connexion can there be, between the place in Lincolnshire, the house in town, the Mercury in powder, and the whereabout of Jo the outlaw with the broom, who had that distant ray of light upon him when he swept the church-yard-step? What connexion can there have been between many people in the innumerable histories of this world, who, from opposite sides of great gulfs, have, nevertheless, been very curiously brought together! (16)

[7] John Forster, *Life of Dickens*, I (Philadelphia, 1873), 112. This passage is discussed by T. S. Eliot in his excellent essay on melodrama in Dickens and Collins: "Wilkie Collins and Dickens," *Selected Essays: 1917–1932* (New York, 1947), p. 378.

This determining contact of people with one another is not abstract and distant, like Mrs. Jellyby's "telescopic philanthropy," or the apparent relation of suitors to the law. It is immediate and intimate, between one person and another, not between person and institution, or between person and person via institution. Mrs. Jellyby's real action in the world is her destructive effect on her husband and children, not her charity to the natives of Borrioboola-Gha, just as Skimpole's real action is on his neglected family, and Lady Dedlock's is on the child she has unwittingly abandoned. This unintentional effect on things and people who are near is perfectly imaged in Mrs. Pardiggle, who, with her "rapacious benevolence" (8), and her "show that was not conciliatory, of doing charity by wholesale, and of dealing in it to a large extent" (8), has the strange power of upsetting things in any room she enters: ". . . she knocked down little chairs with her skirts that were quite a great way off" (8).

*Bleak House* nevertheless contains many cases of an apparently mechanical and impersonal liaison between people who are either ignorant of one another, or who voluntarily refuse responsibility for one another. Skimpole might be speaking for almost all the characters when he says: "I never was responsible in my life — I can't be" (37). The effect of this universal abnegation of responsibility is that many of the characters feel themselves to be caught up in a vast mechanical system of which they are the helpless victims. The system is run by laws, but these laws are unfathomable, and what will happen is altogether unpredictable. So Dickens says of Richard Carstone: ". . . the uncertainties and delays of the Chancery suit had imparted to his nature something of the careless spirit of a gamester, who felt that he was part of a great gaming system" (17). The alienation of such characters is to be unable to come face to face with the human beings who have caused their plight. They are coerced into a transformation which is more physical than moral and cannot be resisted by human means:

. . . it is in the subtle poison of such abuses to breed such diseases. His blood is infected, and objects lose their natural aspects in his sight. It is not *his* fault. (35)

"The system! I am told, on all hands, it's the system. I mustn't look to individuals. It's the system. I mustn't go into Court, and say, 'My Lord, I beg to know this from you — is this right or wrong? Have you the face to tell me I have received justice, and therefore am dismissed?' My Lord knows nothing of it. He sits there, to administer the system." (15)

This sense of being destroyed by an impersonal system may make the characters feel that they are destructively involved, as when Esther in her delirium dreams that "strung together somewhere in great black space, there was a flaming necklace, or ring, or starry circle of some kind, of which I was one of the beads!" (35). Instead of being open to a future of possibility and hope, such a character's relationship to the world is a narrow contact with immediate surroundings which absolutely limit and define. But this enclosure in the world may also appear as the experience of being wholly cut off from the world, wholly *un*involved. Some people seem to have been overlooked by a vast apparatus of impersonal institutions and fixed social structures. So, the "strangeness" of Jo's state is simultaneously to be manipulated, pushed around as though he were an animal, and to be utterly ignored: "To be hustled, and jostled, and moved on; and really to feel that it would appear to be perfectly true that I have no business, here, or there, or anywhere; and yet to be perplexed by the consideration that I *am* here somehow, too, and everybody overlooked me until I became the creature that I am!" (16); "He is of no order and no place; neither of the beasts, nor of humanity" (47).

The effect of this mechanical involvement in the world, an involvement which leaves the inner self of the person untouched and isolated, is a further form of alienation. Such characters lose the sense of their own existence. They feel separated from themselves, or feel that their experiences do not happen to them, but merely to "someone." A wide gap opens between the selves who are involved in the world of impersonal institutions, and the selves they really are, and the latter, lacking all contact with the world, dissolve and disappear into a profound inner void. It is a void of which the characters themselves are not even aware. So Skimpole speaks "of himself as if he were not at all his own affair, as if Skimpole were a third person" (6), "as if he had been mentioning a curious little fact about somebody else" (37). He divides himself into two persons, and in a "fantastic way" "[takes] himself under his own protection and argue[s] about that curious person" (43). This self-division is analogous to the impersonal connection between people involved in the Chancery suit, or in telescopic philanthropy. To be so separated from oneself that one's experiences seem to happen to someone else is to be wholly without a proper inherence in the world. And yet such are the pressures of existence that in sheer self-defense some characters adopt this mode of presence-absence in the world. "You talk of yourself as if you were somebody else," says Jarndyce to George Rouncewell, who has been falsely accused of murder. And George answers, "I don't see how an innocent man is to make up his mind to this kind of thing without knocking his head against the walls, unless he takes it in that point of view" (52).

But, even if it is only negative evidence, such modes of existence in *Bleak House* are important proof that the disintegrative process in which so many of the characters are caught is not necessary, but is the result of the absence of moral relationships. If people are not related morally, they will be related amorally in a vast destructive process. The dominating symbol of this unintentional contact between people is disease — the disease which is bred in the "poisoned air" (11) of Tom-all-Alone's, and spreads from Nemo's graveyard to Jo the crossing sweeper, and then to Esther, Lady Dedlock's daughter and Nemo's daughter too. Corruption multiplies itself in the world of *Bleak House,* and disorder spreads, but only in the absence of a restraining human principle of order. If the world is going to pieces, it is man's fault, and the abandoned world will turn on the irresponsible-responsible ones, and take its revenge: "[Tom] has his revenge. Even the winds are his messengers, and they serve him in these hours of darkness. There is not a drop of Tom's corrupted blood but propagates infection and contagion somewhere. . . . There is not an atom of Tom's slime, not a cubic inch of any pestilential gas in which he lives, not one obscenity or degradation about him, not an ignorance, not a wickedness, not a brutality of his committing, but shall work its retribution, through every order of society, up to the proudest of the proud, and to the highest of the high" (46).

The world, then, is in man's hands. If its decomposition is his fault, it is possible that he might be able to reverse this decay and put the world back together. But how and where is he going to get the strength for this constructive and life-giving act? By himself he seems powerless to stop the rotting away of the world, a rotting which eventually involves him too, and makes of the whole earth, human and material, a single system of self-destruction.

But for some few characters just such a rescuing reconstruction of the world seems possible. The world organizes itself around such characters as orderly, stable, and clarified, as an integrated circle of which they are the center. "Everything about you is in perfect order and discipline," says George Rouncewell to his brother the ironmaster (63), and Richard says of Allan Woodcourt: ". . . the place brightens whenever he comes" (51). "You can," he says, "pursue your art for its own sake; and can put your hand upon the plough, and never turn; and can strike a purpose out of anything" (51). To Esther all the "happiness" of her life seems to "[shine] like a light from one central figure" (Jarndyce) (44). And Caddy Jellyby is able to create a happy home for her husband, "striking out" "a natural, wholesome, loving course of industry and perseverance that [is] quite as good as a Mission" (38). But it is Esther herself who provides the best example of this quasi-magical power to organize and sustain the world. Skimpole describes her as "intent upon the perfect working of the whole little orderly system of which [she is] the centre" (37), and she says of herself: "I thought it best to be as useful as I could, and to render what kind services I could, to those immediately about me; and to try to let that circle of duty gradually and naturally expand itself" (8). She is able to succeed in this magnificently. "Ringing" herself into any new situation with a "merry little peal" of her housekeeping keys, she is able with apparent ease to organize and control the world, to reduce it to order. The world yields resistlessly to her volition and action.

he is what Jarndyce calls her: the "little old woman of the Child's . . . Rhyme" who "sweep[s] the cobwebs out of the ky" (8).

The world in Esther's presence, to her vision of it, has another extremely important quality, a quality which it seems altogether to lack for the other characters. To her it appears to e the abiding place of a beneficent Providence whose strength he shares, and who orders all the world and every event of her fe in the kindly manipulation of her destiny. For her, the world openly reveals its secret spiritual power. This openness, his depth and clarity, and the visible presence in them of an immanent deity, are the keynotes of the scenic perspectives we e through her eyes:

We had one favourite spot, deep in moss and last year's leaves, here there were some felled trees from which the bark was all ripped off. Seated among these, we looked through a green vista pported by thousands of natural columns, the whitened stems of ees, upon a distant prospect made so radiant by its contrast with e shade in which we sat, and made so precious by the arched perective through which we saw it, that it was like a glimpse of the etter land. (18)

O, the solemn woods over which the light and shadow travelled viftly, as if Heavenly wings were sweeping on benignant errands rough the summer air . . . . (18)

The divine power is not simply there in nature, glimpsed by sther as a kind of unattainable transcendence which remains a distance. Rather, it is felt as something close and intimate, esent as much in her own life as in nature. It is immanent id near, and sustains her with its friendly power: "It was and . . . to hear the solemn thunder, and to see the lighting; and while thinking with awe of the tremendous powers which our little lives are encompassed, to consider how beficent they are, and how upon the smallest flower and leaf ere was already a freshness poured from all this seeming rage, hich seemed to make creation new again" (18). This storm the occasion of Esther's first direct contact with her mother. is as though God had intended the storm, and had intended the storms of suffering too that are to make Esther a new person, recreate her as a different self. It is not by accident that Esther's visions of openings in the prospect which reveal a providential presence are in many cases views of Chesney Wold. For it is just in her relationship to her mother and to Chesney Wold that Providence seems to be most clearly working in Esther's life: "I saw very well," she says, "how many things had worked together, for my welfare . . . . I knew I was as innocent of my birth as a queen of hers; and that before my Heavenly Father I should not be punished for birth nor a queen rewarded for it" (36).

Moreover, Esther is able to draw strength from Providence. She is able through prayer to feel, at crucial moments of her life, that divine grace has descended into her own being, and has made it possible for her to endure her life and carry on her work as a bringer of light and order:

I repeated the old childish prayer in its old childish words, and found that its old peace had not departed from it. (35)

I opened my grateful heart to Heaven in thankfulness for its Providence to me and its care of me, and fell asleep. (17)

Esther's power to create a circle of order and meaning around her does not, then, come from herself, but from the God who appears present to her everywhere in the world and in her own life. But does this immanent deity appear in the world to the other characters? Does He appear to the narrator in those times when he withdraws from the human actions he is describing and surveys the world as a totality and as something in which no human consciousness but his own detached awareness is active?

The answer is easy to give. To the cool, uninvolved gaze of the narrator, the world appears again and again as the dwelling place of a light which is rapidly, at this very moment, fading away, withdrawing to an infinite distance, and leaving the world to absolute darkness: "Darkness rests upon Tom-all-Alone's. Dilating and dilating since the sun went down last night, it has gradually swelled until it fills every void in the place. . . . The blackest nightmare in the infernal stables grazes on Tom-all-Alone's, and Tom is fast asleep" (46). And, strangely enough, the narrator has this frightening vision of a world being transformed to formless darkness when perceiving the very scene which brought Esther her apprehension of an immanent Providence. This darkness is seen as the emblem of Lady Dedlock's life, not of Esther's:

. . . the light of the drawing-room seems gradually contracting and dwindling until it shall be no more. (66)

But the fire of the sun is dying. Even now the floor is dusky, and shadow slowly mounts the walls, bringing the Dedlocks down like age and death. And now, upon my lady's picture over the great chimney-piece, a weird shade falls from some old tree, that turns it pale, and flutters it, and looks as if a great arm held a veil or hood, watching an opportunity to draw it over her. Higher and darker rises shadow on the wall — now a red gloom on the ceiling — now the fire is out. (40)

If the narrator sees the light of a spiritual presence at all, he glimpses it precisely as a transcendence rather than as an immanence. It is seen as an inhumanly distant power which refuses, or is unable, to relate itself to the world, and either hovers motionlessly, tantalizingly unattainable, or is caught momentarily in the very act of withdrawing: "All that prospect, which from the terrace looked so near, has moved solemnly away, and changed — not the first nor the last of beautiful things that look so near and will so change — into a distant phantom" (40).

If this receding transcendence enters the human world at all, it enters to renew it by rest, by bringing it a momentary repose. That is to say, to the narrator's eye, it seems that the transcendent light is so incommensurate with the nature of human existence in a corrupt world, that it can only come into this world by bringing a temporary end to that existence, an end of sleep, rest, and forgetfulness which is a rehearsal of death. The world is at peace, it is the presence rather than the absence of God, only when there is no human consciousness left awake to endure awareness of the pain of living, or only a single human consciousness, the consciousness of a watcher who is altogether uninvolved in the world, seeing it in a pure lucidity of perception:

When the moon shines very brilliantly, a solitude and stillness seem to proceed from her, that influence even crowded places full of life. Not only is it a still night on dusty high roads and on hill-summits, whence a wide expanse of country may be seen in repose, quieter and quieter as it spreads away into a fringe of trees against the sky, with the grey ghost of a bloom upon them; . . . not only is it a still night on the deep, and on the shore where the watcher stands to see the ship with her spread wings cross the path of light that appears to be presented to only him; but even on this stranger's wilderness of London there is some rest. (48)

But this presence of a repose which emanates from a divine source is also an absence. It is the total absence of ordinary day-light life. God appears only when the world is seen for a moment from the viewpoint of utter solitude, only when the path of light appears to be presented to a single watcher. This solitary watching is as close as any human being can come to see-ing the world as it would appear if there were no human con-sciousness present in it at all. If man is present as involved in the world, as manipulating it for his own ends, God disappears. If man withdraws from the world, God appears, but only as something wholly foreign to man, as something which is fright-ening proof of man's nonentity. This vision of a world without human presence is seen at Chesney Wold when "the great house, needing habitation more than ever, is like a body with-out life" (40), when there is "no family to come and go, no vis-itors to be the souls of pale cold shapes of rooms" (66). But in the absence of human beings who might give "souls" to inani-mate objects, an inhuman presence appears, a cold light whose life is more disquieting than the complete death of the unin-habited house would have been: "The clear cold sunshine glances into the brittle woods, and approvingly beholds the sharp wind scattering the leaves and drying the moss. It glides over the park after the moving shadows of the clouds, and chases them, and never catches them, all day. It looks in at the windows, and touches the ancestral portraits with bars and patches of brightness, never contemplated by the painters"

(12). At such a time, when the world is seen without a human presence, "it is . . . awful, stealing through [the house], to think of the live people who have slept in the solitary bedrooms: to say nothing of the dead" (40). It is awful to think of the live people because, in their absence, one recognizes suddenly that they are in a way absent even when they are present. One sees that the living are, from the point of view of the transcendent light, or of the wholly detached spectator, the exact equivalent of the dead. The nothingness of human existence appears, then, at the very moment when the existence of some transhuman spirit is recognized. Man and God seem to be altogether incompatible, to cancel one another out. So, in a striking passage, Dickens shows us a Chesney Wold without any inhabitant at all but the pictured forms on the walls, and suggests that the presence of a living Sir Leicester would not change the scene. For a moment the small difference that a human presence seems to make dissolves into complete nothingness. If men "leave no blank to miss them" when they die, are they not really that same blank when they are alive? "Dreary and solemn the old house looks, with so many appliances of habitation, and with no inhabitants except the pictured forms upon the walls. So did these come and go, a Dedlock in possession might have ruminated passing along; so did they see this gallery hushed and quiet, as I see it now; so think, as I think, of the gap that they would make in this domain when they were gone; so find it, as I find it, difficult to believe that it could be, without them; so pass from my world, as I pass from theirs, now closing the reverberating door; so leave no blank to miss them, and so die" (40). The narrator's detached observation of the world leads in *Bleak House,* as in *Martin Chuzzlewit,* but in a different way, to a discovery of the essential nothingness of the human spirit. Here the discovery is posited on the idea of death, a death which somehow moves from its position as the end point of a long life, and undermines, hollows out, that life itself.

Does this mean that Esther's sense of an intimate contact between her life and Providence is a fiction, that she merely thinks she sees something which is not really there at all? Does this mean that the presence of Esther to a world which she makes orderly is necessarily dependent on the absence of God from all that she does? Is it wholly impossible for human action to install God in the world, to bring Him into the world and to keep Him there as its foundation and justification? Apparently so.

And yet the narrator, precisely because of his solitude, is not only able to see the brightness of the divine presence; he is also able to see the human world of the novel in its light. He can identify himself with its perspective, as when he praises Sir Leicester for his fidelity to Lady Dedlock: "His noble earnestness, his fidelity, his gallant shielding of her, his generous conquest of his own wrong and his own pride for her sake, are simply honourable, manly, and true. Nothing less worthy can be seen through the lustre of such qualities in the commonest mechanic, nothing less worthy can be seen in the best-born gentleman. In such a light both aspire alike, both rise alike, both children of the dust shine equally" (58). To see a human action or event from this point of view is to see it in terms of the nullity of all social distinctions, of all worldly values. If it is not to see the divine transcendence as inherent in the social world, it is at least to see that human actions may have some value for this transcendence. It is to see the world from the viewpoint of a total disengagement from all earthly aims and expectations, a disengagement which allows true values suddenly to appear. Are there any characters in *Bleak House* who achieve this disengagement and this clarification?

Just such clarifications occur for Jo and for Richard Carstone at the moment of their deaths. ". . . he is," Chadband says of Jo, "devoid of the light that shines in upon some of us. What is that light? What is it? I ask you what is that light?" (25). This light, Dickens tells us, is what would appear "if the Chadbands, removing their own persons from the light, would but show it thee in simple reverence" (25). As he lies dying Jo says, "It's turned wery dark, sir," and asks, "Is there any light a-comin?" And at the moment of Jo's death, when he has left this obscure world altogether, Dickens says of him: "The light is come upon the dark benighted way" (47).

For Richard Carstone, this clarification comes just before his death, while he is still momentarily in the human world. His blindness has been precisely his infatuation, "the clouded, eager, seeking look" (37) that went with having "no care, no mind, no heart, no soul, but for one thing" (45). But, like Racine's Phèdre, Richard is permitted a few moments of clear vision just before he dies, moments which are possible only because he has been liberated from his infatuation by the fatal ending of the suit. Now he can see that his life has been "a troubled dream" (65), and Jarndyce can say for him: ". . . the clouds have cleared away, and it is bright now. We can see now. We were all bewildered, . . . more or less" (65). Richard feels that he is now at last able to "begin the world," but of course it is too late, and the world he begins is "not this world." It is "the world that sets this right" (65).

The light, we recognize, appears only to those people who for some reason have abandoned all hope in an earthly judgment. Only such people can relate themselves to the true Justice, can make that Justice come into being for this world. This reversal is a double one. By being disabused of a narrow, enclosed faith in the world, the characters achieve a clarification, a breadth of view which is in a sense an appropriation of the world. It is Esther's good fortune to be already, at the beginning of her life, because of the social alienation of her illegitimacy (strongly impressed upon her by her foster mother), disengaged from the social world and unblinded by any false expectations from it.

In *Bleak House,* then, Dickens shows the possibility of a truly moral life. In the early novels the choices were passive expectancy or selfish activity. To act was, except for semi-divine human providences, like Mr. Brownlow or old Martin Chuzzlewit, inevitably to act immorally, to impose a rigorous and coercive form on the world and on other people. It was to deceive them, and to be either self-deceived or consciously deceiving. Now, in *Bleak House,* Dickens goes beyond this. He sees that there is something between these two extremes, that there is a way in which human beings can act morally. Between the two extremes of a passivity which allows the world to return to primeval slime, or a rigid and coercive will which imposes an inhuman fixity on the world, there is glimpsed the possibility of a voluntary action which constitutes the world as an order. The premise for this possibility is the idea that human beings inhere in the world, that man and the world participate in one another. It is only because human beings are detached from the world that it appears fragmentary and disconnected. Moreover, if human beings detach themselves from the world, it will become more and more disordered and fragmentary.

And there is a true Providence in *Bleak House*. It does not, however, work within things, nor does it work within all men, nor in any man all of the time. It appears to be intermittent even though it may secretly be continuous. It is only after this grace and the responsibility someone takes to accept it have permitted the creation of a limited circle of duty that this enclosed place can be seen as orderly and intelligible, can be seen as providential. Providence is powerless to work in things for man and can only work through the heart of man himself. God has withdrawn himself from the world of *Bleak House*. He apparently does not exist immanently within things as an ubiquitous Providence ordering all events for good in mysterious ways. He does not exist in many events at all. He has left the human world and the objective world to human beings. It is their responsibility.

But what sort of voluntary action will succeed in bringing God to earth? It is not a question of forming a rigid plan and coercively carrying it out by forceful action. It is much easier to misuse the will than to use it correctly. The will, for Dickens must always act in accordance with the nature of things as they already are. Each person is thrown into a world and into a situation in the world which he has not chosen. All his attempts to deny this, to reject the nature of the world as it is, are doomed to failure. Too much will, the inhumanly fixed will of Lady Dedlock and Tulkinghorn or of Sir Leicester's conservatism, attempts to hold the world to an inhuman permanence. The will cannot act in this positive way. On the other hand, the alternative of no will, of mere passive expectation, such as we find in Miss Flite, Skimpole, or Richard Carstone, is no more effective. Richard's failure is a failure, precisely, of will. "I shall have to work my own way," he says, echoing Jarndyce, who had said, ". . . he must make some choice for himself" (8). But instead of choosing and acting he "build[s] as many castles in the air as would man the great wall of China" (14). He is continually wiping the slate clean of all that he has done so far, and continually deciding to "make a clear beginning altogether" (24). He is like Mr. Jellyby, who "sometimes half took his coat off, as if with an intention of helping by a great exertion; but he never got any further. His sole occupation was to sit with his head against the wall . . ." (50). But, just as it is fatal to expect a judgment from the human court, so it is equally fatal to expect God to do it all. God helps those who help themselves. "Trust in nothing," says Jarndyce, "but in Providence and your own efforts" (13). To trust either of these separately will fail. God's grace can operate only through those who, like Esther and Jarndyce, take matters into their own hands.

The extremes of violent frontal attack and passive expectancy inevitably fail. Just what form, then, must this shouldering of responsibility take to be successful? It is not machinery, not the actual doing or making of anything. Esther's creation of a small area of order and significance around her is primarily a spiritual act. The human will must accept the fact that its action must be continuous and perpetual. The world must be held together from moment to moment. Esther's success comes from the fact that she submits to the human condition which she so vividly imagines in her delirious dream: ". . . I laboured up colossal staircases, ever striving to reach the top, and ever turned, as I have seen a worm in a garden path, by some obstruction, and labouring again" (35). The human will must act negatively rather than coercively and positively. It must act by a yielding to time and to tradition, rather than through an attempt to freeze the former or break from the latter.

The nature and results of this yielding can be seen in the good households in the novel. The good household possesses the orderly multiplicity and diversity of Bleak House, with its many rooms and passages, its "quaint variety" (6), its continual surprises: "It was one of those delightfully irregular houses where you go up and down steps out of one room into another, and where you come upon more rooms when you think you have seen all there are, and where there is a bountiful provision of little halls and passages, and where you find still older cottage-rooms in unexpected places, with lattice windows and green growth pressing through them" (6). Such a "pleasantly irregular" house allows full room for the freedom and privacy of those living there. And yet, though there is no sense of a mechanical regimen, everything is orderly and planned.

The temporal existence of such a household will be like that of Boythorn's dwelling, which is very unlike Boythorn himself. His milieu is a world of repose, but not of paralyzed fixity. Its temporal duration is a slow maturing which is the very opposite of the process of disintegration accelerating toward death which is so nearly ubiquitous in *Bleak House*. Rather than being the loss of utility and value in the part and of structure in the whole, it is a progressive enrichment through time. Nothing of the past is lost. The past still exists as the enhancement of the present, and the present therefore contains an inexhaustible multiplicity and abundance. The temporal dimension of Boythorn's house is an almost organic growth in which the past exists not only as the outward signs of fruitfulness and life, but as an inward warmth which is the stored up vitality of long years. It is a world of mellowness and plenitude:

He lived in a pretty house, formerly the Parsonage-house, with a lawn in front, a bright flower-garden at the side, and a well-stocked orchard and kitchen-garden in the rear, enclosed with a venerable wall that had of itself a ripened ruddy look. But, indeed, everything about the place wore an aspect of maturity and abundance. . . . [T]he very shadows of the cherry-trees and apple-trees were heavy with fruit, the gooseberry-bushes were so laden that their branches arched and rested on the earth, the strawberries and raspberries grew in like profusion, and the peaches basked by the hundred on the wall. . . . [T]here were such heaps of drooping pods, and marrows, and cucumbers, that every foot of ground appeared a vegetable treasury . . . . [T]he wall had such a ripening influence that where, here and there high up, a disused nail and scrap of list still clung to it, it was easy to fancy that they had mellowed with the changing seasons, and that they had rusted and decayed according to the common fate. (18)

But the "common fate" here is not, like the fate of the suitors in Chancery, to be slowly used up and destroyed. Even the rusting of nails and the decay of wood is, within Boythorn's precincts, the accretion of value, an organic growth and maturing, rather than a dissolution.

With such a yielding to time's maturing movement goes a reverence for the past which makes of the present a living repetition of the past. Such are the celebrations of Mrs. Bagnet's birthdays. These celebrations are a repeated ceremony through which value is gained rather than emptied out: "The auspicious event is always commemorated according to certain forms, settled and prescribed by Mr. Bagnet some years since" (49). Mrs. Bagnet herself, like the family community of which she is the center, "is like a thoroughly fine day. Gets finer as she gets on" (27). And the entire Bagnet household, as the result of a constant maintaining of "discipline," the continual renewal of a constructive activity which is based on family love and solidarity, is a model of order and cleanliness (27).

But for Esther the moral and orderly world must be created rather than accepted from the past. In the necessary conditions of this creation we can see another form of the theme of repetition after an intervening gap which we found to be so important in *Oliver Twist* and *Martin Chuzzlewit*. Nothing is more striking in Dickens than the way many characters who are freed from traditional morality or from a determined place in society simply reaffirm a traditional and narrow morality. Their only freedom is to have chosen this morality rather than having had it imposed upon them by force. The simplicity, the timidity, the conservatism, the domesticity, of the moral life of many of Dickens' good characters, all testify to Dickens' fear of a moral life of breadth, imagination, or novelty. Dickens sometimes seems to believe that only with this narrowness is the moral life likely to be successful. In a way Esther is, like Tom

Pinch in *Martin Chuzzlewit,* seen from the outside by some-one who recognizes her as an ideal, but as a limited ideal. It is an ideal which is impossible for the narrator because he is not so innocent as she is, because he is able to juxtapose her world against all the other worlds of the other characters, and against his own neutral, fragmented, optic world. There is, then, a subtle irony in Dickens' attitude toward Esther as narrator. He does not wholly identify himself with her experience or judg-ment. The acceptance of the bourgeois Protestant ethical prin-ciples of duty, public service, domesticity, responsibility, fru-gality, thrift, cleanliness, orderliness, and self-discipline is qualified and in a way undermined by the juxtaposition of the two modes of narration. The suggestion is that the world can only be seen as Esther sees it, as moral, as containing an imma-nent Providence, through her eyes. The narrator cannot see the world in this way through his own neutral point of view. More-over, in Lady Dedlock, Dickens presents someone who has had a chance at the broad, imaginative moral life with all its com-plexities. But Lady Dedlock's struggles with the kind of moral problems which will command the center of Henry James' novels, and even of Meredith's, are only at the periphery of *Bleak House.* Her real decision has taken place long before the novel begins. And she is, of course, destroyed by the ambiguous moral position into which she has put herself by first becoming the lover of Captain Hawdon and then marrying Sir Leicester. For Esther, the moral life is simpler, the world yields more easily to spirit, than is shown to be the case by the novel as a whole. For Esther duty, kindness, self-sacrifice make the world orderly, and in the end everything she has given up is given back to her. But for Lady Dedlock, who has made a break-through to a complex, ambiguous, moral world, things are not so easy. Things are for her impossible of solution. To Dickens the fear of a broad, imaginative, daring moral life seems to have presented itself as a sense that the will would find great diffi-culty in operating at all, or in operating other than destruc-tively, once it was liberated into self-consciousness. Therefore the unself-conscious, instinctive goodness of Esther seemed to him the only possibility.

But it was absolutely necessary, for Dickens, that Esther should be free to reaffirm this narrow and conventional morality. Against the dead duration of the Smallweeds, which is a hypnotized repetition, or the progressive duration of Richard or Gridley, which is a single curve of descent deeper and deeper into the pit of darkness, or the reaffirmation of her true self by Lady Dedlock, which necessarily coincides with her death, there is the radically transforming discovery of her true self by Esther. As opposed to the other characters, Esther's historical existence is a truly dramatic progression with a climax centering on the reversal of her orientation when she discovers her origin, and on her liberation into an authentic life when she chooses to accept the self she finds herself to be. Her "reiteration" of herself, like Oliver's and Martin's, is broken by a long interval of separation from herself, a separation which is not, like Lady Dedlock's, voluntary, but is caused by her real ignorance of who she is.

But Esther is not wholly self-sufficient. Her final happiness depends on the existence of two people who are, as she is, free from any faith in society and its values, and who choose to act morally toward her. The marriage of Allan and Esther is the marriage of two people who have no imposed ties with one another, and who freely choose one another. Final happiness for Esther can come not through her own efforts alone, but through Allan Woodcourt's voluntary surrender of all social determination of his choice of a wife. It is the liberating act of love. But even love does not break the law of Dickens' moral world which says that there is no ceasing to be the self one already is, no transformation with impunity into an entirely new self. Allan's love transforms Esther not by making her cease to be illegitimate and therefore socially alienated, but by choosing her as she is. The novel ends with a scene in which Allan tells Esther that the disfiguration of her face, caused by her illness, and the symbolic sign of her illegitimacy, has made her "prettier than [she] ever [was]" (67). The full presentation of this theme is, however, obscured by the role of Jarndyce. He sacrifices his claim on Esther, and, like old Martin Chuzzlewit, gives the lovers to one another, and sets them up in a new

Bleak House which is an exact repetition of the old. He thus makes it unnecessary for the lovers to accept full responsibility for their asocial act. But Woodcourt's choice of Esther, like Lady Dedlock's and Esther's choice of themselves, is an act of free volition. Dickens has now come to recognize that salvation cannot possibly come through mere passive waiting and the eventual acceptance of an identity and a place in the world given from the outside. It comes, Dickens sees now, only through an act of voluntary liberation. But this all-important act of will may turn out to be extremely difficult, as *Little Dorrit* is brilliantly to show.

## Chapter VII

# HARD TIMES

# LITTLE DORRIT

# A TALE OF TWO CITIES

Between *Bleak House* and *Great Expectations* Dickens wrote three novels: *Hard Times, Little Dorrit,* and *A Tale of Two Cities. Hard Times* and *Little Dorrit,* especially the latter, are among his finest novels. Considerations of space, however, make full discussion of them impossible here. *Little Dorrit* stands between *Bleak House* and *Our Mutual Friend* as the second of Dickens' three great panoramic novels. Each of these novels presents a broad picture of all levels of society and their interactions. *Little Dorrit* repeats with differences many of the themes and symbols of *Bleak House.* Like the latter it shows a civilization in which people are at once enclosed blindly within their own lives and at the same time inextricably involved, often without knowing it, in the destinies of those around them. But *Little Dorrit* in many ways goes beyond its predecessors in its analysis of the conditions of life of commercial and urban man, and in the symbolic unity of its conception. In the discussion here of *Little Dorrit,* and in briefer remarks about *Hard Times* and *A Tale of Two Cities,* I shall attempt to identify the elements in these novels which represent an advance beyond *Bleak House.*

Each of these three novels is concerned with the conflict between two forms of relationship: relation to society, and direct, intimate relation to other individuals. In all three the choice of the relation to society as a source of selfhood is shown to fail, and to lead rather to the loss of identity. Society turns out to be a fraud (like the Merdle enterprises in *Little Dorrit*). It breaks beneath the pressure put on it by the individual, and reveals its nonentity. Society is only a projection of the selfish desires of individuals; it is all too human. Society is fictive, a game of false appearances, and he who puts confidence in it is absorbed into its unreality. But this brittle façade has power too, and the elaborate machinery of a false civilization can enslave the individual, turn him into an object. Against this destructive relation Dickens sets an increasingly profound analysis of the mystery of a direct relation between two people without intermediary: the relation of love.

I

In *Hard Times* Dickens dramatizes in strikingly symbolic terms the opposition between a soul-destroying relation to a utilitarian, industrial civilization (in which everything is weighed, measured, has its price, and in which emotion is banished), and the reciprocal interchange of love. If the perpetually clanking machinery of the Coketown mills, which turns men into "hands," is the symbol of one, the "horse-riding," as in Picasso's *Saltimbanques,* is the dominant symbol of the other: "The father of one of the families was in the habit of balancing the father of another of the families on the top of a great pole; the father of a third family often made a pyramid of both those fathers, with Master Kidderminster for the apex, and himself for the base . . . . They all assumed to be mighty rakish and knowing, they were not very tidy in their private dresses, they were not at all orderly in their domestic arrangements, and the combined literature of the whole company would have produced but a poor letter on any subject. Yet there was a remarkable gentleness and childishness about these people, a special inaptitude for any kind of sharp practice, and an untiring readiness to help and pity one another . . ." (I, 6). But the circus here is still only a symbol of a good *society,* that is, of communion around a third thing, the "act." In this relation contact with others is still in a way impersonal, and the individual is still defined by his role, by his cooperative submission to a common activity and goal. In the circus act, as in even the best society, the otherness of other people tends to be submerged.

II

*Little Dorrit* is without doubt Dickens' darkest novel. No other of his novels has such a somber unity of tone. Though we move from house to house and from one extremity of society to the other we never lose for more than a moment the sense of shadowed, suffocating enclosure which oppresses us from the beginning. Mrs. Clennam's gloomy house in London, the Marshalsea prison, Casby's stuffy, silent house — ". . . one might have fancied it to have been stifled by Mutes in the Eastern manner" (I, 13) — Miss Wade's dreary apartment in Calais, the fashionable homes of the Merdles, Barnacles or Sparklers, all "stuffed and close" and smelly (II, 24), all these milieus simply repeat with variations the interior of the "villainous prison" in Marseilles to which we are introduced in the opening pages of the novel.

But one does not need to be within doors to experience this feeling of suffocating enclosure. The entire city of London is itself a prison, and keeps off the freedom and purity of the country air as completely as do the walls of the Marshalsea. We are introduced to the real scene of the novel in the description of Arthur Clennam's return to London after a twenty year absence. It is a passage whose powerful picture of the gloom of the city and the despair of people within it is Baudelairean in its intensity (and indeed parallels many of the key images of Baudelaire's dark city scenes):

It was a Sunday evening in London, gloomy, close and stale. Maddening church bells of all degrees of dissonance, sharp and flat, cracked and clear, fast and slow, made the brick-and-mortar echoes hideous. Melancholy streets in a penitential garb of soot, steeped the souls of the people who were condemned to look at them out of windows, in dire despondency. In every thoroughfare, up almost every alley, and down almost every turning, some doleful bell was throbbing, jerking, tolling, as if the Plague were in the city and the dead-carts were going round. Everything was bolted and barred that could by possibility furnish relief to an overworked people. . . . Nothing to see but streets, streets, streets. Nothing to breathe but streets, streets, streets. Nothing to change the brooding mind, or raise it up. . . .

Ten thousand responsible houses surrounded [Arthur Clennam], frowning . . . heavily on the streets they composed . . . . Fifty thousand lairs surrounded him where people lived so unwholesomely, that fair water put into their crowded rooms on Saturday night, would be corrupt on Sunday morning . . . . Miles of close wells and pits of houses, where the inhabitants gasped for air, stretched far away towards every point of the compass. Through the heart of the town a deadly sewer ebbed and flowed, in the place of a fine fresh river. . . .

He sat in the same place as the day died, looking at the dull houses opposite, and thinking, if the disembodied spirits of former inhabitants were ever conscious of them, how they must pity themselves for their old places of imprisonment. Sometimes a face would appear behind the dingy glass of a window, and would fade away into the gloom as if it had seen enough of life and had vanished out of it. Presently the rain began to fall in slanting lines between him and those houses, and people began to collect under cover of the public passage opposite, and to look out hopelessly at the sky as the rain dropped thicker and faster. (I, 3)

Dickens, then, has found for this novel a profound symbol for the universal condition of life in the world of his imagination: imprisonment. The enclosure, the narrowness, the blindness, of the lives of most of the characters in all Dickens' novels receive here their most dramatic expression. And, lest we should imagine that this condition is really peculiar to one time or place or kind of civilization, Dickens in one passage explicitly defines human life in any place or time as imprisonment: "aslant across the city, over its jumbled roofs, and through the open tracery of its church towers, struck the long bright rays [of the early morning sun], bars of the prison of this lower world" (II, 30). All the world's a prison, and even the bright sunshine itself is only a barrier cutting this lower world off from heaven. Imprisonment has, we can see, a religious or metaphysical meaning for Dickens as well as a psychological or social one. To be in this world at all, whether one is good or bad, rich or poor, a lord of the Circumlocution Office or a debtor in the Marshalsea, is to be in prison, and this condition will apparently persist as long as life itself.

But, even in its psychological or social context, imprisonment is in *Little Dorrit* not simply a powerful symbol of enclosure or limitation imposed from without by an indifferent or unjust society administering impersonally its absurd or wicked laws. As Edmund Wilson has observed, *Little Dorrit* advances beyond Dickens' earlier novels in the way it shows so persuasively that imprisonment is a state of mind. The word "shadow" is Dickens' key term linking physical imprisonment and imprisoning states of soul. Like the word "gentleman" and the word "secret," the word "shadow" recurs again and again in *Little Dorrit* in the most diverse contexts. These words tie together the lives of all the various characters we meet and remind us that they are all like one another. Each use of the key words reflects on all the others, and eventually these words take on a subtly ironic meaning contracting in a single node all the complex themes of the novel. So the ambiguities of "Society" are defined by the interaction of various uses of the word "gentleman": "Gentleman" is the word the diabolically villainous Blandois uses to describe himself; the Circumlocution Office is a "school for gentlemen" (I, 26); old Dorrit's progressive degradation in the Marshalsea is marked by his increasing insistence on his "forlorn gentility" (I, 7); and after Merdle's suicide the clairvoyant Chief Butler says: "Sir, Mr. Merdle never was the gentleman, and no ungentlemanly act on Mr. Merdle's part would surprise me" (II, 25).[1] And so the

---

[1] When the Chief Butler says Merdle's act is ungentlemanly he implies that it is gentlemanly to be a great thief, but ungenteel to kill yourself when you are found out. This is a variant of Blandois' linking of gentility with criminality or diabolism. It is used in the Chief Butler's case with a dramatic irony which is an effective attack on the "Society" whose opinion the Chief Butler represents. Once again Dickens has dramatized an ironic relation between low-class criminality and upper-class fraud or sham, a relation which recalls that in Gay's *Beggar's Opera*. So Blandois can defend himself by saying: "I sell anything that commands a price. How do your lawyers live, your politicians, your intriguers, your men of the Exchange! . . . Society sells itself and sells me: and I sell Society" (II, 28). And indeed "Bar"

word "secret" is used again and again to express the isolation of
the characters from one another either in their inturned selfishness or in their self-effacing goodness. But "shadow" is the most
frequently recurring of these key words. It is used most obviously to express the literal shadow of the Marshalsea, but it
appears, often metaphorically, in connection with almost all
the characters and eventually we understand that the real
shadow here is "a deeper shadow than the shadow of the
Marshalsea Wall" (II, 19), and that to be "shadowed" by some
sadness or blindness or delusion or deliberate choice of the
worse rather than the better course is the universal condition
of all the dwellers in this prison of a lower world. The
"shadow," then, is spiritual rather than physical. It is only by
recognizing this crucial extension of imprisonment from physical to spiritual incarceration that we can understand, for example, that Mrs. Clennam is as effectively imprisoned within
the walls of her false interpretation of Christianity as Little
Dorrit's father is imprisoned by the walls of the Marshalsea. It
is just as true to say that Mr. Dorrit's literal imprisonment is
only the physical correlative of his imprisonment within the
labyrinth of his own weakness, vacillation, and selfishness as it
is to say that Mrs. Clennam's physical paralysis and enclosure
in her dark house are the expression and result of her mental
condition.

Indeed, all the many forms of imprisonment in this novel
are primarily spiritual rather than physical: Miss Wade's imprisonment within the narrow circle of her sadism toward
others and masochism toward herself; Merdle's suicidal anxiety, evident in his way of oozing "sluggishly and muddily" (II,
12) around the rooms of his luxurious mansion and in his unconsciously symbolic habit of taking himself in custody as if
he were a criminal — which he is; Flora Casby's imprisonment

---

quotes the *Beggar's Opera* itself, with unconscious appositeness, in Mr.
Merdle's drawing room:

> Since laws were made for every degree,
> To curb vice in others as well as in me,
> I wonder we ha'n't better company
> Upon Tyburn Tree (II, 12)

within the mad sequences of her own involuntary mental associations and within the perpetual reënactment of her lost past; Blandois' wicked imprisonment in his idea of himself as a gentleman "by right and by nature" (I, 30); John Chivery's constant anticipation of his own death, comically expressed in his habit of composing epitaphs for his own tombstone; Pancks' slavery to his master, Casby, always conjugating in the present tense, imperative mood, the verb "to keep at it"; Mrs. Merdle's servitude to society; the sprightly Ferdinand Barnacle's willing acquiescence in the sham of the Circumlocution Office; Little Dorrit's brother's corruption by the prison atmosphere, so that "[w]herever he went, this foredoomed Tip appeared to take the prison walls with him, and to set them up in such trade or calling; and to prowl about within their narrow limits in the old slip-shod, purposeless, down-at-heel way . . ." (I, 7).

But the central event of *Little Dorrit* is itself an explicit dramatization of this discovery that imprisonment is not accidental and exterior, but inner and permanent. Little Dorrit's father, after his imprisonment for debt, "languidly [slips] into [a] smooth descent, and never more [takes] one step upward" (I, 6), until finally he reaches a complete state of degradation, "now boasting, now despairing, in either fit a captive with the jail-rot upon him, and the impurity of his prison worn into the grain of his soul" (I, 19). Then suddenly, and just as unpredictably as he was first imprisoned, Dorrit is discovered to be the inheritor of a great fortune, and becomes a free and wealthy man. But his story is not merely another expression of Dickens' notion that life in the city is commanded by incomprehensible forces. Its real significance is defined by Little Dorrit's "sorrowful" acknowledgment "that no space in the life of man could overcome that quarter of a century behind the prison bars" (II, 5). And there is no more poignant or effective expression of the theme of *Little Dorrit* than old Dorrit's dying speech. He suffers a stroke at a fashionable dinner party, and, imagining himself back in the Marshalsea, welcomes the dinner guests to what is symbolically their true abode: "Ladies and gentlemen, the duty — ha — devolves upon me of — hum — welcoming you to the Marshalsea. Welcome to the Marshalsea!

The space is — ha — limited — limited — the parade might be wider; but you will find it apparently grow larger after a time — a time, ladies and gentlemen — and the air is, all things considered, very good" (II, 19).

Old Dorrit, then, does not escape from the Marshalsea when he leaves its walls, and like all the characters in the novel is doomed to carry his prison with him wherever he goes. But the image of static enclosure, the prison cell, is interwoven with two other images which are almost as important as definitions of life in the world of *Little Dorrit:* the image of a labyrinth and the image of life as a journey.

The image of a labyrinth suggests that life is not immobile enclosure but is endless wandering within a maze whose beginning, ending, or pattern cannot be perceived. Since all places within the maze are the same, its prisoner moves freely but without getting anywhere, and without coming any closer to an understanding of his place in the world or of the forces determining his life. So Little Dorrit's Uncle Frederick, who is, people say, "dead without being aware of it" (I, 20), accepts without comprehension "every incident of the labyrinthian world in which he [has] got lost" (I, 19); Miss Wade lives in a "labyrinth" of little stately-melancholy streets near Park Lane (I, 27); and Dickens speaks of "the multiplicity of paths in the labyrinth trodden by the sons of Adam" (II, 12).[2] The image of the labyrinth is Dickens' way of expressing the idea that the human world is an incomprehensible tangle. People find it even more impossible here than in *Bleak House* to understand how things got the way they are or what is the meaning of the present situation. *Little Dorrit* was originally to be called *Nobody's Fault,* which is another way of saying it is everybody's fault, that the sad state of this world is the result of a collective human crime of selfishness, hypocrisy, weakness of will, or

[2] Elsewhere we read of "this labyrinth of a world" (I, 2), of "the gloomy labyrinth of [Mrs. Clennam's] thoughts" (I, 5), of "a maze of shabby streets, which went about and about" (I, 12), of "a labyrinth of bare passages and pillared galleries" (II, 3), and at Pet Meagles' ill-fated marriage we meet Lord Decimus Tite Barnacle "trotting, with the complacency of an idiotic elephant, among howling labyrinths of sentences, which he seemed to take for high roads, and never so much as wanted to get out of" (I, 34).

sham. No specific cause or explanation of any individual's suffering can be found. Thus Mr. Dorrit has no idea how much
money he owes to whom or what he might do to get out of
prison, and Mr. Plornish's perplexed monologue on the life of
the poor and unemployed inhabitants of Bleeding Heart Yard
ends with another version of the image of a labyrinth: "As to
who was to blame for it, Mr. Plornish didn't know who was to
blame for it. He could tell you who suffered, but he couldn't
tell you whose fault it was. It wasn't *his* place to find out, and
who'd mind what he said, if he did find out? He only know'd
that it wasn't put right by them what undertook that line of
business, and that it didn't come right of itself. And in brief his
illogical opinion was, that if you couldn't do nothing for him,
you had better take nothing from him for doing of it; so far as
he could make out, that was about what it come to. Thus, in a
prolix, gently-growling, foolish way, did Plornish turn the tangled skein of his estate about and about, like a blind man who
was trying to find some beginning or end to it . . ." (I, 12).

Little Dorrit creates a disquieting sense of the selfish indifference diffused everywhere in things and people. By making certain characters vessels for the concentration of this guilt, it
allays our terror and gives us something concrete to hate and
fear. Mrs. Clennam, Merdle, Blandois, and Casby are materi-
alizations of this undefined evil, but in *Little Dorrit,* nevertheless, evil exceeds any particularization of it, and we are left at
the end with an undefined and unpurged sense of menace.
The image of the labyrinth is one of Dickens' chief ways of expressing the mystery of evil. The most striking appearance in
*Little Dorrit* of the symbolic labyrinth is the Circumlocution
Office, with its inextricably tangled halls, offices, passageways,
and levels of authority through which Arthur Clennam and
Daniel Doyce meander hopelessly, filling out reams of forms
and making appeal after appeal without coming any closer to a
satisfactory answer to their question: "Numbers of people were
lost in the Circumlocution Office. . . . [T]hey melted away.
In short, all the business of the country went through the Circumlocution Office, except the business that never came out of
it; and *its* name was Legion" (I, 10). As in the stories of Kafka,

though without quite Kafka's deliberate universalization of the labyrinth as a symbol of the metaphysical alienation of man, the individual's relation in *Little Dorrit* to any sort of tangible earthly authority is expressed as an impossible appeal for judgment on his case, an appeal addressed to an infinitely complex bureaucracy dedicated to the science of "how not to do it." Like one of Kafka's heroes, Daniel Doyce is made to feel like a criminal as soon as he becomes related to the Circumlocution Office, though he is not conscious of having done wrong, and Arthur Clennam's appeal to the Circumlocution Office on behalf of his friend never receives any definite response at all. In *Bleak House* the case of Jarndyce and Jarndyce at least finally came to an end, though only because all the money was consumed in costs, but Clennam's search for an answer from the Circumlocution Office remains at the end of *Little Dorrit* like a loose thread of the plot dangling unresolved. The Circumlocution Office is the labyrinthine prison transformed into an institution of government. Produced by the irresponsibility and greed of the upper class, with its legion of parasitical "Barnacles," the Circumlocution Office can imprison a man in its endless corridors and miles of red tape as securely as any Marshalsea or as any moral flaw. The ominous portrait of the Circumlocution Office is one of those elements of *Little Dorrit* which have led Marxist critics to find Marxism in Dickens and which led G. B. Shaw to say that *Little Dorrit* made him a socialist. Dickens was neither socialist nor Marxist, but his judgment of the Circumlocution Office is as near as he ever gets to asserting the radical instability of the present social order: "As they went along, certainly one of the party, and probably more than one, thought that Bleeding Heart Yard was no inappropriate destination for a man who had been in official correspondence with my lords and the Barnacles — and perhaps had a misgiving also that Britannia herself might come to look for lodgings in Bleeding Heart Yard, some ugly day or other, if she over-did the Circumlocution Office" (I, 10).

If the symbol of imprisonment expresses Dickens' sense of human life as enclosed and limited, whether by physical or spiritual walls, and if the image of life as a labyrinth expresses his sense that human beings are all lost inextricably in a maze without beginning, end, or pattern, the recurrent image of "travelers on the pilgrimage of life" expresses the idea that people are fatefully intertwined in one another's lives, often without knowing it or intending it. It also expresses Dickens' sense that a human life is not motionless but is perpetually flowing on with the river of time toward its destined adventures and toward the ultimate ocean of death: "And thus ever, by day and night, under the sun and under the stars, climbing the dusty hills and toiling along the weary plains, journeying by land and journeying by sea, coming and going so strangely, to meet and to act and react on one another, move all we restless travellers through the pilgrimage of life" (I, 2). The image of life as a long arduous journey, like images of prisons and labyrinths, recurs again and again in *Little Dorrit*. It reinforces the others by suggesting that this world is a lonely place where man is a stranger passing continually on in search of a haven which is not to be found anywhere in the "prison of this lower world." Taken all together, these three images, the basic symbolic metaphors of the novel, present a terrifyingly bleak picture of human life.

But what is perhaps darkest of all here is Dickens' new way of showing many of his characters altogether aware of their spiritual states and even deliberately choosing them. There is a great increase here over the earlier novels in the self-consciousness and articulateness of suffering or malice, an increase of which the extraordinary chapter of "The History of a Self Tormentor" is only the most striking example. Of this chapter Dickens wrote to the uncomprehending Forster, who found it "the least interesting part of *Little Dorrit*": "In Miss Wade I had an idea, which I thought a new one, of making the introduced story so fit into surroundings impossible of separation from the main story, as to make the blood of the book circulate through both." [3] We can indeed see that the lifeblood of *Little Dorrit* flows through Miss Wade's interpolated story when we recognize how frequently her coldly lucid justification of a life of self-destructive selfishness is echoed in various ways in other

[3] Forster, *Life of Dickens*, III, 162.

characters: in Merdle and Mrs. Merdle, in Henry Gowan and
Ferdinand Barnacle, in Mrs. Clennam's justification of her distorted Christianity, and in Casby's deliberate cultivation of a
hypocritical surface of benignity. Of all Dickens' novels it is
true to say that many of the characters exist in a nightmare of
unreality, committed to lives of self-seeking, sham, or vacillation. But the novelty of *Little Dorrit* lies in the fact that many
characters are perfectly aware of this, and therefore live in a
condition of continual restlessness or anxiety, even of despair
or paralysis of will, incapable, like Arthur Clennam, of deciding what to do with their lives, or incapable, like old Dorrit, of
making the least motion of spiritual ascent.

There seems, then, no escape from shadow in the world of
*Little Dorrit.* Whether the characters are literally imprisoned
or not, they are condemned to an endless wandering in a narrow dark labyrinth whose stations repeat one another as Calais
and Italy repeat the Marshalsea (II, 20 and 7). Little Dorrit
will never really "see" her father in her life (I, 19); whether
he is in jail or out he will always be "a captive with the jail-rot
upon him."

### III

But there does seem to be one part of the lower world which
is at peace and has no tinge of the restlessness and anxiety of
the city. Bob the turnkey takes Little Dorrit as a child to the
country to see meadows and green lanes, buttercups and daisies
(I, 7); her favorite resting place as an adult is the Iron Bridge
where she can watch the river and see the free sky and the
clouds above the crowded city; and it is in the country that
Arthur Clennam recognizes the radical difference between nature and human nature: "Within view was the peaceful river
and the ferry-boat, to moralise to all the inmates, saying: . . .
Year after year, . . . so many miles an hour the flowing of the
stream, here the rushes, there the lilies, nothing uncertain or
unquiet, upon this road that steadily runs away; while you,
upon your flowing road of time, are so capricious and distracted" (I, 16); "He had that sense of peace, and of being
lightened of a weight of care, which country quiet awakens in

the breasts of dwellers in towns" (I, 28). Whereas the city is cut off altogether from the divine, the country is close to heaven, as close as life is to death, or as close as trees by the riverside are to their shadowy reflections in the water: "Between the real landscape and its shadow in the water, there was no division; both were so untroubled and clear, and, while so fraught with solemn mystery of life and death, so hopefully reassuring to the gazer's soothed heart, because so tenderly and mercifully beautiful" (I, 28). The temptation is not simply to let the restful peace of the country "sink into" one's soul, but to try here and now, in the human world, to imitate the "divine calm" (I, 28) of nature. Such is the escape Arthur Clennam imagines from the painful anxiety and indecision of his life: "Why should he be vexed or sore at heart? . . . And he thought — who has not thought for a moment, sometimes — that it might be better to flow away monotonously, like the river, and to compound for its insensibility to happiness with its insensibility to pain" (I, 16).

But, alas, anxiety and responsibility are the lot of man, and the only rest available here is the dangerous peace of acquiescence in the false quiet of the prison and its easy path downward into deeper and deeper moral disintegration. This peace is only a horrible parody of the divine calm, as hell is an inversion of heaven. So Arthur Clennam when he finds himself in the Marshalsea as a prisoner experiences the "unnatural peace of having gone through the dreaded arrest, and got there, — the first change of feeling which the prison most commonly induced, and from which dangerous resting-place so many men had slipped down to the depths of degradation and disgrace, by so many ways" (II, 27). And so Dr. Haggage, the dirty, drunken prisoner who officiates at Little Dorrit's birth, delivers her father a sermon on the advantages of the Marshalsea: "We are quiet here; we don't get badgered here; there's no knocker here, sir, to be hammered at by creditors and bring a man's heart into his mouth. Nobody comes here to ask if a man's at home, and to say he'll stand on the door mat till he is. Nobody writes threatening letters about money to this place. It's freedom, sir, it's freedom! . . . Elsewhere, people are restless, worried, hurried about, anxious respecting one thing, anxious respecting another. Nothing of the kind here, sir. We have done all that — we know the worst of it; we have got to the bottom, we can't fall, and what have we found? Peace. That's the word for it. Peace" (I, 6).

Apparently one must endure the anxiety and suffering of the human condition without any hope of respite. But there is, of course, one way to leave this world altogether: death, the final escape from the "contradictions, vacillations, inconsistencies, the little peevish perplexities of this ignorant life," all of which are "mists which the morning without a night only can clear away" (II, 19). It is to this morning without a night that the Dorrit brothers return at last: "The two brothers were before their Father; far beyond the twilight judgments of this world; high above its mists and obscurities" (II, 19). There is, then, a world beyond this one, a light beyond the darkness, freedom and peace beyond the shadows and anxiety of this imprisoned world. But, though this light is the very radiant center and source of this world, it exists in its purity, in *Little Dorrit* as in *Bleak House,* only as something transcendent, as a promise of reconciliation either at the end of an individual life or at the end of the world itself: "The beauties of the sunset had not faded from the long light films of cloud that lay at peace in the horizon. From a radiant centre over the whole length and breadth of the tranquil firmament, great shoots of light streamed among the early stars, like signs of the blessed later covenant of peace and hope that changed the crown of thorns into a glory" (II, 31).

Dickens, however, as we have seen throughout his work, is interested in finding some way to make life in *this* world tolerable. One of his chief objections to Mrs. Clennam's perverted Christianity is to its otherworldliness, its willingness to barter a life of narrow and bitter repression here for some supposed benefit in the life hereafter. Arthur Clennam has escaped from his mother's dismal doctrine by accepting a morality centered on right action in this world: ". . . the first article in his code of morals was, that he must begin in practical humility, with looking well to his feet on Earth, and that he could never mount on wings of words to Heaven. Duty on Earth, restitution on earth, action on earth; these first, as the first steep steps upward" (I, 27). But what sort of right action is possible if every human institution, profession, or mode of life is darkened by the shadow of selfishness or imposture? Is there nothing to do but suffer passively through life, subject in one way or another to the illusions and injustices of the prison of the lower world, and waiting only for the escape at death into the morning without night? Is Dickens' a wholly Manichean world, divided absolutely between the darkness of earth and the brightness of heaven?

The answer is given in Dickens' description of the death of old Dorrit: "Quietly, quietly, the ruled and cross-ruled countenance . . . became fair and blank. Quietly, quietly, the reflected marks of the prison bars and of the zig-zag iron on the wall-top, faded away. Quietly, quietly, the face subsided into a far [4] younger likeness of [Little Dorrit's] own than she had ever seen under the grey hair, and sank to rest" (II, 19). To die is to return momentarily to the self one was as a child, and to reveal the fact that the innocence of childhood is the one stage of life which escapes from the shadow of the prison. The purity of childhood is the only part of a man which is really worthy to be taken up into the "morning without a night," and it is this nucleus, miraculously preserved in the depths of the human spirit, untouched throughout all the vicissitudes and delusions of life, which returns to the surface at the last moment and displaces the shams and weaknesses which have made the face a distorted mask. If so disfigured a character as old Dorrit returns to the goodness of childhood at his death, we can accept the notion that all of the people in *Little Dorrit,* without exception, were innocent and good as children. The horror is that so many of them have been able to alienate themselves almost completely from this kernel of authenticity, and to live as pure self-seeking, illusion, surface, convention, what Dickens calls "varnish." The tragedy of *Little Dorrit,* then, is the tragedy of childhood distorted, betrayed, forgotten, buried so far down that it no longer seems to exist. Dickens' world is not Manich-

[4] The Nonesuch edition has "fair" here, obviously a misprint for "far."

ean at all. Rather, he sees in all but the most exceptional individuals (such as Blandois in this novel) a mixture of good and evil, of reality and sham, and he is ready to believe that even the most hardened and corrupt persons may perhaps reëstablish contact at last with the incorruptible goodness within them, as Mrs. Clennam saves herself by her tardy confession to Little Dorrit, and as the grubby Pancks asserts himself at last by unmasking his employer, the fake Patriarch Casby. The "Prince of this World" in *Little Dorrit* is no positive devil, but is rather a negative illusion which will be dissipated in a moment when the mists are cleared away at death. If he exists embodied in a single person, as in Blandois in this novel, that person will be powerless against the good, an impotent posturing pasteboard figure who is destroyed in the end by his own selfishness, as Blandois is crushed in the collapse of the Clennam house.

Nevertheless, the power of the world for soilure and corruption is very great, and very great too its power to cover childhood with layer upon layer of forgetfulness and distraction. A world in which the goodness of childhood is doomed to be hidden away and rendered inactive by the mask of adulthood is almost as bad as a world in which childhood can be destroyed altogether. But it is just here that we recognize the crucial importance for the whole work of Dickens of his conception of Little Dorrit. She has the place in Dickens' imaginative world that Prince Myshkin has in Dostoevsky's work. Dickens has in Little Dorrit, even more than in Esther Summerson or in the other good women in his novels, dared to imagine a person who is altogether good. And this miraculous goodness is imagined as the persistence into adult life of the purity of childhood. Little Dorrit is again and again spoken of as a child, and is taken as childlike by all of the characters, including Clennam. She is Dickens' dramatization of the idea expressed in Christ's words: "Except ye . . . become as little children, ye shall not enter into the kingdom of heaven. Whosoever therefore shall humble himself as this little child, the same is greatest in the kingdom of heaven" (Matt., 18:3, 4). Little Dorrit derives all her power to help her father and others around her from her preservation of the simplicity, loving-kindness, and faithful perseverance of childhood.

But the ambiguity of Little Dorrit's condition, as of Mysh-kin's, lies in the fact that she is not a child. She is an adult, and human after all, with an adult's knowledge of evil, and an adult's need to combine sexual and spiritual love. This am-biguity is dramatized in her relation to Arthur Clennam. Throughout most of the novel she loves him, not as a child, but as a woman, and to her secret sorrow Clennam persists in think-ing of her as really a child. It is only when he understands that she is both good *and* adult that his fatherly affection gives way to another kind of love and the novel can end with them hap-pily married. Clennam's mistake is to identify Little Dorrit's goodness with childhood. It derives from that indeed, but Lit-tle Dorrit's mystery is that she has been able, unlike any other character in the novel, to carry the innocence and spontaneous love of childhood into adult life. Her innocence is thus even more miraculous, for it is an innocence which knows and un-derstands the wickedness of the world, and is able to accept and love even that. The ambiguities of Little Dorrit's nature are most subtly expressed in a scene early in the novel. She is locked out of her home in the Marshalsea and forced to spend a night in the streets, with only Maggy, a hulking idiot girl with the mind of a ten-year-old, for "protection." They meet a pros-titute on the streets who at first takes Little Dorrit for a child, and then recoils in horror when she realizes she has been treat-ing a woman as if she were a child:

"Poor thing!" said the woman. "Have you no feeling, that you keep her out in the cruel streets at such a time as this? Have you no eyes, that you don't see how delicate and slender she is? Have you no sense (you don't look as if you had much) that you don't take more pity on this cold and trembling little hand?"

She had stepped across to that side, and held the hand between her own two, chafing it. "Kiss a poor lost creature, dear," she said, bending her face, "and tell me where she's taking you."

Little Dorrit turned towards her.

"Why, my God!" she said, recoiling, "you're a woman!"

"Don't mind that!" said Little Dorrit, clasping one of her hands that had suddenly released hers. "I am not afraid of you."

"Then you had better be," she answered. "Have you no mother?"

"No."

"No father?"

"Yes, a very dear one."

"Go home to him, and be afraid of me. Let me go. Good night!"

"I must thank you first; let me speak to you as if I really were a child."

"You can't do it," said the woman. "You are kind and innocent; but you can't look at me out of a child's eyes. I never should have touched you, but I thought that you were a child." And with a strange, wild cry, she went away. (I, 14)

This is one of the most poignant scenes in *Little Dorrit* — perhaps in all Dickens. Here are juxtaposed an adult innocence so pure it is almost childlike and the impurity of the fallen woman. But the juxtaposition shows us that even Little Dorrit cannot really remain a child. She is a woman, with a woman's knowledge, and therefore the prostitute cannot gain, as she expects, a moment's peace and innocence for herself by kissing her. A real child would not know what she is, and therefore could not hurt her or be hurt by her. Here Dickens approaches Dostoevsky's recognition of the complicated relations of good and evil in a world in which evil subtly corrupts and frustrates good and even the worst evil is qualified by a small measure of good.

But to recall the analogy between Little Dorrit and Prince Myshkin is to see immediately how much less subtle than Dostoevsky's is Dickens' conception of the drama of absolute human goodness. The distinction lies in the quality of suffering imagined in each case. To oversimplify the comparison one might say that Myshkin is immeasurably more intelligent than Little Dorrit, that his suffering derives from the terrifying clairvoyance which forces him to look into the depths of the souls of those around him and to take upon himself their pain. Little Dorrit suffers, and even suffers through her understanding of her father's nature, but she does not have Myshkin's terrible lucidity of vision. Moreover, Myshkin is torn to pieces by the incompatibility between his own goodness and the fallen world in which he finds himself, and by the split in his own soul between earthly and divine love, whereas Dickens can imagine Little Dorrit living happily ever after with Arthur Clennam.

Nevertheless, Dickens has reached one of the peaks of his own artistic success in being able to persuade us to accept so completely the mystery of divine goodness incarnate in a human person. Moreover, *Little Dorrit* contains what is for Dickens a new and far more profound idea of the reality of love between two human beings. The happy ending of *Little Dorrit* is made possible through the mutual love of Arthur Clennam and Little Dorrit. But Dickens' new conception of love goes far beyond that presented in any of his earlier novels.

### IV

*Little Dorrit,* like *A Tale of Two Cities,* has at its center a recognition of the inalienable secrecy and otherness of every human being. Here Dickens makes explicit his repudiation of the idea that another person can be a kind of transparent alter ego whom I can know and possess without the intervention of any shadow of mystery or strangeness. In these novels one has a diffused consciousness of the opacity of other people. This opacity is present as a kind of heavy thickness in the air, an impenetrable "shadow" of secrecy. The unknown secrets separating even those closest to one another are related by Dickens to the final secrecy of death. The river of life flows inexorably toward the boundless sea of death, but the river too has its secret depths, and the heart of each living person reaches down to an anonymous and mysterious realm, a realm which even that person himself is not able to explore to its bottom. So important are these ideas for the understanding of a fundamental change in Dickens that the two central passages, one from each novel, must be quoted here at some length:

As he went along, upon a dreary night, the dim streets by which he went, seemed all depositories of oppressive secrets. The deserted counting-houses, with their secrets of books and papers locked up in chests and safes; the banking-houses, with their secrets of strong rooms and wells, the keys of which were in a very few secret pockets and a very few secret breasts; the secrets of all the dispersed grinders in the vast mill, among whom there were doubtless plunderers, forgers, and trust-betrayers of many sorts, whom the light of any day that dawned might reveal; he could have fancied that these

things, in hiding, imparted a heaviness to the air. The shadow
thickening and thickening as he approached its source, he thought
of the secrets of the lonely church-vaults, where the people who
had hoarded and secreted in iron coffers were in their turn similarly hoarded, not yet at rest from doing harm; and then of the
secrets of the river, as it rolled its turbid tide between two frowning
wildernesses of secrets, extending, thick and dense, for many miles,
and warding off the free air and the free country swept by winds
and wings of birds. (*LD*, II, 10)

A wonderful fact to reflect upon, that every human creature is
constituted to be that profound secret and mystery to every other. A
solemn consideration, when I enter a great city by night, that every
one of those darkly clustered houses encloses its own secret; that
every room in every one of them encloses its own secret; that every
beating heart in the hundreds of thousands of breasts there, is, in
some of its imaginings, a secret to the heart nearest it! Something of
the awfulness, even of Death itself, is referable to this. . . . No
more can I look into the depths of this unfathomable water
wherein, as momentary lights glanced into it, I have had glimpses
of buried treasure and other things submerged. . . . It was appointed that the water should be locked in an eternal frost, when
the light was playing on its surface, and I stood in ignorance on the
shore. My friend is dead, my neighbour is dead, my love, the dar-
ling of my soul, is dead; it is the inexorable consolidation and perpetuation of the secret that was always in that individuality, and
which I shall carry in mine to my life's end. In any of the burial
places of this city through which I pass, is there a sleeper more inscrutable than its busy inhabitants are, in their innermost personality, to me, or than I am to them? (*TTC*, I, 3)

*Little Dorrit* centers on the secrecy, the otherness, of Little
Dorrit herself. Whereas Esther Summerson got her strength to
order the world around her through intermittent contact with
the divine transcendence, Little Dorrit is the mystery of incarnate goodness. She does not need to be shown receiving
strength from God's grace, because goodness is permanently immanent in her life, though Dickens does tell us that she is
something different from everyone and everything about her
only because she has been "inspired . . . to be that something, different and laborious, for the sake of the rest" (I, 7)

Her grace to remain good, Dickens says, is exactly like "the inspiration of a poet or a priest" (*ibid.*). Little Dorrit is Esther Summerson presented, as it were, through the eyes of Allan Woodcourt. Arthur Clennam, the Woodcourt of *Little Dorrit,* functions as one of the chief protagonists and the central point of view of his novel. At first, when he returns to London after twenty years absence in China, Clennam's will is paralyzed; he cannot make the least motion of voluntary and directed action; he cannot plan what to do with his life: "I am such a waif and stray everywhere, that I am liable to be drifted where any current may set. . . . I have no will. That is to say, . . . next to none that I can put in action now. Trained by main force; broken, not bent; heavily ironed with an object on which I was never consulted and which was never mine; . . . always grinding in a mill I always hated; what is to be expected from *me* in middle life? Will, purpose, hope? All those lights were extinguished before I could sound the words" (I, 2). Indeed, as we have seen, the novel is full of people whose wills are paralyzed, who are, like Miss Wade, "self-tormentors," but the central dramatic action is Arthur's own search for some means by which his will may be reconstituted. He tests various modes of relation to society. They all fail, and he finally discovers that the pivot of his world, the center to which all roads lead, is "the least, the quietest, and weakest of Heaven's creatures" (I, 9), Little Dorrit:

To review his life, was like descending a green tree in fruit and flower, and seeing all the branches wither and drop off one by one, as he came down towards them.

"From the unhappy suppression of my youngest days, through the rigid and unloving home that followed them, through my departure, my long exile, my return, my mother's welcome, my intercourse with her since, down to the afternoon of this day with poor Flora," said Arthur Clennam, "what have I found!"

His door was softly opened, and these spoken words startled him, and came as if they were an answer:

"Little Dorrit." (I, 13)

Looking back upon his own poor story, she was its vanishing-point. Every thing in its perspective led to her innocent figure. He had travelled thousands of miles towards it; previous unquiet hopes and doubts had worked themselves out before it; it was the centre of the interest of his life; it was the termination of everything that was good and pleasant in it; beyond there was nothing but mere waste and darkened sky. (II, 27)

Without Little Dorrit, Clennam would be, like so many other people in the novel, lost in a patternless maze. Only Little Dorrit gives form to his world and an orientation to his life. She is their center, just as God himself is the hidden radiant center of the larger world.

Clennam's relation to Little Dorrit is a direct relation to the area of mystery in another person. She keeps the secret of his family's guilt toward her. She is the center which is absent, the abnegation of perfect charity. By being the absence of self-assertion, total unselfishness, the voluntary refusal to will, she succeeds in dominating the world, or at least a small area of i , whereas total failure results from all the direct selfish attempts either to spread outward and dominate all (like Merdle, or Blandois, or Pancks), or to create or accept voluntarily a private imprisoning circle protected from the world, an enclosure where one will be safe and in complete control of one's sur-roundings (Mrs. Clennam, Miss Wade, old Dorrit). Little Dorrit sustains Clennam when everything else collapses be-neath him. Indeed, she is really a human incarnation of divine goodness. The latter is present in the novel, but unavailable; it is seen in recurrent glimpses of nature beyond or above the imprisoning city streets. Clennam's relation to Little Dorrit is a relation to the unattainable divine through her mediation. It is only through Little Dorrit that Clennam can escape from the spiritual (and literal) imprisonment and deathlike stagnation to which his life finally comes:

Changeless and barren, looking ignorantly at all the seasons with its fixed, pinched face of poverty and care, the prison had not a touch of any . . . beauties on it. Blossom what would, its bricks and bars bore uniformly the same dead crop. Yet Clennam, listen-ing to the voice as it read to him, heard in it all that great Nature was doing, heard in it all the soothing songs she sings to man. At no Mother's knee but hers, had he ever dwelt in his youth on hopeful promises, on playful fancies, on the harvests of tenderness and humility that lie hidden in the early-fostered seeds of the imagination . . . . But, in the tones of the voice that read to him, there were memories of an old feeling of such things, and echoes of every merciful and loving whisper that had ever stolen to him in his life. (II, 34, and see II, 29)

But if Clennam can escape from the valley of the shadow only through the miraculous goodness of Little Dorrit, she herself can escape from her isolation only through Clennam's return of her love, and because he too has kept intact a kernel of his childhood innocence and belief in good. The novel, then, ends happily with the usual Dickensian scene of reciprocal love, as Arthur Clennam and Little Dorrit leave the Marshalsea for the last time to be married. But here there is even less emphasis than usual on the completeness of the lovers' escape from the shadow, and there is a firm assertion that their happiness is limited to themselves alone and leaves the selfish, restless, and deluded multitudes still locked in the prison of the world: "They went quietly down into the roaring streets, inseparable and blessed; and as they passed along in sunshine and shade, the noisy and the eager, and the arrogant and the froward and the vain, fretted, and chafed, and made their usual uproar" (II, 34).

<h2 style="text-align:center">v</h2>

*A Tale of Two Cities* follows *Little Dorrit* chronologically. It dramatizes Dickens' new concept of love against the background of the French Revolution. Love and war are here metaphorically related. Each is a specific case of a more general process through which what is merely human — the masquerade of the *ancien régime* (II, 7), or the purposelessness of Sydney Carton, "waste forces within him, and a desert all around" (II, 5) — is put in touch with what is beyond the human, and therefore potentially made true and real. But, within the novel, France remains a self-destructive chaos, torn by violent passions liberated after long repression and injustice, and Sydney Carton's only release from purposelessness and impotence of will is death. The novel is dominated by images of blood, storm, death, and, most of all, by literal or metaphorical "risings of fire and risings of sea" (II, 24). These express the bursting forth into the human world of what is beyond the human, and they are applied both to the revolutionists and to the characters in the love story. But Dickens can, at this stage of his career, see direct contact with the transhuman as leading only to death. The mediator is destroyed by his act of mediation. In order to fulfill the theme of "resurrection" (that is, descent into death and return from it to a life at last given a meaning), Dickens must divide his hero into two persons: Charles Darnay and his "double" Carton. Carton must die in Darnay's place so that Darnay may live happily ever after with Lucie. Here, Little Dorrit's act of self-abnegation is seen to require, in order to be efficacious, the supreme sacrifice of life itself. Dickens is no longer able to reconcile the idea of perfect love with the idea of continued life, and it is only in *Our Mutual Friend* that he is able to put the two motions of resurrection, descent into death and return, together in a single person.

In *A Tale of Two Cities* Dickens succeeds, nevertheless, in seeing the act of self-sacrifice from the inside. He thereby investigates at a much deeper level the saving relation of love. The problem now will be to show a reciprocal relation between two persons which does not involve the complete abnegation of one, as in the case of Little Dorrit or Sydney Carton, but which is the simultaneous affirmation and renunciation of two persons who mutually create one another's selfhood. *Great Expectations* gives all these themes definitive expression. It raises the problems in their most intense form by making one last energetic attempt to combine the relation to society with the direct relation to another person.

## Chapter VIII

# GREAT EXPECTATIONS

## I

MY first most vivid and broad impression of the identity of things, seems to me to have been gained on a memorable raw after-noon towards evening. At such a time I found out for certain, that this bleak place overgrown with nettles was the churchyard; and that Philip Pirrip, late of this parish, and also Georgiana wife of the above, were dead and buried; and that Alexander, Bartholo-mew, Abraham, Tobias, and Roger, infant children of the afore-said, were also dead and buried; and that the dark flat wilderness beyond the churchyard, intersected with dykes and mounds and gates, with scattered cattle feeding on it, was the marshes; and that the low leaden line beyond was the river; and that the distant sav-age lair from which the wind was rushing, was the sea; and that the small bundle of shivers growing afraid of it all and beginning to cry, was Pip. ( 1 )

GREAT Expectations is the most unified and concentrated expression of Dickens' abiding sense of the world, and Pip might be called the archetypal Dickens hero. In Great Expec-tations Dickens' particular view of things is expressed with a concreteness and symbolic intensity he never surpassed. Per-haps the restrictions of shorter length and of weekly rather than monthly publication led Dickens to present his story more in symbolic than in discursive form. The result is not a narrowing and rarefying of meaning, but rather a large increase in inten-sity and complexity. What it took Dickens in 1850 the first hundred pages of David Copperfield to say is presented far more powerfully in the first few pages of *Great Expectations*: the lonely boy becoming aware of his desolation on the dark marshes in the midst of a hostile universe, standing by the graves of his mother, father, and brothers, aware that he will be beaten by his foster mother when he returns home, and suddenly terrified by the apparition of the "fearful man" "starting up from among the graves" (1). What had been presented seriatim in the earlier novels is here said with poetic compression. And in following Pip's adventures we perhaps come closest to the intimate center of Dickens' apprehension of the world and of his mode of existence within it. *Great Expectations* makes available, as does no other of Dickens' novels, the central experiences of the universal Dickensian hero.

Never, perhaps, was the form of a great novel conceived as the response to so practical a demand. In the early fall of 1860 the sales of *All the Year Round* were dropping sadly because of the unpopularity of Charles Lever's *The Day's Ride*. Dickens "dashed" in (*Let.*, III, 183) with *Great Expectations* in order to save circulation. At first *Great Expectations* was a "little piece" (*ibid.*, p. 182). Then, as the idea grew — "such a very fine, new, and grotesque idea" (*ibid.*) — it was planned as a monthly serial of twenty numbers, like *Bleak House* or *Little Dorrit*. Then, because of the falling-off of the sales of *All the Year Round*, Dickens decided to write it in the much briefer form of a serial in weekly numbers for that journal.

Dickens' own language for what he was doing scarcely reveals its importance. The central motif of *Great Expectations*, the *donnée* with which Dickens began, was the secret manipulation of Pip's life by Magwitch the convict — a striking idea, which goes to the roots of several key nineteenth-century notions about human existence. Dickens' phrase for it was "the grotesque tragi-comic conception that first encouraged me" (*ibid.*, p. 186). We have only one important sign of the depths which Dickens was plumbing in the conception of the basic motif of *Great Expectations*: "To be quite sure I had fallen into no unconscious repetitions, I read David Copperfield again the other day, and was affected by it to a degree you would hardly believe" (*ibid.*). This is a valuable reinforcement of the sense we get from the novel itself that Dickens was here drawing again, as in *David Copperfield*, on his most intimate personal experiences. They are transformed into a "fable," perhaps, but still retain the essential form of Dickens' sense of the meaning of his own life.

What form does this meaning take?

*Great Expectations*, like most of Dickens' novels, does not begin with a description of the perfect bliss of childhood, the period when the world and the self are identified, and the parents are seen as benign gods whose care and whose overlooking judgment protect and justify the child. Like Oedipus, who, as a newborn baby, was put out in the fields to die, Dickens' heroes and heroines have never experienced this perfect security. Each becomes aware of himself as isolated from all that is outside of himself. The Dickensian hero is separated from nature. The world appears to him as cold and unfriendly, as a "wilderness" or a graveyard. In Dickens there is no Wordsworthian theory of the child's filial bond with nature. There is no moment of primitive or infantile identification of subject and object, self and world, followed by a "fall" into the cruel realm of time and division. The self is not initially the plenitude of a union with the entire universe, but is already narrowed down to "the small bundle of shivers growing afraid of it all and beginning to cry." The Dickensian hero is also alienated from the human community. He has no familial tie. He is an orphan, or illegitimate, or both. He has no status in the community, no inherited role which he can accept with dignity. He is characterized by desire, rather than by possession. His spiritual state is one of an expectation founded on a present consciousness of lack, of deprivation. He is, in Wallace Stevens' phrase, "an emptiness that would be filled."

Furthermore, the Dickensian hero becomes aware of himself as guilty. His very existence is a matter of reproach and a shameful thing. Esther Summerson's foster mother tells her that it would have been better if she had never been born, and Pip says of himself: "I was always treated as if I had insisted on being born in opposition to the dictates of reason, religion, and morality, and against the dissuading arguments of my best friends" (4). It is mere accident that he is alive at all, and is not buried beside his brothers in the lonely churchyard by the sea. "As to you," says Joe of his first glimpse of the infant Pip, "if you could have been aware how small and flabby and mean you was, dear me, you'd have formed the most contemptible opinions of yourself!" (7). And Mrs. Joe recalls "all the times she had wished [Pip] in [his] grave, and [he] had contumaciously refused to go there" (4). The typical Dickens hero, like Pip, feels guilty because he has no given status or relation to nature, to family, or to the community. He is, in everyone's eyes, in the way, superfluous. He is either ignored by society altogether, thrown into the streets to beg or starve, or he is taken care of by the state or by his foster parents in an impersonal way which deprives him of any real identity. To submit to this "care" is to be transformed into an object. He may, alternatively, accept a job as a functionary in the vast system of money-getting which dominates urban society. This will as effectively dehumanize him as going to the poorhouse. Dickens shows that, for his characters at least, no "natural right" exists, no "state" in the sense that Rousseau and Matthew Arnold meant it: something above all hereditary legitimacies and distinctions, something to which the individual may tie himself and submit, as to his own best self. For Dickens, such submission means to lose all one's specifically human qualities of self-consciousness and freedom. Submission to the collective process of making and selling, of "beggaring your neighbor" lest he "beggar" you, is to be in danger of becoming dehumanized, like Wemmick, who is "a dry man, . . . with a square wooden face, whose expression seem[s] to have been imperfectly chipped out with a dull-edged chisel" (21). Or, even worse, the individual may be destroyed altogether by society, and remain behind only as the trophy of somebody's successful manipulations, like Jaggers' clients, who have been transformed into "dreadful casts on a shelf, of faces peculiarly swollen, and twitchy about the nose" (20).

Since the Dickensian hero has initially no real role, any status he attains in the world will be the result of his own efforts. He will be totally responsible, himself, for any identity he achieves, and thus "guilty" in the sense of being the source of his own values. He has no hope of ever being justified by any external approval. He will be, whatever he does, a "self-made man," a man who has made himself his own goal and end. This will be true in spite of any efforts on his part to escape his superfluity. The world has simply refused to give him any assigned place, and any place he gets will have to be seized.

Given such a situation, the hero can remove himself from the world in which he has no place, withdraw into a solitary enclosure. Suicide is not really an option for Dickens' characters, except for those who are completely evil, but withdrawal and passivity are possible. In different ways, for example, Arthur Clennam, Mrs. Clennam, John Harmon, and Miss Havisham attempt to escape from the threat of dehumanization by willing not to will, by abnegation, by a passive drifting which will, they vainly hope, relieve them of the guilt of action. On the other hand, the Dickensian hero can submit to the complete dehumanization which society or his stepparents would practice upon him, or, finally, he can take upon himself the responsibility and guilt of a selfhood which is to be made, not accepted from the outside. In one case, he tries to hide from himself his freedom by submitting to the role society would have him play. He thus becomes one of Dickens' comic automatons, like Wemmick, who at first seems to be a wooden puppet manipulated by external forces, wholly lacking in real human qualities, mouthing the dead language of cliché and slogan: "My guiding star," says Wemmick, "is: Get hold of Portable Property." In the other case, he consciously sets himself up as an end in himself. He is then in danger of becoming, like Blandois in *Little Dorrit,* a demonic individualist whose hand is against his neighbor, and who hopes to achieve personal identity by the destruction of everything that is. But Dickens' true heroes and heroines, those characters at the centers of his novels, seek some intermediary between these extremes. They seek some way out that will make possible the achievement of true selfhood, while not necessitating the extreme of anarchic individualism. These protagonists try various ways, some proper, some improper, of attaining the reconciliation of freedom and security. The single great development in Dickens' world view is the change in the kinds of expedients which are deemed to be proper or possible. *Great Expectations* is the novel in which the various alternatives are most clearly presented and opposed.

## II

In a world where the only possible relation to other people seems to be that of oppressor to oppressed, or oppressed to oppressor, those who are born into oppression may try to seize the role of oppressor. If one must be either master or slave, it seems better to be master than slave. But the choice of Blandois, in *Little Dorrit,* the choice of an open attempt to be master ("It is my character to dominate," says Blandois), is not possible without the consciousness of guilt. Only those who are born members of the upper class can rule guiltlessly, by "divine right," as it were, and the outcast knows that neither God nor the collective approval of society will justify any open attempts on his part to reverse the role, and to become oppressor rather than oppressed. So he tries various ways to attain the same movement up in the social scale without incurring guilt for it.

He may simply dominate those beneath him in the social chain of being, as Wemmick, himself a victim of the great legal organization, treats those beneath him, Jaggers' clients, condemned jailbirds, as though they were the plants in his flower garden, or as Abel Magwitch, escaped convict, at the extreme point of his exclusion from society, coerces Pip into feeding him. He is "beneath" everyone in the world except Pip, whom he seizes and turns upside down, as though to reverse their roles. Much later in the novel, when Pip is being browbeaten by Jaggers (surely "master" rather than "slave" in the world of the novel), he says: "I felt at a disadvantage, which reminded me of that old time when I had been put upon a tombstone" (36). The inadequacies of this expedient are obvious. The "exploiter" cannot hide from himself the fact that he has unjustifiably seized power over another human being.

But two other more surreptitious ways are attempted by characters in *Great Expectations*. In the first case, one person manipulates another not as his victim, but as the agent of his revenge on society. In one way or another several characters in *Great Expectations* try to "make" other characters. They do not try to make them into mere dehumanized tools, but to make them into members of the upper class who will have all the prerogatives of justified exploitation which they themselves lack. Thus Magwitch boasts that Pip is "the gentleman what I made." If he cannot himself ever be anything but a transported felon, "hunted dunghill dog," perhaps he can secretly create a gentleman through whom he will vicariously enjoy all the powers he could never attain himself: "I says to myself, 'If I ain't a gentleman, nor yet ain't got no learning, I'm the owner of such. All on you owns stock and land; which on you owns a brought-up London gentleman?' " (39). Magwitch is a nightmare permutation of Mr. Brownlow and Mr. Jarndyce. He is the benevolent guardian, secretly manipulating the fortunes of the hero and protecting him, turned into a condemned felon who, like a horrible old dog, gloats over his victim.

There is at least one comic parody of this theme: Pumblechook boasts that he is the "founder" of Pip's fortune, and he shakes Pip's hand again and again on the day his great expectations are announced. Pumblechook's action is an ominous anticipation of Magwitch's symbolic gesture of appropriation when he appears at Pip's door, and grasps his hands. Indeed, as John H. Hagan, Jr. has observed, Pumblechook, as one of those who have schooled Pip in the attitudes which prepare him for his delusion, can claim with justice to be the founder of Pip's fortune.[1]

But Miss Havisham is a more important parallel to Magwitch. Her heart has been broken by Compeyson, the archvillain who lies behind all the evil in the story. She has withdrawn forever from the world, and has renounced all attempts to act in her own person. Miss Havisham has attempted to stop time at the moment she received the news that her bridegroom-to-be had deceived and deserted her. She does not try to stop

---

[1] See pp. 172, 173 of "The Poor Labyrinth: The Theme of Social Injustice in Dickens's 'Great Expectations,' " *Nineteenth-Century Fiction*, IX (1954), 169–178.

time at the moment *before* she heard the news. No, she does not want to escape the harsh reality of her betrayal, and return to the time when she was living in an illusory world of innocence, security, and, as she thought, reciprocal love. She wants, rather, to crystallize her grief and bereavement into an eternal moment of shock and sorrow, like those of Faulkner's characters who remain immobilized with their backs to the future, facing some terrible event in the past which has determined the meaning of their lives.

Miss Havisham has two motives for her attempt to freeze time. She wants to make certain that her betrayal will be the whole meaning of her life, that nothing more will happen to change her destiny as it existed at the moment of betrayal. She does not want it to be possible for her to stop suffering, to forget, to turn her attention to other things and other people, and so cease to be the Miss Havisham who was cruelly abandoned on the day of her wedding. If she allows herself to change at all that self may become a thing of the past, a matter of history, a self she no longer is. She may slip back into time, which means to slip back into a human existence which is conditioned in its essence by temporality. And to be essentially conditioned by time means never to reach a stopping place in one's life, to be "ever more about to be," to be not yet what one is going to be, and never finally what one is. Miss Havisham's attempt to freeze time implies a recognition of the same harsh truth that drove Quentin Compson in Faulkner's *The Sound and the Fury* to suicide: "You are not thinking of finitude," says Quentin's father, "you are contemplating an apotheosis in which a temporary state of mind will become symmetrical above the flesh and aware both of itself and of the flesh it will not quite discard you will not even be dead . . . you cannot bear to think that someday it will no longer hurt you like this . . . no man ever does that [commits suicide] under the first fury of despair or remorse or bereavement he does it only when he has realised that even the despair or remorse or bereavement is not particularly important to the dark diceman." [2]

[2] William Faulkner, *The Sound and the Fury & As I Lay Dying* (Modern Library ed., New York, n.d.), pp. 195, 196.

Miss Havisham, like Quentin, wants to achieve an inhuman fixity, to escape time and to live as if her life were finished, as if she had survived herself, and could look back at her life as everyone else does, regarding it as a "destiny" and as a completed meaning. Dickens judges Miss Havisham as harshly as any of his characters, though he abandons his apparent intention to have her hang herself (8): "in shutting out the light of day, she had shut out infinitely more; . . . in seclusion, she had secluded herself from a thousand natural and healing influences; . . . her mind, brooding solitary, had grown diseased, as all minds do and must and will that reverse the appointed order of their Maker . . ." (49). Moreover, Miss Havisham's attempt is doomed to failure. For in willing to freeze her life at the moment the annihilating blow came from the outside, she changes her abandonment from a "cruel fate" to a chosen role. It is Miss Havisham herself who chooses to make her betrayal the central event and meaning of her life. And in so choosing she makes herself responsible for it. She tries to flee forever out of the realm of freedom, unpredictability, and change, but she only succeeds in making herself responsible for ruining her own life, and for nearly ruining Estella's and Pip's.

Miss Havisham's second motive for attempting to freeze time at the moment of her betrayal is the motive of revenge. She had loved Compeyson with a love she herself defines as "blind devotion, unquestioning self-humiliation, utter submission, trust and belief against yourself and against the whole world, giving up your whole heart and soul to the smiter . . ." (29). "There is no doubt," says Herbert Pocket, "that she perfectly idolised him" (22). Miss Havisham tries to carry the same kind of all or nothing quality into her new life. Her revenge is to make her betrayal into the very meaning of her life, and to make her resulting death-in-life a curse on her heartless lover: " 'When the ruin is complete,' said she, with a ghastly look, 'and when they lay me dead, in my bride's dress on the bride's table — which shall be done, and which will be the finished curse upon him — so much the better if it is done on this day!' " (11). ("This day" is the anniversary of her betrayal.) If she slips one instant in her determination to make her whole life a reproach and a curse on Compeyson, her revenge will be incomplete. Her frozen life is not the result of a failure of will, but of a will strong as iron to "reverse the appointed order of [her] Maker" by closing every last aperture of her life through which change might come, just as she has closed all the windows and doors in Satis House through which the natural light and air might enter.

Miss Havisham's other method of revenge is Estella. ". . . with my praises, and with my jewels, and with my teachings, and with this figure of myself always before her," says Miss Havisham of Estella, ". . . I stole her heart away and put ice in its place" (49). Just as Magwitch, another victim of Compeyson, creates in Pip an "instrument" of his revenge on society, so Miss Havisham "mould[s] [Estella] into the form that her wild resentment, spurned affection, and wounded pride, found vengeance in" (49). Estella will draw men as a candle attracts moths, but, being without a heart, she will treat them as Compeyson treated Miss Havisham: "How does she use you, Pip, how does she use you?" asks Miss Havisham. She had deluded herself into thinking she is taking no direct revenge on mankind, but only letting her state of abandonment be a punishment. Through Estella she will take an indirect and therefore guiltless revenge, and break a hundred hearts for her own one heart that was broken.

This transformation of the master-slave relation is apparently a reconciliation of irreconcilables. Miss Havisham and Magwitch hope to attain vicariously all that they lack. They will enjoy the power of the oppressor without being guilty of having unjustifiably seized that power. No one will be able to blame Magwitch for the arrogance of Pip the gentleman, and no one will blame Miss Havisham for the cruelties Estella practices on her suitors. Since the low origin of his great expectations is hidden from Pip, he will have the sense of "divine right" that is enjoyed by a gentleman born. His transformation from "common" blacksmith's boy to London gentleman will seem to him like a "destiny," something at any rate for which he is not guiltily responsible. And Estella will be brought up to feel that men are her natural enemies. She will experience no remorse for breaking their hearts because she will have no heart herself. She will be like a superhuman goddess, unable to understand the sorrows of mere mortals.

This attempt to transcend isolation without guilt, by paradoxically both being and not being another person whom one has created, in both cases fails.

For Miss Havisham love reduces itself to the extreme of masochistic submission to the iron heel of the lover. For her, human relations are inevitably a conflict, a war to the death, and love to her is simply an extreme form of that possession and manipulation of another person which we see in the relations of Magwitch and Pip, Miss Havisham and Estella, Jaggers and his clients, and so on. Love, for Miss Havisham, is another form of "fettering," and cannot escape from the universal law which says, "I shall either dehumanize my neighbor, or be dehumanized by him, either be master or slave." But Miss Havisham proves in her own experience the hard truth that the relation of master and slave is frustration, suffering, and alienation for master as well as for slave. For if the master succeeds in driving away all the human qualities of his victim, as Miss Havisham has succeeded with Estella, then in a single stroke the victim as human being evaporates, and with him the validation of selfhood which the master had structured on his relation to the slave. "You stock and stone! . . . You cold, cold heart!" says Miss Havisham in the anguish of her realization that as a result of her upbringing Estella is altogether incapable of returning her "burning love, inseparable from jealousy at all times" (38). Miss Havisham is not telling all the truth earlier when she says her motive in attaching Estella to herself is to make possible a perfect revenge on men for her betrayal. She also wants to create between herself and her creature Estella a perfect relation as a substitute for the one which so failed her when her lover abandoned her. Then she had set her whole heart on Compeyson, and had been reduced to spiritual nothingness when he betrayed her. Now she still wants a perfect relation to another person, a relation which will fill up the void left in her heart by the tragedy of her youth. But she wants to achieve that relation without risk. Miss Havisham imagines

that she can escape the uncertainty of all authentic human relationships if she takes a young girl, before her personality has
been formed, and brings her up to look only to her guardian for
protection and love. She wants Estella to love her only, so that
in the dark, airless confines of Satis House they may dwell safe
from all the world, and be sufficient to one another. Miss Havisham succeeds in making Estella wholly her "creation," but,
at the same time, she destroys any possibility of a return of her
love. The kind of relation Miss Havisham wants cannot be
achieved without risk, without an acceptance of the unpredictability and insecurity of all real human relations. At the very
moment Miss Havisham makes sure of Estella, Estella will,
paradoxically, reverse roles and become Miss Havisham's master: " 'But to be proud and hard to *me!*' Miss Havisham quite
shrieked, as she stretched out her arms. 'Estella, Estella, Estella,
to be proud and hard to *me!*' " (38).

In the same way Magwitch cannot resist the temptation to
return from New South Wales, even at the risk of his life, to
see with his own eyes the gentleman he has made: "I've come
to the old country fur to see my gentleman spend his money
*like* a gentleman. That'll be *my* pleasure. *My* pleasure 'ull be
fur to see him do it. And blast you all! . . . blast you every
one, from the judge in his wig, to the colonist a stirring up the
dust, I'll show a better gentleman than the whole kit on you
put together!" (40). Magwitch has returned to let Pip know
the real source of his transformation into a gentleman. His
project cannot succeed because Pip must both know and not
know that Magwitch has "made" him. He must not know, in
order to remain a true gentleman, conscious of enjoying his
status by right. He must know in order really to be Magwitch's
representative, the creature he has manufactured to wreak his
vengeance on society: "Once more he took me by both hands
and surveyed me with an air of admiring proprietorship . . ."
(40). Magwitch wants to enjoy directly his sense of power, and
he wants Pip to know that all his acts are as the vicar of Magwitch. But of course as soon as Pip knows the source of his
great expectations he no longer thinks of himself as a gentleman. Rather he repudiates with horror his connection with

Magwitch, and looks upon himself as Magwitch's dupe, manipulated, as Magwitch was by Compeyson, for his criminal assault upon society. Neither Estella nor Pip can embody in their own persons the contradictory needs of their creators' projects for them.

<h3 style="text-align:center">III</h3>

She had adopted Estella, she had as good as adopted me, and it could not fail to be her intention to bring us together. She reserved it for me to restore the desolate house, admit the sunshine into the dark rooms, set the clocks a going and the cold hearths a blazing, tear down the cobwebs, destroy the vermin — in short, do all the shining deeds of the young Knight of romance, and marry the Princess. (29)

Neither way out of alienation will work, neither the attempt to become an oppressor of those below even while being oppressed from above, nor the attempt to endow someone else with the power to be an oppressor while one remains innocently passive oneself. One other way remains, a way that even more subtly than the others hides its radical defect: The disinherited one may accept "great expectations." That is, he may believe that, in spite of his apparent lack of status, and of any real reason for existing, there is a hidden place for him, a destined role among those who enjoy the dignity and security of being masters. Pip repudiates what he is now with the utmost horror: He denies that he is an orphan, "brought up by hand," destined to be apprenticed to Joe and to spend the rest of his life as a country blacksmith. No, he is not what he appears to be. He is really the secret self which lies unfulfilled in the future, beyond the shadowy mists of his great expectations. Now, he is not what he is, and he is what he is not. Pip's acceptance of great expectations does not mean seizing recognition of his usefulness by force. It means believing that he will be miraculously given a place in society as though it were his natural right, as though the world had for some unaccountable reason conspired to keep his real place hidden, only to bestow it at last as a free gift. Such are Pip's hopes. He believes that Estella and all the privileges possessed by a gentleman are destined for him by Miss Havisham. He will not need to dirty his hands with the crime of appropriating a place among the oppressors. He will suddenly be transformed from the class of the exploited to the class of the exploiters. There will be an absolute discontinuity between his initial given condition of alienation and isolation, and the suddenly attained possession of a secure place in society. The new man will be both free (cannot Pip buy anything he wants?), and at the same time wholly consecrated in his new role by the approval of society.

Although Pip is of course the main example of the theme of "great expectations," a number of other characters are comic parodies of Pip's attempt to transcend his first situation. If Pip seeks escape in the unconditioned possession of Estella and the rights of a gentleman, Wemmick's goal is the unlimited possession of "Portable Property." Wopsle lives in the unquenchable expectation of reviving the drama, with himself as a famous actor, receiving the applause of multitudes. Mrs. Pocket is the daughter of a very small nobleman, and has been "brought up from her cradle as one who in the nature of things must marry a title" (23). As a result she has "grown up highly ornamental, but perfectly helpless and useless" (23). And Herbert Pocket has even greater expectations than Pip does. Although he is a mere miserable apprentice in a counting house, in his own mind he has already made his fortune, and is "a capitalist — an Insurer of Ships" (22).

Pip might have moved beyond awareness that the family and the social order are based on the notion that there are two distinct kinds of being. He might have rejected the whole structure. But no; he accepts the situation, and simply "expects" to move from one status to the other. When Jaggers announces the great expectations, he tells Pip what he has been hoping for all along: his benefactor wishes "that he be immediately removed from his present sphere of life and from this place, and be brought up as a gentleman — in a word, as a young fellow of great expectations" (18). When Joe and Biddy express "wonder" at the notion of Pip as a gentleman, he doesn't "half like it" (18). To him the good fortune is merely the recognition of the true Pip, the Pip who has heretofore by accident been hidden from view. The new Pip feels, like a supernatural being, a "sublime compassion for the poor creatures who were destined to go there [to the country church], Sunday after Sunday, all their lives through, and to lie obscurely at last among the low green mounds" (19). To the new godlike Pip the country people seem less than human. They are like beasts of the field who live a merely natural life, unconsciously passing on to an obscure death, like the "mute inglorious" countrymen of Gray's "Elegy." Pip plans a great feast for the village, in which he, the *grand seigneur,* will stoop from his godlike height and bestow "a dinner of roast-beef and plum-pudding, a pint of ale, and a gallon of condescension, upon everybody in the village" (19). As for Pip: "henceforth [he is] for London and greatness" (19).

It is at first difficult to see why Pip's great expectations do not seem to him another form of the degrading manipulation by society, another subtler form of alienation. They do appear that way to Joe and Biddy, who accept their status with the proud independence of the lower class. When Pip suggests to Biddy that he might "remove Joe into a higher sphere" (19) (a parody of what Jaggers said when he announced the great expectations), she says, "He may be too proud to let any one take him out of a place that he is competent to fill, and fills well and with respect" (19). Why then does Pip accept so readily a change in status which to Joe seems an affront to his pride and independence? It is a very different thing to have as one's given place in society the status of a gentleman rather than the status of a blacksmith. It approaches the reconciliation of freedom and security which Pip seeks. Moreover, the circumstances of mystery which surround the great expectations make it possible to manipulate their meaning ambiguously. Pip thinks they come from Miss Havisham, but he is not certain, and this uncertainty allows him to interpret them as at once a willful choice on someone's part to change his place in society, or as a reward for faithful service, or as recognition that he has too noble a nature to be a blacksmith. Because of the mystery about the gift Pip can look upon his great expectations as at once earned and gratuitously bestowed. The more pleasant interpretation is the one which makes them the recognition by society of what his inmost nature has been all along. The flattering Pumble-chook chooses this interpretation of Pip's rise in the world: "I give you joy of your good fortune," he says. "Well deserved, well deserved!" (19). And he tells Pip he has always said of him: "That boy is no common boy, and mark me, his fortun' will be no common fortun' " (19). The word "common" here has a good deal of nuance. "Coarse and common" was what Estella had called him; these were the words that made him dissatisfied with his lot as a blacksmith's apprentice.

Indeed, Pip's first visit to Miss Havisham's determines every-thing which follows in his life, because it determines the way he reacts to everything which happens to him thereafter: "That was a memorable day to me, for it made great changes in me. But it is the same with any life. Imagine one selected day struck out of it, and think how different its course would have been. Pause you who read this, and think for a moment of the long chain of iron or gold, of thorns or flowers, that would never have bound you, but for the formation of the first link on one memorable day" (9). Pip is "bound" by his reaction to the ex-periences of this day, as firmly as he is bound apprentice to Joe, and as firmly as the captured Magwitch is bound by his fetters. On this day he makes the original choice of a desired self, and binds his destiny inextricably to Estella. Pip is able to understand this only much later, on the day when, aware that he has lost Estella, he first confesses his love for her: "You are part of my existence, part of myself. You have been in every line I have ever read, since I first came here, the rough common boy whose poor heart you wounded even then. You have been in every prospect I have ever seen since — on the river, on the sails of the ships, on the marshes, in the clouds, in the light, in the darkness, in the wind, in the woods, in the sea, in the streets. You have been the embodiment of every graceful fancy that my mind has ever become acquainted with. The stones of which the strongest London buildings are made, are not more real, or more impossible to be displaced by your hands, than your presence and influence have been to me, there and every-where, and will be" (44). Pip's desire to possess Estella, in spite of his recognition of her nature, is identified with his deepest project of selfhood. It is, he says, "the clue by which I am to be followed into my poor labyrinth" (29), "the innermost life of my life" (29). In choosing Estella, Pip alters and defines the entire world, and gives it a permanent structure pervaded by her presence. He is true to the determining choice of his life, the choice that was made when, "humiliated, hurt, spurned, offended, angry, sorry" (8), he reacted to the taunts of Estella not by hating and rejecting her, but by accepting her judgment of him, and by spontaneously rejecting all the pieties of the forge. Before he went to Satis House the forge had been sacred. His prospective relation to it had justified his life as completely as a Christian is justified by his conversion and by his sense of receiving God's grace: "I had believed in the best parlour as a most elegant saloon; I had believed in the front door, as a mysterious portal of the Temple of State whose solemn opening was attended with a sacrifice of roast fowls; I had believed in the kitchen as a chaste though not magnificent apartment; I had believed in the forge as the glowing road to manhood and independence" (14). Now all that is changed. The old gods have been rejected, and Pip is ashamed of home: "Within a single year all this was changed. Now, it was all coarse and common, and I would not have had Miss Havisham and Estella see it on any account" (14). It is only in response to his acceptance of Estella's judgment of him that Pip's great expectations come into existence. It is only because Estella has become part of "every prospect" that Pip makes the otherwise unlikely mistake of assuming Miss Havisham is the source of his great expectations and intends Estella for him. Just as he has rejected as far as possible his relation to Magwitch — being "on secret terms of conspiracy with convicts" is to Pip a "guiltily coarse and common thing," "a feature in [his] low career that [he] had previously forgotten" (10) — so he interprets everything that happens to him in terms of Estella and Miss Havisham. He is not fooled; he fools himself: "All other swindlers upon earth are nothing to the self-swindlers, and with such pretences did I cheat myself" (28).

Pip's love of Estella is by its very nature a self-deception, because it is a love which is based on its own impossibility. It depends in its intimate nature on the fact that it can never be satisfied. On the one hand, Pip says, ". . . I loved her against reason, against promise, against peace, against hope, against happiness, against all discouragement that could be" (29), and, on the other hand, he can say, "Then, a burst of gratitude came upon me, that she should be destined for me, once the blacksmith's boy" (29). From the beginning Estella is the judge who scornfully labels Pip "a common labouring-boy," who looks down on him from a great height like a cold star, and fixes everything eternally in its place, as everything seems eternally immobilized under the winter stars. To Pip, Estella seems always "immeasurably above [him]," and treats him "as insolently as if [he] were a dog in disgrace" (8). But he does not wish to escape from this relationship to Estella, any more than he wishes to escape from his submission to society in those "wretched hankerings after money and gentility" which cannot be dissociated from "her presence" (29). Rather, he imagines that when Estella is given to him as his wife he will succeed in possessing his judge. She is "destined" for him, and therefore he expects to bring down his star from the sky, to have in Estella at once judge and submissive wife.

Pip has succeeded through Estella, if not in escaping his initial state, then at least in defining himself as the lack of something particular. His essence is defined entirely by negations (he lacks the education, language, manners, and fine clothes of a gentleman; he fails to possess Estella — she is "inaccessible"), but even a definition in terms of what he is not is better than no definition at all. Pip in his relation to Estella achieves the only kind of definiteness, it may be, which is available to man: the definition of a desired future self. In spite of her infinite distance and inaccessibility, and in a way because of them, Estella is the source of all the meaning and coherence of Pip's life. To Pip it is a great relief to be judged. The criminal seeks out his own punishment. If his crime remains a secret and he is accepted by everyone as though he were still the person he was before the crime, he has a horrible sense of his own unreality. The gap between what he is for himself, and what other people think he is, causes intolerable suffering. The criminal will give himself up in order to be reintegrated into the human community, even if being reintegrated means to be condemned to death. In the same way, Pip never hesitates a moment to accept Estella's judgment of him, even though it means accepting a much less admirable self than he is in the eyes of Biddy. To Biddy he is an honest blacksmith's apprentice faithful to his duty. But to accept Biddy's judgment rather than Estella's means accepting the role which has become identified for Pip with his initial state of isolation and subjection. On the other hand, Estella's judgment that he is coarse and common implies a very definite self which he fails to be, and which would transcend his first state if he could reach it. It is no wonder that he repudiates Herbert's suggestion that he give her up because she will never make him happy. To give up Estella would be to give up the very meaning of his life. Pip can abandon this relationship to Estella only when the entire structure of his world has been destroyed by the return of Magwitch.

But why did Dickens choose to have his hero enchanted by such a person as Miss Havisham? What is the relation between Pip and Miss Havisham? And why should Estella be identified with the desolation of Satis House? Satis House is an elaborate example of a figurative technique constantly employed by Dickens: the use of houses to symbolize states of soul. Again and again in Dickens' novels we find houses which are the mirror images of their masters or mistresses. But Satis House expresses far more than merely Miss Havisham's nature. Miss Havisham and her house are the images of a fixed social order, the power which can judge Pip at first as coarse and common, and later as a gentleman. The name "Satis House," as Estella tells Pip, "meant, when it was given, that whoever had this house, could want nothing else" (8). That Pip becomes fascinated by such a vision of the upper class and of its norms is all the stronger testimony to the falsity of his desire to be a gentleman. Miss Havisham's house of darkness, decay, and frozen time is a symbol of the upper class, paralyzed in its codified mores and prejudices, as much as it is a symbol of the spiritual condition of Miss Havisham. When Pip sees in "the stopped clock, . . . the withered articles of bridal dress upon

the table and the ground, . . . in the falls of the cobwebs
from the centre-piece, in the crawlings of the spiders on the
cloth," "in everything the construction that [his] mind [has]
come to, repeated and thrown back to [him]" (38), he is con-
fessing to the effect of his infatuation with the idea of being a
gentleman as much as to the effect of his submission to Miss
Havisham or to Estella as persons. Pip in London, living in the
eternally unsatisfied pursuit of Estella and of the "pleasure" of
London high society, is as much the victim of his desire to be
a gentleman as he is of his love for Estella, or of his "enchantment" by Miss Havisham. Miss Havisham and her house, then,
are the concrete symbols of that place in the upper class Pip
has been led to want by Estella's judgment of him. They express his fatuity as no abstract analysis could do. Pip is willing
to barter all the spontaneity and charity of his relations to Joe
for the coldness, formality, and decay of Miss Havisham's
house, and for the life as a gentleman he thinks she has given
him.

But Pip finds that being a gentleman is no escape from uncertainty and guilt. One of the conditions of his great expectations is that he shall still go by the name of Pip, the name he
gave himself in his early childhood. This is a symbol of the
fact that he cannot make a full break with the past, and in a
way hints of the terrible revelation which will shatter his expectations. But even when he has received his expectations, is
living as a gentleman in London, and has not received the
blow which will destroy his hopes, he is not at peace: "I cannot tell you how dependent and uncertain I feel, and how exposed to hundreds of chances" (30); "I lived in a state of
chronic uneasiness respecting my behaviour to Joe" (34);
". . . a weariness on my spirits" (*ibid.*); ". . . restlessness
and disquiet of mind" (*ibid.*). This is partly, no doubt, because
of Pip's uncertainty about Estella, but it is also part of the very
condition of being a gentleman — as Dickens showed in his
other portraits of idle and uneasy aristocrats (such as Eugene
Wrayburn or Henry Gowan). These young gentlemen all suffer from ennui, and from an inability to choose a course of ac-

tion. Paralysis of will seizes them precisely because they have unlimited possibilities. There are so many courses open to them that they are wholly unable to choose one. Far from realizing the peace of a reconciliation of freedom and security, Pip's transformation into a gentleman only plunges him into deeper disquietude and weariness of spirits — deeper because he is even further than ever away from the discovery of some externally imposed duty which will tell him what to do and who he is.

IV

There comes a moment, then, when Pip discovers the futility and hollowness of his expectations. Already he has discovered that the mere unlimited possession of money is not "enough." When he is learning to be a gentleman in London with Herbert Pocket he gets further and further into debt, and his device of projecting the debt limit further and further by leaving a "margin" is an effective dramatization of the ever-receding character of his attempt to achieve peace and stability through money. Each time he runs into debt immediately "to the full extent of the margin, and sometimes, in the sense of freedom and solvency it impart[s], [gets] pretty far on into another margin" (34). The more money Pip spends, the more he needs, and the goal of satisfaction recedes further and further, like the end of the rainbow. The actual possession of the tangible evidence of his great expectations leaves him what he has always been: "restless aspiring discontented me" (14). Dickens is dramatizing here his recognition of the bankruptcy of the idea of the gentleman, who rules by inherited right, but owes protection and help to those beneath. Since society has ceased, in Dickens' view, to be an organic structure, being a gentleman means chiefly having the money to buy education and luxuries. It no more means being part of a community than does being sent to the hulks, like Magwitch, or being bound apprentice, like Pip. Pip the gentleman, spending money in London, enjoying the frivolities of his club, the Finches of the Grove, has no authentic relation to anybody. Instead of improving his condition, he has substituted for a dehumanizing relation to society no relation at all.[3]

Moreover, Pip discovers when he at last openly admits his love for Estella that she cannot at the same time be both distant judge, and possessed and enjoyed as a wife. As transcendent judge she is not really human at all, but a superhuman goddess, and as a woman she could not play the role of judge. It is not until Pip learns that Estella is not "destined" for him that he really faces the fact that she has no heart, and cannot love him. Until then he has believed, in the *hubris* of his great expectations, that she would be able to combine the two incompatible roles. Whenever she has appeared particularly cold, proud, or unfeeling, he has been able to assure himself that after all she is destined for him. It is only when he realizes that Miss Havisham does not "mean" them for one another that he can understand Estella when she says: "When you say you love me, I know what you mean, as a form of words; but nothing more. You address nothing in my breast, you touch nothing there. I don't care for what you say at all" (44).

Finally, Pip discovers the emptiness of his hope of being given a justified place in the ruling class. He discovers that his real benefactor is not Miss Havisham, the representative of society, but the pariah Magwitch, "hunted dunghill dog." This discovery is really a discovery of the self-deception of his great expectations, his recognition that they were based on an irreconcilable contradiction. Pip has been climbing slowly toward Estella and toward the freedom and security of gentility. Now the ladder has collapsed, and he finds himself back at his origin again, back where he was at the opening of the story. Then he had received his "first most vivid and broad impression of

[3] Dickens shares with other Victorian novelists a concern for the validity and meaning of the term "gentleman." In *Great Expectations,* as in the ironies of *Little Dorrit,* he tends to repudiate the term altogether. For him it is a mere expression of the impostures and injustices of society. However, as G. N. Ray has shown in *Thackeray: The Uses of Adversity, 1811–1846* (New York, 1955), Thackeray believes that the idea of the gentleman is undergoing a profound revaluation, but still is an indispensable concept, whereas the more conservative Trollope feels that right ethical actions are performed spontaneously only by those who possess by nature the unanalyzable qualities of a gentleman or lady.

the identity of things," including himself, on the day he stole food from his home to feed an escaped convict. Now he has discovered that the source of his "expectations" is not Miss Havisham, but that same convict. Moreover, he has discovered that Estella, the star of his expectations and the symbol of his desire for gentility, is really the daughter of Magwitch. All that he thought was taking him further and further from his shameful beginning has only been bringing him inexorably back to his starting point. He is like a man lost in the woods who struggles for hours to find his way out, only to discover suddenly that he has returned by a circuitous route to the exact spot where he first realized that he did not know where he was.

But Pip's return is to an origin which has been transformed into its opposite. Then the tie to Magwitch was repudiated as sinful, as the guilty secret of a crime against home, as a shameful bond to the dregs of society, and as the pain of moral isolation. Now that same tie is about to be revalued. As Pip starts down the Thames on the desperate attempt to save the life of the convict who has broken parole to return to him, "a veil [seems] to be drawn from the river, and millions of sparkles burst out upon its waters," and "[f]rom [Pip], too, a veil [seems] to be drawn" (53). The mists that rose from the marshes as he started off for London (19) have been dissipated at last, and Pip stands ready to face the truth which lies at the very center of *Great Expectations:* all the claims made by wealth, social rank, and culture to endow the individual with true selfhood are absolutely false. However far he apparently travels from his origin he will still be akin to the mud and briars of the marshes and to the terrible man he met there on the day he became aware of himself as Pip, the Pip who has named himself because there is no person and no institution that cares enough for him to give him a name. And, at the same time, Pip discovers that he himself has initiated the series of events which he believed were descending on him from the outside through a mysterious grace. He it was who committed the act of aggression against his family, stole for the convict, did not give him up to the soldiers, and formed the secret "taint of prison and crime" which has stuck to him all his life. He it is who is himself the source of all that has happened to him, all that he has believed was not his responsibility. The appearance of Magwitch to claim the "gentleman what he has made" reveals to the horrified Pip that he has not been free, that he has been secretly manipulated as though he were a passive tool, or puppet, or a mechanical man created for Magwitch's revenge on society. But it also reminds him that he has himself been guilty of the act of kindness, outside the bounds of all socially approved morality, which formed his tie to the convict. Moreover, he has also been Miss Havisham's "tool." She has not been secretly planning to bestow on him Estella and her jewels as a reward for his intrinsic nobility of character. No, she has rather been using him as something for Estella to practice her techniques of heart-breaking on. Pip's voyage, his attempt to sustain himself above all coercion and determination, and yet not to accept any responsibility for this, has ended in utter shipwreck: "Miss Havisham's intentions towards me, all a mere dream; Estella not designed for me; I only suffered in Satis House as a convenience, a sting for the greedy relations, a model with a mechanical heart to practise on when no other practice was at hand; those were the first smarts I had. But, sharpest and deepest pain of all — it was for the convict, guilty of I knew not what crimes, and liable to be taken out of those rooms where I sat thinking, and hanged at the Old Bailey door, that I had deserted Joe" (39).

Pip's life as a gentleman turns out to have combined the worst possible aspects of both sides of the human condition: its unjustifiable freedom, and its imprisonment in a given situation. On the one hand, Pip's life as a gentleman has been a fraud practiced on society. He has in effect pushed and elbowed his way into a place in the upper class — gratuitously and under false pretenses. He must experience the bad conscience of the social climber, the parvenu. Pip is thrown back, therefore, on his initial isolation. There is nothing outside himself that judges, approves, consecrates his existence. On the other hand, Pip discovers that his life as a gentleman has been unwittingly a return to the life of a manipulated object he had so hated when he was a child being brought up "by hand." He is returned to his alienation, and to his submission to what is imposed on him by force from the outside, and determines his actions, his place in the world, and even his nature: "The imaginary student pursued by the misshapen creature he had impiously made, was not more wretched than I, pursued by the creature who had made me, and recoiling from him with a stronger repulsion, the more he admired me and the fonder he was of me" (40). Indeed, as this passage implies, Pip is both Frankenstein's monster and Frankenstein himself. He has without knowing it been the creature of Magwitch's project of revenge, but at the same time he himself has made this possible by the initial act of pity and kindness which inextricably linked Magwitch's life to his. Magwitch chose to make Pip a gentleman only because Pip had "kep life in [him]" when he was a "hunted dunghill dog" (39). "Look'ee here, Pip," says Magwitch. "I'm your second father. You're my son — more to me nor any son!" (39) — "more" because in this case the son has been as much maker of his father as father the maker of son. From the height of his great expectations, Pip is cast down again into the depths of disinheritance. He has indeed acted freely in forming his filial bond to Magwitch, freely in the sense that he has acted outside every social law. His freedom has been horrifyingly transformed into a wholesale assault and fraud on society. He is, in fact, even more disinherited than he was at the beginning, for now he knows the full meaning of his state, and he is able to compare this realization that he is nothing except what he has made himself with the self-deceiving hope of the great expectations he has so recently lost. At "the end of the second stage of [his] expectations" (39), Pip is at the deepest point of his wretchedness: ". . . it was not until I began to think," he says, "that I began fully to know how wrecked I was, and how the ship in which I had sailed was gone to pieces" (39).

V

The third part of "Pip's Expectations" traces the slow rise of the hero's fortunes. He moves out of the depths of despair in which he finds himself at the end of the second part. Love is the cause of this reversal of fortune. For Dickens, as for the general tradition of ethical thought, love is the only successful escape from the unhappiness of singularity, the unhappiness of being this unique and isolated person, Pip.

For Dickens, as for generations of Christian moralists, love means sacrifice. Pip must abandon all the proud hopes which have formed the secret core of his life. He must abandon forever his project of being a gentleman, the belief that somewhere there is a place for him which he can possess by right. He must accept the fact that he can in no way transcend the gap between "the small bundle of shivers growing afraid of it all and beginning to cry" and the wind, sea, sky, and marshland, the alien universe — in no way, that is, but by willingly accepting this separation. And to accept this means to accept Magwitch, who springs up with "a terrible voice" from the marshes at the moment Pip becomes aware of his separateness.

Pip learns about love, then, not through Estella, but through the slow change in his relation to Magwitch. Only this change makes possible a transformation of his relation to Estella. Otherwise, Pip would have remained, even if he had possessed Estella, the submissive worshipper of a cold and distant authority. Just as Mrs. Joe atones for her cruelties to Pip and Joe by bowing down to Orlick, so Pip can escape from despair, from the total loss of his great expectations, only by a change in his attitude toward Magwitch. His acceptance of Magwitch is not only the relinquishment of his great expectations; it is also the replacement of these by a positive assertion that he, Pip alone, will be the source of the meaning of his own life. Pip finally accepts as the foundation of his life the guilt which has always haunted him: his secret and gratuitous act of charity to the escaped convict. Pip slowly realizes that if he betrays Magwitch as Razumov betrays Victor Haldin in Conrad's *Under Western Eyes,* it will be to betray himself, to betray the possible foundation of himself by self-denial, by the abandonment of his egoistic expectations. And to betray Magwitch will be to plunge Magwitch back into the nothingness of the complete outcast. It is a case of the hunter hunted. Pip had been seeking in social position and in Estella a basis for his identity. Now he finds

hat he himself has been sought. Just as Razumov finds that he
annot escape having *some* relation to Victor Haldin, even
hough he has not sought any (since Haldin has "taken" him
is a revolutionary, he must be either faithful to the image of
imself the other has formed, or he must betray it), so Pip has
een seized, will-nilly, by Magwitch, and, whatever he does
henceforth, cannot avoid his tie to Magwitch. In Dickens'
vorld, as in Conrad's, people exist in the exact degree that they
xist in other people's eyes. And for Dickens, as for Conrad, one
erson can impose on another, whether he wishes it or not, the
esponsibility of betraying him or being faithful to him. Pip at-
empts all through his life, until his change, to remain neutral
oward Magwitch, to "beat the dust of Newgate out of his
lothes," to wipe out of existence the charitable theft for Mag-
vitch which happened so long ago in his childhood. But he can-
ot erase this act from existence. He can only betray it, or re-
ffirm it. His whole life has been determined by that initial act.
n spite of himself Pip is forced into complicity with convicts.
Ie is forced to make a choice: either give Magwitch up to the
olice, or commit against society the crime of harboring an es-
aped felon.

Whereas Razumov betrays Haldin, Pip is faithful to Mag-
itch, and perhaps this marks the difference between the two
ovelists, and between the two centuries. But it is only slowly
hat Pip realizes what his faithfulness means. It means facing
ie fact that he and Magwitch are in the same position of isola-
on. If they do not help one another, no one will. It means dis-
overing that each can help the other by offering himself as the
oundation of the other's selfhood, Pip by sacrificing all his
opes, Magwitch by his change from a fierce desire to "make"
gentleman for revenge, to the desire to help Pip be a gentle-
an for Pip's own sake: "For now my repugnance to him had
l melted away, and in the hunted wounded shackled creature
ho held my hand in his, I only saw a man who had meant to
e my benefactor, and who had felt affectionately, gratefully,
d generously, towards me with great constancy through a
ries of years" (54). Magwitch's handclasp, originally a sym-
olic appropriation of Pip as his creation and possession, now

becomes the symbol of their mutual love, and of their willingness to sacrifice all for one another. This transformation is complete after the unsuccessful attempt to get Magwitch safely out of the country. Thereafter, Magwitch thinks only of Pip and not at all of the "society" he had so hated, and Pip thinks only of Magwitch (56).

Pip remains faithful to Magwitch, publicly manifesting his allegiance throughout Magwitch's imprisonment, trial, and death. He hides from Magwitch the fact that all his money will be forfeited to the crown, and that his hopes of leaving Pip a gentleman will fail. And just before Magwitch dies Pip tells him that Estella, his child, is still alive, "is a lady and very beautiful. And I love her!" (56). This is in a way his greatest sacrifice. He admits that he even owes Estella to Magwitch, and brings all the hope and dreams which had centered on Estella completely into the orbit of his relation to Magwitch. Magwitch is the source of everything he has and is.

By choosing his servitude to Magwitch, Pip transforms it into freedom. The dialectic of love in Dickens is more like the Kierkegaardian choice of oneself than like Sartre's endlessly frustrated conflict between two freedoms striving to be both free and secure at the same time. In place of the self-assertive love which requires the other to make himself the basis of one's selfhood, there is substituted by Magwitch and Pip the mutual sacrifice of their dearest claims to selfhood. For Dickens, as for Kierkegaard, the self can only affirm itself through self-sacrifice. But what was for Kierkegaard the relation of man to God becomes in Dickens the relation of man to man. No character in Dickens finally achieves authentic selfhood by establishing direct relation to God. Only the mutually self-denying self-creating relationship of love succeeds, whereas the active assertion of will and the passive hope of great expectations both fail.

The divine power functions in *Great Expectations* primarily as the supreme judge before whom all social distinctions are as nothing: "The sun was striking in at the great windows of the court, through the glittering drops of rain upon the glass, and it made a broad shaft of light between the two-and-thirty [criminals] and the Judge, linking both together, and perhaps reminding some among the audience, how both were passing on, with absolute equality, to the greater Judgment that knoweth all things and cannot err" (56). There is a true religious motif here. The light is God's judgment before which earthly judge and earthly judged, gentleman and common thief, are equal. But the meaning of the passage is as much social as religious. It is a final dramatization of the fact that social eminence such as Pip had sought and social judgments such as have hounded Magwitch all his life are altogether unimportant as sources of selfhood. At the center of Dickens' novels is a recognition of the bankruptcy of the relation of the individual to society as it now exists, the objective structure of given institutions and values. Only what an individual makes of himself, in charitable relations to others, counts. And this self-creation tends to require open revolt against the pressures of society. Human beings are themselves the source of the transcendence of their isolation.

Once Pip has established his new relationship to Magwitch he is able at last to win Estella. Pip's final love for Estella is a single complex relation which is both identification with the loved person (he is no longer conscious of a lack, a void of unfulfilled desire), and separation (he is still aware of himself as a self, as a separate identity; he does not melt into the loved person, and lose himself altogether). As in *Little Dorrit* and *A Tale of Two Cities,* the irreducible otherness, the permanent area of mystery in the loved one, is recognized and maintained.

Pip and Estella have experienced before their union their most complete separation, Pip in the agony of his discovery that Estella is not destined for him and that Magwitch is his real benefactor, and Estella in her unhappy marriage to Bentley Drummle, who has "used her with great cruelty," just as Pip has been "used" by Estella. These experiences have transformed them both. It is only when Estella has been tamed by the cruelty of her bad husband that she and Pip can enter into a wholy different relationship. Only when Estella's proud, cold glance is transformed into "the saddened softened light of the once proud eyes" (59) can she and Pip transform the fettering of slave by master into the handclasp of love. Estella too must

suffer the slave's loss of selfhood in order to be herself transformed. Both have come back from a kind of death to meet and
join in the moonlight in Miss Havisham's ruined garden. The
second ending is, in my opinion, the best. Not only was it, after
all, the one Dickens published (would he really have acceded
to Mrs. Grundy in the mask of Bulwer-Lytton without reasons
of his own?), but, it seems to me, the second ending, in joining
Pip and Estella, is much truer to the real direction of the story.
The paragraphs which, in the second version of the ending,
close the novel remind us, in their echo of Milton, that Estella
and Pip are accepting their exile from the garden of false
hopes. Now that the mists of infatuation have cleared away Pip
and Estella are different persons. They go forth from the ruined garden into a fallen world. In this world their lives will
be given meaning only by their own acts and by their dependence on one another. Pip now has all that he wanted, Estella
and her jewels, but what he has is altogether different from
what he expected. Rather than possessing the impossible reconciliation of freedom and security he had sought in Estella and
in gentility, he now loves and is loved by another fallible and
imperfect being like himself:

The silvery mist was touched with the first rays of the moonlight, and the same rays touched the tears that dropped from her
eyes. . . .
I took her hand in mine, and we went out of the ruined place;
and, as the morning mists had risen long ago when I first left the
forge, so, the evening mists were rising now, and in all the broad
expanse of tranquil light they showed to me, I saw no shadow of
another parting from her. (59)

## Chapter IX

# OUR MUTUAL FRIEND

### I

IF *Little Dorrit* shows that, for Dickens, a man can be success-fully reintegrated into the world only through the medium of another person, *Great Expectations* seems to indicate that this saving relation can only come into being entirely outside the context of society. The individual's place in society can only determine an inauthentic existence. But *Our Mutual Friend* everywhere gives evidence that for Dickens in his last com-pleted novel no one can escape his given place. Of all the char-acters in this novel it would be true to say what Dickens says of John Harmon: "He had lapsed into the condition in which he found himself, as many a man lapses into many a condi-tion, without perceiving the accumulative power of its sepa-rate circumstances" (II, 14). A man cannot perceive the power of circumstances because they are identical with his own life, and it is impossible to withdraw to a detached perspective and see them as they are. Man is not detached. He is entwined with the world, and the world is permeated with his presence. Man is his world. The condition of the characters in *Our Mutual Friend* thus differs radically from that of the protagonists of *Oliver Twist* or *Martin Chuzzlewit,* or from that of all the other orphans and outcasts in Dickens. Oliver Twist began his life alienated from the world, excluded from it. He sought some place in society as the only means of securing selfhood. In *Our Mutual Friend,* by the time the characters reach the age of self-reflection they find themselves already enmeshed in a situ-ation. It is altogether impossible to withdraw completely from that situation and to create out of nothing a new self and a new engagement in the world. There is no realm of pure spirit or pure freedom. *Our Mutual Friend* presents a fully elaborated definition of what it means to be interlaced with the world.

But what are the dimensions of this world whose frontiers are also the characters' frontiers of being?

It might seem that *Our Mutual Friend* simply presents again on a wider canvas the way of being in the world characteristic of Mr. Mould in *Martin Chuzzlewit* or, indeed, of a great many other characters in Dickens' novels. Character after character is presented living imprisoned in his own nature and in his own milieu. Each personage, on all occasions, could be said to be like Mr. Dolls, who "brought his own atmosphere with him" (III, 17). Thus Rogue Riderhood is as much enclosed as Mr. Mould. He dwells "deep and dark in Limehouse Hole, among the riggers, and the mast, oar and block makers, and the boat-builders, and the sail-lofts, as in a kind of ship's hold stored full of waterside characters" (II, 12). And so the Veneerings are defined by their surroundings. Dickens does not have to present them from the inside. What they are is entirely visible from the outside. The observer does not need to be told that the Veneerings, like the Lammles, "have no antecedents, no established character, no cultivation, no ideas, no manners" (I, 10). Their inner natures are altogether present in what is exterior to them: "Mr. and Mrs. Veneering were bran-new people in a bran-new house in a bran-new quarter of London. Everything about the Veneerings was spick and span new. All their furniture was new, all their friends were new, all their servants were new, their plate was new, their carriage was new, . . . they themselves were new, they were as newly married as was lawfully compatible with their having a bran-new baby, and if they had set up a great-grandfather, he would have come home in matting from the Pantechnicon, without a scratch upon him, French-polished to the crown of his head. . . . And what was observable in the furniture, was observable in the Veneerings — the surface smelt a little too much of the workshop and was a trifle sticky" (I, 2).

*Our Mutual Friend,* then, apparently differs from its predecessors only in that it presents a greater number of characters in terms of the intermingling of their inner natures and outer surroundings. There is no central protagonist in *Our Mutual Friend*. Far more even than *Bleak House* it is a multi-plotted novel. There a few characters were obviously central, but in *Our Mutual Friend,* though some characters are more complex or more elaborately treated than others, a very large number, almost all those who appear, are shown in the full span of their lives, not from their birth but from an initial presentation of the person rooted in his situation to some conclusive working out of that situation and its transformation into the destiny of the character.

Nevertheless in *Our Mutual Friend* we do not simply see the characters in the midst of their milieus, trapped eternally like flies in amber. We see them actively living their situations through time and making them into the definitive meaning of their lives. In *Our Mutual Friend* Dickens describes what we never saw in the case of Mr. Mould: the very formation of milieus. The environments of these characters have a crowded, built-up quality. The characters are slowly fabricating a thick texture of humanized things around themselves, as, for example, Mr. Venus is surrounded by the products of his craft, the bones which he is articulating piece by piece with the care of a jeweler. But his shop is not static and complete. His world is not finished. It is in process. Along with the finished skeletons there is a great collection of disarticulated bones which have yet to be put together. And the Harmon dust-heaps, a dominant symbol in the novel, have been thrown up bit by bit as a kind of projection of their maker. Old Harmon has literally produced his own geographical surroundings. He was "a tremendous old rascal who . . . grew rich as a Dust Contractor, and lived in a hollow in a hilly country entirely composed of Dust. On his own small estate the growling old vagabond threw up his own mountain range, like an old volcano, and its geological formation was Dust" (I, 2). Moreover, it is no longer possible to say that most of Dickens' characters are unself-conscious, so wrapped up in an unchanging identity and its appropriate environment that they are unable to make even the least motion of self-reflection. All the characters in *Our Mutual Friend* are perfectly self-aware. We hear almost all of them, even the more or less unintelligent characters like Betty Higden, talking about themselves, or even see them from the inside in soliloquy. This self-consciousness takes a special form: the characters are shown as aware of their situations, of their given engagements in the world. And they are shown assuming these situations, accepting them as ineluctable matters of fact, as Jenny Wren accepts her drunken father and her crippled back, and as Pleasant Riderhood accepts her inheritance, though she has not chosen it: "Pleasant she found herself, and she couldn't help it. She had not been consulted on the question, any more than on the question of her coming into these terrestrial parts, to want a name. Similarly, she found herself possessed of what is colloquially termed a swivel eye (derived from her father), which she might perhaps have declined if her sentiments on the subject had been taken" (II, 12). All of the characters are, like Pleasant Riderhood, aware that they have been thrown willy-nilly into a particular place in the world, and have found themselves already committed rather than able to commit themselves freely. The identity the characters have as members of a certain level of society is as much part of them as the psychological characteristics with which they were born: "Our old selves weren't people of fortune; our new selves are," says Mr. Boffin in explanation of his changed way of life, and, to Lizzie Hexam, Eugene Wrayburn is inseparable from his place in society: "If my mind could put you on equal terms with me, you could not be yourself" (IV, 6). But the characters have given psychological natures too. They are aware that part of their inheritance is an inalterable identity. Their situations cannot be escaped, and neither can the psychological identity in terms of which they live that situation. Thus Eugene Wrayburn says of Lizzie Hexam: "She cannot choose for herself to be strong in this fancy, wavering in that, and weak in the other. She must go through with her nature, as I must go through with mine" (IV, 6).

Since the characters are conscious of themselves and of their situations, it is not possible for them to live, as did some charac

ters in *Bleak House,* completely cut off from their pasts in a repetitive present which cannot even be recognized as repetitive.
As their immediate involvements in the world are vividly present to them, so their pasts too are present, and are constantly
relived by the characters as intimate parts of their lives. Just
as the present situation cannot be withdrawn from and escaped, so the characters make no pretense of being able to escape from their own pasts. A crucial incident in Bella Wilfer's
past seems to her, as she tells her father, to be constantly reënacted as her life continues: ". . . if you knew how much I
think this morning of what you told me once, about the first
time of our seeing old Mr. Harmon, when I stamped and
screamed and beat you with my detestable little bonnet! I feel
as if I had been stamping and screaming and beating you with
my hateful little bonnet, ever since I was born . . ." (IV, 4).
In fact, the characters' awareness of their pasts depends intimately on their awareness of their entanglement in an inescapable present situation. This scene from Bella's childhood
still seems part of her present existence because it was the very
moment when old Mr. Harmon first saw Bella and decided to
will her to his son. The past moment has caused her present relation to the world, and is equally present in her memory and
in the particular world which organizes itself around her. Each
character in *Our Mutual Friend,* then, is the unique possessor
of a circumambient world which is both spatial and temporal.
This world surrounds them and is as intimately present to them
as their own self-consciousness.

The uniqueness of each character's involvement in the world
is apparent in the way Dickens maintains a special tone or
style for each character or homogeneous group of characters:
the hard, detached present tense narration for the "Society" of
the Veneerings, Podsnaps, and Lammles, the slightly hallucinated, nightmarish tone of the grotesque colloquies between
Wegg and Venus, the farcical comedy of the Wilfer home, the
self-destructive intensity of Bradley Headstone's speech and action, and so on. The unique style of life of each character is visible in all the language Dickens uses about him, and to move
from a chapter about the Veneerings to a chapter about Wegg

and Boffin is to move into an entirely different world. The narrator respects the irreducible particularity of each character or group. The basic structural technique of the novel is the complete transformation of tone and milieu from chapter to chapter. Even more than *Bleak House, Our Mutual Friend* might be compared to cubist collage. Its structure is formed by the juxtaposition of incompatible fragments in a pattern of disharmony or mutual contradiction. Apparently, then, *Our Mutual Friend* is a multi-plotted novel presenting a collection of unrelated lives each fulfilling itself privately, enclosed in its own personal world. The novel seems to be a large group of impenetrable milieus with characters buried untouchably at their centers. These milieus exist side by side, but do not organize themselves into a larger whole.

## II

It was the queerest of rooms, fitted and furnished more like a luxurious amateur tap-room than anything else within the ken of Silas Wegg. There were two wooden settles by the fire, one on either side of it, with a corresponding table before each. . . . Facing the fire between the settles, a sofa, a footstool, and a little table, formed a centrepiece devoted to Mrs. Boffin. They were garish in taste and colour, but were expensive articles of drawing-room furniture that had a very odd look beside the settles and the flaring gaslight pendent from the ceiling. There was a flowery carpet on the floor; but, instead of reaching to the fireside, its glowing vegetation stopped short at Mrs. Boffin's footstool, and gave place to a region of sand and sawdust. (I, 5)

Nothing could be less like the presentation in *Martin Chuzzlewit* of Mr. Mould and his surroundings. There everything, including other people, was a reflection of a single subjectivity. But here there are three subjectivities, each possessing in its own way the room. The irreducible isolation of each consciousness is recognized. Though Mr. and Mrs. Boffin are man and wife they do not share a common milieu. Each has produced a projection of his own personality in the room, Boffin's amateur taproom and Mrs. Boffin's garish drawing room. But there are no impenetrable walls surrounding each milieu. The Bof-

fins are present and available to one another in the room they
share. The room is both single and double at once. Moreover,
there is an intermediate area, a kind of no man's land, where
the two milieus come into contact with one another, conflict,
and for a brief distance interpenetrate. Mrs. Boffin's flowery
carpet *gives place* to a region of sand and sawdust. It is surrounded, and, so to speak, embraced by Mr. Boffin's part of the
room. The room and its contents are a perfect objective model
of a reciprocal relation between two subjectivities. Each person
keeps his own integrity, but each is in intimate contact with the
other via the material objects with which they have surrounded
themselves. As Mr. Boffin explains, the bizarre furnishings of
the room are not evidence of the marital disharmony of the
couple, but are made by mutual consent: "These arrangements
is made by mutual consent between Mrs. Boffin and me. Mrs.
Boffin, as I've mentioned, is a highflyer at Fashion; at present
I'm not. I don't go higher than comfort, and comfort of the
sort that I'm equal to the enjoyment of. Well then. Where
would be the good of Mrs. Boffin and me quarrelling over it?"
(I, 5). Each person possesses the other's milieu, and recognizes
it as representing in some sense part of his own personality. It
is always possible that the boundaries will, by mutual agreement, be moved in one direction or another. They are fluid
and kept in place not by the pressure of a single personality,
but by the balance between two personalities which are in intimate contact. Wherever the boundaries may be, this strange
room expresses not only the irreconcilability of "Fashion" and
"Comfort," but also the "Sociability," symbolized by a kiss,
which unifies the two: "So Mrs. Boffin, she keeps up her part
of the room, in her way; I keep up my part of the room in
mine. In consequence of which we have at once, Sociability (I
should go melancholy mad without Mrs. Boffin), Fashion, and
Comfort. If I get by degrees to be a highflyer at Fashion, then
Mrs. Boffin will by degrees come for'arder. If Mrs. Boffin
should ever be less of a dab at Fashion than she is at the present
time, then Mrs. Boffin's carpet would go back'arder. If we
should both continny as we are, why then *here* we are, and give
us a kiss, old lady" (I, 5).

Moreover, the room is presented not as seen by a detached observer (Dickens' usual strategy), but through the eyes of someone from the outside who nevertheless participates in the scene. Wegg, a stranger here, sees the room as the arena of his own potential activity of appropriation. The objects in Mould's room communicate only with him, but here inanimate objects speak to the outsider, and offer themselves to him: ". . . certain squat case-bottles of inviting appearance seemed to stand on tiptoe to exchange glances with Mr. Wegg over a front row of tumblers and a basin of white sugar" (I, 5). Wegg is, in his own way, as much interwoven with the objects in the room as are Mr. and Mrs. Boffin.

*Our Mutual Friend,* then, is not really a collection of impenetrable milieus with characters buried unattainably at their centers. Each character lives in intimate contact with all of the other characters. The characters coexist. The milieu of each is not his own private surroundings, but the world shared in common by all of the characters. This world is both physical and spiritual, or, rather, it is the nonhuman world as collectively humanized by all of the people living within it. Rather than forming a screen which cuts one off from the world, one's own material premises are a unique perspective on all the other premises, and on the lives that are lived within them. So the dust mounds are private mountains shutting off the world, but they also afford a view of the neighborhood, a possession of the world which extends far beyond Harmon's own domain: "There's a serpentining walk up each of the mounds, that gives you the yard and neighbourhood changing every moment When you get to the top, there's a view of the neighbouring premises, not to be surpassed. The premises of Mrs. Boffin's late father . . . , you look down into, as if they was your own' (I, 5). In *Bleak House* the fog was a nonconducting medium cutting the characters off from one another, but the city of *Our Mutual Friend* is integrated by the river. And just as the river flows through all the city and is shared in common by all so the Harmon murder is not altogether a secret. It is a public object too, and exists as what all the people in all the different levels of society know and think about it: "Thus, like the tides on which it had been borne to the knowledge of men, the Harmon Murder — as it came to be popularly called — went up and down, and ebbed and flowed, now in the town, now in the country, now among palaces, now among hovels, now among lords and ladies and gentlefolks, now among labourers and hammerers and ballast-heavers, until at last, after a long interval of slack water, it got out to sea and drifted away" (I, 3).

The characters in *Our Mutual Friend* know about the other characters, even those existing in very different levels of society. And they are aware that they are known by the others. Dickens again and again gives us a perspective on one character or set of characters from the point of view of other characters in other social levels. Thus, we first hear of the Harmon murder and of its circumstances at the Veneering dinner table, and we are constantly throughout the novel seeing the waterside characters or the Boffins and Wilfers from the point of view of "Society." And, on the other hand, Bella Wilfer is acutely conscious of the way she is "made the property of strangers" (II, 13): ". . . when the Harmon murder was all over the town, and people were speculating on its being suicide, I dare say those impudent wretches at the clubs and places made jokes about the miserable creature's having preferred a watery grave to me" (I, 4).

Furthermore, characters from all levels constantly meet and interact with one another. There is a great deal more genuine interrelation and cross contact here than in *Bleak House*. In *Bleak House* all the characters were related, but often in an external way, as all involved in the Chancery suit or in the Dedlock mystery. And in *Bleak House* meetings tended to be the collisions of inalterable characters locked in their private selves. But here there are dozens of encounters which change both persons. The novel might be seen as a kind of slow dance in which all the possibilities of interaction are displayed one by one. Even characters who are not to have decisive effects on one another's lives are shown meeting and changing one another, for example, Fascination Fledgeby and Jenny Wren, Bella Wilfer and Lizzie Hexam, Mr. and Mrs. Lammle and the

Boffins. There is nothing abstract or impersonal about these meetings. They are direct and intimate, and have the effect of causing each character to manifest himself in a way he could only do through contact with just this other person. Thus the central dramatic actions work themselves out in a context which ultimately includes all of the other characters in the novel. The novel is an immense network of interrelations, none of which has an isolated existence.

The human world made by the transformation of matter into utensils, values, and meanings is the vehicle of an intercommunication which liberates all of the characters from the prison of their subjectivity. Since each of the characters penetrates and possesses a material world which extends far beyond his private milieu, all of the characters are in touch with each other. The true mode of existence in *Our Mutual Friend* is intersubjectivity. The consciousness of each character is interwoven not only with the nonhuman matter around it, but also, by means of that matter, with the consciousness of the other characters. The inner self of another person is not here, as it was in *Martin Chuzzlewit,* impenetrably hidden behind the masks of his home, costume, or body. It is open, accessible, almost as much present as one's own consciousness.

Consequently, there is no drama of bewilderment and discovery such as dominated *Pickwick Papers, Oliver Twist,* or *Martin Chuzzlewit,* no obsession with secrets as in *Little Dorrit.* Even the central secret of *Our Mutual Friend* is not meant to be a secret from the reader, and it plays a very different role in the interrelations of the characters from that played by the secrets in the earlier novels. "I was at great pains," says Dickens in his postscript, "to suggest . . . that Mr. John Harmon was not slain, and that Mr. John Rokesmith was he" (p. 926). Even when the full truth about one character is hidden from another, an intuitive understanding of the other's general nature and situation is available at a glance. Bradley Headstone is one of the most secret characters in *Our Mutual Friend,* and takes elaborate pains to keep his self-destructive passion hidden. Yet try as he may, he cannot keep John Harmon from learning something of the depths of his inner turmoil: "The

Secretary thought, as he glanced at the schoolmaster's face, that he had opened a channel here indeed, and that it was an unexpectedly dark and deep and stormy one, and difficult to sound. All at once, in the midst of his turbulent emotions, Bradley stopped and seemed to challenge his look. Much as though he suddenly asked him, 'What do you see in me?' " (II, 14). Even Rogue Riderhood has no difficulty reading Bradley's mind, and strangers in a low tavern understand him immediately: "not one of the night-birds hovering about the sloppy bar failed to discern at a glance in the passion-wasted night-bird with respectable feathers, the worst night-bird of all" (III, 11). There are no real secrets in *Our Mutual Friend*. The characters are immediately available to one another, primarily, perhaps, through language, but also through gestures and mute body-language which are perfectly comprehensible, like Jenny Wren's habit of stabbing the air with her needle, as if she were piercing someone's eyes, or Boffin's pantomimic colloquies with his walking stick (IV, 3), or the white dints that come and go around Lammle's nose (IV, 2). Lammle's coarse falsity is instantly perceptible in a quality of excessiveness that pervades his appearance. His big nose unmistakably betrays his mind and his manners: "Too much of him in every way; pervadingly too much nose of a coarse wrong shape, and his nose in his mind and his manners; too much smile to be real; too much frown to be false; too many large teeth to be visible at once without suggesting a bite" (II, 16). Lammle is even able to gesture with his shirt-front (IV, 2), and Mrs. Lammle's "appealing look" (IV, 2) at the Boffins is instantly understood, while the struggle within her as she leaves the Boffins is expressed not in language but "in the depth of the few last lines of the parasol point indented into the tablecloth" (IV, 2).

People exist in the universe of *Our Mutual Friend* as a kind of magnetic emanation which goes out from their inner selves through their bodies and behavior to permeate the world around them. These emanations cannot be avoided by other people. They effect a qualitative change in the minds and even appearances of others. Thus the "very presence" of Eugene Wrayburn beside Lizzie Hexam "in the dark common street" is "like glimpses of an enchanted world" (II, 15); an old lady has "an infection of absurdity about her, that communicate[s] itself to everything with which, and everybody with whom, she [comes] in contact" (IV, 11); and the effects of Mrs. Wilfer's glares are visible on the faces of those she glares at: "A magnetic result of such glaring was, that the person glared at could not by any means successfully pretend to be ignorant of the fact: so that a by-stander, without beholding Mrs. Wilfer at all, must have known at whom she was glaring, by seeing her refracted from the countenance of the beglared one" (III, 16). And so Bradley Headstone is wholly unable to escape the unwitting effect the personality of Lizzie Hexam has had upon him: "You draw me to you. If I were shut up in a strong prison, you would draw me out. I should break through the wall to come to you. If I were lying on a sick bed, you would draw me up — to stagger to your feet and fall there" (II, 15).

The narrator of *Our Mutual Friend* is in exactly the same position as the characters of the novel in relation to one another. For the narrator, the characters' inner lives are there, available, in what he can see and hear of them, their bodies, gestures, behavior, and surroundings. The reader is neither wholly outside of Wegg or Venus or Boffin, nor wholly inside. He is both outside and inside at once. Dickens keeps the objectivity of the third-person narrator. He does not give us the streams of consciousness of the characters, but presents, from the outside, their supposed consciousnesses, as in the narrative of the death of Betty Higden: "So, keeping to by-ways, and shunning human approach, this troublesome old woman hid herself, and fared on all through the dreary day. Yet so unlike was she to vagrant hiders in general, that sometimes, as the day advanced, there was a bright fire in her eyes, and a quicker beating at her feeble heart, as though she said exultingly, 'The Lord will see me through it!' . . . 'Water-meadows, or such like,' she had sometimes murmured, on the day's pilgrimage, when she had raised her head and taken any note of the real objects about her. There now arose in the darkness, a great building full of lighted windows. . . . Between her and the building lay a piece of water, in which the lighted windows were reflected, and on its nearest margin was a plantation of trees. 'I humbly thank the Power and the Glory,' said Betty Higden, holding up her withered hands, 'that I have come to my journey's end!' " (III, 8). Consciousness is not presented here as something purely subjective. We are at once inside ("a quicker beating at her feeble heart") and outside ("there was a bright fire in her eyes"). Betty's mere appearance is a language. It is as though she spoke. The medium between the narrator's consciousness and Betty's is the objective world (including Betty's body and her murmured words). This world is really there, and would be really there for any spectator. The narrator can see it with his own eyes, and thus can see it by projection through Betty Higden's eyes too, as she makes the real scene before her an emblem of her approach to the promised land of death. Since the character is inseparably identified with his environment, even in the extreme moment of death, we are at all times permitted access to his subjectivity.

In *Our Mutual Friend,* neither narrator nor characters are alone in a phenomenal world inhabited by strange creatures whose inner lives are altogether mysterious. The proper model of the universe of *Our Mutual Friend* is not that of a non-Euclidean space filled with incommensurate local monads entirely isolated from one another. It is rather that of a large number of interlocking perspectives on the world, each what Whitehead would call a special *prehension* of the same totality. But Dickens can never present the totality as it is in itself. Indeed, there is no such thing as the world in itself. There is no world without some consciousness at the center to organize it in some unique way. *Our Mutual Friend* is, like the initial scene of *Bleak House,* a non-Euclidean space in that it is a plurality of worlds rather than a single world. It is different, however, in that each of these worlds is a particular constitution of the same unattainable substratum, rather than being wholly isolated. But there is no set of coordinates which would have priority over all the others and liberate the spectator from the falsifications of a point of view. A summation of all the perspectives would not produce a supra-perspective. It would only be a finite number out of an infinite number of possibilities.

The narrator here never claims to see his characters from some point of view outside the world. He is as much engaged in the world and limited by his perspective as any of the characters. He too cannot liberate himself from his concrete existence and put himself somewhere outside it. But since the narrator is not himself in a real situation in the world of the novel, he can only see the world as it appears from the perspective of some particular personage or group of personages who are not, as he is, mere spectators, but are actively engaged in the world. Without this acceptance of a vicarious inherence in the world, it would be a mere blank for the narrator. Dickens' need for an involved narrator is testified to by his frequent use of a minor character as a vicarious point of view. Thus the Veneering dinner parties are seen filtered through Twemlow's consciousness, and, in the case of Bella's wedding, Dickens invents a character used only on this occasion, old Gruff and Glum, a wooden-legged Greenwich pensioner. The wedding is described as seen through his eyes.

In presenting in the very structure of his novel a rejection of the idea that the world has a unity in itself, outside of any distorting perspectives, *Our Mutual Friend* destroys a major premise of the traditional English novel, and anticipates twentieth-century fiction. Whereas *Bleak House* in the end put an apparently dispersed world back together, *Our Mutual Friend* remains true to its rejection of the idea that there is an ideal unity of the world transcending the differences between individual lives, and perceptible from the outside by Providence or by the omniscient eye of the narrator. *Bleak House* was in various ways unified by the use of the first-person narrative of Esther, by the Chancery case in which everyone is involved, and by the emergence of Esther's story as the central one. But here there is no unifying center and no final scene which shows the chief protagonists looking forward to living happily ever after. The final chapters of *Our Mutual Friend* run quickly through the various irreconcilable milieus without pretending that they can be merged, and the last chapter returns us to the most dispersive environment of all, the dining room of the Veneerings. If *Pickwick Papers* was a farewell to the eighteenth century

*Our Mutual Friend* is on the threshold of the twentieth. Dickens is one of the first great novelists to define the peculiar conditions of urban life. For him, the city is, first of all, the copresence of an unimaginable number of people in an entirely humanized world. And, as entirely humanized, the city can contain no transcendence, Christian or romantic. Since everything has been transformed into something humanly significant or useful or into a means of human intercommunication, there is nothing which does not share the limitations of the human condition. The city is a triumph of the human spirit, but in this triumph the unity of the world as something extrahuman has altogether disappeared. If it exists, it is wholly unavailable to any man.

This concept of the city as an unknown quantity, uniquely organized by each of the lives which interpenetrates it, is overtly asserted in a passage in the "memorandum book" which Dickens kept between 1855 and 1865, while he was writing, among other novels, *Our Mutual Friend*. In this note Dickens imagines a story "representing London — or Paris, or any other great place — in the new light of being actually unknown to all the people in the story, and only taking the colour of their fears and fancies and opinions. So getting a new aspect, and being unlike itself. An *odd* unlikeness of itself" (*Let.*, III, 788). Anyone's experience of the world transforms it from what it is in itself into a *view* of the world, a view which gives it a new "aspect" and makes it an "odd" distortion of itself. But, as *Our Mutual Friend* consistently shows, the city as it is in itself cannot be seen by anyone, not even by the narrator himself.

### III

"There is nothing new this morning, I suppose?" says Twemlow . . . .

Fledgeby has not heard of anything.

"No, there's not a word of news," says Lammle.
"Not a particle," adds Boots.
"Not an atom," chimes in Brewer. (II, 16)

It would seem that the triumphant reduction of the world to man's measure would solve all human problems. As in the

Marxist millennium, there is nothing which has not yielded to the uniquely human power of negation. This power transmutes everything with which it comes in contact from what it is in itself into value or meaning or use. Nowhere is there left any realm of opacity or mystery or threatening otherness. Even the very dust of disintegrated human artefacts exists as value, as worth so many thousand pounds. Gold, as Dickens repeatedly says in one way or another in *Our Mutual Friend,* is dust, and dust is thus money:

. . . the coaly (but to him gold-dusty) little steamer got her steam up in London. (IV, 4)

There was a golden surface on the brown cliffs but now, and behold they are only damp earth. (I, 10)

"I would rather he thought well of me . . . than that you did, though you splashed the mud upon him from the wheels of a chariot of pure gold. . . ." (III, 15)

" 'One of Mr. Dancer's richest escritoires was found to be a dungheap in the cowhouse; a sum but little short of two thousand five hundred pounds was contained in this rich piece of ma- nure . . . .' " (III, 6)

Dust, then, (or mud, or even dung) is gold, gold is dust, and Mr. Boffin is the "Golden Dustman." Money, the ascription of nominal value to what has no value in itself, is the central sym- bol in *Our Mutual Friend* of the successful humanization of the world. This symbol is constantly before us, as the money of the dust mounds and of the Harmon will, as the money which Bella Wilfer wants, as the money which Gaffer Hexam steals from drowned bodies, as the money which has made the Ve- neerings out of nothing. Given the universal acceptance of money as the measure of all worth — "A man may do anything lawful, for money," says the Voice of Society. "But for no money! — Bosh!" (IV, 17) — the individual will have no dif- ficulty in understanding other people or in identifying himself. Other people are immediately comprehensible as worth so much money, and a man *is* his own bank account, or what he can sell himself for. Dominated by the universality of money, the world becomes transparent, without mystery or depth. It becomes a vast system of interchanges of coin for coin, the same for the same, in which, in the end, individualized persons and objects no longer exist, only the monetary simulacra which make them all equivalent or reduced to common measure. In such a world, everyone will say, with Bella Wilfer: "I have money always in my thoughts and my desires; and the whole life I place before myself is money, money, money, and what money can make of life!" (III, 4).

Money, however, is only an extreme example of what exists everywhere in the urban world of *Our Mutual Friend*. Nature is buried invisibly behind a thick surface of roads, streets, buildings, utensils, signs, values, meanings.[1] The characters do not fall naked into a naked world, but find themselves in a world which everywhere already has a sense. This meaning has been given to it by the past generations of the dead. The world is everywhere heavy with the debris of history. It is as though one had been set down in the midst of the ruins of an ancient city and were forced to live the dead life appropriate to it because everything around was still fabricated and valued.

There is no stronger symbol in *Our Mutual Friend* of the great inescapable weight of history than the Harmon dust mounds themselves. They are not mere formless dust. They are "coal-dust, vegetable-dust, bone-dust, crockery dust, rough dust, and sifted dust — all manner of Dust" (I, 2). They are not, or not yet, a symbol of the natural, nonhuman matter behind fabricated things. They are full of objects, objects broken and useless, but still possessing a human meaning and a human value. These objects are dead indeed, but still have power to dominate the lives that are lived in their midst. In *Hard Times* Dickens had already made an identification of dustheaps with the inherited institutions which structure the life of the nation. Mr. Gradgrind is described as "sifting and sifting at his parliamentary cinder-heap in London (without being observed to turn up many precious articles among the rubbish)" (II, 9). Parliamentary procedure has no more life than a dustheap, yet it still determines the way things are done, and reaches out to desic-

[1] Compare the description of Coketown in *Hard Times:* "Nature was as strongly bricked out as killing airs and gases were bricked in . . ." (I, 10).

cate the lives of everyone with its atmosphere of death. And now in *Our Mutual Friend* we see Silas Wegg, surrounded by the Harmon dust mounds, reading *The Decline and Fall of the Roman Empire*. It is clear that, for Dickens, nineteenth-century England is repeating the fall of Rome, and that we may read a double reference in his statement that "those enervated and corrupted masters of the world . . . were by this time on their last legs" (II, 7). It is also clear that Dickens assigns a precise cause to this catastrophe. Modern England, like ancient Rome, is being slowly destroyed because it cannot find strength to rid itself of the tangible, material presence of the dead forms of the past.

Everyone in *Our Mutual Friend* is in the sad condition of poor little Miss Podsnap, who has been victimized and reduced to spiritual inertia by the mere presence of massive furniture: "Miss Podsnap's life had been, from her first appearance on this planet, altogether of a shady order; for, Mr. Podsnap's young person was likely to get little good out of association with other young persons, and had therefore been restricted to companionship with not very congenial older persons, and with massive furniture" (I, 11). There has been no need to indoctrinate Miss Podsnap in Podsnappery. Her father's furniture has been able, without direct human intervention, to impose upon her a certain view of life: "Miss Podsnap's early views of life being principally derived from the reflections of it in her father's boots, and in the walnut and rosewood tables of the dim drawing-rooms, and in their swarthy giants of looking-glasses, were of a sombre cast . . ." (*ibid.*).

But Miss Podsnap's father is no better off. Even though he has chosen his own furniture, he is victimized by its "hideous solidity" (*ibid.*), and lives in a world that is immovably locked in rigid conventions and opinions. There is no change or freshness in his world, as there is none in the life of his rocking-horse wife who is trained in the "act of prancing in a stately manner without ever getting on" (*ibid.*). For Podsnap the entire world "gets up at eight, shaves close at a quarter-past, breakfasts at nine, goes to the City at ten, comes home at half-past five, and dines at seven" (*ibid.*). Of anything outside this rig-

idly repetitive round Podsnap says: "Nothing else To Be —
anywhere!" (*ibid.*). Even though the world has succumbed
completely to Podsnap's coercive will, he is not in contact with
reality. For all its fixity, his world lacks solidity because there
is no contact between its rigid conventions and the reality of
life underneath, whether human or nonhuman. His world is
the same in the end as that of the Veneerings.

The Veneerings, as their name implies, have no inner reality
at all, not even, we discover in the end, the money which their
appearance claims. They have no past, but have sprung up
"bran-new" overnight, and nothing of what they apparently are
is supported by anything authentic underneath. If the Podsnaps are hideous solidity, cast in an unchangeable mold, the
Veneerings are pure surface, a frail crust which cannot be
changed without breaking it. They are like the horrible old
Lady Tippins, who is "dyed and varnished" (I, 10) too, and
who, like the Veneerings, is a fabricated self supported by nothing real: "Whereabout in the bonnet and drapery announced
by her name, any fragment of the real woman may be concealed, is perhaps known to her maid; but you could easily buy
all you see of her, in Bond-street: or you might scalp her, and
peel her, and scrape her, and make two Lady Tippinses out of
her, and yet not penetrate to the genuine article" (*ibid.*).

One might think that the Veneerings would be given reality
by the objects with which they have surrounded themselves:
house and furniture, carriage and plate. But it is just here that
the ultimate flaw in the project of humanizing the world appears. For the action of giving value cannot without contradiction go in both directions at once. Either the objects already
have a value and meaning which they impart to the human beings living in their midst, or the human beings give meaning to
the objects. The urbanites of *Our Mutual Friend* have chosen
the latter course, since they no longer believe the former is open
to them. The fabricated objects which they possess exist only
as reflected in the human life which uses them and values
them. They are not outside, independent and self-sufficient,
but are interiorized, and therefore are not other than the human culture which inhabits them. Such objects have just as

much meaning and reality as do the people who give them value — and no more. But the Veneerings, as everyone in Society knows, are "bran-new people." They have no authentic reality or meaning in themselves. The mundane realm becomes eventually, then, the reflection of nothing by nothing. It is a closed circuit formed by the vain reflections back and forth between the people, who are nothing in themselves, and a world they have completely transformed into their image, therefore into nothing. There is no escape in any direction, neither toward nonhuman nature, nor toward the reality in the depths of the human beings themselves. Man has absorbed the world into himself, and the transformed world has absorbed him into itself, in an endless multiplication of nothing by nothing.

This sense of the nullity of both the Veneerings and their possessions is brilliantly suggested by Dickens in the description of a Veneering dinner party. The Veneerings and their possessions, seen reflected in a looking-glass which is itself one of the possessions, lose reality and solidity. We see them momentarily as what they really are, altogether false and empty, and this insight derives from our recognition of the fact that neither objects nor people here have power to endow the other with value and authenticity: "The great looking-glass above the sideboard reflects the table and the company. Reflects the new Veneering crest, in gold and eke in silver, frosted and also thawed, a camel of all work. The Heralds' College found out a Crusading ancestor for Veneering who bore a camel on his shield (or might have done it if he had thought of it), and a caravan of camels take charge of the fruits and flowers and candles, and kneel down to be loaded with the salt. Reflects Veneering; forty, wavy-haired, dark, tending to corpulence, sly, mysterious, filmy . . . . Reflects Mrs. Veneering; . . . gorgeous in raiment and jewels, enthusiastic, propitiatory, conscious that a corner of her husband's veil is over herself" (I, 2). The weight of gold and silver camels, Mrs. Veneering's clothes and jewels, her husband's corpulence, are, in spite of their apparent solidity, thin, filmy veils which hide the inner falseness behind, but in the mirror the truth is betrayed, and we see that the Veneerings are a frail image of reality, an image which is pure dissimulation altogether lacking in substance.

The act of transforming nonhuman matter into human objects is the human action par excellence, but this action eventually destroys the otherness of the world and leaves people faced everywhere with an impenetrable screen of dead husks. Everything has a meaning, but it is a dead meaning, and the people living imprisoned within this humanized world suffocate from lack of contact with anything real, anything other than merely human:

Very little life was to be seen on either bank, windows and doors were shut, and the staring black and white letters upon wharves and warehouses "looked," said Eugene to Mortimer, "like inscriptions over the graves of dead businesses." (I, 14)

A grey dusty withered evening in London city has not a hopeful aspect. The closed warehouses and offices have an air of death about them, and the national dread of colour has an air of mourning. The towers and steeples of the many house-encompassed churches, dark and dingy as the sky that seems descending on them, are no relief to the general gloom; a sun-dial on a church-wall has the look, in its useless black shade, of having failed in its business enterprise and stopped payment for ever . . . . The set of humanity outward from the City is as a set of prisoners departing from jail, and dismal Newgate seems quite as fit a stronghold for the mighty Lord Mayor as his own state-dwelling. (II, 15)

But other characters in *Our Mutual Friend* do not merely find themselves imprisoned in an empty world they have made for themselves. They are not simply forced to live their lives in accordance with a certain culture already formed and inherited from the past. They find themselves in a world full of streets, roads, signs, and the coercive schemes of certain definite actions and ways of life. But they also find that they are not free to choose which of the already existing paths they will follow. A certain route has already been mapped out for them, and everyone expects them to follow its itinerary. Bella Wilfer, John Harmon, Eugene Wrayburn, even Mortimer Lightwood, Miss Podsnap, and poor feeble Twemlow are not simply in situations which entangle them inextricably in the world. They are in situations which bereave them of all freedom and initiative. Instead of being a reciprocal interchange in which the person actively assumes his engagement in the world and gives it meaning and life, each of these situations is a one-way current of constrictive pressures all converging from the world on the person at the center and denying all authenticity to his life. So Mortimer Lightwood's "small income . . . has been an effective Something, in the way of preventing [him] from turning to at Anything" (IV, 16); Twemlow has all his life been waiting in vain for leave from his noble kinsman, Lord Snigsworth, "to do something, or be something, in life" (II, 16); and Eugene Wrayburn's spiritual emptiness derives from the fact that his father has "always in the clearest manner provided (as he calls it) for his children by pre-arranging from the hour of the birth of each, and sometimes from an earlier period, what the devoted little victim's calling and course in life should be" (I, 12). The Harmon will, which left a great fortune to John Harmon on condition that he marry Bella Wilfer, is only the most striking example of a situation which is ubiquitous in *Our Mutual Friend.*

The state of mind of the victims of this power in parents or ancestors is not the despair, conscious or unconscious, which is the dominant spiritual condition of the characters in *Little Dorrit.* Here the dominant state is *boredom,* an oppressive sense of the absurdity and emptiness of one's life, an inability to act which results from sheer ennui. The character feels that his life is altogether ridiculous because every move in it has been decided beforehand, and he is prevented from acting because he feels that, for him, all human relationships are doomed to failure:

. . . they were haggardly weary of one another, of themselves, and of all this world. (IV, 2)

"Could I possibly support it? I, so soon bored, so constantly, so fatally?" (I, 12)

"I am in a ridiculous humour," quoth Eugene; "I am a ridiculous fellow. Everything is ridiculous." (I, 13)

There never was such a hard case! I shouldn't care so much if it wasn't so ridiculous. It was ridiculous . . . to have a stranger coming over to marry me, whether he liked it or not. It was ridiculous . . . to know what an embarrassing meeting it would be, and how we never could pretend to have an inclination of our own, either of us. (I, 4) [2]

Instead of solving the problem of self-identification and communication, the complete humanization of the world ends by making these problems more acute. Within society, there is no possibility of ever coming into real contact with another person. The other is hidden, as nonhuman matter is hidden, and if he is not seen as an object, he is seen as wholly institutionalized, wholly clothed, wholly defined by his imposed social role. On the other hand, each character feels himself being transformed into an object: ". . . how *could* I like him," asks Bella, "left to him in a will, like a dozen of spoons . . ." (I, 4). Or, worse yet, he loses all certainty about his own identity. Nothing certain or real can be discovered either inside or out, and the character gives up as hopeless the attempt to find out who he is: "You know what I am, my dear Mortimer. You know how dreadfully susceptible I am to boredom. You know that when I became enough of a man to find myself an embodied conundrum, I bored myself to the last degree by trying to find out what I meant. You know that at length I gave it up, and declined to guess any more" (II, 6). In the end, then, boredom becomes anguish, the anguished recognition of the joint nothingness of self and world. A person suffering this anguish sees the insignificance, the emptiness, the nullity, of things within the closed circuit of the humanized world. Everything returns the self to itself, therefore to nothing. Such a character becomes "like one cast away, for the want of something to trust in, and care for, and think well of" (II, 11).

[2] This theme is repeated in *The Mystery of Edwin Drood* in the reaction of Edwin Drood and Rosa Bud to the fact that they have been betrothed as children by their fathers. "It *is* so absurd to be an engaged orphan," says Rosa (3); "*Your* life is not laid down to scale, and lined and dotted out for you, like a surveyor's plan," says Edwin to his uncle. "*You* have no uncomfortable suspicion that you are forced upon anybody, nor has anybody an uncomfortable suspicion that she is forced upon you, or that you are forced upon her. *You* can choose for yourself" (2).

### IV

The characters of *Our Mutual Friend* are lost, then, unless they can find something other than themselves to depend on, some way out of the earthly hell of the quotidian, the endless circling repetition of the same meaningless acts. Having absorbed the world into themselves, they are finally absorbed into the world. Their lives becomes wholly inauthentic, wholly at the mercy of the "voice of society." Dickens' phrase for the one thing needful is "*something* to trust in, and care for, and think well of." Not somebody, some other human being, but some *thing,* that is, something outside the human and the humanized. But, as in the "unhappy consciousness" of Hegel, it would seem that for Dickens in *Our Mutual Friend* there is no exit from the human. Whatever consciousness comes in contact with it transforms into itself, and is therefore left alone. And alone it is not sufficient unto itself. It falls into its own void of nothingness and boredom, and what had at first seemed a triumph becomes the disaster of a progressive volatilization and thinning out of the world. Nowhere is there anything substantial which will support the human world and give it solidity.

But the novel itself is in one sense an act of liberation from this imprisonment in the all too human. These people, if we imagine them as real, are entrapped in situations which, even if they are intolerable or meaningless, are altogether inescapable and concrete. Bradley Headstone is tormented not by his nothingness, but by the positive presence to himself of his consciousness and of his particular involvement in the world. He is tormented by the fact that he is *there,* present to the world, and wholly unable either to escape his situation or to assume the burden of his existence other than self-destructively: "The overweighted beast of burden, or the overweighted slave, can for certain instants shift the physical load, and find some slight respite even in enforcing additional pain upon such a set of muscles or such a limb. Not even that poor mockery of relief could the wretched man obtain, under the steady pressure of the infernal atmosphere into which he had entered" (IV, 15). The interpenetration of Bradley Headstone and his situation is perfectly real, and, though he feels driven and trapped, it is not by external forces, but precisely by the conjunction of self and situation. Only if he could be liberated from his situation could he be saved. But this, it seems, cannot happen.

Nevertheless, in describing Bradley and all the other characters in the novel, in making a verbal image of their lives and of the world they live in, Dickens produces a gap between the reader and this world, a gap which suffices to liberate at least the reader from it. The reader at least is able to recognize these lives as null, and therefore to escape from the situation which traps the characters if we imagine them as real. The very operation of making a verbal image of the urban world, like the Veneerings' mirror, reveals its nature more clearly than it can be seen by any people actually living in the midst of it.

To put it another way, the characters of *Our Mutual Friend* do not exist as motives, personalities, psychological natures, actions. The world they live in does not possess an objective reality. The characters and their world exist as words. Their mode of existence is permeated through and through with the ambiguous character of words. *Our Mutual Friend* is not, any more than any other novel, a novel of reality, in spite of Dickens' more or less naturalistic and conventional theory of the methods and aims of fiction.[3] It is a work of literature, and, like any work of literature, has a verbal existence. This would be no less true even if it could be shown that every character and every scene is a copy or projection of some real character or scene in Victorian England. The verbal copy of a reality is not, one hardly needs to say, the reality itself. But it also in some sense presupposes the distancing for the readers of the reality copied. Instead of the reality, we are given the reality transformed into a verbal image, and this perspective liberates the readers, at least, from the inescapable prison the characters inhabit.

We can possess this image in a way no reality can be pos-

[3] See Monroe Engel, "Dickens on Art," *Modern Philology*, LIII (1955), 25–38, for a discussion of Dickens' pronouncements on this subject in *Household Words, The Household Narrative, All the Year Round,* and in his letters.

sessed. Such possession takes a particular form. The reader's consciousness must make itself into a kind of virtual space, and allow itself to be altogether filled up and inhabited by the verbal image. Nothing will exist for him except the words and their meanings. And if these meanings point to possible experiences in the "real" world, the images formed by the words of the novel indicate everywhere the absence of these realities rather than their presence. To read *Our Mutual Friend* is to leave the real world, both the real world of the reader and the real world from which the novel sprang as Dickens wrote it. It is to enter a world of verbalized consciousness.

These remarks might be applied to literature in general. All novels or poems are a liberation from the real world. But there is a characteristic of the style of *Our Mutual Friend* which reminds us constantly of its fictitious character. The novel makes a special use of metaphor which, though present throughout Dickens' work, comes more and more to dominate the style of his later novels. This might be called "non-ontological metaphor." It does not rest on any comparison or analogy between things or people in the novel, but only on a free leap of the imagination from the primary level of "reality" in the book to another purely fanciful level. The metaphor rests on nothing but itself. It hangs in the void of consciousness.

The characters themselves use such metaphors. Their language is one of the chief signs that they have transformed the material world into something entirely human. Their metaphors do not import meaning and solidity from the nonhuman world into the human one, but simply manipulate the names of material objects freely to express a psychological meaning. These material objects have no given meaning, guaranteed by their own natures or by some divine symbolist, but are assigned meanings by the characters themselves. These non-ontological metaphors are one source of the comedy of *Our Mutual Friend,* one source of our feeling that the characters' sense of the world around them is slightly askew, is in excess of its "reality," that is, of the reality it might have for another person. But such metaphors are used by the melodramatic characters too, and in the end are simply testimony that nowhere here is there any undistorted reality, only the characters' particular ways of assuming that reality into their own lives:

He is made of venomous insults and affronts, from the crown of his head to the sole of his foot. (III, 11)

In the meanwhile let it be fully understood that I shall not neglect bringing the grindstone to bear, nor yet bringing Dusty Boffin's nose to it. His nose once brought to it, shall be held to it by these hands, Mr. Venus, till the sparks flies out in showers. (III, 14)

. . . he is here to submit to you that the time has arrived when, with our hearts in our glasses, with tears in our eyes, with blessings on our lips, and in a general way with a profusion of gammon and spinach in our emotional larders, we should one and all drink to our dear friends the Lammles. . . . (II, 16)

There is no ontological substratum in these metaphors. They have only a human meaning. There is no real grindstone, and no hearts in the glasses. Nothing exists except as the meaning which the human beings give it. The peculiarity of these metaphors is that their unreality persists, expands, and penetrates the characters themselves and the primary level of the novel. The characters exist in terms of metaphors. That is what they are. The use of such metaphors is a powerful tool in Dickens' hands for making us recognize the nullity of the lives of his characters. Thus Dickens tells us of "other friends of [the Podsnaps'] souls who were not entitled to be asked to dinner, but had a claim to be invited to come and take a haunch of mutton vapour-bath at half-past nine" (I, 11). This seems to be merely a vivid way of saying that the late guests will be able to smell the dinner they did not eat, but, when the dinner itself comes to be described, what had been initially only a metaphor turns out to have overwhelmed the reality and transformed it into its own insubstantial mode of being. The result is a surrealistic scene whose triumph is to force us into an unrelieved tension between an attempt to imagine the naturalistic reality behind the words, and a recognition that there is no naturalistic reality anywhere here, only a verbal realm in which it is quite possible to have bathers in the drawing room: "And now the haunch of mutton vapour-bath having received a gamey infusion, and a few last touches of sweets and coffee, was quite ready, and the bathers came. . . . Bald bathers folded their arms and talked to Mr. Podsnap on the hearth-rug; sleek-whiskered bathers, with hats in their hands, lunged at Mrs. Podsnap and retreated; prowling bathers went about looking into ornamental boxes and bowls as if they had suspicions of larceny on the part of the Podsnaps, and expected to find something they had lost at the bottom; bathers of the gentler sex sat silently comparing ivory shoulders" (I, 11).

This leap from reality metaphorically described to a world altogether fictive often takes place by a transition from simile to metaphor. Thus the Veneerings' butler is initially *"like* a gloomy Analytical Chemist" (I, 2), but thereafter is simply "the Analytical Chemist." The character comes to exist entirely as the figure of speech which at first merely seemed to be a witty way to describe him. It would be possible to make an elaborate list of such metaphors. Gaffer Hexam is a bird of prey, Mr. Wilfer is a cherub, Mrs. Podsnap is a rocking horse, and so on. But to give an exhaustive list would be to quote much of the novel, for all of the characters and all of the scenes are permeated by this overtly fictive quality, reminding us constantly of the presence of the consciousness of Dickens creating the reality of his novel out of the insubstantial stuff of words. The novel really exists, as thought has a real existence, but it no more exists objectively or refers to an objective existence than a woman can ever be a rocking horse. It is at once there and not there, like consciousness itself. Dickens earlier had tended to qualify such metaphorical transformations by the use of the locution "as if." For example, in *Martin Chuzzlewit* we read of "water-pipes . . . which at unexpected times in the night, when other things were quiet, clicked and gurgled suddenly, as if they were choking" (46), and of "poultry . . . [which] disappeared as rapidly as if every bird had had the use of its wings, and had flown in desperation down a human throat" (16). Such a qualification testified to the disjunction between the reality of the novel and the spectator's view of it. But Dickens in his last novels comes increasingly to dispense with the "as if," and to merge reality and the narator's consciousness of it. This is implicit recognition that here is in the novel neither objective reality nor detached conciousness, but only consciousness *of* the entirely imaginary people, events, and objects of the novel. This style gives its peculiar clarity to *Our Mutual Friend* and to *The Mystery of Edwin Drood*. The effect is of transparent lucidity, for there is no longer felt to be a tension between words and a reality which they can never completely express or efface. There is no background of secrecy and opacity, as in earlier novels, but a sense that everything there is to be given can be given in the words. At its best this style produces a kind of pure poetry. The reader delights in the play of language without caring any more to invent a naturalistic world behind it. He enters completely a surrealistic world in which the words produce their own self-contained reality:

Mr. Sampson perceiving his frail bark to be labouring among shoals and breakers, thought it safest not to refer back to any particular thing that he had been told, lest he should refer back to the wrong thing. With admirable seamanship he got his bark into deep water by murmuring, "Yes indeed." (III, 16)

Veneering . . . is much occupied with the Fathers too, piously retiring with them into the conservatory, from which retreat the word "Committee" is occasionally heard, and where the Fathers instruct Veneering how he must leave the valley of the piano on his left, take the level of the mantel-piece, cross by an open cutting at the candelabra, seize the carrying traffic at the console, and cut up the opposition root and branch at the window curtains. (III, 17)

This implicit recognition of the fictive, verbal nature of the novel perfectly matches the wholly human character of the world of which it is the image. It makes that human quality available to the reader, but it does not indicate any escape from it, only a detached recognition of the nullity of the urban world. It is an escape into nothing. It does not suggest the possibility of ever coming into contact with anything nonhuman.

Even so, this withdrawal is better than an enclosure within the wholly human world which does not allow any detached perspective upon it whatsoever. And certain characters in the

novel achieve a withdrawal from their situations parallel to that
of the narrator and reader. Such characters live their lives in
image, that is, they transform their real situations into fictive
situations which free them from the "steady pressure" of real
ity. They change their real identities into roles, and live their
lives as if they were a play or a game. Thus Bella and her father
enact and reënact a ritual in which Mr. Wilfer is transformed
into a schoolboy with Bella as his mother; Jenny Wren and her
drunken father have, in the same way, reversed roles; and
Jenny and Riah pretend to be Cinderella and the fairy god
mother. A similar break between character and situation is
made in one way or another by the many examples of double
or disguised identities in the novel (John Harmon, Mr. Boffin,
Bradley Headstone, and Rogue Riderhood). Mr. Boffin, for
example, is apparently transformed by riches into a miser, but
we discover afterward that what seemed to be action and
speech as honest and sincere as that of the other characters, as
complete an identification of self and world, was really only
pretense. Boffin was not really what he appeared to be. He
might be said to have been defining himself as the refusal to be
his situation, his appearance, his speech, his actions. He was
not what he was. The Veneerings and Lammles are playing
roles too, pretending to a reality which they do not possess. But
their assumption of roles rests on nothing, and is a way of es
caping from reality rather than of facing it. The play-acting of
Jenny, Mr. Boffin, or John Harmon, on the other hand, is a way
of assuming their real situations, and yet of transforming them
from something merely imposed to something in a sense free
and chosen. The situation is recognized and accepted, and the
act of changing it into an imaginative version of itself is a
means of dealing with it. Nevertheless, though pretending to
be her father's mother may help Jenny lead her difficult life, it
does not provide an escape from that life, and she remains en
closed in a world which everywhere reflects back to her her
own image. The only possible escape from this world would be
some kind of fissure, a rupture of the closed circuit between
man and the world which would allow the nonhuman world to
show through. Only then could man see the world as it was be

fore everything was transformed into value or use. But this is apparently impossible.

## V

Hideous solidity was the characteristic of the Podsnap plate. Everything was made to look as heavy as it could, and to take up as much room as possible. Everything said boastfully, "Here you have as much of me in my ugliness as if I were only lead; but I am so many ounces of precious metal worth so much an ounce; — wouldn't you like to melt me down?" A corpulent straddling epergne, blotched all over as if it had broken out in an eruption rather than been ornamented, delivered this address from an unsightly silver platform in the centre of the table. Four silver wine-coolers, each furnished with four staring heads, each head obtrusively carrying a big silver ring in each of its ears, conveyed the sentiment up and down the table, and handed it on to the pot-bellied silver salt-cellars. (I, 11)

Suddenly, there is a crack in the façade, and what is behind breaks through in a kind of eruption: sheer, gross, heavy, impenetrable matter, the mere weight and presence of it, like an implacable stare, meaningless, massive, unsightly, entirely unchanged by the form into which it has been cast, altogether resisting man's attempts to assimilate it into his world. The deliberate ugliness of Victorian objects, intended to reveal their intrinsic worth without the veneer of mere prettiness, has overreached itself, and has inadvertently revealed the nudity, the absurdity, the otherness of matter. These hideous objects of Victorian décor are displaced slightly from the spectator's view, and put before us in the manner of a Max Ernst collage, wrested from their context, as so many pounds of metal cast into a meaningless shape. They appear to be silver, but might as well be lead, since their sheer material presence is more important than its specific form. Behind the superficial shape appears the unformed, irrational reality, yielding itself to any mold, but giving authenticity to none. The sight of the metal behind the epergne puts Podsnap's dining room in touch with the formless matter of the dust heaps, and with the river full of "ooze and scum" (IV, 15) and rotting corpses, and bordered by the "accumulated scum of humanity . . . washed from higher grounds, like so much moral sewage, and . . . pausing until its own weight force[s] it over the bank and [sinks] it in the river" (I, 3). Even humanity is included in this sudden recognition of the elementary matter which is present everywhere in the world behind the façade of meanings and shapes. Once a single fissure has opened the secret is out, and we become aware of the omnipresence of the nonhuman, even where it has been successfully hidden. Only through the experience of seeing things in the image of themselves, broken off from man and remaining mutely and statically at a distance, only through the sudden destruction of the unity of man and the world, can man come in contact with nonhuman reality. The attempted transformation of the world into meaning and usefulness has not really succeeded at all. It has left impassible matter untouched and ready in a moment to reassert itself when the volitions keeping the world human relax or are wrongly used. Thus, in the neighborhood of Bradley Headstone's school the construction of streets and houses hiding the natural world has not been altogether successful, and sheer matter shows through as a "disorder of frouziness and fog" beyond the "unfinished street already in ruins" (II, 1). And the nudity of matter has begun to show through in Boffin's bower during the long years it has not been inhabited by normal human life. Only constant use can keep matter which has been transformed into utensil and meaning from falling back into a naked and formless state: "Whatever is built by man for man's occupation, must, like natural creations, fulfil the intention of its existence, or soon perish. This old house had wasted more from desuetude than it would have wasted from use, twenty years for one. A certain leanness falls upon houses not sufficiently imbued with life (as if they were nourished upon it), which was very noticeable here. The staircase, balustrades, and rails, had a spare look — an air of being denuded to the bone — which the panels of the walls and the jambs of the doors and windows also bore. The scanty moveables partook of it; save for the cleanliness of the place, the dust into which they were all resolving would have lain thick on the floors . . ." (I, 15).

Beneath all the forms which relate matter to our consciousness and make it comprehensible as specific objects, is the
formless dust from which all things come and to which they
are returning. If the Veneerings' world is a frail surface, rigidly
imposed, which cannot be changed without breaking, and the
Podsnaps' world is weight, solidity, cast in an unchangeable
mold hiding, or trying to hide, the formless stuff of things, the
dust too is on the surface. It is a kind of solid fluid, made up of
powdery, anonymous particles, infinitely divisible, able to take
any form, but to hold none. It is a manifestation of perpetual
change, and can be removed, or can blow away, no one knows
whither. But if everything returns to dust, everything comes
too from the dust, and though it is visible on the surface of
things it comes from their profound depths. It makes manifest
in the daylight world the indistinct pullulation at the heart of
matter, the incessant flux behind all solid and rationalized
forms. As opposed to the other kinds of façade in the novel, the
dust brings the surface in touch with the depths. It brings the
depths to the surface where they can, perhaps, be seen and
manipulated by man. So, for Dickens, the dust and its kindred
form, paper scraps, are not simply present in the Harmon dust
mounds, but are a kind of mobile, ubiquitous presence, brought
from some unknown place by the east wind. They are a mysterious currency. This metaphor relates the dust to money, that
daylight form of the perpetual interchange of like with like, in
which everything is ultimately absorbed into an anonymous
universal. The extremes of the human and of the inhuman are
equally the return to a realm of indistinction: "The grating
wind sawed rather than blew; and as it sawed, the sawdust
whirled about the sawpit. Every street was a sawpit, and there
were no top-sawyers; every passenger was an under-sawyer,
with the sawdust blinding him and choking him. That mysterious paper currency which circulates in London when the
wind blows, gyrated here and there and everywhere. Whence
can it come, whither can it go? It hangs on every bush, flutters
in every tree, is caught flying by the electric wires, haunts every
enclosure, drinks at every pump, cowers at every grating, shud-
ders upon every plot of grass, seeks rest in vain behind the

legions of iron rails. . . . The wind sawed, and the sawdust whirled" (I, 12).

This wind, which brings the dust and wears everything to dust, is itself one of the basic symbols in *Our Mutual Friend* of the fundamental otherness of nature. The wind comes from the sky and from the indistinct blackness of night. In one extraordinary passage the night wind is seen as absorbing the entire city into the formless darkness of the sky: "The blast went by, and the moon contended with the fast-flying clouds, and the wild disorder reigning up there made the pitiful little tumults in the streets of no account. It was not that the wind swept all the brawlers into places of shelter, as it had swept the hail still lingering in heaps wherever there was refuge for it; but that it seemed as if the streets were absorbed by the sky, and the night were all in the air" (I, 12). Nature here is no longer, as in *Bleak House,* the abiding place of a gentle and beneficent Providence, interested in man and supporting his values. It utterly denies those values and man's sufferings, and makes them "of no account." It is a place of chaos, of "wild disorder," of a perpetual aimless whirling of shapeless forms in the blackness. It offers no support to anything human.

But it is the river which is, in *Our Mutual Friend,* the most important symbol of the otherness of nature. Related to the dust through their merged form, mud, it is not the mere passive limit from which all things come and to which they go. Even more frighteningly, it has, like the night wind, the power to destroy all recognizable forms and to transmute them into its own formlessness: "Not a lumbering black barge, with its cracked and blistered side impending over them, but seemed to suck at the river with a thirst for sucking them under. And everything so vaunted the spoiling influences of water — discoloured copper, rotten wood, honey-combed stone, green dank deposit — that the after-consequences of being crushed, sucked under, and drawn down, looked as ugly to the imagination as the main event" (I, 14). If one symbolic center of *Our Mutual Friend* is a Biblical theme — "All are of the dust, and all turn to dust again" (Eccles. 3:20) — another is the idea that all life comes from the ocean and returns to it. Like the wind, the voices" of "falling water" and "the sea" are "an outer memory to a contemplative listener" (IV, 1), that is, they connect man with his past and with his mysterious origins in the depths of that past. Thus Bella's baby comes from the ocean (IV, 5). But the ocean is also death, the terminal point toward which all human lives are flowing: "To [Father Time] it is no matter what living waters run high or low, reflect the heavenly lights and darknesses, produce their little growth of weeds and flowers, turn here, turn there, are noisy or still, are troubled or at rest, for their course has one sure termination, though their sources and devices are many. . . . [T]he solemn river [steals] away by night, as all things steal away, by night and by day, so quietly yielding to the attraction of the loadstone rock of Eternity . . ." (IV, 11).

The dust, the wind, and the river, then, are primary forms of that otherness, that chthonian reality, which the characters, caught in the closed space of a wholly human world, so urgently need. But to recognize the absolute otherness of matter is to recognize something which altogether denies and subverts the human world. Man has come in contact at last with the real, but it is a reality which seems utterly to deny him the possibility of an authentic life. He has gone from the devil of the quotidian to the deep black sea of the unformed profundity of matter. To experience the nocturnal reverse of the world, when everything is the spectral image of itself, is to recognize the impersonal, expressionless strangeness of things. It is also to recognize the omnipresence of death: "The moon had gone down, and a mist crept along the banks of the river, seen through which the trees were the ghosts of trees, and the water was the ghost of water. This earth looked spectral, and so did the pale stars: while the cold eastern glare, expressionless as to heat or colour, with the eye of the firmament quenched, might have been likened to the stare of the dead" (IV, 7).

And to recognize the omnipresence of death is to recognize that each human life is bounded by nothingness, and thus undermined in its very nature: ". . . they are living and must die" (III, 3); ". . . we brought nothing into this world, and it is certain we can take nothing out" (IV, 9).

## VI

"Ah!" said Jenny. "But it's so high. And you see the clouds rushing on above the narrow streets, not minding them, and you see the golden arrows pointing at the mountains in the sky from which the wind comes, and you feel as if you were dead."

. . . "How do you feel when you are dead?" asked Fledgeby, much perplexed.

"Oh, so tranquil!" cried the little creature, smiling. "Oh, so peaceful and so thankful! And you hear the people who are alive, crying, and working, and calling to one another down in the close dark streets, and you seem to pity them so! And such a chain has fallen from you, and such a strange good sorrowful happiness comes upon you!"

Her eyes fell on the old man, who, with his hands folded, quietly looked on.

"Why it was only just now," said the little creature, pointing at him, "that I fancied I saw him come out of his grave! He toiled out at that low door so bent and worn, and then he took his breath and stood upright, and looked all round him at the sky, and the wind blew upon him, and his life down in the dark was over! — Till he was called back to life," she added, looking round at Fledgeby with that lower look of sharpness. . . . "But *you* are not dead, you know," said Jenny Wren. "Get down to life!"

. . . As Riah followed to attend him down the stairs, the little creature called out to the Jew in a silvery tone, "Don't be long gone. Come back, and be dead!" And still as they went down they heard the little sweet voice, more and more faintly, half calling and half singing, "Come back and be dead, Come back and be dead!" (II, 5)

No passage in *Our Mutual Friend* is of greater importance. These sentences are a kind of focal center around which the rest of the novel organizes itself and becomes comprehensible. The rooftop of Pubsey and Co., where Jenny and Lizzie come for "rest," "quiet," and "air" (II, 5), is a place from which the various possibilities of life in the novel may be clearly seen.

Jenny opposes death to life, but equivocally. From one point of view, to be on the rooftop, near the indifference and impersonality of the wind and the mountains in the sky, is to be alto-

gether out of life. It defines a possible mode of existence which
is withdrawn from the ordinary engagements of life, and is
close to death. But, from another point of view, life down in the
"close dark streets," "crying, and working, and calling to one
another," is death. Riah comes up on the roof as if he were
coming out of his grave, and his life down below is a tenebrous
rehearsal of death-in-life, as are all lives governed by the voice
of society and caught in the meaningless round of financial ex-
changes. Fledgeby, the meanest, most selfish, narrow, and
blind, of all the society people, is "not dead." He is wholly unable to escape from the all too human world, and Jenny's judgment of Fledgeby is a kind of final condemnation by Dickens of
all those people in his novels who cannot in some way die to
the quotidian world and to all its values and conventions.
Though they do not express orthodox Christian doctrine, Dickens' novels are religious in that they demand the regeneration
of man and society through contact with something transcending the merely human. Riah's life in the dark streets below, we
feel, is somehow made significant and good, as are Jenny's
and Lizzie's, by the fact that, unlike Fledgeby, they can "be
dead." Their lives are constantly in contact with the alien and
inhuman, present in the sky, the water, the mountains, and
the wind, and, though this means that they are in touch with
what from the human point of view is death, such contact
somehow gives an authenticity to their lives which is wholly
lacking to those remaining within the human world. Life, the
daylight world of action, interrelations between people, and the
collective historical process of humanizing the world, must remain close to all that denies it, death, night, and the nonhuman, as Lizzie Hexam's life has been in contact with the indifferent Thames: "How can you be so thankless to your best
friend, Lizzie?" says her father. "The very fire that warmed you
when you were a baby, was picked out of the river alongside
the coal barges. The very basket that you slept in, the tide
washed ashore. The very rockers that I put it upon to make a
cradle of it, I cut out of a piece of wood that drifted from some
ship or another. . . . As if it wasn't meat and drink to you!"
(I, 1). This relation between death and life is not really dia-

lectical, in the ordinary sense of the word. It is rather the non-logical derivation of one thing from its opposite in a constant intimate interchange of sameness and difference. Death is the mysterious origin of life, and no life that ignores its origin can be other than empty and false. And, as life's origin, death is always part of life and everywhere underlies it. Yet death is the complete negation of life rather than its dialectical opposite. The problem, then, is how to assume death into life — without simply and literally dying.

Surely G. K. Chesterton, when he claimed that *Our Mutual Friend* is "a sort of Indian summer of [Dickens'] farce," [4] was mistaking the dominant tone of the novel. Though it does not have the oppressive gloom of, say, *Little Dorrit,* no other novel by Dickens is so obsessed with death. The quality of the lives of all the characters is judged from the point of view of death, and death is present everywhere — in the Harmon dust *mounds* (the word recalls, perhaps intentionally, burial mounds), in the piled bones of Venus' dark shop, as well as in the fact that a great many characters die or nearly die: John Harmon, Bradley Headstone, Gaffer Hexam, Rogue Riderhood, "Mr. Dolls," little Johnny, Eugene Wrayburn, and old Betty Higden. All of these characters but Johnny and Mr. Dolls die or nearly die in the river or in close proximity to the river. The atmosphere of the initial chapter, describing Gaffer Hexam and his daughter at work seeking drowned bodies in the Thames, hangs over the entire novel, and one might say, paradoxically, that the characters who do *not* die are the most dead. The real house of death in the novel is the Veneering mansion.

Some characters achieve an authentic life by making death not simply the end point of their lives, but the fulfillment of life. Thus the death of little Johnny is only the last of a long series of deaths of children in the works of Dickens. It testifies again to the close connection Dickens felt between the innocence and purity of children, as yet untouched by the world, and the peace of death. And Mr. Dolls, the father-child of Jenny Wren, reaches a dignity and calm in death which his life has never had. His death is the inevitable end of his drunken

4 In his introduction to the Everyman edition (London, 1941), p. vii.

irresponsible life, and gives it as much meaning as it can have. But these deaths are not deliberate. They seize their victims unaware, and the meaning they give to life is not apprehended by the one who dies.

More subtle and significant is the death of Betty Higden. Just as John Harmon has fled into an incognito to escape the pressure of the role society has imposed upon him, so Betty makes it the whole goal of her life to keep out of the institutionalized coercion of the poorhouse. She consciously makes it the aim of her life to die well, that is, to die her own independent death with money left to pay for her burial. She centers all her waning energies on her death, and accepts that death as a release from the pain of life. Every moment of her life is one step closer to death: "If I was young, it would all have to be gone through again, and the end would be a weary way off . . ." (II, 14). But death is not merely an escape for her. She assumes death into her life, and makes the reaching of a good death the fundamental project of her life. When she dies it is as "true to one purpose to the very last" (IV, 6), and she dies close to the river which is for Dickens the material image of the impersonality of death (III, 8).

But her death is simply the transition to that impersonality, and though her anticipation of her own death has given meaning to her life, its quality has not been made available to her in life, or to others through her. The most important deaths or near deaths in *Our Mutual Friend* put either the dying person himself or others into direct contact with the very substance of death. They make death available to life, and in making a breach through life to death they perform a fundamentally vivifying function for the world of the novel.

Death is present in the impersonality of matter, especially the dark water of the river, with its inhuman coldness and formlessness, but death is also present in the depths of each spirit, depths which are several times in the novel compared to the profound interior of the river or the sea. These inner human depths may be reached by the proximity of real death, or by the unbidden ascent of thoughts from the unknown deeps of a human spirit:

This was the subject-matter in his thoughts; in which, too, there came lumbering up, by times, like any half-floating and half-sinking rubbish in the river, the question, Was it done by accident? (IV, 1)

If you are not gone for good, Mr. Riderhood, it would be something to know where you are hiding at present. This flabby lump of mortality that we work so hard at with such patient perseverance, yields no sign of you. If you are gone for good, Rogue, it is very solemn, and if you are coming back, it is hardly less so. . . . The low, bad, unimpressible face is coming up from the depths of the river, or what other depths, to the surface again. (III, 3)

The rippling of the river seemed to cause a correspondent stir in his uneasy reflections. He would have laid them asleep if he could, but they were in movement, like the stream, and all tending one way with a strong current. As the ripple under the moon broke unexpectedly now and then, and palely flashed in a new shape and with a new sound, so parts of his thoughts started, unbidden, from the rest, and revealed their wickedness. (IV, 6)

This frequent rising of a drowning man from the deep, to sink again, was dreadful to the beholders. (IV, 10. This is a description of the way Eugene drifts back and forth from consciousness to unconsciousness as he lies near death from Bradley Headstone's bludgeoning.)

Analogous to the material otherness of the river, then, there is the mysterious depth of the human spirit, and a person hovering between life and death or surprised by a thought from his own subconsciousness gives glimpses to himself or to others of the realm of death. But a corpse too, in which the dead man' soul is strangely both present and absent, may be an avenue putting the living in touch with death. The characters in *Our Mutual Friend* only become mysterious for one another when they are dead or dying. Until then they are altogether transparent, comprehensible, without secrets. But when they are dead they seem to be in touch with a far away somewhere else of which their bodies are now the shadow. Thus the body of Gaffer Hexam, taken from the river as he has taken so many corpses, has been "baptized unto Death." He has gone where no human speech can reach him, and, as he lies soaking into the formless earth, he has entered into mysterious communication with the wind, messenger, as we have seen, of the realm of the nonhuman:

The wind sweeps jeeringly over Father, whips him with the frayed ends of his dress and his jagged hair, tries to turn him where he lies stark on his back, and force his face towards the rising sun, that he may be shamed the more. A lull, and the wind is secret and prying with him; lifts and lets fall a rag; hides palpitating under another rag; runs nimbly through his hair and beard. Then, in a rush, it cruelly taunts him. Father, was that you calling me? Was it you, the voiceless and the dead? Was it you, thus buffeted as you lie here in a heap? Was it you, thus baptized unto Death, with these flying impurities now flung upon your face? Why not speak, Father? Soaking into this filthy ground as you lie here, is your own shape. Did you never see such a shape soaked into your boat? Speak, Father. Speak to us, the winds, the only listeners left you! (I, 14)

The drownings or near drownings of Gaffer Hexam, Eugene Wrayburn, Rogue Riderhood, Bradley Headstone, and John Harmon put the daylight realm of life in touch with death. But to reach death is to reach what denies life, and has no meaning for life. There is no more striking proof of this than the life and death of Bradley Headstone. On the surface, Bradley's mind is "a place of mechanical stowage" (II, 1), full of dry facts he has learned as a schoolteacher. But beneath this dead surface, which corresponds to the superficial life of the Veneerings or Lammles, there are unsuspected depths. Bradley's devouring, self-destructive love for Lizzie Hexam brings to the surface the deep passions hidden under the rigid veneer of his forced learning: " 'No man knows till the time comes, what depths are within him. To some men it never comes; let them rest and be thankful! To me, you brought it; on me, you forced it; and the bottom of this raging sea,' striking himself upon the breast, 'has been heaved up ever since' " (II, 15).

After this, Bradley at least no longer lives as a false surface, as do the Veneerings, but his tragedy is evidence that it is impossible for men to live entirely in terms of their depths. These depths are entirely asocial, entirely destructive and self-destructive. To accept them without transmuting them in some way is inevitably to be swallowed up by the interior storm. Thus, in Dickens' last unfinished novel, *The Mystery of Edwin Drood,* John Jasper, Lay Precentor in a placid provincial cathedral town, is driven to murder by an amorous passion rising from the stormy depths of his being to overwhelm and engulf the quiet surface of his life. What had been a subsidiary theme in *Our Mutual Friend* here holds the center of the stage. Dickens for the first time in his life was writing a novel in which the major protagonist was a villain, murdering others and eventually destroying himself. The climax of *Drood,* if Dickens had lived to write it, was to be, according to Forster, the confrontation, in the death-cell, of the divided halves of Jasper's personality, the arraignment of the murderer half by the respectable half: "The story," says Forster, ". . . was to be that of the murder of a nephew by his uncle; the originality of which was to consist in the review of the murderer's career by himself at the close, when its temptations were to be dwelt upon as if, not he the culprit, but some other man, were the tempted. The last chapters were to be written in the condemned cell, to which his wickedness, all elaborately elicited from him as if told of another, had brought him." [5] These chapters, if they had been written, would have been a striking dramatization of the self-destructive conflict of surface and depth within a single personality. The theme of the double, so pervasive in *Our Mutual Friend,* would have received its most tragic expression: the complete division of a self unable to assimilate its two halves. But the part of *Drood* finished before Dickens died is itself dominated throughout by fundamental thematic and imagistic oppositions between the conventional and clarified life of a quiet English cathedral town, and the real depths below, the darkness of opium fumes, of hallucinatory visions and of the fanaticisms of the Orient, of the cathedral crypt, of night, dust, windstorms, and death by drowning or suffocation, of the evil city, of fiery or savage passions, and, as in *Our Mutual Friend,* of the shadowy river "winding down from the mist on the horizon, as though that were its source, and already heaving with a

[5] Forster, *Life of Dickens,* III, 463.

restless knowledge of its approach towards the sea" (*ED*, 12). What is beneath the surface, in *Drood*, is completely destructive, completely other than the daytime life of the surface. In no other novel by Dickens are the symbolic opposites further from one another and less reconcilable. Throughout the novel, in a thousand major and minor details, the sparkling daylight world of childish innocence, of the river surface, and of the paradisiacal garden by the river's upper reaches is set against the inhuman abysses underground, in the unfathomable depths of the river, and in the darkness of the human heart:

Mr. Crisparkle, Minor Canon, fair and rosy, and perpetually pitching himself head-foremost into all the deep running water in the surrounding country . . . . (*ED*, 2)

Possessing an exhaustless well of affection in her nature, its sparkling waters had freshened and brightened the Nuns' House for years, and yet its depths had never yet been moved: what might betide when that came to pass; what developing changes might fall upon the heedless head, and light heart, then; remained to be seen. (*ED*, 9)

A monotonous, silent city, deriving an earthy flavour throughout from its cathedral crypt, and so abounding in vestiges of monastic graves, that the Cloisterham children grow small salad in the dust of abbots and abbesses, and make dirt-pies of nuns and friars . . . . (*ED*, 3)

. . . all too soon, the great black city cast its shadow on the waters, and its dark bridges spanned them as death spans life, and the everlastingly-green garden seemed to be left for everlasting, unregainable and far away. (*ED*, 22)

"A hazardous and perilous journey, over abysses where a slip would be destruction. Look down, look down!" (*ED*, 23)

If *The Mystery of Edwin Drood* had been completed it might have marked a new departure for Dickens, a radical rejection of any possibility of the reconciliation of surface and depth, of "celestial" and "devilish" (*ED*, 2). The last work of Dickens recognizes that life within the daylight world is precariously balanced over unfathomable abysses. And indeed the story of Bradley Headstone itself seems to prepare for a confrontation of irreconcilable contradictions in the nature of man and the world. Drawn by love, the motivation that had in *Great Expectations* provided the only escape from inauthenticity, Bradley Headstone is led further and further away from life in the ordinary world, and deeper and deeper into the realm of death. He fulfils his destiny and his name when he lies a rotting corpse in the "ooze and scum" of the river bed (IV, 15).

To enter the realm of death is to enter the realm of an immense attraction, and, once there, it is extremely difficult to find strength to return to the daylight world: "He is struggling to come back. Now he is almost here, now he is far away again. Now he is struggling harder to get back. And yet — like us all, when we swoon — like us all, every day of our lives when we wake — he is instinctively unwilling to be restored to the consciousness of this existence, and would be left dormant, if he could" (III, 3). The only possibility of a relation to death which would sustain life would be some reconciliation of depth and surface. Only someone who could descend into the depths and return to reaffirm in a new form his engagement in the daytime world could put life in a true relation to death. But are there any such characters in *Our Mutual Friend?*

### VII

". . . there are spaces between . . . that I know nothing about, and they are not pervaded by any idea of time. . . . I could not have said that my name was John Harmon — I could not have thought it — I didn't know it . . . . [I]t was not I. There was no such thing as I, within my knowledge." (II, 13)

In *Dombey and Son* or *David Copperfield* water was representative of the final fusion in which isolation is transcended, and true selfhood is found. In *Our Mutual Friend* the dark water of the Thames is the moving, indifferent milieu in which people are lost. When John Harmon and Eugene Wrayburn nearly drown, they enter an impersonal and anonymous realm. In the murky water of the river they go outside of themselves, and lose all sense of their own distinct identities. They forget themselves, and become wholly other. Death, for them, is the place where one is no one, nobody. But within the region of death John and Eugene also lose all sense of their concrete involvement in the social world. John forgets the intolerable conditions of his father's will, and Eugene forgets the impasse of his relations with Lizzie. The realm of death is the realm of a complete escape from both self and world. To enter it is to be swallowed up by a vast space without time, and without distinct objects of any kind. In a moment, one is at an immense distance, in a completely indefinite place. Rather, it should be said, one is in places, for death is the realm of endless wandering. It is a place of interminable motion, where one goes constantly from place to place without ever getting anywhere, because each place is exactly like all the others, that is, altogether empty. Each new place is the return of the same. Within the space of death, one is a wholly anonymous awareness of a wholly indeterminate place, an awareness which is filled with an empty, gnawing anxiety, an anxiety about nothing: "Sometimes his eyes were open, sometimes closed. When they were open, there was no meaning in their unwinking stare at one spot straight before them, unless for a moment the brow knitted into a faint expression of anger, or surprise . . . , so evanescent that it was like a shape made in water. . . . 'I begin to be sensible that I have just come back, and that I shall lose myself again . . . . If you knew the harassing anxiety that gnaws and wears me when I am wandering in those places — where are those endless places . . . ? They must be at an immense distance!' " (IV, 10).

From these places, it is possible to return, like Lazarus back from the dead (I, 3), as both John and Eugene return to life, and as Rogue Riderhood comes back from his first "drowning." But Rogue returns unchanged by his sojourn on the "dark road," even though his daughter has had "some vague idea that the old evil is drowned out of him, and that if he should happily come back to resume his occupation of the empty form that lies upon the bed, his spirit will be altered" (III, 3). John and Eugene, though, *are* altered. For them, the shapeless water is the place of absolute change, and their immersion makes possible a break with their past life, and a return from the dead as entirely different persons. Thus John Harmon dies in the dark water of the Thames, and lies buried "fathoms deep" (II, 13). An entirely new person, John Rokesmith, swims out on the other side of the river. And the bored, indecisive aristocrat, Eugene Wrayburn, unable to bring himself to marry beneath his station, is replaced in the watery realm of metamorphosis by a new Eugene determined to marry Lizzie, and possessing now "a mine of purpose and energy" (IV, 11).

But this transformation by water takes a special form. It makes possible a new way of being in the world. The social world is pure reflection; there, the inside is outside, and the outside is inside. But death and the river are not reflection. It is altogether impossible to appropriate them into the human world, and to assign them meaning as utensil or value. Everything which comes in contact with them is absorbed into their quality and transformed into the spectral image of itself. But those who have endured the annihilating plunge into the river can have a special form of engagement in the world, a form impossible to those who have not died to the world. They can live both inside life and out of it. They can live their lives in terms of death, assume death into their involvement in the world as something which permits them to see that engagement as what it really is, that is, as something negated by death, by the nonhuman reality outside the social world. Thus John Harmon turned into John Rokesmith feels like a lonely ghost returned from the grave. He lives a shadowy life which is undermined by his awareness of its falsity: "It is a sensation not experienced by many mortals," he says, "to be looking into a churchyard on a wild windy night, and to feel that I no more hold a place among the living than these dead do, and even to know that I lie buried somewhere else, as they lie buried here. Nothing uses me to it. A spirit that was once a man could hardly feel stranger or lonelier, going unrecognised among mankind than I feel" (II, 13). And, like his evanescent expressions as he lies unconscious, all Eugene's actions and experiences after his sojourn in death will be "shapes made in water," that is, they will lose the apparent reality and solidity of actions and experiences within the closed circuit of society. They will remain in touch with the fluidity of water. They will be seen as deriving from the neutrality of death, as being both supported by death, and negated by death. The contact of the human with the transcendent otherness which simultaneously denies and gives authenticity to human life will be maintained.

But the characters who are "baptized unto Death" and return to life do not return to a world that is entirely open and free. They do not freely choose an altogether new self and a new role in society. The all-important peculiarity of their reëngagement in the world is that they reaffirm a new form of just that situation they were already in. Their near death permits a transformation of that situation, not an escape from it, or a total rejection of it. It is a liberation from the absurdity, the coerciveness of that situation, a liberation which allows their former lives to begin again. But now, rather than being made by their situations, such characters make their places in the world and give them value.

This liberation of self from situation is absolutely necessary. It permits a change in orientation from past to future. Before, an identity and a relation to the world were imposed from the outside and from the past. Now, after the intervention of a sojourn in the realm of death, self and situation are inside and future. The world is open, and the characters are free to reaffirm themselves as the selves and situations they were. Only those who are Lazarus back from the dead can be reconciled to their inescapable enclosure in society. So Eugene reaffirms the love for Lizzie which has "struck" his "cursed carelessness" "dead" (IV, 6), and so John Harmon fulfils the conditions of the will: he marries Bella and accepts his inheritance. The descent into the waters of death is the last and most significant version of a constant motif in Dickens, a motif going back to *Oliver Twist:* the reaffirmation of one's given role after an interval of separation from it. This is Dickens' own special form of the theme of repetition. Like members of a primitive or traditional society, Dickens' characters are profoundly fearful of self-initiated novelty. They find their most authentic selves by accepting, after an interval of dissociation, their original given places in the world. Their most real and valid actions are repetitions, reaffirmations. Dickens' good people take upon themselves the responsibility for making history. They accept their immediate roles in the collective historical drama. But they do not conceive of history, in the Hegelian or progressionist way, as the constant and free introduction of absolute novelty into the world.

The transformation of Bella Wilfer herself, which holds a central place in *Our Mutual Friend,* repeats this drama of withdrawal and reaffirmation, though without the literal immersion in the water of death. Bella must be brought to see that her acceptance of "money, money, money," as the only goal of her life, has been acceptance of what is illusory and empty. She is brought to see this by being introduced into an altogether false and deceptive world, a world in which the good Mr. Boffin is apparently transformed into a miser, and in which nothing is what it seems. She must be brought through this experience to accept John Harmon for what he is in himself without any reference to his place in society, and she must accept without question all that is equivocal and inexplicable about her husband. The climax of this experience is a recognition of the strangeness and mystery of the world around her. This experience is a less extreme version of the near deaths of John and Eugene: ". . . when . . . she and John, at towards nine o'clock of a winter evening, went to London, and began driving from London Bridge, among low-lying water-side wharves and docks and strange places, Bella was in the state of a dreamer; perfectly unable to account for her being there, perfectly unable to forecast what would happen next, or whither she was going, or why; certain of nothing in the immediate present, but that she confided in John, and that John seemed somehow to be getting more triumphant" (IV, 12). Bella here is, like John Harmon transformed into John Rokesmith, absent from the world and seeing it as the strange image of itself. Her enclosure within a perfectly comprehensible world has been broken. She too passes through a stage of vacancy when she is between two selves, a period when the present is incomprehensible and the future unpredictable. And just as Lizzie has the power to recall Eugene from death after they are married (IV, 11), so Bella's single tie with the world here is her trust in John.

But Bella, like the others, is not transformed into something entirely new. Her new attitudes are not attitudes in a vacuum. She does not hate the love of money in general. She hates her past self and the miserly Boffin. And by rejecting her original values, she regains all that she had originally cared for, the Harmon fortune and a high place in society. Her discovery that Boffin was not really a miser and that in marrying John Rokesmith she has married John Harmon has a fairy-tale quality, but it is a fable of something perfectly true. Her assumption and endurance of her situation has transformed it. Her story affirms a central truth of the universe of *Our Mutual Friend:* When one has recognized that gold is dust, one can go on to make gold of dust. Out of dust can come gold, out of death, life. Gold forced upon us, or accepted as an absolute value in itself, is dust, but so long as we are free to value the world we can make gold of dust. Only when Bella recognizes that the true source of value is the human spirit itself does she recapture the gold she had lost. The real gold is Bella herself, who is "true golden gold at heart" (IV, 13), and worth "all the gold in the world" to her husband (IV, 5). Her recognition of this makes the Harmon gold "[turn] bright again, after a long, long rust in the dark, and . . . at last [begin] to sparkle in the sunlight" (IV, 13). And if Bella is gold for John, he brings gold into the world for her. The human spirit, in the reciprocity of self-sacrificing love, has the magical power to transform any situation and make any wishes come true, but only through the full acceptance of that situation. ". . . your wishes," says Bella to John, "are as real to me as the wishes in the Fairy story, that were all fulfilled as soon as spoken. Wish me everything that you can wish for the woman you dearly love, and I have as good as got it, John. I have better than got it . . . !" (IV, 5).

## Chapter X

# CONCLUSION

THIS study has attempted to trace the development of Dickens' imagination. Each novel has been viewed as the transformation of the real world of Dickens' experience into an imaginary world with certain special qualities of its own, qualities which reveal in their own irreplaceable way Dickens' vision of things. But certain elements persist through his work. Among the most important of these are the general situation of the protagonist at the beginning of the story and the general nature of the world he lives in. Each protagonist confronts, from moment to moment, a certain kind of world, a world in which inanimate objects, space and time, other people, and his own inner life have certain given modes of existence. These entities are initially, in most cases, distant from the protagonist, inimical, without comprehensible relation to him. The nonhuman world seems menacing and apparently has a secret life of its own, unfriendly to man, while the social world is an inexplicable game or ritual, in which people solemnly enact their parts in an absurd drama governed by mysterious conventions. Each Dickensian hero, then, lives like Paul Dombey, "with an aching void in his young heart, and all outside so cold, and bare, and strange" (DS, 11). He is even alienated from himself, and views his own consciousness as something mysterious and separated from himself. Beginning in isolation, each protagonist moves through successive adventures, adventures which I have tried to describe and define. These adventures are essentially attempts to understand the world, to integrate himself in it, and by that integration to find a real self. In this interchange between mind and world there is in Dickens' characters and in the novels themselves as wholes a constant attempt to reach something transcendent, something more real than one's own consciousness or than the too solid everyday material world. This supra-reality is perhaps caught in fleeting glimpses at the horizon of the material world, or in the depths beneath the upper layers of consciousness. In those depths are the regions of dreams, or of that hallucinated vision of things and people which is so characteristic of Dickens. The realm of images, where self is given a material form, and where things are transmuted into emblems of the self, is the very domain where the reality beyond or within reality may be momentarily apprehended. To put self and the sensible world it possesses as image in touch with these depths would be to transfigure the self, thus to validate it. Dickens' protagonists, initially creatures of poverty and indigence, are constantly in search of something outside the self, something other than the self, and even something other than human, something which will support and maintain the self without vaporizing and engulfing it. Dickens' novels, then, as I have tried to show, form a whole, a unified totality. Within this whole a single problem, the search for viable identity, is stated and restated with increasing approximation to the hidden center, Dickens' deepest apprehension of the nature of the world and of the human condition within it.

Dickens' recognition of the indifference or positive evil of much of the world was obscured by the high spirits of *Pickwick Papers,* so that Oliver Twist is the first of Dickens' heroes to dramatize unequivocally the plight of the disinherited orphan, lost in a dark and alien world. Oliver is rescued and the novel given a happy ending by a resolution which is standard for dozens of Victorian novels: the secrets of the orphan's birth are discovered and he inherits a secure place in the world. Only the intensity with which Dickens imagines and shares Oliver's sufferings gives authenticity to this conventional plot. So powerful is Dickens' fear of suggesting that the alienated hero should take matters into his own hands that he accepts a denouement which emphasizes the infantile passivity of his hero.

Oliver is willing to accept a definition of his identity which comes from the outside and from the past.

The novels which follow *Oliver Twist* show that a sense of the grotesque idiosyncrasies of people, their incommensurability with one another, is a central element in Dickens' vision of the world. But this partial shift from the melodrama of *Oliver Twist* back to the comedy of *Pickwick Papers* does not alter the fact that the central characters of *Nicholas Nickleby, The Old Curiosity Shop,* and *Barnaby Rudge* are, like Oliver, isolated in an inimical world. Indeed, the vision of people as wholly unlike one another and locked in the distortions of personal eccentricities is one of Dickens' most powerful ways of dramatizing the theme of isolation, and the inexhaustible power to bring into existence large numbers of comic or melodramatic grotesques, each alive with his own peculiar intensity of life, is perhaps Dickens' most extraordinary talent as a novelist. Though *Nicholas Nickleby, The Old Curiosity Shop,* and *Barnaby Rudge,* like *Oliver Twist,* depend for their resolutions on the discovery of something coming from the past and from outside the hero's own action, there is increasing recognition, especially in *The Old Curiosity Shop,* that the only complete escape from the alien city is through death. The death of Nell near the graveyard of a country church reflects back on Oliver's retreat to a happy rural paradise and suggests that it was an evasion of Dickens' problem, not a real solution.

In *Martin Chuzzlewit* Dickens faces this problem more squarely by bringing his hero into the open arena of society, and by minimizing the help he can get from his parents, grandparents, or ancestors. Here one of Dickens' central themes is fully expressed: the impossibility of achieving other than a sham identity by dependence on a society which is a masquerade of imposture and disguised self-seeking. Dickens sees in *Martin Chuzzlewit* that the purely human, cut off from any contact with what is above or beyond it and setting itself up as an end in itself, is factitious. Martin must learn to repudiate all selfishness and hypocrisy and depend on what is most real in human nature: its spontaneous feelings of affection or loving-kindness for others. But this idea is blurred by an ending which recalls in some ways that of *Oliver Twist*.

*Dombey and Son* and *David Copperfield*, the novels which directly follow *Martin Chuzzlewit*, complete one of the most important transformations of Dickens' imaginative vision: a movement from dependence on the child-parent relation as an escape from isolation to a dependence on the more adult solution of romantic love. *Dombey and Son* is Dickens' first mature analysis of the child-parent relation. It shows that to know and possess one's parents can be as much a cause of suffering as to be a friendless orphan. But Florence Dombey achieves real happiness not through the change in her father's attitude, but through her love for Walter Gay and his love for her, just as the center of *David Copperfield*, Dickens' most intimately personal novel, is the relation of David to Agnes. However, the opposition in *David Copperfield* between the hero's private memory and the power of Providence as alternative sources of the world's coherence, like the image of the "wild waves" in *Dombey and Son*, anticipates a central issue of Dickens' later novels: the question of the relation between man and the divine transcendence.

*Bleak House*, the first of Dickens' novels whose real protagonist is an entire society, shows people imprisoned by forces descending from the past, rather than liberated by them, as was the case in *Oliver Twist*. The only escape from the smothering fog of the Court of Chancery is Esther Summerson's power to make order in her immediate surroundings through the self-sacrifice and devotion of love. But Esther derives this power from her direct relation, through prayer, to divine grace. Esther is the avenue through which God's goodness, otherwise transcendent, descends into the human world. *Bleak House*, then, marks another transmutation in the nature of Dickens' imaginative world. Instead of waiting passively for a satisfactory place in society to descend upon her from the mysteries of the past, Esther must "trust in nothing, but in Providence and her own efforts." She must change the world around her through her own independent action in the present. Esther's discovery of her origin is an ironic reversal of the similar discovery in *Oliver Twist.* It liberates her from having any false expectations of society, and forces her to assume full responsibility for her own life.

The novels which follow *Bleak House,* however, show that this assumption of responsibility and the abnegating love it presupposes may not be so simply attained as they were for Esther. Dickens' later novels see the world as more and more shadowed and enclosed by the self-generating cruelty, injustice, and imposture of mankind. *Little Dorrit,* Dickens' darkest novel, is also his most profound exploration of the theme of perfect human goodness. All levels of society are so imprisoned in their selfish delusions that only the mystery of divine goodness incarnate in the childlike form of *Little Dorrit* can be a liberating force. But even *Little Dorrit* ends with the happy marriage of its heroine, whereas *A Tale of Two Cities* affirms that the self-sacrifice of perfect love, in order to be efficacious, may need the full sacrifice of life itself. *Great Expectations* pursues even further this exploration of the ambiguities of love. While *Hard Times* attempts to reconcile in the symbol of the "horse-riding" an image of the good society and the direct relation of love, *Great Expectations,* perhaps Dickens' most satisfactory treatment of the theme of romantic love, sees an irreconcilable opposition between Pip's relation to society and the final form of his love for Estella. Pip must choose between his "great expectations" and Estella. Moreover love is no longer seen as wholly guiltless and pure. Pip's initial love for Estella is as ambiguous in motivation as his "great expectations" from society, and his final relation to her is the mutual responsibility for one another's lives of two fallible and fallen people. Dickens' later novels give increasing recognition to the devastating and even anarchic power of love.

Still another reversal in orientation was reserved for Dickens' very last novels. This final surprising change in the nature of Dickens' vision of the world brings him in some ways closer to twentieth-century attitudes and themes than he had ever been before. It makes *Our Mutual Friend* the novel by Dickens perhaps most interesting to a contemporary reader, and makes us sorry that he did not live to finish *The Mystery of Edwin Drood*. This last change is a double one. It is a new notion that the transcendent spiritual power glimpsed at the margins or in the depths of the material world is not really a positive support for human values, even for good ones, but is the negation and reduction to nothing of all the human world indiscriminately. And it is a belief, deriving from this new vision of transcendence, that the human condition, with all its sufferings and unreality, can in no way be completely escaped, as long as life lasts. The human world is itself the only real support for human values. There is only one world for man. Dickens' last heroes and heroines come back to life after a purifying descent into the dark waters of death, but they come back to assume just that situation which was their given one in society. The difference is that their contact with the negative transcendence has liberated them to a new attitude toward their situation, an attitude which recognizes that value radiates not from any thing or power outside the human, but outward from the human spirit itself.

These, then, are the <u>chief stages</u> of Dickens' development. However, the most important single change in Dickens' novels, and the true turning point of his <u>imaginative development</u>, is a reversal which corresponds to a fundamental transformation of attitude in his century. This change can be defined as the rejection of the past, the given, and the exterior as sources of selfhood, and a reorientation toward the future and toward the free human spirit itself as the only true sources of value. To affirm this is to recognize the otherness of the nonhuman world, and the fact that it does not in itself offer any support to the creation of a humanly significant world. Rather than receiving selfhood as a gift from the outside and from the past, man, in Dickens' last novels, imposes value on himself and on the world as he assumes his future, including his death, in a dynamic process of living. The terminal point of *Our Mutual Friend,* as of the work of Dickens as a whole, is man's reaffirmation, after withdrawal, of his particular, limited, engagement in the world and in society. This engagement takes the form of an acceptance of intimate relations with other people, and of a concrete, forward-moving action, oriented toward the future. Such action manipulates and gives value to the world at the same time that it derives value and identity from the solidity of that world. A man can transform his situation by assuming it, and only thus can the self find an external support for its identity and reconcile at last freedom and substantiality. Only by living in the mode of present participles can the self have an authentic existence, that is, only by living in the mode of an immediate present which is becoming future, and in the mode of a verbal action which is in the very process of becoming substantial and real as it alters the world and identifies itself with it: "Bella was fast developing a perfect genius for home. All the loves and graces seemed (her husband thought) to have taken domestic service with her, and to help her to make home engaging. . . . Such weighing and mixing and chopping and grating, such dusting and washing and polishing, such snipping and weeding and trowelling and other small gardening, such making and mending and folding and airing, such diverse arrangements . . . !" (IV, 5).

It is only by "such diverse arrangements" of the world that Bella ceases to be the "doll in the doll's house" (IV, 5: the phrase gave Ibsen a title and a theme). And it is only by such a perpetual dynamic interaction between self and world that all men, for Dickens, can escape from the dilemma of either having no identity, or having one imposed from the outside on its passive recipient. Each man, in this way, can give himself a life which is constantly renewing itself, constantly perpetuating itself. To take responsibility for arranging the world is to take responsibility for making the self, and to escape at last from the grim alternatives of guilty action, passivity, or isolation which are initially the sole possibilities in the imaginative universe of Dickens.

# BIBLIOGRAPHY
# INDEX

# BIBLIOGRAPHY

The following bibliography is not at all meant to be complete, but only to list salient examples of the various kinds of recent studies mentioned in the introduction. For further discussion see Fred W. Boege, "Recent Criticism of Dickens," *Nineteenth-Century Fiction*, VIII (1953), 171–187; Edgar Johnson, "The Present State of Dickensian Studies," *Victorian News Letter*, No. 7 (1955), 4–9; Morton Dauwen Zabel, "Dickens: The Reputation Revised," *Craft and Character . . . in Modern Fiction* (New York, 1957), pp. 3–15.

"Alain" [Émile Chartier], *En lisant Dickens* (Paris, 1945).

Benjamin, Edwin B., "The Structure of *Martin Chuzzlewit*," *Philological Quarterly*, XXXIV (1955), 39–47.

Boege, Fred W., "Point of View in Dickens," *Publications of the Modern Language Association*, LXV (1950), 90–105.

Brown, E. K., "*David Copperfield*," *Yale Review*, XXXVII (1948), 650–666.

Butt, John, "*Bleak House* in the Context of 1851," *Nineteenth-Century Fiction*, X (1955), 1–21.

—— "*David Copperfield*: From Manuscript to Print," *Review of English Studies*, new ser., I (1950), 247–251.

—— "Dickens's Notes for his Serial Parts," *The Dickensian*, XLV (1949), 129–138.

—— "Dickens's Plan for the Conclusion of 'Great Expectations,'" *The Dickensian*, XLV (1949), 78–80.

Butt, John and Tillotson, Kathleen, *Dickens at Work* (Fair Lawn, N. J., 1958).

—— "Dickens at Work on *Dombey and Son*," *Essays and Studies: 1951*, ed. for the English Assoc. by Geoffrey Tillotson, pp. 70–93.

Churchill, R. C., "Dickens, Drama and Tradition," *Scrutiny*, X (1942), 358–375, reprinted in *The Importance of Scrutiny*, ed. Eric Bentley (New York, 1948), pp. 182–202.

Connolly, Thomas E., "Technique in *Great Expectations*," *Philological Quarterly*, XXXIV (1955), 48–55.

Cruikshank, R. J., *Charles Dickens and Early Victorian England* (London, 1949; New York, 1950).

Eisenstein, Sergei, "Dickens, Griffith, and the Film Today," *Film Form and The Film Sense* (New York, 1957), pp. 195–255, earlier published separately in *Film Form* (Harcourt, Brace, 1949).

Eliot, T. S., "Wilkie Collins and Dickens," *Selected Essays, 1917–1932* (New York, 1932), pp. 373–382.

Engel, Monroe, "Dickens on Art," *Modern Philology*, LIII (1955), 25–38.

—— "The Politics of Dickens' Novels," *Publications of the Modern Language Association*, LXXI (1956), 945–974.

Ford, George H., *Dickens and His Readers: Aspects of Novel-Criticism since 1836* (Princeton, N. J., 1955).

Grenander, M. E., "The Mystery and the Moral: Point of View in Dickens's *Bleak House*," *Nineteenth-Century Fiction*, X (1956), 301–305.

Hagan, John H., Jr., "Structural Patterns in Dickens's *Great Expectations*," *ELH*, XXI (1954), 54–66.

—— "The Poor Labyrinth: The Theme of Social Injustice in Dickens's 'Great Expectations,'" *Nineteenth-Century Fiction*, IX (1954), 169–178.

House, Humphry, *The Dickens World* (London, 1941).

Jackson, T. A., *Charles Dickens: The Progress of a Radical* (London, 1937).

Johnson, Edgar, *Charles Dickens: His Tragedy and Triumph* (2 vols., New York, 1952).

Leavis, F. R., "'Hard Times': An Analytic Note," *The Great Tradition* (London, 1950).

Lindsay, Jack, *Charles Dickens: A Biographical and Critical Study* (New York, 1950).

Monod, Sylvère, *Dickens romancier* (Paris, 1954).

Morse, Robert, "*Our Mutual Friend*," *Partisan Review*, XVI (1949), 277–289.

Needham, Gwendolyn B., "The Undisciplined Heart of David Copperfield," *Nineteenth-Century Fiction*, IX (1954), 81–107.

Nisbet, Ada, *Dickens and Ellen Ternan* (Berkeley, Calif., 1952).

Orwell, George, "Charles Dickens," *A Collection of Essays* (New York, 1954), pp. 55–111, earlier published in *Inside the Whale* (London, 1940), in *Dickens, Dali and Others* (New York, 1946), and in *Critical Essays* (London, 1946).

Pearson, Hesketh, *Dickens: His Character, Comedy, and Career* (New York, 1949).

Pope-Hennessy, Una, *Charles Dickens: 1812–1870* (London, 1945).

raz, Mario, "Charles Dickens," *The Hero in Eclipse in Victorian Fiction,* trans. Angus Davidson (London, 1956), pp. 127–188.

antavaara, Irma, *Dickens in the Light of English Criticism* (Helsinki, 1944).

aw, G. B., "Introduction" to the Limited Editions Club Edition of *Great Expectations* (1937).

ange, G. Robert, "Expectations Well Lost: Dickens' Fable for His Time," *College English,* XVI (1954), 9–17.

one, Harry, "Dickens' Use of his American Experiences in *Martin Chuzzlewit,*" *Publications of the Modern Language Association,* LXXII (1957), 464–478.

illotson, Kathleen, *Novels of the Eighteen-Forties* (London, 1954).

rilling, Lionel, "*Little Dorrit,*" *Kenyon Review,* XV (1953), 577–590.

an Ghent, Dorothy, "On *Great Expectations,*" *The English Novel: Form and Function* (New York, 1953), pp. 125–138.

—— "The Dickens World: A View from Todgers's," *Sewanee Review,* LVIII (1950), 419–438.

ilson, Edmund, "Dickens: The Two Scrooges," *Eight Essays* (New York, 1954), pp. 11–91, first published in *The Wound and the Bow* (Boston, 1941).

abel, Morton Dauwen, "Dickens: The Revolutionary Fate; *A Tale of Two Cities,*" *Craft and Character . . . in Modern Fiction* (New York, 1957), pp. 49–69.

—— "Introduction" to the Riverside Edition of *Bleak House* (Boston, 1956), pp. v–xxix, also printed as "Dickens: The Undivided Imagination; *Bleak House*" in *Craft and Character . . . in Modern Fiction,* pp. 15–49.

# INDEX

Characters are indexed under the names by which they are commonly known. The initials in parentheses after each name identify the novel in which it appears. See the Introduction, p. xii, for a key to abbreviations. Some important place names are also included.

# A selected list of MIDLAND BOOKS

*(continued on next page)*

# MIDLAND BOOKS

# CHARLES DICKENS
## *The World of His Novels*
### *By* J. Hillis Miller

George Orwell once said of Dickens' work: "It's not so much a series of books, it is more like a world." Mr. Miller attempts to identify this "world", to show how a single view of life pervades every novel that Dickens wrote, and to trace the development of this view throughout the chronological span of Dickens' career. There are full critical analyses of six of the novels: *Pickwick Papers, Oliver Twist, Martin Chuzzlewit, Bleak House, Great Expectations,* and *Our Mutual Friend,* with shorter discussions of many of the others. Each is viewed as the transformation of the real world of Dickens' experience into an imaginary world with special qualities of its own.

"It suggests investigations into relatively unexamined phases of Dickens' art-phases which, if studied objectively, may well yield new and rewarding insights into the novels."
—J. L. Bradley, *Christian Science Monitor*

"The most important Dickens' study since Edmund Wilson's *The Wound and the Bow.*"
—E. F. Walbridge, *Library Journal*

J. HILLIS MILLER is Professor of English at The Johns Hopkins University.

INDIANA UNIVERSITY PRESS
BLOOMINGTON & LONDON

COVER DESIGN BY *Peter Oldenburg*